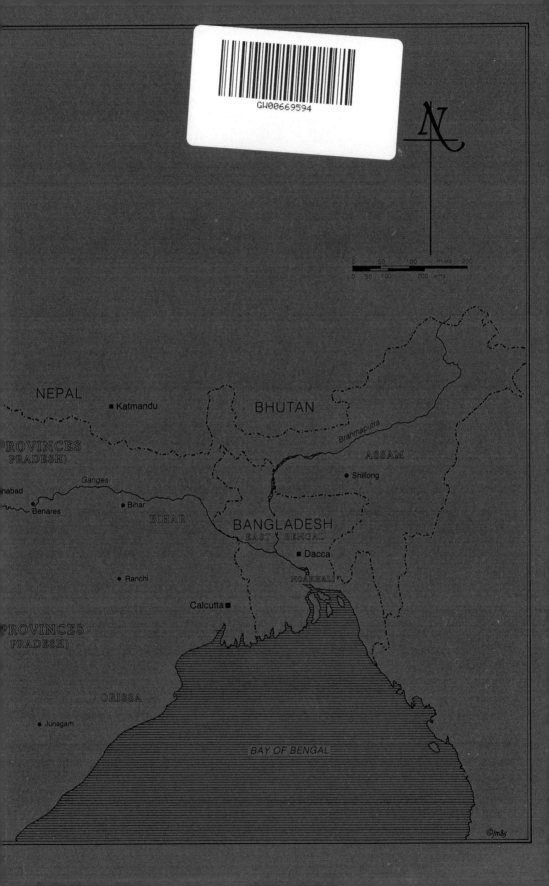

NEPAL

■ Katmandu

BHUTAN

PROVINCES
(PRADESH)

Brahmaputra

ASSAM

● Shillong

Ganges

nabad

● Bihar

● Benares

BIHAR

BANGLADESH

EAST BENGAL

● Dacca

● Ranchi

NOAKHALI

Calcutta ■

PROVINCES
(PRADESH)

ORISSA

● Junagarh

BAY OF BENGAL

©jm85

0   50   100   miles   200
0   50   100   200   kms

Disastrous Twilight

The sun . . . .
In dim eclipse disastrous twilight sheds
On half the nations, and with fear of change
Perplexes monarchs.

Milton, *Paradise Lost* Book I

Disastrous Twilight

A PERSONAL RECORD OF
THE PARTITION OF INDIA

Major-General Shahid Hamid

PRIVATE SECRETARY TO FIELD-MARSHAL
SIR CLAUDE AUCHINLECK
1946–47

With a Foreword by
PHILIP ZIEGLER

LEO COOPER
in association with
SECKER & WARBURG

First published in Great Britain 1986 by Leo Cooper
in association with Martin Secker & Warburg Limited
54 Poland Street, London W1V 3DF

ISBN 0-436-19077-X

Printed in Great Britain by
Mackays of Chatham Ltd, Kent
Plates printed by BAS Printers
Over Wallop, Hampshire

In Memory of
Field-Marshal Sir Claude Auchinleck
GCB, GCIE, CSI, DSO, OBE

The Last Commander-in-Chief in India

Contents

Illustrations

Between pages 236 and 237

The Auk with the author and his children.

The Auk with Ayub Khan on the way to review the Parade of the 1st Punjab Regiment.

The Auk with the author's younger daughter Chootu during a visit to Pakistan.

The Auk, the author and his wife at the Auk's 90th birthday party at the Hurlingham Club.

A letter from the Auk to one of the author's children.

Foreword

by Philip Ziegler

Major-General Shahid Hamid is a shining example of that type of man whom the English have in mind when they observe, with the air of one conferring the ultimate in accolades, that really, he might almost have been an Englishman. By this they mean that he is straightforward, loyal, honourable and courageous: all qualities which they like to believe the lesser breeds have in mind when they refer to "the English gentleman" (if, indeed, anyone does still refer to English gentlemen in this most ungentlemanly age). General Hamid also exhibits another characteristic of the species – a tendency to see one thing at a time with the utmost clarity, to the almost complete exclusion of anything else.

In March, 1946, Shahid Hamid was appointed Private Secretary to Sir Claude Auchinleck, Commander-in-Chief of the Indian Army. He remained with the Field-Marshal until August, 1947, and was still in close touch with him up to the time that Auchinleck left India some three months later. Throughout this period he kept a diary in which he recorded the events of the day and his reflections on the issues involved. As is almost bound to be the case with such instant records, its judgments are based on information which is usually incomplete and often inaccurate. It was written in the heat of the moment (and, to judge by General Hamid's epilogue, the fires have died down very little in the intervening years). It makes no effort to achieve objectivity and the prejudices that it demonstrates seem to me to be generally wrong-headed. Nevertheless, it is a transparently honest statement of a point of view which, rightly or wrongly, many people held at the time and still hold today. It is right that it should be made generally available.

General Hamid's voice is the more valuable for being one that is comparatively rarely heard. He is a Muslim and a loyal servant of Pakistan, and on the whole the voice of the Hindu and of India has been heard more vociferously in Britain. He is a soldier, and it is the politician or the civil servant whose opinions are most commonly expressed. Above all, he was a devoted admirer and servant of Auchinleck, and that most inarticulate and withdrawn of men has chosen to let his case go, if not by default, then at least without any

attempt to propagate his point of view. The Auk needed a champion and he
has found a doughty one in Shahid Hamid.

The picture of Auchinleck that emerges from these pages is an attractive
one. The bleak, somewhat unapproachable figure viewed with trepidation by
so many of his subordinates is revealed among his intimates as warm-hearted
and welcoming. "The Auk is a simple man with a zest for living, having
unsophisticated habits and unadulterated joys. He enjoys the little pleasures
life has to offer." He relished schoolboy games, laughed heartily at the most
unassuming pleasantries and had a weakness for rumbustious practical
jokes. Himself lonely and with his self-confidence sapped by the defection of
his wife, he responded to the obvious affection and admiration of the young
Hamids and joyfully let himself be drawn into their family circle. "The
children are very fond of him, and he of them. He has practically adopted
them as his own. . . . Whenever the children want a special toy, they let him
know. To them the Auk is known as 'Chiefi'." He treated his Private
Secretary as a trusted friend. "I have been short-tempered, unreasonable
and petty at times," he confessed in his farewell letter. "I know my faults and
deplore them but my flesh is weak."

But the real significance of this book lies in the picture that it paints of the
negotiations that led up to the independence of India and Pakistan, the
massacres that followed, and the teething pains of the two new countries, as
seen by a Muslim officer who had the ear and enjoyed the confidence of the
Commander-in-Chief. Shahid Hamid's fundamental assumptions are pre-
dictable: the Muslim leaders were honourable and undemanding; their
Congress counterparts were wily, grasping and unscrupulous; Mountbatten
was the puppet of the latter, manipulated by the subtle Hindus who knew
how to play on his vanity and his ambition. But even allowing for this, the
sort of misconceptions that seem to have prevailed in Auchinleck's headquarters are still disconcerting and could have been extremely damaging.

To take one example: "Under Nehru's instructions," wrote Shahid
Hamid on 19 June, 1947, "Mountbatten left for Kashmir to pressurize the
Maharajah to throw in his lot with India." In fact Mountbatten went to
Kashmir against Nehru's strongly expressed wishes and in the hope of
pressurizing the Maharajah to throw in his lot with Pakistan – a mission
which, in the event, proved singularly fruitless. It mattered little that a junior
officer should have got things so completely back to front. It would not have
mattered very much if Auchinleck had reached the same conclusion. But
things may have gone further than that. Hamid saw it as part of his duty to
tell Jinnah what was going on. "In the evening Mountbatten came to see
the Auk," he wrote in his diary for 19 April. "He was of the view that the
emergence of Pakistan cannot be avoided. I informed the Quaid accordingly." If Jinnah had heard from what he might reasonably have supposed
to be, if not the horse's mouth, then at least something pretty close to it,
that Mountbatten was going to Kashmir to talk the Maharajah into accession

with India, then what chance was there that he would trust the Viceroy on that or any other issue? Yet if he had instead accepted that Mountbatten was working to achieve the exact opposite, and had indeed persuaded Nehru that Kashmir's accession to Pakistan was proper and inevitable, then he might never have inspired the Pathan invasion and the Maharajah would not have been panicked into joining India. To pin on Shahid Hamid even part of the responsibility for the long-drawn tragedy of Kashmir would be extravagant, but his comments illustrate vividly how prejudice and fear can breed the very perils that they are anxious to avert.

Given Hamid's total dedication to the cause of Auchinleck, it was inevitable that Montgomery would get even shorter shrift than Mountbatten in his diary. "Monty is extremely ambitious and ruthless," is the entry when the Chief of the Imperial General Staff arrives in Delhi in June, 1946. "He knows in his heart-of-hearts that the Auk is a superior person and a better soldier than himself." Montgomery had already made up his mind that Auchinleck had outstayed his time in India and should be got rid of as soon as possible, to be replaced by Slim (an idea that Hamid wrongly attributes to Mountbatten, who in fact was determined that Slim should succeed Montgomery as CIGS). The two men were incompatible, disliked each other cordially, and made little effort to conceal the fact. Hamid had no doubt where his loyalties lay. Montgomery's Private Secretary told him that his master did not like to see anyone smoking in his presence. "When Monty arrived I made certain that I had a cigar in my hand . . . Not a word was said."

It was not only the Muslim army officers who felt sickened and betrayed by the destruction of the Service to which they had given their lives. Shahid Hamid's is the age-old protest of the straightforward soldier against the devious politician, of the idealist against the pragmatist, of the traditionalist against the progressive. It is not necessary to accept the premises of his argument to feel sympathy for the raw pain and anger that permeate this chronicle. His book deserves to be widely read. Any student of the period who accepted it as the whole truth would be gravely misled, but if he were to ignore it altogether he would be missing a statement of real importance.

Philip Ziegler

Acknowledgements

I am grateful to the following for the generous help given to me in the preparation of the book:

Mr Barry Bloomfield of the India Office Library and Records, to Mr Boris Mollo of the Army National Museum and especially to Dr M. A. Pegg of the Manchester University Library for allowing me to reproduce from their records. I am also grateful to Dr Lionel Carter of the centre of South Asian Studies, University of Cambridge for his advice on the form of the book.

I am particularly thankful to Lady Savory and Major A. C. S. Savory for giving me permission to quote from General Savory's papers.

Unpublished crown copyright material in the India Office Records reproduced in this book appears by permission of the Controller of Her Majesty's Stationery Office.

The photographs reproduced in the book are from my personal collection acquired over many years.

I am grateful to the family of Field-Marshal Sir Claude Auchinleck, and especially to Major Mark Auchinleck, for giving me permission to write about their kinsman and for allowing me to quote from his papers. I am also indebted to Peter Willy for his help and advice.

I owe a debt of gratitude to Leo Cooper for publishing my book and to Tom Hartman for editing it.

I am indebted to my family for encouraging me to write the account of this period and especially to my younger daughter Shama for editing the manuscript in the first place.

I am also grateful to Shakir Jaffery for arranging the photographs and to Bunyad for typing the manuscript.

My thanks to *The Times* and *Daily Mail* for permission to quote from articles originally published in those newspapers.

This book could not have been completed without the help, understanding and hospitality which I received from Margo and John Dent. Their home has always been my retreat in England and it was there that I put the finishing touches to my manuscript.

Finally I would like to thank Philip Ziegler for writing such a stimulating foreword to my book and to assure him that my admiration and affection for him are not one whit diminished by what he says. He will, I am sure, agree that history can never be entirely objective, but even with the benefit of hindsight, and having read his excellent biography of Lord Mountbatten, I still stand by every word that I wrote nearly forty years ago.

Introduction

I had never met Field-Marshal Sir Claude Auchinleck before I was selected to be his first Indian Private Secretary. In fact I had not served at GHQ, India nor met any of the top brass. Why I was selected for the post I do not know.

Well-informed people, including Lord Douglas-Home, have told me that a true and factual account of the events that led up to the partition of the Indian subcontinent has not yet been written. In whatever has been written, Auchinleck has been maligned and made a scapegoat. His greatness lay in not wanting to defend himself during his lifetime, leaving History to judge his actions. On the contrary Mountbatten took every conceivable opportunity to justify his stand.

Few people knew the Auk at such close quarters as I did. I came to know him as a Commander and as a human being. Few had this opportunity. He took me into his confidence and kept me abreast of events. As I became aware of the fact that the time we were passing through was going to be important in the history of the subcontinent I began to keep a diary. The Auk gave me permission to make copies of documents I wanted in this connection though he asked me not to publish anything during his lifetime.

Many an account has been written of the Auk's exploits as a soldier. Very little has been said of his personal and human side. I have endeavoured to bring out this aspect of his character so that future historians may see the 'Whole Man'.

I was fortunate to witness many historic events, and also to meet the men who made them possible. This gave me a unique insight into the character of the leaders and their approach to the national problems that were facing them. I was able to record their opinions, expressed both privately and in the open, alongside my own.

In brief, I witnessed the dwindling glow of the British Empire. I saw small men entrusted with great jobs, playing with the destiny of millions.

This book has been written incorporating the diary I kept diligently during those days. It is not just a record of events, but includes my reactions to what

I saw, what I heard and what came across my desk. After the Auk's death I gave the final touches to my diary and procured copies of some of the documents which were incomplete.

My book is a tribute to his memory.

While this book was being prepared for the printer, Philip Ziegler's official biography of Earl Mountbatten was published. I have read the pages which relate to Mountbatten's time in India and see no reason to qualify anything which I wrote at the time.

On my relinquishing the assignment the Auk wrote to me as follows:

COMMANDER-IN-CHIEF'S HOUSE
NEW DELHI
25th August '47

My dear Shahid,

I was greatly touched by your kind and generous letter. It is a very great help and comfort to me to feel that I have such a good and loyal friend in you, and I can only say that I could not have had a better staff officer in what, as you know, have been very difficult times.

As I hope you know, I have always looked on you as a friend and a partner rather than as a subordinate officer and you have fully justified the complete confidence I placed in you.

In these troublous days during which you and I have worked together – I hope for the good of India and our Army – I have kept practically nothing from you and this has been a tremendous help to me – I mean that I was able to do this because of my faith in your loyalty and discretion. Things which I may have kept from you – and they were very very few – I had to keep from other people – like PSOs – also!! You have had, I know, a most difficult and delicate task and I do realise how much you have protected me from many worries and anxieties, which a less competent Secretary would have failed to do. This has meant a very great deal to me and also enabled me to keep on functioning under very heavy strain. I have been short-tempered, unreasonable and petty at times – I know my faults and deplore them but my flesh, like that of most of the sons of Adam, is weak! You have been very patient and good and I thank you. I can not say more. I shall miss you sadly – in fact I am missing you daily now. I am so glad we were able to do so many interesting journeys together in so many parts of the world – made easy and pleasant by your good management and refusal to get bothered or annoyed – great qualities of yours! Never lose them!! I look back on our journeyings together with the greatest pleasure and with profound sorrow that we are to do no more of them.

As to Tahira and the children – they have helped enormously too and it has been a real joy and comfort to me to have known them and learned to love them. I shall miss them terribly for the few months that remain to me here. The house and garden will never be the same without them. You are truly blessed in having them. I hope they will have long years of happiness and peace before them. Now that Tahira is going, who will come to my rescue when difficult guests are to be charmed and made at home!!!

As to you, I wish you every success and all the luck you deserve in your new service. There are, I fear, difficult times ahead for all in this country, but I feel you will keep your head and your feet and not be swept away by emotion or sentiment or hate or envy. You know that if I can help you or any of the family I will always do my very best. I have many 'God-children' as we call them in England, but none who have the place in my heart that Hassan and Shahnaz hold and now – little Chootu. God keep them safe and happy and free from hate.

This is not goodbye, only a letter of thanks.

We shall meet again soon, I hope. You know that for so long as I am here this house is yours so do not hesitate to use it. Thank you again for the lovely rug – it was naughty of you to give it to me, but I love it all the same.

Yours
AUCHINLECK

'The British are a just people. They have left India in exactly the same state of chaos as they found it.' So said a Magistrate (*The Making of Pakistan* by Richard Symonds).

PART I

The Background

The Political Stalemate

It is helpful to start by explaining the historical and political developments that were taking place in the Indian subcontinent when I went to Delhi in 1946. To this end I have prefaced my diary with several essays, each dealing with a specific topic which was of particular concern at the time. Some of these naturally overlap but it would, I felt, be more confusing to try and weave them together. Those readers already familiar with the situation in India immediately after the Second World War may prefer to skip these introductory essays.

To put the facts in their historical perspective I shall go back to the years when India was ruled by several dynasties of Muslim kings. Last among these were the Moghuls. After a few centuries they were ousted by the English. Eventually the British Empire was firmly established in the sub-continent.

In 1857 the Muslims raised the standard of freedom against their rulers and were crushed by the British who took all possible measures to ensure that the Muslims did not raise their heads again. It also became part of their policy to encourage the Hindus in every way and use them for extending British rule. For example, in 1867, in the United Province, steps were taken to replace Urdu as the main language. Following this, *Band-e-Matram*, a Hindu religious song, was adopted by the Hindus as the future National Anthem of India.

British rule in India was a mixture of pageantry, generosity and benignity, but was based on the principle of 'divide and rule'. Nevertheless they brought law and order to India.

In 1882, at Aligarh, Syed Ahmad Khan propounded the 'Two Nation Theory' as a permanent solution to the problems of the subcontinent, inhabited, as it was, by two different nations with widely disparate cultures. By implication he suggested the division of the subcontinent into Muslim and non-Muslim areas. Gradually this two-nation theory gained ground.

The All-India Congress was formed by the Hindus in 1885 and not supported by the Muslims. It pleaded for self-rule by the Indians.

At the beginning of the century Gandhi appeared on the Indian scene and advocated *Swaraj* (home rule) for India. In 1906 the Muslim League was formed, and in 1916 agreed to work with the Congress towards Indian independence.

Certain reforms were announced by the British in 1917, but these were not acceptable to the Indians. At the end of the First World War the Indians as a whole expected that some type of Home Rule would be given to them. When this was not forthcoming, they resorted to political agitation in various parts of the country. This resulted in the Amritsar massacre of 13th April, 1919. The action taken was extremely severe but it did check further incidents. During 1920 and 1921 *hartals* (strikes) and boycotts became the order of the day. The words 'swaraj' and 'non-cooperation' had already been introduced by Gandhi and had caught on, although Maulana Hasrat Mohani opposed the use of the word 'swaraj', saying that it was ambiguous and did not mean total independence.

In 1921 the Muslim League supported the Congress Non-Cooperative Movement while the Hindus reciprocated by taking part in the Khilafat Movement. In the same year the agitation came to a head in the Mupillas rebellion in Malabar which was ruthlessly put down. Later certain reforms were introduced and the agitation gradually died down.

In 1927 the British Government sent a Commission to India under Sir John Simon to investigate the possibility of further reforms. On their return they suggested holding a Round-Table Conference. This was held in London in 1931 and was attended by all the prominent leaders including Gandhi and Jinnah, the leader of the Muslim League. There was wide difference of opinion between the two.

As a result of the Second Round Table Conference in 1932, an Act, later known as the 'Government of India Act 1935', received the Royal Assent in August, 1935. It came into force on 1st April, 1937 and provided for separate electorates, the separation of Sind from Bombay, weightage for the Muslims in provinces where they were in a minority, and certain safeguards for minorities as a whole. The Muslim League was allotted one-third of the seats. Seats were also reserved for the Indian States. Nehru called the Government of India Act 'a Charter of Slavery'.

At this stage Gandhi became extremely active, even though he had officially retired from the Congress. He often claimed that he was both a Hindu and a Muslim at heart. To prove this, at his prayer meetings he arranged for readings from the Holy Quran as well as from the Bhagvat Gita. But his appeal to the Hindu masses remained just as strong. With all his fads of fastings, drinking goat's milk and observing days of silence, he was pre-eminently a Hindu. Interestingly enough, when he preached non-violence the results were just the opposite.

Gandhi had a tendency to prefer dreams to facts and ideals to reality. By 1937 his fatal self-deception had done serious damage to national unity in

India and eventually became the cause of the split between the Hindus and the Muslims. Gandhi had a low opinion of Jinnah and maintained that he had no following. On the other hand Jinnah was extremely suspicious of all Gandhi's actions and movements. He called him a 'Hindu Revivalist'.

Nineteen thirty-seven was a crucial year for the subcontinent. Elections were held in January and February. Jinnah advocated that the Muslims must stand together and warned the Congress not to interfere in the elections for Muslim seats, so that the Muslims were not divided. In March the Congress passed a resolution which said that they had entered the legislature not to cooperate but to combat the Act, and asked for complete independence for India.

After the elections the Congress formed the Government in the predominantly Hindu provinces – Bombay, Madras, Central Province, United Province, Bihar and Orissa – but refused to include any representative of the League. Jinnah had hoped that the Hindus and the Muslims would be able to work together. He pleaded for Hindu/Muslim unity, but this phase petered out very quickly. The Congress was not in favour of forming coalition ministries. Both Gandhi and Nehru urged the Muslims to stop looking upon themselves as a separate body and offered them absorption rather than partnership. They maintained that the Muslims must become members of the Congress party. Jinnah, however, felt that the Congress was out to establish a 'Hindu Raj' just for the Hindus.

In Punjab Sikandar Hayat formed the Ministry and said there could be nothing worse than the establishment of Pakistan, which he dubbed as 'Jinnahistan' and told the League to keep out of Punjab. This was the beginning of the double rôle played by politicians in the Punjab which carried on up to Partition in 1947.

The Congress having committed the fatal error of not including the Muslim League in the provincial ministries, it was now obvious that the Hindus were not prepared to work side by side with the Muslims. This had long-range consequences and became the prime cause of the creation of Pakistan. Jinnah said, 'Muslims can expect neither justice nor fair play under the Congress Government . . . There is no hope for the Muslims in a Federal Government which is dominated by the Hindus'. He further said, 'All hopes are wrecked on the rocks of Congress Fascism'. Previously Jinnah had been described by the Congress as 'the Ambassador of the Hindu-Muslim unit' but now a new chapter opened, characterized by confrontation rather than cooperation.

The Congress then launched a mass contact movement among rural Muslims to enrol them into the Congress Party. The Muslim League reacted by proclaiming that Islam was in danger and consequently made much headway, absorbing many minor Muslim parties. Nehru had underestimated the strength of the Muslims and the power of Jinnah. However, the future course of events was becoming clearer to him.

In 1938 Nehru declared that the League was a fascist organization and was following Hitler's Nazi policies. Gandhi and Jinnah tried to effect a reconciliation, but the Congress committee condemned the negotiations. In order to increase the influence of the Hindus the Congress introduced the Wardha Education Scheme in the Provinces which increased the influence of the Hindi language. The League maintained that it was not in the interest of the Muslims of the subcontinent and rejected it.

The Viceroy appealed to Jinnah to give the Federal scheme a trial, but Jinnah was opposed to any Federal objective and began working on other constitutional schemes. At the same time he formed a Committee under the Rajah of Pirpur to report on the working of the Congress Ministries in the Provinces. This report showed the anti-Muslim nature of the Congress Provincial governments.

By 1939 the League alone spoke for the Muslims and Jinnah was their undisputed leader. He declared that the Muslims were irrevocably opposed to any federal scheme, and stressed the fact that India comprised two separate nations and therefore should be two states. The Congress provincial ministries resigned in October, 1939, and the League observed 22nd December as the 'Day of Deliverance' from the tyranny, oppression and injustice of Congress rule.

Nineteen hundred and forty, with Britain at war with Germany, was a crucial year for India. On 23rd March the Pakistan Resolution was passed by the All India Muslim League Committee at Lahore, demanding the partition of the subcontinent and the establishment of Pakistan. It also made it quite clear that the Muslim League was the only body qualified to speak for the Muslims. The Sikh leader, Master Tara Singh, said, 'If the Muslim League wants to establish Pakistan they will have to pass through an ocean of Sikh blood'. In the province of Sind Allah Baksh disputed Jinnah's claim and said that he did not speak for the Sindhi Muslims.

L. S. Amery, the Secretary of State for India, announced that the attainment by India of full and equal partnership in the Commonwealth of Nations was the goal of the British policy. Thereupon the Viceroy, the Marquess of Linlithgow, offered India the following:

1) After the war a body would be set up to work out the constitution;
2) The enlargement of the existing Viceroy's Executive Council by the inclusion of political appointments;
3) The setting-up of a War Advisory Council.

Both the Congress and the League rejected these offers. The Governor-General's Council was reconstituted and included eight Indians and three British members and the C-in-C. A National Defence Committee was set up but was given consultative status only.

At this stage Gandhi appealed to all Britons to practice non-violence and lay down their arms. He advocated individual *satyagrahas.** He was arrested on 31 October and sentenced to four years' imprisonment. Immediately after his arrest a Civil Disobedience Movement on an individual basis was launched.

By this time the Congress had realized that the Muslims would not be satisfied with anything other than the establishment of Pakistan. In their heart of hearts they conceded the principle of partition of the subcontinent.

The Civil Disobedience Movement continued in 1941 for some time but with no effect. By the end of December all political prisoners had been released. On 1st July the then General Sir Archibald Wavell was appointed C-in-C of the Indian Army.

By now HMG realized that something must be done towards the attainment of self-rule for India. Winston Churchill decided to send Sir Stafford Cripps to India to recommend constitutional changes and present them to the political leaders before implementation.

Cripps arrived on 22nd March, 1942, and carried with him a draft Declaration. Churchill purposely selected Cripps, a member of the Labour Party, in order to effect his 'Waterloo'. He knew very well that Cripps was incapable of bringing about a settlement because of his Congress leanings. The Declaration said:

1) Immediately on the cessation of hostilities steps are to be taken to set up an elected body charged with the task of framing a constitution for a fully self-governing Indian Union within the Commonwealth. The composition of the elected body was also stated.

2) Any province or provinces or States can stay out of the proposed Indian Union and form separate Unions of their own and would have the same status as the Indian Union.

3) An Interim Government would be formed immediately but control over Defence would rest with the C-in-C who was to be the War Member. However, an Indian representative would be allowed to look after the ancillary department of the Defence Ministry.

4) The British obligations and interests in India were to be settled by a Treaty freely negotiated between HMG and the constitution-making body.

The purport of this proposal was described by Cripps as 'complete and absolute self-determination and self-government for India'. The Viceroy said that it was a solemn pledge by HMG, while Gandhi maintained that it was 'Balkanization' of the subcontinent. Nehru wanted the Defence Member to be an Indian, in place of the C-in-C, who he was prepared to accept as an advisor. Wavell told Nehru if that was his stand then there was

---

*Literally 'defiance'. The term was to describe the deliberate courting of arrest.

nothing further to be discussed. The lone voice among the Congress leaders who advised acceptance of the proposal was that of Rajagopalachari.

However, the Congress, who wanted Independence forthwith and the future of the Muslims to be settled later, rejected the proposal. If the Congress had accepted, the League would have followed suit and a Coalition Government might have been formed and a working relationship between the Hindus and the Muslims would have emerged. Cripps's proposal was the last chance of forming a National Government and the last opportunity for keeping India in one piece. The dream of a United India came to a sad end, due to the lack of wisdom, foresight and statesmanship of the Congress High Command, who failed to appreciate the situation and the opportunity it offered. The blunders which the Congress made between 1937 and 1942 damaged them immensely, damage from which they never recovered. This series of mistakes made the establishment of Pakistan unavoidable. Even the British admitted that there was no other solution. It was a great triumph for Jinnah. Later, Amery announced that the Mission had failed.

Soon after, the Congress Working Committee passed a resolution calling for non-cooperation and for 'non-violent resistance to the invaders' and Gandhi announced that the British should leave India to God. If that was too much, then leave her to anarchy. He said again that as long as the British stayed in India as a third party there would be no solution. He appealed to every Briton to leave India. The Congress advocated a mass Civil Disobedience Movement against the British and said, 'The Jews practised passive resistance and that is what India should do against the British'. Gandhi wrote to Hitler to embrace all mankind irrespective of race, colour and creed. Rajagopalachari resigned from the Congress. On 8th August the All India Congress Committee approved the Quit India Resolution. It amounted to an open insurrection on a nationwide basis at a time when the British had their backs to the wall.

Gandhi believed that the resolution would lead to serious negotiations with the Viceroy. He miscalculated. The Government immediately arrested all the leaders during the night with the result that the Congress could not put its plan into full operation and it went off at half-cock. They did not expect such a quick reaction and it took the wind out of their sails. During August and September there were disturbances throughout the country and in many places the railway lines were ripped up. Troops that were meant for the forward areas had to be used for safe-guarding installations and keeping the lines of communication open.

The Muslim League kept out of the agitation and took no action which would embarrass the Government. In fact they deplored the action of Congress in no uncertain terms and thus gained the sympathy of HMG and that of the Government of India. They improved in strength and influence.

In February, 1943, Gandhi began a fast in prison. This was his usual tactic. Soon after, three members of the Viceroy's Council resigned to show their sympathy with Gandhi. The Government issued a White Paper on the disturbances of 1942, making the Congress responsible for them. On 20th October, 1943, Field-Marshal Wavell became the Viceroy of India and General Auchinleck the C-in-C.

On 17th February, 1944, Field-Marshal Wavell, while addressing a session of the Central Legislature, announced that the Cripps offer was still open. At this stage Rajagopalachari, who was now back in Congress, accepted the 'recognition of Right of Separation of certain areas from the United India'. This was the result of a meeting between him and Jinnah. On 6th May Gandhi was released from prison on medical grounds. Soon afterwards he asked for immediate independence for India. He also met Jinnah and together they produced a formula. Gandhi did not accept the two-nation theory and maintained that after the war a Commission should be appointed to demarcate contiguous areas where the wishes of the people could be obtained by ballot. After this it might be possible to consider the establishment of two separate States. He went further to suggest that between the two States a treaty on common interests could be drawn up. He saw no reason why the two nations could not live in peace and recommended that a mechanism should be worked out to give the suggestions a practical shape. The formula was shortlived and nothing much came out of it. Later Gandhi described the establishment of Pakistan as an 'untruth'. Thereupon Jinnah asked that all the six Provinces should be included in the future Pakistan.

On 23rd March, 1945, Wavell went to the United Kingdom for consultations with HMG and was accompanied by V. P. Menon. On 14th June, in a broadcast, Wavell presented his proposal for advancing India towards self-government and announced the holding of a Conference for all the leaders. The Conference was held at Simla from 25th June to 14th July, but it failed as the League claimed the right to nominate all the Muslim members of the Executive Council. The following month, on 26th July, a Labour Government came into power in Britain. Wavell was again summoned to London and on his return announced his plan for self-government for India. The plan included:

1) the holding of elections for Provincial and Central Assemblies;
2) the establishment of a constitution-making body;
3) the restoration of Provincial autonomy;
4) the reformation of the Viceroy's council.

After the Japanese surrender on 14th August, 1945, the political climate became intense and activities increased all round.

In November the Indian National Army trials began, which gave a very favourable handle to Congress to outwit the British and they took full advantage of it, as will be discussed later.

In late December the results of the elections to the Central Legislature were announced. The League captured all the Muslim seats. In the provinces they won 446 seats out of a total 495. Their only failure was in the North-West Frontier Province. In Punjab they achieved great success, winning 79 Muslim seats while the Unionists retained only ten. This was the end of the Unionist Party. The results went to reinforce Jinnah's claim that he was the leader of Muslim India. If the Congress had recognized this fact earlier a great deal of bad feeling would have been avoided and the Congress and the League could have worked together.

Early in 1946 the Labour Government, in a further effort to resolve the stalemate, decided to send a Parliamentary delegation to India with a view 'to salvaging goodwill towards India'. The delegation toured the subcontinent, met people of all shades of opinion and submitted their reports to Clement Attlee, the Prime Minister.

The Prime Minister was anxious to safeguard the interests of the retiring as well as of serving Indian soldiers, sailors and airmen. He wanted special monetary and other benefits granted to them, hoping that by such measures he would ensure their loyalty to the Crown.

Auchinleck had already informed him that the reliability and morale of the Indian Forces would best be secured by a firm and explicit declaration by His Majesty's Government to the effect that, while HMG maintained its intention to grant self-government to India by constitutional methods, it would not hesitate to put down any armed insurrection, by force if necessary. In such an event the leaders would be punished and the troops acting in the execution of their duties would be protected at that time and thereafter.

The Prime Minister was informed that the Viceroy and the C-in-C were doing all they could to foster loyalty by taking the following steps:

a) When the units returned from active service to their home stations, welcome parades and tea parties were arranged. Indian officers and other ranks who had been decorated for gallantry received official welcomes and special parades were held in their honour. The returning prisoners of war were met and entertained at Bombay by the Governor. A Victory Celebration Week was to be held at Delhi in March. Three Victoria Cross Parades had been held at which the Viceroy has personally decorated the recipients. These were attended by large crowds.

b) The pay had been considerably increased since the beginning of the war but any further increase was not contemplated.

c) A great deal of attention had been paid to the welfare of the Indian troops and they would receive amenities on the same scale as the British troops.

d) Grants of land had been made for good service and gallantry.

e) Every effort was being made to counteract the distorted version of events in India, particularly the false reports published in the Press on the

Indian National Army trials. Regular talks of reconstruction and current problems were being given to the Indian troops. The Indian Soldier Boards had been reactivated and were looking after the soldiers' dependants and their welfare.

f) The old 'Josh Groups', which had existed to inculcate a hatred of the Japanese, had been resurrected as study groups in order to discuss current problems.

g) *'Dilkush Sabhas'* (the Indian equivalent of ENSA) had been giving performances to Indian troops throughout the subcontinent.

In the Forces the politically-conscious technical and administrative personnel were undermining the loyalty of the troops. They were fanning communal trouble with the result that there was a danger of their becoming unreliable. The Indian troops abroad were showing signs of dissastisfaction and wanted to return home. In the event of internal disorder there were enough British troops in India to back the Indian troops, provided they remained loyal. Further reinforcement of British troops was considered inadvisable. Nevertheless some had been earmarked for India in case of an emergency. There was a great shortage of experienced British officers in the Indian units.

In February, 1946, communal trouble broke out in Eastern Command. General Sir Francis Tuker, the GOC-in-C, handled the situation superbly. He knew India better than most senior officers. He understood the people's mentality and knew how to deal with civil disturbances. His intelligence system was excellent; he was better informed than the civil administration, but kept close links with them and did not hesitate to suggest a line of action to them. He anticipated likely trouble spots, made his dispositions in advance and believed in strong and ruthless action before the situation got out of control.

Naturally, the greater the unrest the wider the deployment of the Army on internal security duties. It was therefore essential to ensure that it acted impartially and great responsibilities devolved on the Army High Command to keep the troops out of politics. The Congress had made it clear that the Indian Army as it existed was an Army of aliens and ought to be converted into a political instrument to turn the British out of India. To this end newspapers of all shades of opinion were sent to Army formations and units. It was even suggested that Army personnel should be allowed to attend political meetings, as long as they were in 'mufti'. The communists and the socialists tried hard to infiltrate the Forces and undermine their loyalty.

The Indian Army

The term 'Army in India' embraced all regular British and Indian troops, the Auxiliary Forces, the Territorial Units, the Reserves and the Indian State Forces when placed at the disposal of the government. The Royal Indian Air Force and Royal Indian Navy, the War and Defence departments also came under the C-in-C.

The task of the Defence Forces in India was local defence, maintenance of internal security in India and external defence in cooperation with Imperial and Allied Forces. The Imperial Government and the Government of India were jointly responsible for the external defence of India against major invasions.

The Secretary of State for India, as one of His Majesty's Ministers, had special responsibility with regard to the defence administration in India.

The Secretary of State's principal adviser on Indian military affairs was the Secretary in the Military Department of the India Office. This post was filled by a senior officer of the Indian Army with recent Indian experience. In order to keep in touch with Indian affairs, the Military Secretary was expected to visit India regularly. In addition, by a practice which had obtained for many years, a retired Indian Army officer of high rank had a seat on the Secretary of State's Council.

The superintendence, direction and control of the civil and military government of India were vested in the Governor-General in Council, who was required to pay due obedience to all such orders as he might receive from the Secretary of State. The Viceroy's Executive Council exercised in respect of Defence the same authority as it exercised in other departments of the Government. In the first phase of the representative institutions conferred upon India by the Montagu-Chelmsford Scheme, Defence expenditure and the direction of Defence policy were excluded from the control of the Indian Legislature. As a result of a decision to expand the Viceroy's Executive Council, the Defence Department, which had previously been responsible under the C-in-C for the whole of the Defence Services administration, was divided on 20th July, 1942, into two departments.

The Commander-in-Chief relinquished his title as Defence Member in the Viceroy's Executive Council and became War Member in the same Council and Head of the newly formed War Department. A civilian at the same time became Defence Member on the Executive Council and Head of the reorganized Defence Department.

The C-in-C, besides being a member of the Viceroy's Executive Council, was also a member of the Council of State. As War Member of the Executive Council he was responsible for the RIN, the Indian Army and the Air Force while in India Command, as well as the department which administered these services. Below him came the Secretary to the Government of India in the War Department (War Secretary) who controlled the department, and had constitutional right of access to the Governor-General, and the right to call for papers on any subject assigned to his department (which included all the subjects dealt with at Defence Headquarters, other than those assigned to the Defence Department).

The head of the Defence Department was the Defence Member of the Viceroy's Executive Council, who had under him a Secretary to the Government of India (Defence Secretary), who had the same constitutional rights as his counterpart in the War Department. The Defence Department took over the functions of the former Defence Co-ordination Department, and in addition a number of subjects dealt with by the former Defence Department (later War Department). These included such subjects as cantonments, Imperial prisoners of war, the Indian Soldiers' Board and certain military colleges and schools. When I arrived there was no Defence Member and the C-in-C administered his Department.

The War Department dealt with all army services proper, and also with the administration of the Royal Indian Navy and the Air Force in India, in so far as questions requiring the orders of the Government of India were concerned. It also dealt with all questions connected with the administration of ecclesiastical affairs. The War Department Secretariat had no direct relations with commanders of troops or the staffs of formations subordinate to Army Headquarters. The Army administration was represented in the Legislature by the War Member in the Council of State and by the War Secretary in the Legislative Assembly. The Defence Department was represented in the Executive Council by the Defence Member and in the Assembly by the Defence Secretary.

In 1941, when India assumed considerably wider responsibility for the actual conduct of the War, a Defence Consultative Committee of both the Central Indian legislatures and the National Defence Council was created, on which, besides members of the Legislature, representatives of the States and other public men agreed to serve. Later a Civil Defence Branch was created.

In November, 1943, South-East Asia Command was established; the operational control passed to the new Command and India became a base and training area for SEAC. To deal with their demands the office of the Principal Administrative Officer (India), was created under the C-in-C.

During the War special efforts were made to train more officers, who received 'Emergency War Commissions'. Until then only two types of commission had existed: the 'King's Commission Indian Officer' (those who had passed out of the Royal Military College, Sandhurst,) and the 'Indian Commissioned Officer' (those who had passed out of the Indian Military Academy, Dehra Dun). Under the officers came the Viceroy Commissioned Officers (VCOs) who were like Warrant Officers in the British Army and rose from the ranks.

When Germany and Japan surrendered, the problems of the C-in-C increased out of all proportion and he became, much to his disgust, a major political figure, second in importance only to the Viceroy himself, and found himself involved in a fierce political battle. Due to the impending political changes his main task was to keep the Indian Army in being and to prevent its involvement in any situation which might threaten effectiveness, morale and efficiency. He had to prepare its transition in status, its demobilization and rehabilitation. He had to decide the postwar composition of the army, and the steps to be taken to nationalize the forces. Indian formations were still abroad and they had to be brought back. The British formations and units had to be repatriated and the future of the Gurkhas had to be decided. The after-effects of the mutinies in the Royal Indian Navy and the Royal Indian Air Force had to be erased. The question of the Indian National Army trials loomed large and the Congress politicians were loudly accusing the regular army of being an army of mercenaries.

The C-in-C's problems were further increased by HMG's insistence that India should provide the forces for the defence of South-East Asia, that the sea and air links should be secured and, above all, that India should be made to stay in the Commonwealth.

The Indian National Army

*'The effect of this proposed condonation of crimes of
brutality and violence on the officers of the Army, in my
considered opinion, will be serious. . . . The officers will
regard this action as a betrayal of the principles to which
they have, throughout their service, been taught to adhere.'*

The Auk.

The so-called Indian National Army, known in GHQ as the Japanese Indian
Forces (JIF), was a product of the British military disaster in the East and
India's aspiration for independence. Subhas Chandra Bose was its creator.
He was a Bengali who had topped the list in the Indian Civil Service entrance
examination but later left the service to become a politician. Bose was elected
President of the Indian National Congress in 1938 but, as he believed in the
use of brute force to gain independence for India, he fell out with the more
conservative Congressmen, including Gandhi, who in fact disliked him.

In December, 1940, he stowed away in a Japanese ship from Hooghly to
Yokohama and then found his way to Germany. There he tried to raise a
Legion of 2000 men from Indian prisoners of war in German hands, but his
efforts were poor and he did not find much sympathy or encouragement in
Germany or Italy, as he and his troops refused to swear allegiance to Hitler
or Mussolini. He wanted these countries to declare that India would be
given Independence after the war, which they refused.

In 1942 Rommel declined the services of the Legion in the Western
Desert. In 1943 it was moved to Holland where the men mutinied and were
brought under control with difficulty. The following year it was sent to
Bordeaux in France where it committed many atrocities. The Italians raised
another unit in November, 1944 from the Indian POWs captured in North
Africa and ordered it to Libya but it refused to go.

Bose married an Austrian woman and had a child, but they were later
divorced. Meanwhile all Bose's political and military hopes in Europe were
shattered and he was sent by the Germans in a submarine to South-East
Asia.

At the time Bose left Japan for Germany, Raj Behari Basu, a known
terrorist, found his way to Japan and there married the daughter of Mitsuru

Toyama, the head of the Black Dragon Society. Basu became an adviser on Indian affairs. Singapore fell in February, 1942, and some 60,000 Indian troops became POWs. The Indian other ranks were separated from their British officers and there was nobody to guide them. The Japanese had no difficulty in raising the Indian National Army of 25,000 men under Captain Mohan Singh. Those who resisted were tortured. The Indian officers, junior commissioned officers and other ranks were made to use a common mess.

In 1942 Basu and Mohan Singh, during a visit to Tokyo, tried to persuade the Japanese to support the independence movement in India, which they at first refused to do. However, at a conference in Bangkok in 1942 Bose, then in Germany, was elected as Head of the Provisional Government of India and the Japanese gave way.

The men of the Indian National Army were given menial jobs and deployed to guard the concentration camps, construct airfields and act as camp followers to the Japanese Army. Mohan Singh protested and fell out with the Japanese, who arrested him and disbanded the INA. Many of his men were put in POW camps.

In June, 1943, the INA was revived by Bose, on the eve of the planned Japanese invasion of India. Bose asked the Japanese for funds, arms and ammunition, but his requirements were given a very low priority and the men were only armed with rifles. In October, 1943, Bose set up the Government of Free India (Azad Hind) in Tokyo, appointed himself Head of the State, Foreign Minister and C-in-C., and declared war on the UK and USA. He also sent ambassadors to various countries.

Field-Marshal Count Terauchi, Commander of the Japanese Forces in Burma, at first refused to have any INA units under his command, but, when forced to do so, grudgingly accepted 3,000 of the 23,000 troops offered to him. Originally the Japanese were prepared to accept up to 25,000 men but on scrutiny found only 12,000 fit for combat. Another reason for their non-acceptance was that there was a mutiny among the INA in Singapore and Bose did not know what to do and panicked.

At this time Bose was broadcasting regularly to the Indian troops in Burma and to the public in India, inciting them to throw off the yoke of the British. His broadcasts started with 'Chalo Delhi' (On to Delhi), 'Jai Hind' (Long Live India), etc. But by the summer of 1944 his words rang hollow and the INA itself was upset by his unsubstantiated slogans. The capture of an outpost in the Arakan was big news. Minor engagements were highlighted. To Bose it was a question of the survival of the INA. Out of the original 12,000 men which were accepted 6,000 surrendered in the Arakan.

When the Japanese started their Kohima/Imphal offensive in late 1944 out of the remaining 6000 men only 600 were found fit for duty. The INA had no heart left to fight when the Japanese started suffering reverses.

Bose sent some INA personnel by submarine to Baluchistan to raise a rebellion, but on arrival they gave themselves up. The Japanese and the INA did not hesitate to torture and commit brutalities on officers and men who would not join them. The worst case was that of Captain Durrani of the Bahawalpur State Forces who was put in a cage. By early 1945 the INA had become a farce. In March at Pegu some 2000 surrendered without firing a shot. Finally in April the INA was disbanded and Bose departed from Saigon. On 18th August, on his way to Tokyo, he was killed in an airplane crash.

The total INA personnel killed in battle was two officers and 150 other ranks. Casualties for other reasons were 1500 out of 20,000. This was the record of the INA which the Congress leaders were later to attempt to turn into an epic of heroic proportions.

Most of the men who joined the INA were cowards and were not prepared to face the hardships of the prisoner of war camps. It was an escape from ill-treatment and starvation. Very few joined it for patriotic reasons. Most officers later realized that the INA was a trap, but once in they could not get out. They had no love for the Japanese and maintained that they were let down by them. The atrocities committed by the Kempatai (Japanese Special Military Police) did not help towards better relations. Taking their clue from the Kempatai the INA committed atrocious crimes in the name of patriotism against their own comrades. These are considered among the most degrading crimes in the history of soldiering.

POW Camps were established in the forward areas where a few INA personnel were tried and sentenced. But then a decision was taken to bring them to the Red Fort in Delhi and screen them. They were classified into three categories: 'the Whites' – those who joined under compulsion. These were cleared and sent to their depots. Their total number was 3880; 'the Greys' – those who were 'luke warm' and did not take an active part. These were discharged but forfeited their pay and war gratuities for the period they were POWs. They were allowed to keep the family allowances already paid out and any pension earned other than when they were POWs. Their total number was 13,211; 'the Blacks' – those who were active members. These were dismissed from the service. They forfeited all rights and were considered a danger to the security of India. Their total number was 6177.

Some 'Blacks' were tried by court martial in November, 1945, for the following offences:

a) waging war against their country;
b) abetment to murder;
c) gross brutality against Indian POWs.

However, a lenient view was taken and in many cases they were only cashiered. Tuker was of the opinion that the 'Greys' should also be rehabilitated after a prolonged training period in the depot, otherwise they would swell the ranks of the disgruntled elements.

However, the politicians had decided to exploit the situation, and in this GHQ unwittingly played into their hands. Instead of trying the culprits in the Field Areas, they were brought to the capital and placed in the Red Fort and were tried under a full blaze of publicity. To make matters worse, in one case a Hindu, a Sikh and a Muslim were picked and tried jointly, which unified the different parties and they adopted a common stand.

Those tried were:

> Captain Shahnawaz
> Captain P. K. Sehgal
> Lieutenant G. S. Dhillon

The trial lasted from 3rd November to 31st December, 1945.

It must be said that Auchinleck did not believe in 'trials in secret' and wanted to give the accused the benefit of a full defence and access to their records. The charges against the accused were cast iron and Auchinleck wanted the public to be made aware of them. However, he misjudged the mood of the people and could not have chosen a worse time and place. It was a blunder. Nor did the Labour Government realize that it was becoming a 'political trial' and a trial of strength between them and the Congress. They thought they were holding another Nuremberg trial. When the trial caught the imagination of the people Wavell, Auchinleck and HMG did not know what to do and were anxious to get out of the mess somehow or other, but they were trapped. Auchinleck never really recovered from this loss of prestige.

GHQ was in an embarrassing position too. Auchinleck was the target of all shafts from Congress. Everybody kept pestering him for the release of the detainees. The members of the regular forces did not know where they stood. They felt that they were no longer required and were called mercenaries and toadies.

The disgruntled elements in the forces felt that they could now make trouble and get away with it. This was one of the causes of the mutinies in the Indian Air Force and Royal Indian Navy and some technical units in the Army. At this juncture the Army was truly in a delicate state.

In January, 1946, Nehru visited Singapore as a member of the Congress Medical Mission. A day before his visit orders were issued that no troops would be visible anywhere along the route and were to be confined to barracks.

Soon after his arrival Nehru met the Mountbattens, who went out of their way to cultivate him. Admiral Mountbatten, as C-in-C South East Asia, also thought that he should establish close links with the future leader of India and Edwina Mountbatten used all her charms to captivate him.

Thereupon Mountbatten invited Nehru to visit the unit messes and talk to the officers and issued orders to the garrison commander that the routes leading to the messes should be lined by troops giving him an ovation.

Nehru visisted the 16th Cavalry mess where the CO, Lieutenant-Colonel Peter Wilkinson, a classmate of mine, and the officers of the 19th Lancers were also present. Major Glancy, an officer of the 19th, heckled him over his support for the cause of Indian National Army. Glancy reminded Nehru that while he was in Ahmednagar jail he had condemned the activities of the Indian National Army but was now championing their cause and using it for political purposes. Thereupon Nehru lost his temper and flatly denied it, saying that he had always wanted their release and if they had to be tried it should have been done at Vizagapatam and not in Delhi. Glancy retorted that they were a disgrace to the good name of the Indian Army, upon which Nehru said that the Indian National Army had fought well and he would use his good offices to get them reinstated and placed in their correct order of seniority. He infuriated all officers present by saying that it was a 'British War' and he had little to do with it. India now required a National Army with a national outlook and hinted that Mohan Singh might become C-in-C.

In fact Nehru originally condemned the activities of the INA and had written accordingly to the C-in-C. But after Bose's death and the Japanese surrender he decided to take up their cause. It was a God-sent opportunity for him as it could be exploited for political purposes. He decided to make them into 'Heroes' and 'Patriots'. In September, 1945, the Congress asked for the release of the prisoners and set up a Defence Committee to handle their cases. The Committee included Bhulabhai Desai, Sir Tej Bahadur Sapru, Kailashnath Katju, Asif Ali and Nehru himself.

Bhulabhai Desai was openly saying that the INA trials had given the Congress the best possible weapon for propaganda and if the accused were executed, as was likely, it may lead to an armed revolution which might be supported materially by the Congress.

Colonel K. S. Himmatsinghji, a very senior and respected officer, kept Auchinleck informed of the effect of the trials on army personnel as well as on the public. In February he reported to Auchinleck that 'Never before had the entire country been in such a hostile mood against the British Government as it is today. This is due to political frustration. It is the only issue upon which there is agreement between the Congress and the League. The INA has aroused the imagination of all, including that of the Army. If any punishment is awarded to the INA personnel it would be denounced by all political parties. The future National Government will release all'. Colonel Himmatsinghi finally suggested that all INA prisoners should be released.

A British officer by the name of Major C. W. Cockin, who was Himmat's friend, had suggested that the INA trials should be put in cold storage until an Indian Government was formed as it was wrong for a British officer to judge their conduct. He maintained that the INA stood for freedom for India and they were justified in breaking their oath for patriotic reasons. He maintained that the trials were vindictive.

General Scoones wrote to Auchinleck in no uncertain terms and said, 'Leniency will not attain our immediate objective. . . . We may be blamed for lack of moral courage . . . and the armed forces will get confused'.

In early January the Congress issued invitations to a number of INA leaders to attend various political functions throughout India. The INA formed a Congress Volunteer Corps in the north and the Sikh *gurdwaras* (temples) became the centres of their activities and depots for their arms. This voluntionary Corps set up a number of revolutionary organizations to create unrest in the country and indulge in sabotage. They also worked to sow dissatisfaction among the personnel of the Regular Army and to make them feel that they were the tools of an alien government, while the INA was the army of the future and had the support of the political parties.

When the findings of the first INA trial of Sehgal, Dhillon and Shahnawaz came before the C-in-C, sentencing all three to cashiering, forfeiture of pay and transportation for life, he took a lenient view and wrote, 'I hold that it is our object to dispose of this most difficult problem of how to deal with the so-called INA in such a way as to leave the least amount of bitterness and racial feelings in the minds of the people of India and Britain. . . . . It is no use trying to judge these unfortunate people by the standards which we apply to British officers. . . . It would be quite wrong to expect the same standard of loyalty to their allegiance as from British troops. . . . Bose acquired a tremendous influence over them.' In conclusion he said, 'To confirm the sentence of transportation would make them into martyrs and intensify the political campaign of bitterness and racial antipathy now being waged by Congress in connection with the INA trials.' The C-in-C remitted the sentences of transportation for life but confirmed those of cashiering and forfeiture of pay and allowances. It was a political decision and was not well received by the Army.

Later some fourteen others came up for trial but with no results and Congress pressure increased to do away with the trials altogether.

The C-in-C also asked Formation Commanders for their views on the result of the INA trials. Later he issued a Memorandum on the INA trials to all Commanders. (See Appendix I, p. 303)

When I arrived in Delhi the Congress was jubilant over the result of the trials. The Muslim League was lukewarm and was taking very little interest in the trials.

The lighter side of this dismal situation was that Sir Shanti Surup Bhatnagar, the Director of Scientific and Industrial Research Organization, wrote to Auchinleck and asked for his permission to recommend his name for the Nobel Peace Prize.

A questionnaire was sent to the King's Commissioned Officers obtaining their views on the trial. I also received one and replied as follows:

EFFECT OF THE RESULT OF THE INA TRIAL ON INDIAN COMMISSIONED OFFICERS (ICOs)
(Impressions gathered by a King's Commissioned Indian Officer)

OBJECT
1) The object of this paper is to examine the effect of the result of the INA trial on the serving ICOs and to consider their feeling towards the very lenient punishment given to the three officers of the INA.

TRIAL
2) The general feeling among the ICOs is that the trial has been given undue publicity and should not have been held in Delhi, and for that reason, not even in India. After the original mistake of holding the trial in Delhi had been committed and public opinion roused against it, the authorities should not have yielded to press or party propaganda but should have punished the accused according to existing laws, which would have shown that discipline in the Army is not subject to public opinion. It is felt that if a soldier who has committed an offence can mobilize public opinion in his favour, he will always be able to get away with it. Amending the Indian Army Act and punishing these people leniently have made it obvious that the Government has shown weakness before the Congress party leaders. This has not created a good impression of the ICOs.

3) Up till now the Army was an organization with which the politicians would not dare interfere. But now it is not so. They can even get people set free who have committed serious offences. The Army should be above politics and politicians should not be allowed to meddle with it.

4) It is felt that the C-in-C's hands were forced by the Viceroy in taking this decision, in view of the fact that, at the moment, the authorities are keen to please the politicians so that the Parliamentary delegation, now in India, may get a hearing from all parties and not be boycotted.

NOTE:
It should be mentioned here that the ICOs have an implicit faith in the present C-in-C and feel that he has their interest at heart, but realize that as he is dictated to from above he cannot do as much as he would like to do.

POSITION OF THE ICOs
5) The ICOs feel that loyalty does not always pay. Those who withstood all hardships and torture by the enemy and the INA are not any better off today. Most prisoners are physical wrecks. Those who joined the INA have on the other hand done extremely well. They had a most comfortable existence under the Japs and on return to India have been set free.

6) The Indian public has no sympathy with those who did not join the INA. On the contrary, they are looked down upon. Those who joined INA are considered 'National Heroes' (a misused term) and are regarded as the leaders of the future army. These so-called 'National Heroes' will receive all the sympathies and the support of any National Government formed in India. The ICOs will be considered aliens and traitors to their cause. Efforts will be made to replace them by the 'Heroes'.

POSSIBLE FUTURE ORGANIZATION

7) It is thought that the political organizations, while their hands are tied, will raise some kind of unarmed militia like the German SS Organization in 1936, who, though unarmed, were fully trained to use arms. It is feared the nucleus of officers for this army will be provided by the released INA officers and men. Later, when the National Government is strong enough, they will be armed and equipped and ultimately when their strength is such that they will be able to defend India the Indian Army will be dissolved or merged into the National Army. The ICOs will be excluded from such an Army for being loyal to the British.

CONCLUSION

8) The ICOs feel that the three INA officers have been let off very lightly and the authorities have bowed down to the politicians. This has had an adverse effect on their morale and they do not see much of a future in the Army. Steps should be taken to show that the fears expressed above do not come true.

S. SHAHID HAMID

The Royal Indian Navy Mutiny

*'A man who cannot adjust himself to changed surround-
ings has served his usefulness in life.'*

The Auk.

The Royal Indian Navy Mutiny started in mid-January, 1946, when the
Royal Air Force mutinied in certain stations in India and the Middle East,
demanding early demobilization. Their mutiny remained peaceful and in
due course the men returned to work. The Indian Air Force, which was
modelled on the British pattern, taking the clue from their brothers in the
Royal Air Force, decided to follow suit and demanded the same privileges
as those given to the Royal Air Force. However, strong disciplinary action
was taken and the trouble in the Royal Indian Air Force was nipped in the
bud.

In early February trouble broke out in an Indian Pioneer Unit located
close to an establishment of the Royal Indian Navy in Calcutta. Immediate
action was taken and the culprits court-martialled and sentenced. It was all
done quietly and there was no leakage to the press. Soon after there was
unrest in the Signal Training Centre and the Electrical and Mechanical
Engineering Centre at Jubbulpore. This too was tackled quickly and the
disgruntled elements court-martialled. It was quite apparent that the Congress leaders, and especially the socialists under Jai Parakash Narain, were
inciting service personnel to defy the orders of their officers, specially those
of British officers.

The Formation commanders were facing a difficult situation as the Press
was giving extensive coverage to the activities of the mutineers. Jinnah,
however, kept his balance and did not encourage them. On the other hand
he advised Muslim officers of the Armed Forces to keep away from politics.
Later the Congress leaders got cold feet when the disturbances threatened
to engulf the country and by and large kept aloof. But by this time the fire
had been lit and the easiest targets were the units which were in the big
cities. In Bombay another Indian unit showed signs of indiscipline and was
immediately removed. But the biggest concentration of ships and establishments of the Royal Indian Navy was also at Bombay and the trouble soon
spread to them.

The causes of the RIN Mutiny were many. In 1939 the Navy had 117 vessels, including seven sloops, and had expanded twelvefold by 1943, and twentyfold by 1944. The expansion was too rapid and there were few experienced officers and trained men to lead them. They were extremely short of officers with peacetime experience. Most of the lieutenant-commanders were loaned from the Royal Navy and had no experience of Indian conditions. They knew little about the personnel with the result that discipline and morale deteriorated. Another reason was the recruitment of men from all over India who had no Naval background. The Navy had been initially manned by Punjabi Muslims. When certain personnel were required to operate the newly raised landing-craft units, men from two Army Battalions were transferred to the Navy. They were nicknamed 'Shallow Water Sailors'. The 'Divisional System', as practised in the Royal Navy, was adopted in the Indian Navy and was completely unsuited to Indian conditions. Another unsettling effect was the demobilization and reduction in the Navy and those who wanted to stay in the service found that they had no hope of making the Navy their career.

The Indian Navy had nine mutinies between the years 1942 and 1945.

Admiral John Godfrey was the C-in-C of the Navy, an appointment which he had held from 22nd March, 1943. The Admiralty gave him notice of retirement from September, 1945, but as he had not completed his three years of command, the C-in-C of the Army, who was the Head of the three Services, persuaded the Admiralty to let him stay until 22nd March, 1946, to which they agreed. A notification of retirement was published along with his appointment as Flag Officer Commanding Royal Indian Navy. He, however, said that his relief must be found by March otherwise he would hand over to Admiral Rattray and would leave for the United Kingdom. Godfrey was a spent force and kept putting off all actions, on the plea that his relief would tackle them. So much so that he had not even prepared a demobilization plan, maintaining that the Japanese surrender had come too soon, thus giving him no time to prepare the plan.

Godfrey was against the Indianization of the Navy on the grounds that he would lose the support of the Admiralty and would not be able to get Royal Navy Officers to serve in the Indian Navy. Auchinleck did not agree with him, and said that that was 'nonsense'.

Godfrey lacked tact and the ability to cooperate with others. He was not interested in his job. He was more interested in cultivating the Indian Princes and Congress leaders. His particular friend was Jam Sahib of Jamnagar who he often used to visit. He was also interested in the Women's Auxiliary Organization and did a great deal for them.

Godfrey was also Principal Transport Officer India, Naval Adviser to the War Member and the link between the Indian Navy and the Royal Navy. He had Rear-Admiral A. R. Rattray as his Second-in-Command at Bombay who was commissioned in 1912 and had had a chequered career. The only useful officer he had was Captain J. W. Jefford RIN who was the Controller of Personnel and Post-War Planning.

Godfrey did not see eye to eye with the C-in-C Army and resented being his subordinate. He maintained that the outlook of Auchinleck was purely military but he was the only one who ever took the slightest interest in the Navy. He was of the view that the interests of the Navy were being hindered by being under an Army C-in-C. He used to say that there was nobody to fight his battles with the Finance Ministry who bracketed the Navy with the Army and who were, in return, dominated by the War Department. He even said that a soldier should not be the political Head of his own service. Godfrey maintained that Auchinleck's conferences were 'jagged' as he did not listen to anyone who differed with him. He therefore had decided not to raise any controversial issues and preferred to keep quiet. What annoyed Godfrey most about Auchinleck were his orders to Indianize the Navy and the adoption of the Viceroy Commissioned Officers system as a link between the officers and men. Auchinleck maintained that the petty officers could not fill the gap and had little contact with the men.

Godfrey did not want the Viceroy Commissioned Officers system to be introduced. Auchinleck also urged that the divisional system of the Royal Navy be abolished but Godfrey did not agree. In fact in many instances Godfrey was not supported by his senior officers. The expansion of the Navy had brought in many Reserve officers, both Indian and British, who were mediocre and took little interest in their jobs. Godfrey had no system of evaluating the morale of his officers and men. It was only at the instance of Auchinleck that the Morale Section was established in August, 1945. In November the first report was received which revealed that all was not well in the Navy.

On 8th February in HMIS *Talwar* there were many catcalls against the WRINS. Some personnel were court-martialled but were acquitted. Many slogans like 'Quit India', 'Revolt Now', 'Kill the British White Bastards' were written on the walls of the establishment.

At this time Godfrey decided to visit the Princes in Rajputana. On 17th February the personnel of the HMIS *Talwar* refused to touch food or go on parade. HMIS *Sutlej* and *Jumna* followed suit. It was an open mutiny. Auchinleck ordered Rattray to intervene but it was too late. Flag marches were organized by the mutineers who took over the establishments.

On 18th February Godfrey arrived in Udaipur. On the same day a deputation of the disgruntled elements waited on the Flag Officer Bombay and presented forty complaints which included increase of pay to the level of the Royal Navy and release of the Indian National Army personnel. Auchinleck ordered that there should be no parleying with the mutineers but Rattray turned a blind eye and maintained that it was only a 'strike'.

On 20th February Godfrey arrived in Delhi and then flew to Bombay. HMIS *Narbada* had trained its guns on the Yacht Club at Bombay, disembarked the British and Indian Officers and hoisted the Congress flag. There was great. political tension in Bombay, leading to hooliganism and political unrest. All this created widespread hysteria. The ratings organized a march and the politicians were loud in their praise.

The same day in Karachi the personnel of HMIS *Hindustan* raised 'Jai Hind' slogans and opened fire but some howitzers and mortars silenced them. Seven men were killed and the rest surrendered.

On 21st February in Bombay the Army opened fire to prevent the mutineers fanning out in the city and Godfrey ordered all the officers to leave their ships. At this juncture General Sir Rob Lockhart took over control. He posted guards on HMIS *Talwar* and in the Castle Barracks. An Armoured Brigade was moved into Bombay. RAF Mosquitos also appeared. There was a bonfire of cars in the city. Police officers were burnt alive. Murder and looting were rampant.

The Congress sat in their Headquarters and encouraged the mutineers, the most active of them being Aruna Asaf Ali and Jai Parkash Narain, who maintained that to get rid of the British it was vital to undermine the discipline in the armed forces, the Army being an instrument of suppression, raised as it was from the martial races.

Later Patel got cold feet and started discouraging the mutineers lest it became a prelude to greater disorder. Godfrey broadcast to the Naval personnel without efect.

On the 23rd the Army opened fire, killing one officer and nine ratings, but order was restored. The incident was over by 3rd March.

A Court of Inquiry was instituted with Justice Fazal Ali as Chairman, two judges of the High Court and Admiral Paterson and General Rees as members, to investigate the causes of the mutiny. Their findings covered 598 pages and were unsupported by facts and based on the evidence of the disgruntled and dismissed elements.

Admiral Sir Geoffrey Miles, who replaced Godfrey, maintained that it should have been a departmental enquiry and not a judicial one. The full proceedings were not published but a summary appeared.

The Sikhs

*'The Sikhs are or were good soldiers but they are born
intriguers and care far too much for money.'*

The Auk.

On the downfall of the Mughal Empire, the Sikhs butchered, bayonetted,
strangled, shot down, hacked to pieces and burnt alive every Muslim they
could find!

The Sikhs had accepted British paternal authority and prospered under it.
In the Punjab they always had a privileged position. They were good farmers
and colonists, had the best of the agricultural land and were well-to-do.

There were two million Sikhs in East Punjab and 1.8 million in West
Punjab. In the Army they were over-represented and occupied many senior
posts. They were hard-working and made good technicians.

In 1940 the Sikh squadron of the Central India Horse refused to go
overseas and mutinied in Bombay. It was disbanded. Consequently the
recruitment of the Sikhs in the Indian Army was reduced and they lost their
'favoured treatment'. This was the work of the anti-British 'Akali Dal' party.

A Major Short, a 'dug-out' officer of the XI Sikh Regiment and a great
Sikh enthusiast, was sent for from the United Kingdom. He was appointed
Civil Liaison Officer in Punjab to humour the Sikhs and report on the unrest
which prevailed among them. Cripps made him an unofficial adviser and kept
in touch with him. Short made the Sikhs realize that the only friends they had
were the British. He convinced them that they had nothing in common with
either the Muslims or the Hindus. The Hindus for that matter were not their
equal. The Sikhs were isolated and left friendless by not co-operating with
the British. However, to support the aims and aspirations of the Sikhs a book
was published in Britain called *Betrayal of the Sikhs* by Loudon Sasasfield. In
this way Short managed to rally their support to the war effort.

Short was a great friend of the Maharaja of Patiala and other Sikh rulers.
He knew all the Sikh political leaders intimately. As such he occupied a key
position. He often said 'Settle the Sikhs and you settle India'. To his way of
thinking an understanding with the Sikhs was essential to the peace of the
Punjab. He was of the opinion that they were frightened of becoming a
helpless minority in United Punjab.

After the 1940 Resolution of the League, the Akalis (the party of Master Tara Singh and Gyani Kartar Singh) demanded 'Khalistan'. They felt that if the Muslims had a homeland so could they. However, they had no hope of achieving it unless it was within Pakistan. Short and others, including Baldev Singh, advised them to extract all possible concessions and privileges from Jinnah before they became part of Pakistan. They asked for:

1) A separate Province of East Punjab like that of Sind.
2) Special privileges in West Pakistan.
3) Special rights in Pakistan as a whole.
4) Special representation in the Army.

However, there was little doubt in the minds of the Sikhs that they would ultimately be part of Pakistan and the best way to get concessions was to use 'Khalistan' as a bargaining counter. Even though they knew the strength of their case, Congress ensured that they did not press it.

Jinnah said that he was prepared to come to an understanding with the Sikhs and told them, 'Let us not talk at each other but let us talk to each other', and appealed to them to free themselves from extraneous influences when a reasonable settlement could be reached.

Jinnah time and again assured the Sikhs that their rights would be fully safeguarded and made many gestures to them, but they were not reciprocated.

In Punjab Sir Sikander Hayat kept all parties together. He walked a tightrope and acted as mediator. He had signed a pact between the Unionists and Akalis which was known as the Sikander-Baldev Singh Pact. Short played a leading role in achieving this. His 'Sikh Mission' was successful and he established himself as a 'Sikh expert'. But the pact eventually contributed to the undoing of the Punjab.

On several occasions during 1941 and 1942 Jinnah assured the Sikhs that their right and privileges would be safeguarded in Pakistan. They would have nothing to fear. He invited them to talk to him, settle their differences and come to an understanding with their Muslim brothers. In 1944 Jinnah again said that, 'Every community is entitled to the right of self-determination and I do not want to deny this right to the Sikhs'. However, the Congress made every possible effort to convince them otherwise. Sikhs lacked political wisdom and thought that the Muslims were out to destroy them.

Jinnah also said that a 'sub-national group does not mean that the Sikhs are not a nation. I do not dispute that the Sikhs are a nation' and that 'they should send their proposal to me and give us their considered demand now and forget the past. We are willing to meet them in every way.' Jinnah could not have said more.

Eventually the Sikhs did not get Congress support for the establishment of Khalistan.

In the spring of 1946 any possibility of an agreement with the Sikhs was destroyed when the League was excluded from power in Punjab.

The North-West Frontier

'The officer must be an Indian first and then . . .'

The Auk.

The political situation on the frontier was not stable and the tribesmen were raising their heads.

Some time back a Committee had been appointed to examine the defence and administration problems of the North-West Frontier Province and Baluchistan, including the tribal area. After the Governor of the NWFP had commented on the report it was sent to the C-in-C for his views. In the opening remarks the Governor had posed certain questions – 'Is the responsibility for the tribal areas to be placed on the Central or Provincial Government?' 'If the Centre is to provide the money will they agree to the Provincial Government controlling the expenditure?' 'Should the tribes be allowed within certain limits to choose their own methods of internal Government?' 'Should anything in the nature of a confederation of tribes be encouraged or ought we to aim at linking each tribe with the adjacent settled district?'

The Governor maintained that due to the forthcoming constitutional changes their anwers must be speculative.

Auchinleck's comments were rather sarcastic. He said, 'The political department have been "speculating" on these and other like subjects for some eighty years or so but they still remain in a "speculative" mood, like the Freemasons.'

The Governor was of the view that the situation on the frontier was satisfactory. Auchinleck commented, 'Depends what is meant by "satisfactory". If it means "peace in my time" then it is probably a just claim. If it means "progress" then it is very doubtful.'

The general recommendation of the Committee was that an overall organization be set up to control the Militias. However, the Governor was of the opinion that the elaborate set-up betrayed a misconception of the problem. Auchinleck was of the view that a true conception of the problem depends on a correct definition of the object. What is the object of the Political Departments?

The Governor said that the Committee had proposed the formation of an Army in the guise of Militias to replace the regular army which he was of the view would be resented by the tribesmen; the Militia should function more like a Police Force with light armament and should not be a substitution for the Army. Auchinleck maintained that this was a wrong deduction. The Militias should aim at preventing the necessity for large operations. In any case he could not afford a great number of troops tied up on the Frontier.

A general reorganization of the various Scouts and Militia was suggested in the Report. In Waziristan a 'Central Waziristan Scouts' was to be formed to replace the regular garrison in Razmak. The Kyhber Rifles were to be mustered etc.

It was suggested in the Report that the tribes should be disarmed, but the Governor maintained that if the disarmament was to be accepted as a definite policy then it could only be done by force and provided the Afghan Government took similar and simultaneous action on their side of the border. The Auk was of the view that the External Affairs Department had been trying to disarm them for a long time with no results in spite of the fact that the Afghan Government had offered full cooperation. The Governor also maintained that in view of the impending constitutional changes the disarmament should be put off. Auchinleck's comment was, 'Why? This has been the attitude for fifty years or more and nothing has been done to achieve it.'

The Committee deliberated on the social and economic problems. The Governor remarked that 'the lack of development up to date is not for lack of policy but the real reason is that most tribes have looked upon proposals for development as being a corollary of occupation by the Government.' He went on to say that the tribesmen would rather be free and undeveloped than developed and administered and until they desired development for its own sake, no steps should be taken. He suggested that the first step towards it was to gain their confidence. The C-in-C did not agree with the Governor and asked, 'Have no steps been taken since 1860? If not, why not?' Auchinleck was of the view that if the tribesmen were made aware of the benefits of development they would come forward. He maintained that the Political Department was *non-possumus* as usual. The Committee had suggested that 'some sort of administration' should be suggested to the tribes for running their own affairs but the Governor maintained that it would raise suspicion. Auchinleck's comments were that the Political Department was always afraid to take any action.

It was suggested that the Army garrisons be withdrawn both from Razmak and Wana. Auchinleck agreed to the withdrawal.

It was suggested that local elements of Wazirs and Masuds should be introduced in the Waziristan Scouts but the Governor, on the recommendation of Commandants of the Scouts, said that they should not be enlisted. Auchinleck said that their introduction was essential and the Commandants were quite incompetent to judge in this matter as they lived in blinkers.

It was strongly recommended that a Boys' Company in the Militia should be raised and Auchinleck agreed.

All agreed to locating the Air Force at different stations not only for close support but also for supply dropping and troop carrying.

The rewriting of the 'Grey Book' was recommended. This book gave all the necessary information on the Frontier. Steps were to be taken to simplify it and reduce it in size.

The Gardai Brigade was to be withdrawn as soon as the Khasadars were in a position to protect the Razmak Road.

The Frontier Constabulary was to be left as it was.

In conclusion the Governor expressed the view that the garrison troops should not be withdrawn, while Auchinleck maintained that the Governor had not understood the long-term policy issued by GHQ which envisaged that the tribes police themselves eventually. That should be the firm basis of a Frontier policy.

Auchinleck, with his long experience of the Frontier, had an intimate knowledge of its problems and their implications.

PART II

It Nearly Succeeded

March 1946

'Internal chaos means suffering, misery, loss to everyone, and can only retard progress.'

The Auk.

It was a pleasant February morning in 1946 when the General Officer Commanding the Formation at Saharanpur called me to his office. He showed me a signal from GHQ commanding me to travel to Delhi immediately. I was bewildered and so was the GOC. I did not have the faintest idea what had necessitated the summons. My first impression was that probably some A&Q matters relating to the Division were to be discussed. Therefore I collected all the information which I thought might be required and braced myself for the Delhi encounter.

Arriving in Delhi the next morning I reported to the Military Secretary, General Sir Ross McCay.* In the five minutes I was with him he asked me a few odd unrelated questions. He then told me to go and see the Chief of the General Staff, the Master General of Ordnance, the Quarter-Master General and the Adjutant-General in turn.

I went from office to office meeting each of the senior officers that I had been told to see. We talked about the current situation in the country and abroad. None of them inquired even casually about anything relating to my Formation.

By this time I was getting curious, if not impatient, as to why I was being shunted from one office to another. Then the Military Secretary saw me again and told me to see the Private Secretary to the Commander-in-Chief, a man called Lt-Col Robin Ridgway who, in civilian life, had been a master at Winchester.

The riddle deepened. Wherever I was ordered or guided to I found people scrutinizing me more in meaningful silence than through overt questioning. This, frankly, bewildered me. Ridgway, too, did not discuss anything and I sat musing upon the whole affair.

At about midday, Ridgway suddenly asked me what I was doing for lunch.

---

*Lieut-General Sir Ross McCay (1895–1969) had been Military Secretary, India since 1944. In 1940 he became an Area Commander, India; in 1948 Chief of Staff, Pakistan Army.

I thought he was perhaps going to extend his hospitality. I told him that I was keen to get back to my Formation.

'Come and have lunch with the Commander-in-Chief,' he said in a casual way. For a moment I thought he was pulling my leg, but when he told me to be there by 1 p.m. and that he himself would introduce me to Sir Claude, I realized he was serious. It was the last thing I expected to happen. I told him that I was not properly dressed, 'It doesn't matter much,' he said.

The Commander-in-Chief was universally referred to as the 'Chief'. Sharp on 1 p.m. I arrived at his house. He drove in from his office soon after. He welcomed me with a friendly chat and then we went in to lunch. Apart from him the only other person present was his sister. She was a formidable woman called Mrs Cherry Jackson. We talked about a variety of subjects such as gardening and tree planting. Nothing was said relating to Army matters.

At the end of a very enjoyable lunch I thanked 'the Chief' and returned to my Division. This was my first glimpse of him at close quarters.

Next morning I reported to my own General. He was a very fine commander and was extremely kind to me. When I told him what had happened in Delhi he laughed and said, 'Shahid, you are up for the high jump.'

On 24th February I received the following letter from the Military Secretary at GHQ:

PERSONAL & CONFIDENTIAL
General Headquarters
India
Military Secretary's
Branch
NEW DELHI 21st FEBRUARY 1946

My dear Hamid,

Lieut.-Colonel W. R. P. Ridgway, OBE, whom you met last Tuesday, will be vacating the appointment of Private Secretary to HE. The C-in-C next month, on release from the service.

His Excellency desires to appoint an Indian Army Officer to this post and has instructed me to ask whether you are willing to accept it. I need not, I am sure, emphasize what an important post it is in the working of GHQ.

Naturally the appointment would be officiating to start with to find out whether you and the job suit each other, though I do not think there need be any doubts as to the result. If, as I hope, you agree to accept you will be needed here by 1st March to be put in the picture and learn the ropes.

Yours sincerely
Sd/ – R. C. McCay

Lieut. Colonel S. S. Hamid, RIASC
CRIASC
39 Ind Div
A. P. O. SAHARANPUR

Frankly, I was stunned. I did not know what to make of this new appointment. It was now clear to me that the first call to GHQ was to assess whether, in the words of General McCay, the job and I 'suited each other'. I realized that others too must have gone through the same exercise, before they had finally selected me.

Amidst a spate of congratulatory messages from the Division Commander and the Staff, I packed my few belongings and left the next morning.

From now on most of my narrative will be in first person as this is the diary I kept while on the job itself.

The reader will find me referring to Sir Claude Auchinleck as 'the Auk' or just 'Auk'. This is what we called him amongst ourselves. I have referred to Mohammad Ali Jinnah as the 'Quaid', the short form of Quaid-i-Azam, the title by which he was known to us Muslims.

When revising my diary I have clarified some aspects of it to make it more readable.

4th March: I think that I should begin my diary by describing the Commander-in-Chief's house and the household.

The house itself is enormous. There are some twenty bedrooms and many state rooms, simply but elegantly furnished. Long windows open on the terrace. It is a vast estate with a beautiful garden. Auk's poodle and two cranes roam the estate freely. There is a big vegetable patch for the staff. A swimming pool has been built on top of an old Mughal hunting bower.

The Auk has no Military Secretary. I do that job as well. Major Learmonth is my assistant. There is a Controller of the household, a cousin of the Auk called Jack Auchinleck. There is an Assistant Controller and four ADCs. Next to the house is my residence and that of the Surgeon to the C-in-C.

The house given to me has six bedrooms. We occupy two, leaving the other rooms for our guests. It is a very comfortable house with a lovely garden and spacious lawns. It is situated at the edge of the woods from where wild boars often appear in our compound!

Everything is free for me: the house, the servants, the cars; even the vegetables and poultry which come from the C-in-C's estate. There are horses to ride. In the woods at the back one can always get some game. In other words, it is sheer luxury.

The other day at the house, I had my first real encounter with Auk's sister, Mrs Jackson. This was not without sparks. She spoke to me rather haughtily.

'Are you the new Private Secretary? I did not like your predecessor and I wonder whether I will like you. I also wonder whether you will last in this job.'

This cold reception did shake me a bit though I had already been warned by Robin to take no nonsense from her.

'Yes, Mrs Jackson,' I said, 'I am the new Private Secretary and incidentally a native. I mean to stay in this job. Nobody apart from the C-in-C can remove me.'

She looked straight at me and I stared back. I think I made my point. I hope she realizes that I am not going to take any nonsense from her.

Mrs Jackson is a widow. Her husband was a tea planter in Ceylon. The Auk has called her to act as hostess for him. She is a woman of strange priorities and keeps six dogs with her. Her odd selection of friends includes a woman shopkeeper whom the Auk particularly dislikes. Mrs Jackson is now virtually the second lady of the land. The first is of course the Viceroy's wife. I presume this exalted station has gone to her head.

It is rather a difficult period in Auk's personal life. His wife, Jessie, has decided to marry Air Marshal Sir Richard Peirse.* Jessie's possessions are being packed so that they can be sent to her, as are all the things Auk gave her as gifts.

Jessie left before I began my job here. But I have been told that she could never reconcile herself to the composed and sedate life expected of her as the wife of the C-in-C of the subcontinent. She found Auk's long office hours and dedication to work tiresome and totally unsuited to her taste. She was gay and full of life. I gather Auk never denied her any opportunity to enjoy herself, attend parties and visit whomsoever she wished. Mary Cawthorn, wife of General Cawthorn,† both good friends of the Auk, told me that the Auk adored Jessie. She let him down.

The Auk often discussed his private affairs with Mary. She said that she was next door the night Jessie left. Mary had said a prayer for him. She remembered seeing the Auk in a shop buying jewellery for Jessie not long before. According to her it must have been most embarrassing for the Auk to see Jessie and Richard 'fooling' with each other in public.

Anyhow, at this time the atmosphere at the C-in-C's house is heavy with a brother's personal misery and a sister's social oddities. To get over the sad episode the Auk has plunged more and more into the work.

The office which I have inherited is virtually a 'mad house'. People keep popping in and out endlessly. There is a battery of four telephones on my table which ring incessantly. The ADC and the lady stenographer share my office. Their acquaintances visit them every now and then to exchange social pleasantries.

Robin, who was charged with the task of initiating me into the rituals of office, had scarcely had time before he left to talk to me, much less 'put me wise' to its detailed work.

*Air Chief Marshal Sir Richard Peirse (1892–1970) was AOC-in-C India 1942–43 and Air C-in-C S.E. Asia Command 1943–44.

†Major-General Sir Walter Cawthorn (1896–1970), an Australian, was Director of Intelligence India Command 1941–45; Deputy Chief of Staff, Pakistan Army 1948–51; High Commissioner for Australia in Pakistan 1954–58.

The Auk comes to the office every morning regularly in an old, weather-beaten car and without an escort. It is a great honour to serve this distinguished Commander, who had the distinction of being the first to inflict a defeat on the Germans in the midst of their astounding military successes.

When I took over the assignment, I inherited an engagement diary from my predecessor. To keep this up is part of the job. I have never kept a diary myself. Until now I have considered it to be an unnecessary drill.

The days that lie ahead will become an important part in our history, too important to be consigned to the frailties of human memory. So I have decided to record them fresh, and preserve them. I have also decided that I might keep copies of important secret documents and have asked the Chief's permission to do so. He has no objection but said that if I ever intended to publish them it should not be during his lifetime.

In view of all this I have begun to keep a detailed account of day-to-day events, alongside the engagement diary.

I collect the more interesting papers and store them away in deference to his wishes.

I must say here that I am deeply impressed by the Chief's personality, his courteous manners and his forthright approach. At no stage do I feel that I am talking to the Commander-in-Chief. He puts me at ease right at the outset with a smile and a friendly handshake. He does not talk down to me being the head of the mighty military machine, but as a brother officer.

General Savory,* who has been commanding the British Forces in Persia, has arrived to stay. He is to take over the appointment of Adjutant-General to the Forces. He is a tough soldier and the Auk likes him immensely.

We attended a performance of *Fauji Dilkush Sabha*. This organization is similar to that of ENSA which entertains British troops. It is very popular among Indian Troops. Various groups go round all over the subcontinent and give performances.

5th March: Delhi Victory Week has started. There was a full dress rehearsal of the Viceroy Parade today.

Lord Mountbatten, the Supreme Allied Commander South-East Asia, has arrived to stay. This was my first glimpse of him. Apart from being a good conversationalist, he is good-looking and well turned-out, an impressive figure.

In the evening we attented a reception given by His Highness the Maharaja of Patiala where some 300 Sikhs were present.

6th March: The C-in-C gave a flag to the Boy's Company of the Royal Garhwal Rifles. There has been a great shortage of technicians in the Armed

*Lt-General Sir Reginald Savory (1894–1980) commanded the 23rd Indian Division 1942–43; Director of Infantry, India 1943–45; Adjutant-General in India 1946–47.

Force. As the Army becomes more and more mechanized the demand has become greater. The C-in-C is convinced that to meet this requirement the only course open is to enlist boys, whose training would be carried out within the various regimental centres. In due course they would become first-class technicians in their own units. Every Boys' Company has to have a flag designed by the boys themselves but approved by the Auk who often alters them.

The Auk is a member of the Council of States and attends its meetings regularly. He answers questions on the Armed Forces. He is very friendly with all the other members. The Auk is no orator but an excellent speaker, direct, clear and convincing.

The C-in-C had set up a Committee under the Chairmanship of Lt-Gen. Sir H. B. D. Willcox.* This Committee was to consider the question of the future organization of the High Command of the three services in India. It submitted its report at the beginning of the year and is now being considered by the C-in-C.

The Committee recommended:

a) The Armed Forces should be headed by a Supreme Commander and under him be placed the three Commanders-in-Chief.
b) The Supreme Commander should act as an adviser to the Government of India.
c) The War Department should be headed by a War Member or a Political Minister and the Supreme Commander should be responsible to him.
d) A Supreme Commander's Committee with the three Commanders-in-Chief should be established.
e) An organization should be created to deal with the administration of all the three Services.
f) A Defence Committee of the Cabinet should be established with the Prime Minister as its Chairman, the War Member as the Deputy Chairman and the Finance, Foreign and some other ministers as its members.

7th March: The Army Commander's Conference was held today at the house.

At 1500 hours I went with the Commander-in-Chief to watch the victory parade. The salute was taken by Lord Wavell. It was really a magnificent show and the turn-out of the men, vehicles and animals was meticulous. It did my heart good to watch this magnificent body of men march past. The parade went extremely well and the timings were perfect though it lasted nearly two hours. I must say that Wavell stood there like the great Commander which he is. His face reflected the pride and satisfaction which he must have felt. The Auk was looking very pleased and happy at the sight of the men whom he had also trained, and who had fought so well in the war.

*Lieut-General Sir Henry Willcox (1889–1968).

The Congress did not approve of the Victory Celebration as they have already committed themselves to the cause of the INA. Not only did they boycott the Parade but also staged demonstrations in the city. Violence broke out. The Town Hall and many other buildings were burnt down. The police had to open fire on the rioters, causing many casualties.

Wavell was very annoyed with the politicians who had boycotted the Parade, and did not mince his words. He told them what he thought about them. He said that this was the most magnificent Parade he had ever seen in his life and it was a great pity that they were not there to see this superb body of men who were responsible for defending the subcontinent against the Japanese invasion.

Incidentally, after the victory over the Germans, the Auk made a broadcast to the troops.

There were fireworks in the evening in the true Mughal style. The C-in-C gave a dinner party at the house for the Army Commanders and others.

8th March: The Auk presided over the Defence Consultative Committee. The last time he addressed them he was very clear about the intending developments in the forces. In today's meeting the stand he took was similar.

9th March: The Auk received a letter from General Mayne* who is the Military Secretary to the Secretary of State for India. In this he mentioned that there had been discussions between the 'Big Three' – Pethick-Lawrence† Alexander‡ and Cripps§ – on the future constitutional changes in India. He also stated that the Prime Minister wanted the future government or governments to give an undertaking to provide Defence Forces to the Commonwealth for the defence of 'South-East Asia Area'.

How can anybody give such an undertaking? The Auk himself is against such a request being made to the leaders. He has sent the letter to the Viceroy for his information.

Admiral Godfrey, the C-in-C RIN, left India.

---

*General Sir Mosley Mayne (1889–1955) was GOC-in-C Eastern Command India 1943–44; Principal Staff Officer, India Office, 1945–46.

†Frederick William, 1st Baron Pethick-Lawrence (1871–1961) was raised to the peerage in 1945. Educated at Eton, he was a Labour MP 1923–31 and 1935–45; he was Secretary of State for India and Burma 1945–47. He had been a member of the Indian Round Table Conference in 1931.

‡Albert Victor, 1st Earl Alexander of Hillsborough (1885–1965) was raised to the peerage as a Viscount in 1950 and created an Earl in 1963. Educated at an Elementary School in Bristol, he was First Lord of the Admiralty 1929–31, 1940–45 and 1945–46; Minister of Defence 1947–50.

§Sir Stafford Cripps (1889–1952) was educated at Winchester and was Labour MP for E. Bristol 1931–50; British Ambassador to Russia 1940–42; Minister of Aircraft Production 1942–45; Chancellor of the Exchequer 1947–50.

At 0830 hours Mountbatten gave a lecture on South-East Asia in the Cinema Hall and talked about the wonderful work he had done! It was an exercise in publicity. He is meeting many Congress leaders.

There was an Investiture at the Viceroy's House at 10.30 am. I was introduced to Wavell, presumably to get his OK to my appointment. Major-General C. O. Harvey,* Military Adviser to the Indian State Forces, was knighted. Incidentally, he is a famous polo player. In the afternoon there was an Air Pageant and in the evening at 9 pm we witnessed the Tattoo.

10th March: The Viceroy gave a party in the Mughal gardens for soldiers, airmen and the naval personnel who participated in the Victory Parade. A lovely spectacle, highlighting the British love for pageantry.

The C-in-C gave a lavish '*Barakhana*' (feast) to some of the participating troops. He ate with them sitting on the ground. Many prominent personalities were also present. His Honorary ADC, Captain Tikka Khan, was in attendance. The dinner was followed by music.

11th March: The Auk is due to go to the Chief of the Imperial General Staff's Conference, and to attend the Exercise 'New Concept' in London.

Robin Ridgway wants to accompany him and then get demobbed in UK. He asked for my permission. I said I had no objection to him accompanying the Auk.

Though poor Robin tried his best to put me in the picture, he has had no time. Robin and I had been together for a week. Today was his last day. He said some interesting things.

'Old boy, you have seen the mad house. I am very sorry that I could not carry out proper handing-and-taking over, but I am sure that you will manage the job. However, I will tell you one important aspect about the C-in-C's house. For whatever it is worth, I did not get on with the Auk's sister Mrs Jackson. She disliked me immensely. I could not understand her but I hope that you will get on with her and put her in her place. From now on it is all yours.'

My appointment as PS(C) has come as a surprise to the whole of the subcontinent. It was commonly believed that a 'native' would never be appointed to such a sensitive post. I have received telegrams, letters, messages from all over the subcontinent wishing me God-speed and good luck. Among the telegrams there is one from General Irwin,† Commandant of Staff College, Quetta, where I was an instructor:

*Major-General Sir Charles Harvey (1888–1969) was Military Secretary to the Viceroy of India 1926–31; commanded South Indian Division 1940–42; Military Adviser to the Indian State Forces, 1943–46.

†Major-General Stephen Irwin (1895–1964) was Chief of Staff to Commander 14th Army, Burma 1943–44; Commandant of the Staff College, Quetta, 1945–46; Deputy Chief of General Staff, India, 1946–47.

'Congratulations from all 'Owls' on your appointment.' (The Owl is supposed to be the wisest amongst birds and figures prominently in the Staff College crest). Azam Jah, the heir apparent to the Nizam of Hyderabad and a personal friend, as well as General Cariappa, sent me congratulatory messages.

The newspapers and All-India Radio commended the far-sightedness of the C-in-C in appointing an Indian to this all-important job.

It is very heartening indeed. The most profound joy I have felt was from my mother's letter.

'Had your father been alive today, he would have felt proud of you.' Then, imparting an oriental touch to her message, she continued, 'Remember, the more a bough is laden with fruit, the more it bends to the ground.' It was another way of saying 'Blessed are the meek'. With these words ringing in my ears, I have embarked upon my fascinating job.

12th March: The Auk left for UK and Air Marshal Sir Roderick Carr,* the Air Officer Commanding, became the officiating C-in-C. He has occupied the Commander-in-Chief's Office. Visitors continue to pour in. I went through files to ensure they were in order, and sent them to the Air Marshal. They remained with him for hours. Later they were returned without any comments, as well as being unsigned.

Then again I sent them in and they were returned the same way. The third time I took them in personally.

'Sir, you have not approved or disapproved the proposals which have been submitted to you.'

'You read them. If they are in order and you agree with them, bring them in personally, and I will sign.' This has really shaken me.

Today was my first day in the chair. I am not yet fully acquainted with the working of GHQ. In fact it means more homework for me. I must record that, true to his words, Sir Roderick signs all the papers blindly.

We get on extremely well. He is a gentleman, and a distinguished airman, but hates office work. However, his method of working is doing me immense good. I have to study each file in depth and am gradually picking up the working of the War Department and GHQ. It is also giving me confidence, which, as a novice to an important assignment, I badly need. I hope that I will have a complete picture of the situation by the time the Auk returns.

The Air C-in-C takes all things quietly. He does not go out of his way to create work. He just does enough to keep the mighty GHQ ticking over, and

*Air Marshal Sir Roderick Carr (1891–1971) a New Zealander, was with Shackleton's Antarctic Expedition 1921–22; Deputy Chief of Staff (Air) Supreme HQ Allied Expeditionary Force 1945; AOC-in-C India 1946.

no more. The Chief of the General Staff, General Sir Arthur Smith* (called 'Salvation Arthur' by Auk) attends the Viceroy's conferences. He is also sent by the Viceroy to meet the political leaders, especially to discuss the INA trials and their consequences.

23rd March: The League held the Pakistan Day Rally in Delhi.

The Sikhs have become a source of trouble and their demands are many and varied.

The Viceroy is facing political as well as administrative problems. The internal situation in the subcontinent is becoming extremely delicate. Communal violence has erupted in many places.

Before the C-in-C left for UK he had asked the Formation Commanders for their views on the results of the INA trials. Later he issued a Memorandum on the INA trials to all Commanders. (See Appendix I, p. 303)

24th March: There has been extensive political activity and a great many conjectures as to how the Cabinet Mission is going to function. No one is quite certain whether they are coming with any definite proposals or are just on a fact-finding mission, making up their minds later. In any case, they are going to talk to various Indian leaders.

Today the Cabinet Mission has arrived. Wavell has called them 'The Three Magi'. Others call them 'Three Wise Men'. It consists of Lord Pethick-Lawrence, Secretary of State for India, Sir Stafford Cripps, President of the Board of Trade, and Mr. A. V. Alexander, First Lord of the Admiralty. Out of these, Cripps is the real negotiator. Lord Pethick-Lawrence, an old sedate politician, looks pathetic in the midst of a political tempest. He is already known as 'Pathetic-Lawrence'. He has the appearance of a padre, and is considered a disciple of the Gandhian philosophy. Cripps is a socialist and is known to be close to Hindus. He is the liveliest of the group and is called 'Father Cripps'. He gives the impression that he is a know-all and in control of the situation. He looks mainly through the Hindu eye and regards the Muslims as an aggravating minority. Alexander is placid and reticent. He is the only member capable of considering things in their correct perspective.

Major Short, a retired officer of the Sikh Regiment and a great favourite of the Sikh community, has accompanied the mission as Cripps's personal assistant. This is to give the Sikhs the impression that their interests are being looked after. The three gentlemen are lodged at 2 Willingdon Crescent, very close to our house and have established their office in the South Wing of the Viceroy's House.

---

*Lt-General Sir Arthur Smith (1890–1977) was GOC-in-C Eastern Command, India, 1945–46; Chief of General Staff, India, 1946; Deputy C-in-C India 1947; Commander of British Forces in India and Pakistan 1947–48.

The Mission is to assist Wavell in bringing about an agreement on the method of framing a constitution and in the formation of an interim Government. The mission has undoubtedly given the impression that HMG means business and that Independence is within the grasp of the Indians. It has also made it clear that if the parties do not agree, and do not cooperate, then the Labour Government will not hesitate to propound their own scheme.

The Viceroy doubts whether they have come with any definite plans, though they have given him the impression that the delegation had something up its sleeve. The Mission has given an ineffective press conference, though they answered many questions. From the outset Cripps has humoured Gandhi and Nehru. It is well-known that the Labour Government which he represents has always been close to the Congress Party and is impressed by them. He has a tendency to believe Congress and is reluctant to regard Pakistan as a really serious proposition or even a live issue. The Labour Government believes that 'Pakistan' is being used as a bargaining counter to get the best deal for the Muslims.

Savory said that it was a 'Fateful Day for India and possibly for the Empire'. We may have Independence this year, a critical year. The Auk's role is to help to guide the Indian Army through transition in a spirit of calm discipline. There may be trouble, but then I am a pessimist. The Congress and the League are becoming acutely aware that before long they will be responsible themselves for keeping law and order. They are unlikely to stir up further trouble among the armed forces. They have, I think, seen the red light, though I cannot tell definitely.

27th March: A great deal of discussion on the future of the British troops in India. Naturally nobody wants the British troops to get involved in a quarrel between the future Dominions or in any other ill-fated incidents. But while the British hold India, they have a job to perform.

In the autumn of 1945 the retention of the British troops in India was being questioned and it was maintained that they were not necessary as the country was going to be given self-government. Besides, the cost of maintaining them was much greater than that of the Indian troops. Previously they have been used to hold India for the British Government and to stiffen the Indian troops.

Some were of the view that in case of communal disturbances the Indian troops would prove unreliable due to religious feelings and the British troops would still be required due to their impartiality. But now this can only be decided by an autonomous Government of India.

The British have used them to protect airfields, ports and other strategic points important to the Empire. They have considered that for the good of the Commonwealth it was essential that the British and the Indian troops work, play and train together. This would ensure cooperation and understanding in case of a war.

People of all shades of opinion, except certain politicians for selfish reasons, subscribe to the belief that the British troops should be retained. Many feel that it is the responsibility of the British Government to maintain law and order until they withdraw. It is emphasised that the subcontinent must be handed over in an orderly fashion to give the future government a good start. Some politicians feel that HMG is retaining them in India to prolong their rule, and even for re-establishing their authority. Therefore they want to make sure that the British troops leave the soil as soon as possible. The way to ensure their departure is to give the impression that the British troops are redundant, and no longer required for internal security duties. At the same time the Congress politicians want British prestige to suffer in the eyes of the world. They want to show them up as being incapable of maintaining law and order. They also feel that they can bully Britain as it is no longer a world power. The Congress is even prepared to see chaos rather than use the British troops in aid of the civil power.

It is quite evident that the British are leaving India as soon as a political settlement is reached. This is not in too distant a future. Incidentally Wavell has continuously asked HMG to fix a date for the handing over which he feels will create confidence among the politicians.

28th March: The Viceroy has called the Governors of the Provinces to meet the Cabinet Mission. All Indian leaders are in Delhi. The Princes' Standing Committee is in session and so is the Editors' Standing Committee. It is quite a gathering and there are many speculations.

The Auk had prepared a radio broadcast on 'Your Great Duty' to the officers of the Army. This was broadcast by the Adjutant-General. The text was sent to all officers and is printed as Appendix II on p. 307.

Tuker* submitted a paper to the Auk. He is of the opinion that sooner or later communalism must infiltrate into the Indian Army. The men are being subjected to nationalist propaganda, attending political meetings and coming in contact with political agitators. The vernacular press is inciting them and calling them 'stooges of the British'. Communal disturbances in their home areas and the tales of atrocities are a source of constant worry to them. Tuker maintains that anyone who disagrees with the above assessment is out of touch and living in a world of make-believe.

Mixed Indian units when used on internal security duties have come in for criticism. He states that in order to avoid any breakdown in discipline it is vital to change them into one-sect units as soon as possible. They could then be easy to handle and would be effective in protecting the minorities during the disturbances.

*Lt-General Sir Francis Tuker (1894–1967) commanded 4th Indian Division 1942–44; 4th Indian Corps 1945; GOC-in-C Eastern Command, India 1946–47. Known as 'Gertie', he was a writer of distinction, perhaps best remembered for his autobiography *While Memory Serves*.

Besides, as the division of the subcontinent is imminent, it is in the fitness of things that the sooner the units are reorganized into one-class units, the smoother would be the transition. All this must be completed before the Partition Plan is put in operation. Otherwise there will be the danger of a civil war. One-class units have existed before and even now there are many in the Army. Through them it will be easier to keep peace, as well as form nuclei of the future armies of Pakistan and Hindustan. Auk does not agree. A pity.

Tuker had already discussed the Plan with the Parliamentary Delegation in January, 1946, but with no results.

Tuker is the most outstanding officer I have ever met. He is a fighting soldier as well as a great strategist, and is completely relaxed in a difficult situation. He is a great friend of Wavell, with whom he shares a love for poetry. He even attends Urdu *Mushairas* (recitations of poetry). In fact, he is fond of all the arts. He is himself a good painter as well. He told me that when he was a Brigade Major his Brigade Commander did not approve of his writing poetry or of his painting efforts and said that these trends did not suit a soldier.

30th March: Today the *Hindustan Times* commented editorially on the Auk's appeal to the Indian Army. 'There is no doubt whatever that if the transfer of power is not quickly brought about, the foreign rulers of India cannot count upon the loyalty of the Indian Army. Nor can Nationalist [India] attach importance to such loyalty.' The *Hindustan Times* ridiculed the Auk's statement that certain disruptive forces were at work to undermine the discipline of the Indian forces. It said that the immediate danger is to be expected from foreign vested interests, by which they meant the British officers of the Indian Army who might create trouble. It is a dirty insinuation as the British officers are doing their level best to keep sanity in the Indian Army. To blame them and to doubt their loyalty at this stage is to dishearten them. Probably that is the very purpose of the article.

The *Hindustan Times* also advocated the cause of the Indian National Army. It mentioned that the C-in-C and his advisors were betrayed into a grievous error of judgement by enforcing a public discussion regarding the duty of a soldier when faced with a conflict between his patriotism and professional discipline. The *Hindustan Times* ignored the fact that the INA officers were being tried for acts of brutality against their own comrades.

Durga Dass, who is the Editor of *Hindustan Times*, believes in 'yellow' and 'keyhole' journalism. He is a great friend of Patel and is therefore disliked by Nehru.

31st March: General Savory made a pertinent comment which is worth mentioning here: 'Let's see how things turn out. There is a divinity that shapes our ends and too much worrying and planning in these uncertain days is without profit.'

April 1946

'The Army is the anchor of the country.'
The Auk.

2nd April: A Pay Committee has been formed under Major-General S. F. Irwin. He was Commandant at Staff College when I was instructing there. I know he is a brilliant officer.

GHQ had asked Tuker to submit his thoughts on 'the military implications of Pakistan'. The paper was later sent to Wavell with a note from the Auk that it will be impossible to defend a partitioned India. As a result of this Tuker was called in by the Cabinet Mission. He advocated the presence of a neutral force to defend the subcontinent.

3rd April: Auk returned to work after his trip to UK.

The whole country is governed by the Viceroy and his Executive Council. The Auk is the War Member. Wavell leans heavily on him and takes his advice. In fact, together they run the country. Auk comes next only to the Viceroy in importance. Before his name appears the prefix 'His Excellency'. He is commonly known as the *'Jangi Lat'* (*Jangi* meaning 'war' and *Lat* being the vulgarization of 'Lord'). He keeps abreast of political thinking and developments in the subcontinent. As such he leads an extremely busy life.

In the morning the Auk goes to GHQ and presides over a meeting or committee, of which there are any number. He also has to attend the Viceroy's Executive Committee meeting as well as the Council of State. At both places he has to answer questions on defence and allied matters. He gives special interviews to the politicians and to visitors from abroad. The Principal Staff Officers see him practically every day. The Directors see him once a week. A lecture is given in the Cinema hall by some distinguished person each week. The subjects range from military topics to world affairs. The Auk attends this too. He also presides over the Defence Consultative Committee which is comprised of civilians.

Because the Viceroy and the Auk work so closely together, my job has become complex and intricate.

The Viceroy has a Private Secretary who is officially known as the PS(V),

'V' for Viceroy. Similarly, I am called PS(C), 'C' for Commander-in-Chief. Both of us work in close coordination. Ambrose Dundas* is the Defence Secretary with Bhalja as Additional Secretary. Philip Mason† and Iskander Mirza‡ are Joint Secretaries and Choudry Mohammad Ali§ is the Financial Adviser. Our offices are on the same floor close to each other. I am quite confident doing this job. In fact I feel quite at home.

The correspondence that passes through my office has many diverse headings. Here listed are the unusual ones, the meanings of which I have yet to decipher:

a) Not to be passed through any office.
b) For . . . . Absolutely Secret to be deciphered by the personal assistant.
c) Destroy when read.
d) NGO – not to go out of office.
e) Eyes only . . . .
f) Very Specially Secret.
g) Very Personal and Confidential.
h) Strictly Personal and Secret.
i) Top Secret & Personal.
j) Guard.

When going through the files submitted by the PSOs and others, the Auk has allowed me to write my own views. In this way I can bring some particular point to his attention. I write it on a slip of paper which I pin to the file. When it comes back to me after he writes his remarks I remove it. Before this job I seldom had the opportunity to comment on a file.

4th April: Several issues, especially that of the Indian National Army, were discussed when the Commander-in-Chief met the Viceroy today. The recent mutiny at Jubbulpore was also scrutinized. The subject of the employment of British troops for internal security duties in case the subcontinent was divided into Pakistan and Hindustan provided much argument.

In the afternoon His Highness the Nawab of Bhopal came to consult the Auk. The Nawab is the Chancellor of the Chamber of Princes. He is playing a significant role in political talks on behalf of the Indian States.

*Sir Ambrose Dundas (1899–1973) entered the Indian Civil Service in 1922; Governor, North-West Frontier Province, 1948–49; Lieut-Governor, Isle of Man, 1952–59.

†Philip Mason (b. 1906) was a member of the Indian Civil Service from 1928 to 1947. He is a distinguished and prolific author.

‡Later Governor-General of Pakistan.

§Later Prime Minister of Pakistan.

5th April: An overbearing woman called Miss Slade came to see the Auk. Since she became a disciple of Gandhi, she changed her name to Miraben. She is a Labour leader and wanted to discuss Labour representation in the future Government.

6th April: The Auk pays a great deal of attention to the rehabilitation of demobilized soldiers. A Post-War Benevolent Fund had been created for their resettlement after they leave the forces. The General in charge of welfare has a Civilian Adviser to help him in this regard. He is F. L. Brayne* ICS, a great exponent of 'village uplift'.

I remember Brayne when he visited my regiment in 1936 at Ferozepore. He gave a lecture to the troops on village uplift. Among other points, he said it was imperative that village houses must have ventilators for fresh air. He believed that by doing so it would bring health and prosperity to the families of the village. At the end of the lecture, a Sowar stood up. He came from Gurgaon, where Brayne had been Deputy Commissioner. He said that the Sahib had given a similar lecture years ago in his village and he had done the needful. On hearing this Brayne's face lit up with joy. But the man ruefully broke the news that the very same night a thief made his way into the house through the ventilator and stole all his valuables!

Nonetheless, Brayne is doing a magnificent job. All units and formations have been ordered by GHQ to run rehabilitation courses within the unit. They have also been ordered to make personnel attend technical courses run by the civil government.

8th April: The C-in-C attended the Council of State. A resolution had been moved by Pandit Kunzru‡ that a time limit be laid down for the nationalization of the Indian Army.

When it was the C-in-C's turn to speak, he was explicit. 'Our aim is to create a completely national army, that is, an army officered and manned throughout by Indians in the shortest possible space of time without lowering the very high standard of efficiency which obtains in the Indian Army today.'

He went further to say that he had no doubt that India could eventually produce sufficient Indians of the right type to provide all the officers likely to be needed. He, however, maintained that it would take some time. It was a fallacy to think that a wartime junior leader must of necessity make a good officer in peace. This, he said, was a dangerous misconception. A very high-quality officer is required in peacetime to enable the Army to expand in time of emergency. He must have a high degree of balanced knowledge,

---

*Frank Brayne (1882–1952) was a member of the ICS from 1905 to 1941. He wrote, among several others, a book called *Village Uplift in India*.

‡Pandit Kunzru was a member of Council of State (Upper House) and of the Defence Consultative Committee.

not only technical but a deeper knowledge of men and things. This can only come from long experience and contact with men.

The C-in-C said that, taking all the officers available, there would still be a shortage of 4000 officers unless we are prepared to lower the standard of selection. He stressed that the essential minimum efficiency in peace must be maintained.

For the training of such a large number of officers it was proposed to establish a new National War Academy which would produce some 500 to 600 officers annually. However, before the full complement is available, and to fill the gap, British officers would have to be seconded to the Indian Army. Full use of the emergency commissioned officers and the short service commissioned officers would also have to be made. He said that it will take some ten years to make up the backlog. However, no British officers will be appointed to the lower ranks.

The C-in-C accepted that some Indian officers should be given accelerated promotion but in his mind there should not be undue haste unless we are prepared to accept lower standards in the Army.

The Auk presided over the PSO's Coordination Committee and discussed Plan 287. This is the 'Plan for Demobilization of the Indian Army'. The Inter-Services Demobilization Planning Staff attended. The Plan gives the detailed composition of the eventual peacetime Army in India and its strength by units together with a guide for future mobilization.

9th April: In the afternoon the great politician Mahatma Gandhi arrived. He was accompanied by Rajkumari Amrit Kaur.*

For the first time I watched this great exponent of non-violence who does not hesitate to convert it for violent purposes when it suits him. He supports it as a 'moral act'. I kept watching him closely and tried to analyse his words and his reasoning. He tried to act as an apostle and at the same time as a man who belongs to mankind and who has their welfare at heart. He said so many contradictory things in one breath that it left one bewildered and one does not know what they meant. His approach is masterly and it confuses the listeners.

He indulged in generalities and adopted a very subtle approach, saying, 'I am nobody . . . I can only pray . . . Nobody listens to me, etc.' I often looked at the Auk's face wondering whether he was absorbing what was said. He was quiet and just listened, but he was getting impatient as naturally he wanted to find out the purpose of Gandhi's visit. Later it came out. He wanted to find out what action the C-in-C was going to take against his 'poor misguided patriotic' Indian National Army prisoners. When the Auk told him what they had done it made no impression on him.

The C-in-C issued a Training Directive. The preface of this was as follows:

---

*Rajkumari Amrit Kaur was a disciple of Gandhi and later became a Minister in the Government of India.

'This Directive contains the principles upon which your approach to training and man-management is to be based during the period of demobilization and reorganization on which we have now embarked.

'I wish leaders of all grades throughout the Army to give the Directive careful study and thought, and to pay particular and continuous attention to creating and maintaining in every formation and unit the highest standard of mutual respect between officer and man.'

In the training directive the C-in-C stressed that the present period demanded a high standard of leadership and management by all in authority. This was a transitory period. On it would depend the emergence of a proper Regular Indian Army and an efficient Army. He said that from now onwards all post-recruit training would become the responsibility of units and Formation Commanders. Up till now the object of training had been simple and clear-cut. From now onwards it would be less well-defined and difficult for many soldiers to understand. Therefore the Commanders must adopt a psychological approach and explain the present objectives to their men. Under no circumstances should the importance of maintaining discipline be ignored. The recreation aspect must also be kept in view, together with the release-period education.

10th April: This has been a very long day. The Auk could not attend the Viceroy's Executive Council in the evening as he was not feeling well. George Abell* came to see him to ascertain the effect on the Indian Army of the Indian National Army Trials.

Sir Ahmed Said Khan, Nawab of Chhatari, came to lunch. He is the Prime Minister of Hyderabad and was a great friend of my late father.

The Auk told me that the Viceroy is planning to tell Gandhi in no uncertain terms that the personnel of the INA were cowards. They were not fit to be called soldiers. From what he said I also got the impression that all was not well between Cripps and Wavell. The former has been using underhand tactics and negotiating directly with the Congress behind the Viceroy's back. It seems Cripps is anxious to please.

13th April: The Auk asked me to get hold of a Captain Durrani who had been a Prisoner of War in Japan and bring him to lunch. He was now in the Fort. Apart from being skin and bones, he seemed far from normal. He could hardly talk. The Auk told me afterwards that he was going to receive the George Cross.

14th April: The Auk gave a tea party for the Prisoners of War who returned from the East. It was a great success and well-attended. I introduced Risaldar Major Ismail Khan of my Regiment, the 3rd Cavalry, to the C-in-C.

*Sir George Abell (b. 1904) entered the ICS in 1928; Private Secretary to the Viceroy 1945–47.

'He literally taught me soldiering,' I told him. The Auk had a smile on his face. With a twinkle in his eye he said to Ismail Khan 'Look, your pupil has not done too badly, has he?'

Great changes are impending in the Army. The British officers are to leave. A great many have become very attached to their men and to their units. One feels sorry for them as they will have to start a new career. They must get a fair deal.

Nehru is looking overwhelmed and lost. I suppose this is due to the many responsibilities which are coming to him.

Bill Slim's name is being mentioned as the Auk's successor. This is probably due to the fact that the Auk has threatened to resign on the Indian National Army issue. Besides, the Labour Government is not partial to the Auk. They think that he has served his usefulness.

Slim is a great soldier and well respected. He will make a good successor to the Auk but the job is an unpleasant one at this juncture. In my view it will be suicidal to replace the Auk at this stage.

16th April: A Selection Board under the C-in-C was held. Messervy, Tuker, Lockhart, Smith, Savory and Loch attended.

The Board could not reach an agreement on who should be in the C-in-C of the Indian Army. The choice was between Cariappa* and Rajindra Singhji.† The majority were in the favour of Rajindra Singhji as they considered that Cariappa did not posses the degree of stability essential to the officer who has to hold the appointment of head of the Army.

However, they both were recommended to be Army Commanders along with Brigadier Akbar Khan‡ and Nathu Singh.§ Shri Srinagesh‖ was recommended to become the Chief of the General Staff, Rudhra¶ to be the Adjutant-General and Chimni** as Quartermaster-General. Except for Rajindra Singhji and Srinagesh the rest are a poor selection.

The Cabinet delegation met the Quaid.

17th April: The Commander-in-Chief gave a dinner in honour of the Cabinet Mission. All the Army Commanders and the Principal Staff Officers were present. This gave the members of the Cabinet Mission an opportunity to talk to the hierarchy of the Armed Forces. The members were not too communicative and hence there were not many questions asked. However, Alexander was good fun and kept us amused throughout the dinner.

---

* Cariappa later became the C-in-C of the Indian Army.
† Rajindra Singhji later became the C-in-C of the Indian Army.
‡ Akbar Khan commanded a division in Pakistan Army.
§ Nathu Singh commanded a corps in the Indian Army.
‖ Srinagesh became Chief of General Staff in the Indian Army.
¶ Rudhra became Adjutant-General in the Indian Army.
** Chimni became Quartermaster-General in the Indian Army.

18th April: General Mayne, who was Moochu Chowdhry's Divisional Commander in Africa, had written to Auk and recommended that Moochu should be given accelerated promotion. He suggested that Moochu should be the first Indian Officer to attain higher rank. I must say he looks a sharp and slippery customer.

19th April: Master Tara Singh, the Sikh leader, came to see the C-in-C in the afternoon. He said that he was not satisfied with the Sikh representation in the Armed Forces. He is a great force in his community but is dogmatic and has a somewhat blurred perspective of the whole idea of partition.

20th April: The C-in-C presided over the Defence Consultative Committee. It is held quarterly and the session lasted the whole day. The members, except for Pandit Kunzru, have no views or opinion on defence matters. A poor lot. Their ignorance is difficult to believe. They mistrust each other as well as all the actions of GHQ. They asked the most naive questions and it was obvious that they had not done their homework. Instead of discussing policy matters they kept bringing up minor issues.

It has been decided that there are to be no future trials of the Indian National Army personnel.

Khan Bahadur Kuli Khan, from the Frontier, came to lunch. He is now turning into a politician and talked on all matters under the sun to impress the Auk.

Auk saw the Viceroy in the evening and gave his views on the Plan submitted by Cripps. He told the Viceroy that Asif Ali* was aspiring to become the War Member. He discussed the Frontier policy which is to be decided at a Conference in Peshawar at a later date.

A Plan called 'Madhouse' has been prepared which will be put into operation in case the Indian Army becomes unreliable and another Plan called 'Bedlam' in case it becomes hostile.

22nd April: We flew to Peshawar and then drove to Kohat to attend Exercise 'MANNA'.

The Auk is excellent company when he is touring. He knows the Frontier extremely well and often tells delightful stories of the operations in which he has participated.

Desmond Young, the Director of Public Relations, travelled with us in the same car. He does not know this area at all. The Auk almost frightened him. Pointing to some '*Khasadars*' (Watchmen) on top of a hill, the Auk said they were probably snipers up there, quite likely to have a potshot at us.

*Asif Ali later became the first Indian Ambassador to the USA.

On arrival at the camp we were met by Major-General Denys Reid* who is conducting the exercise. During the war he distinguished himself in Italy and is a fighting soldier with a great sense of humour.

The main object of the exercise was to practise, under Frontier conditions, the freedom of action and movement conferred on a Brigade group with air support in all its forms. Secondly, to try out certain tactical methods and various equipment.

It was a very big exercise. We witnessed direct air support, supply dropping, construction of air strips for light aircraft, marking of dropping zones and the evacuation of casualties by air. All these were carried out by day as well as by night. CDL (Canal Defence Light) tanks illuminated the landing and dropping zones for night landings and supply dropping. They also pin-pointed the targets for a night attack, dazzling the defenders.

Animal transport was reduced to the minimum. 3.7 inch Howitzers were transported on the carriers. Attempts were also made to keep a fully mechanized group supplied by air. During the Exercise the troops were kept on various rations – emergency ration, 24-hours ration, and the composite (6-man) pack, to ascertain their suitability.

24th April: On our return to Peshawar today a conference was held at Government House to discuss a plan for regrouping and for the substitution of the Civil Armed Forces for regular troops in the tribal areas.

The conference was attended by the Governor NWFP, AOC-in-C, Agent to the Governor-General, Baluchistan, His Majesty's Minister at Kabul, and other military and civil officers. It was agreed that the constitutional future of the tribes was uncertain until the outcome of the Cabinet Mission's Plan. Meanwhile it was essential that the regrouping of the forces should be carried out, provided it was done cautiously and on the basis of trial and error. It was decided that no formal announcement to the *Jirgas* (tribal assembly) about the regrouping of the forces would be made. The Gardai Brigade was to be withdrawn earliest but it depended on the provision of officers for the Khasadar units.

There was complete agreement that Razmak and the Takki Zam line† must be held by properly organized and equipped Civil Armed Forces. Complete withdrawal could be misunderstood by the Afghan Government. The Central Waziristan Scouts are to be raised and provided with heavy armaments. The C-in-C was not prepared to leave light tanks in tribal areas to be attached to the Civil Armed Force. The reorganization was to be carried out gradually. It was suggested that the Scouts should have an Air Wing but no decision was taken. It was agreed to withdraw the Wana and Razmak Brigades in due course. The Malakand Battalion was to be retrained.

*Major-General Denys Reid (1897–1970) had commanded the 10th Indian Division in Italy.

†Razmak and the Takki Zam line were the main defence lines against Afghanistan.

The C-in-C informed those present that the application of the new tactics to tribal warfare had not been studied. Its implementation will depend on the availability of aircraft and equipment. These tactics in the first instance would be tried against the Madda Khel tribe, which he felt the Afghan Government would welcome.

It was decided to step up the Indianization of the officers' cadre in the Scouts.

The Governor and the political officers did not relish the move of the Army Commander's HQ from Rawalpindi to Lahore. However, the C-in-C explained that a Military and an Air Force Commander of suitable rank would be located in Peshawar.

It was agreed that air support would be available to the Civil Armed Forces. In this connection the maintenance of the air strips in the tribal territory was important. On the whole the Conference was a great success and the uniformity of the views was encouraging.

Sir George Cunningham* is a great friend of the Auk. They get on very well together. Sir George's knowledge of the Frontier is astounding. What he does not know about Frontier is not worth knowing! He was a splendid host. He is very fond of the Pathans and greatly respected by them.

26th April: We witnessed the raising of the Khyber Rifles at Landikotal. Those who had been in the Khyber Rifles before it was disbanded were invited. They were all very pleased that the Rifles were being re-raised. Auk spoke to the gathering in fluent Pushtu.

Back in Peshawar the Auk showed me the house in which he lived as a Brigade Commander. The house, he told me, was a hundred years old. He often says that the command he enjoyed most was that of the Peshawar Brigade. The Auk is extremely popular on the Frontier and has a vast number of friends and admirers.

27th April: We visited the Armoured Brigade at Risalpur before returning to Delhi today. The Cabinet Mission has departed for Simla where they are going to hold a Conference with the leaders. The basis of the negotiations are:

a) All-India Union Government controlling Foreign Affairs, Defence and Communications.
b) Two groups of Provinces based on the majority principle and to deal with such common subjects as the Provinces desired.
c) The Provinces to deal with all the other subjects. They were also to have the Sovereign Rights.
d) The Indian States were to negotiate their future.

*Sir George Cunningham (1888–1964) entered the ICS in 1911; Private Secretary to the Viceroy 1926–31; Governor of N.W. Frontier Province 1937–46 and 1947–48; Rector of St. Andrews University 1946–49.

The Congress objected to any feature which carried the faintest impression of the establishment of Pakistan.

28th April: The Congress is examining the Cabinet proposals. Azad wrote a letter to the Cabinet Mission without the approval of the Working Committee.

Azad has found similarity between his ideas of the solution of the communal problems and those of the Cabinet Mission. Azad wants the maximum decentralization of power in the Federal structure and the Provinces to enjoy the largest measure of autonomy in all subjects expect Foreign Affairs, Defence and Communications. The Cabinet Mission found a strong ally and friend in Azad. However, Sudhir Ghosh* is sabotaging his plans. He is considered by all as a great exponent of India's future unity.

29th April: We flew to Bareilly to see the Victory Contingent which is due to leave for UK to participate in the Victory Parade. The Contingent was a magnificent body of hand-picked men from various units.

There is some talk of a 'breakdown' plan which will come into operation if the Congress usurp power without accommodating the Muslims. It envisages the British withdrawal to the Provinces of Punjab less Ambala, NWFP, Sind, Baluchistan and East Bengal less Calcutta. Some are calling the area 'Medium Pakistan'.

Since I began my job here in Delhi I have been very busy. In spite of that I did manage to go and see the Quaid at his residence at 10, Aurangzeb Road. He was pleased that I had been appointed Private Secretary to the Commander-in-Chief and asked me to keep in touch with him and Liaquat Ali Khan. He told me that I could come and see him at any time and required no prior appointment.

I first met the Quaid-i-Azam in 1932 when I was at the Royal Military College, Sandhurst. My brother-in-law, Qazi Isa, and some of our other friends used to get together in the Park Lane Hotel every Saturday for a cup of tea.

On one occasion we were all sitting in the lounge when we noticed a man entering the hall. He was elegantly dressed and extremely self-composed. He did not quite look a man of the soil and we wondered who he was. While we were still wondering he passed close to our table. Noticing a questioning look in our faces, he stopped. He introduced himself as Mohammad Ali Jinnah. We, out of respect for his age, stood up and introduced ourselves as well. We requested him to have tea with us and he accepted our invitation. During our conversation he asked us about our studies and our various interests. Thereafter we met at various receptions given to delegates of the Round Table Conference.

*Sudhir Ghosh was Gandhi's contact man with HMG and carried out secret negotiations between the two.

I did not see him again till 1939. But Isa, who had already decided to enter politics, had kept in close touch with him. At that time I was doing a course in Poona when Isa rang me up and wanted me to spend a week-end with him in Bombay.

Together we went to the Quaid's house on the Malabar Hill and had tea with him. I asked him for his advice to Army officers. He replied without hesitation:

'Learn your profession.' He was gracious enough to give me a photograph of himself, signed 'yours very sincerely'. From then onwards I met him on several occasions with Isa but it was not until I arrived in Delhi that I came to know him really well.

My sister Jamila, married to Shaukat Omar (who is working in Calcutta), has come to stay with us. She is a forceful public speaker and deeply interested in politics. She is well read and has the courage of her convictions. At that time she was critical of the policies of the League and had leftist leanings. She wanted to meet the Quaid.

When Jamila and I arrived at Quaid's residence he received us with affection. Jamila asked a number of questions, some of which were not tactful at all. I objected to her asking them, but the Quaid told me to let her have her say. With great patience he took up her queries one by one, and answered them convincingly. Once or twice I begged permission to leave for I knew he was a busy man. We had been with him for over an hour already. But he would not let us. After a while I noticed that Jamila was getting convinced of his sincerity and logic. Eventually she stood up, kissed his hand and said that she had been converted to his way of thinking.

'Look my boy, I have not wasted my time. I have gained a worker,' he said with a smile.

May 1946

*'There is no doubt that today there is a danger of strike
and disorder in the country. . . . You all know the good
that comes from discipline and toleration.'*

The Auk.

1st May: There was a meeting of the Viceroy's Executive Council. Later,
the Viceroy discussed the INA trials with the Auk. The Viceroy said that he
had told Nehru clearly that the INA personnel were weaklings and deserters,
and that their release would adversely affect the morale of the Army. Wavell
does not mince his words and is forthright.

2nd May: Sir Jamshed Ali Khan, Nawab of Baghpat, came to lunch. He has
a portly figure and a striking moustache which he keeps waxed! He is a man
of the old order and greatly respected by everyone. He talks a great deal of
sense, but is very upset over the current political situation.

4th May: We left for Simla via Lahore where the Cabinet Mission has again
started its deliberations.

The Congress is represented by Azad,* Nehru, Patel† and Ghaffar
Khan.‡ The League is represented by Jinnah, Liaquat,§ Ismail Khan‖ and
Nishter.¶ Gandhi has also arrived to blackmail Wavell and the Cabinet
Mission. He is accompanied by Sudhir Ghosh, his 'Mercury'.

The Viceroy showed the Auk the final draft of the Cabinet Mission Plan.
Wavell asked him whether it would in any way upset the Armed Forces. The
Auk replied in the negative. Nevertheless he said it must be explained to
them in detail.

Simla is packed with politicians and the whole town is buzzing with
political conjectures.

---

* Azad was the President of the Indian National Congress.
† Patel was the strong hand of the Indian National Congress.
‡ Ghaffar Khan was a Nationalist Muslim and a member of the Congress.
§ Liaquat became the first Prime Minister of Pakistan.
‖ Ismail Khan did not come to Pakistan.
¶ Nishter became the Governor of Punjab.

As usual we are staying at Snowden, a gorgeous chateau built by Kitchener. Apparently it was his private property. The ceilings of the various rooms are beautiful. It is said that they were modelled from the pulp of old army files!

The Auk has received a letter from Nehru thanking him for his decision to withdraw all trials of Indian National Army personnel. Nehru in his letter admitted that the Regular Indian Army had been largely ignored, the reason being that they were looked upon as agents of foreign authority. So long as political conditions in India do not change completely and the Army considers itself a real national army, this approach will remain. He admitted that a number of people who joined the Indian National Army did not necessarily do so for patriotic motives but he still decided to lionize them.

The letter went on to say that, though the Congress Party is supposed to have exploited the Indian National Army trials for political purposes, this was not true. Congress had not even thought of it. He said it did not strike him at all that political advantage could be taken of this affair. The trials had fanned the aggressive mood of the people providing them with an excuse to give expression to that mood. Finally Nehru admitted that his pleading the cause of the Indian National Army had injured the Regular Indian Army, but he said, such risks had to be taken. He also said that a very large number of Regular Indian Army officers and men held the same views. God knows whom he means, unless it is Master Kaul (Lt-Col B. M. Kaul) – his blue-eyed boy!

Never in my life have I read a letter which was such an extensive exercise in equivocation. It was a sickening sermon. Did Nehru think that he was writing it to an oaf? His advocacy of the cause of the Indian National Army personnel has been as clear as daylight. He has supported it by many public statements. I never thought he was a hypocrite with such double standards! I lost whatever respect I had for him by reading the letter.

5th May: The Conference with the politicians has started.

Nehru came to see the Auk today. When he arrived he was riding a *bazzar tat* (pony) and was dressed in an *achkan* (long coat) and *choori dar pyjama* (tight-fitting pyjamas). A rose was stuck to his front button.

Nehru seemed rather apologetic as a result of his advocating the cancellation of the Indian National Army trials. He probably realizes for the first time what effect the cancellation of trials will have on the Regular Army. This is the same Army that stood firm and fought well during the war while the Indian National Army indulged in atrocities against their comrades. During the conversation he seemed to make his peace with the Auk and even tried to humour him.

The Viceroy saw the C-in-C and again assured him that the Cabinet Mission Award will have no disturbing effect on the Army. He has full confidence in the Auk and keeps him in the picture. He takes his advice as well. Wavell also told him that Patel wanted a showdown with the Muslim League but had been warned against doing so. Eventually the Auk showed the Viceroy the letter that he had received from Nehru.

Poor Cripps fainted during one of the discussions with the Viceroy. The intricacies of the conference must have been too much for him!

10th May: The Army Commanders have been summoned. They will be briefed on the present political situation and on the intended Award by the Cabinet Mission.

11th May: Bukhari, the Imam of Jama Masjid, called on the C-in-C. He is greatly respected in the Muslim community because of his balanced views. He is well-informed and knows what is happening in political circles.

Every afternoon the ADC collects my two older children Hassan and Shahnaz (known fondly as Hassu and Gurya) and takes them to the C-in-C's house. While the Auk is working in the garden he makes my children do the same. He has given them small garden implements. The children are very fond of him, and he of them. He has practically adopted them as his own. Whenever he goes out on tour and happens to be in a city, he finds time to visit a big store to buy toys. By now they have so many from him that we do not know where to keep them. Whenever the children want a special toy, they let him know. To them the Auk is known as 'Chiefi'.

Recently little Gurya was walking through the house. Her shoes were dirty and Mrs Jackson stopped and scolded her, saying that she must not come inside the house. Gurya promptly replied, 'You are nobody to stop me.' She went straight to the Auk and promptly told him what Mrs Jackson had said. The Auk laughed and said, 'You should not take notice of her'.

The official Cadillac is locked up and rarely brought out unless my children want to have a ride in it. The Auk then sits in the middle with Hassu and Gurya on either side. While in the car, they make a nuisance of themselves, pressing one button for the window glass to go up and the other to bring it down. The Auk enjoys watching them have such fun. In fact he comes and plays all manner of games with them whenever we have a children's party.

12th May: Today the Cabinet Mission's negotations with the political parties broke down. This was owing to the ill-advised and ill-timed actions of the Secretary of State and Cripps.

15th May: Jam Sahib of Jamnagar has arrived to stay. Jam Sahib is one of the enlightened princes and conducts a good administration. He is well-informed and fond of the British way of life. He told us that he has 157 cars and that his wife has 1700 saris. These days he is on 'Hay diet' to reduce his weight.

16th May: The Executive Council met this morning. Wavell discussed with the Auk the possibility of the Congress launching a mass Civil Disobedience Movement against the 'Award'. The Auk told him that it was most unlikely. I think he is right.

17th May: The Cabinet Mission has announced the long-term as well as the Interim Plan which is as follows:

1) Formation of an All-Indian Union Government with a Central Legislature comprising the representatives of British India and the Princely States. Foreign Affairs, Defence and Communications will remain as Central subjects.

2) The Provincial Governments will retain the remaining subjects.

3) The Provinces will be grouped into three groups (sections) and will have their own Legislature and Executive:
   The Grouping will be:
   'A' Hindu majority provinces Bombay, Madras, CP, UP, Bihar and Orissa.
   'B' Punjab, Sind, NWFP, Baluchistan.
   'C' Bengal and Assam.

4) A Constituent Assembly, which will be elected by the Members of the Provincial Assembly together with the respresentatives of the States, will frame a Constitution. The Assembly will be divided into three Sections and will draw up the Constitution for the Provinces. It will also decide whether a group should be formed and if so what subject should be allotted to it and what powers should the Legislature carry.
   The Provinces will have the right to opt out of the group. Later the Constituent Assembly will meet as a whole and decide the Union Constitution.

5) An Interim Government will be formed and all the Members including the War Member will be Indian. Invitations were issued to fourteen persons to form the Government.

Cripps gave a pathetic press conference. Everyone who attended was dissatisfied with it.

The League and Princes accepted the Plan while the Congress wanted the 'complete picture' before they accepted. Later the Viceroy mentioned to the Auk the lack of reality in Congress circles as regards their insistence that the Government of India should be handed over to one party, i.e. the Congress itself.

The Nawab of Bhopal called in the evening. He is very upset and is fast losing his control over the Princes.

The C-in-C broadcast to the Indian Armed Forces over the All-India Radio in Urdu. The following is the text:

'As you have heard from His Excellency The Viceroy, the British Government have put forward a scheme to enable Indians to make their own constitution and set up an independent Indian Government. As you all know too, members of the British Government and the Viceroy have for some time past been discussing with the leaders of the Muslim League and of the Congress. They have been trying to decide what kind of Government shall be set up in India. Their object is to make good the promise of the British Government that in future India shall be governed entirely by her own people, free from all control by Britain, and free to remain within the British Commonwealth or to go outside as she likes.

'In spite of every attempt to find a form of Government which would be acceptable to the Congress and the Muslim League, no agreement has been reached.

'The Muslim League considers that there must be two independent and separate Governments in India, Pakistan for the Muslims and Hindustan for the Hindus. The Congress thinks that India must not be divided and that there should be one Central Government with the Provinces controlling their own affairs to the greatest possible extent.

'This very briefly is the position taken up by the two main political parties.

'It was hoped that between the two points of view some compromise acceptable to both parties might be found. This has, however, not been found possible, although both parties have, for the sake of goodwill, modified their views to a considerable extent.

'The British Government, therefore, having failed to get the two principal political parties to agree, has decided that it is their duty to the people of India to lay down what shall be done in order to give India her independence as soon as possible in an orderly and peaceful manner, so that the mass of the people may be put to the least inconvenience and disturbance.

'In making these arrangements the British Government has tried to ensure justice and freedom for the smaller as well as for the larger sections of the people of India.

'The British Government realizes that the Muslims have a real fear that they may be forced to live for always under a Hindu Government and that any new form of Government must be such as to make this fear groundless for all time.

'With this in view, the possibility of setting up a completely separate and independent Muslim State of Pakistan has been most carefully considered from every point of view and without any partiality at all.

'As a result of this examination the British Government has been forced to conclude that the setting-up of completely independent States not linked together in any way would not result in a settlement of the differences between Hindu and Muslim.

'The setting-up of two or more independent Governments would also, in their opinion, result in great loss and danger to India in the future.

'They, therefore, cannot agree to divide India into separate States, though they do think that some way must be found for the predominantly Muslim areas to govern themselves if they wish to do so and to live their own lives. This is also recognized by the Hindus and the Congress Party.

'The British Government, therefore, have approved neither the setting-up of completely separate States nor the retention of all power at the Centre. They consider that, although the different areas should have a large measure of independence if the people desire it, the responsibility for the Army, Navy and Air Force and for the defence of the whole of India in war, must rest with one authority for the whole of India.

'Apart from this, they have accepted the principle that each Province or group of Provinces may have full powers to manage its own affairs as desired by its own people without interference from the centre.

'These proposals are meant to ensure that all creeds and classes shall have their say in how they are to be governed and also to prevent any one section of the people being forced to live under the rule of any other section, without being sure that they will have the right to live their lives in their own way without fear or persecution.

'The details of this new system of government for India must be worked out by the people of India themselves. It is not the task of the British Government to do this.

'To carry on the administration of the country while a new system of government is worked out the Viceroy proposes to form an Interim Government composed of himself and of leaders of Indian political opinion who have the confidence of the people.

'In this temporary Government, the post of War Member which is at present held by the Commander-in-Chief (that is myself) will be held by a civilian who will be an Indian. I shall continue to be responsible for the command and welfare of the Army, Navy and Air Force but all political matters will be in the hands of the new War Member under whom I shall serve, just as the Commanders in Britain serve under civilian Ministers.

'While this temporary Government carries on the daily business of governing the country, it is proposed that there should be set up three Assemblies composed of representatives of all parties and creeds and classes, and elected by the Provincial Legislatures.

'It will be the task of these three Assemblies together with representatives from the Indian States to decide how India will be governed in the future.

'The British Government hopes that in this way peace and security will come to India under the rule of her own leaders and that she will become as great and prosperous as she deserves.

'While these discussions and meetings are going on it is the duty of the Navy, Army and Air Force to continue to serve the Government and to carry out its orders.

'As I have said, this temporary Government will be an Indian Government composed of members chosen from the leaders of the main political parties in the country who have the full confidence of the people.

'There is no doubt that today there is danger of strife and disorder in the country. Whether you are in the Army, the Navy or the Air Force, you all know the good that comes from discipline and toleration. You have also learned to live together, Hindu, Muslim, Sikh and Christian, in the service of your country without quarrelling or jealousy.

'You have learnt each to respect the other and to work side by side for one object – the good of your country.

'In this you have set an example to all India.

'I trust you, as I have always trusted you, to go on setting this example and to do your duty, as you have always done it in war and peace.

'I for my part shall do the same. So long as I am here you may rely on me to safeguard your interests in the future as in the past.'

19th May: Mountbatten has come to stay. He is trying to find out what is going on, taking a deep interest in the politics of the subcontinent.

There have been riots in Bengal.

However strait-jacketed I am as a Private Secretary, I can still find some respite to indulge in my 'native pursuits'. I have many opportunities of praying at the Mazars of the Saints in and around Delhi. I visit these places late at night and all by myself when I can pray and meditate.

Delhi, after Lucknow, is the home of music, *Qawwalis, Mushairas* and all that goes with the Muslim culture. We have a fortnightly session at our house to which a great many friends are invited. This breaks the monotony of office work. It is the only diversion which I can possibly manage in a routine dominated by visitors. The list is long. There are Congressmen, Leaguers, communists, businessmen and Maharajasi! Among the ruling Princes, Jaipur and Gwalior are my favourites.

Lucknow and Allahabad are the centre and home of all Indian politics. When I was first posted to Allahabad in 1933 and was serving in a British unit I was often appointed a liaison officer with the civil authorities during the disturbances. I thus came in direct touch with the Congress leaders. Among them were Pandit Jawaharlal Nehru, Sir Tej Bahadur Sapru, Dr Kailash Nath Katju, Mrs Pandit* and a host of others.

In 1937 I was again posted to Allahabad where my regiment had a squadron. During the anti-Government disturbances, the squadron was called upon to disperse a crowd which was led by Congressmen. I tried to

*Mrs Pandit is Nehru's sister.

persuade them to see reason but it had no effect. Thereupon I charged them with drawn sabres, knowing full well that all would run away on the approach of galloping horses. This is precisely what happened. However, I was later officially ticked off by the Brigade Commander. At the same time he gave me a private pat on the back for not inflicting any casualties.

To be on tour with the Auk is an exhausting though exhilarating experience. It is a break from the normal routine and a very educating one. He tours extensively, mostly by air, because of which he is known as 'the airborne C-in-C'.

We usually leave Palam before sunrise, and invariably get to our destination before the morning work has begun.

Tours are a full day's work, as the Auk insists on seeing everything. His visits are thorough, yet informal. I work out all the details for him in advance. This requires a great deal of preparation. I make a small booklet which he can refer to. It includes all the relevant information on the senior officers and the formations they command.

The Auk told me that in his younger days he participated in various recruitment drives in rural areas. During this time he lived and fed with the men, thus acquiring an insight into their problems and their thinking. It is difficult to realize how deeply the influence of just one man can go. Even now he keeps himself informed of the recruiting potential of various classes and their recruiting areas. When he is with the Indian troops, he is the happiest of men. He talks to them without any formality, man to man, taking an interest in their welfare, wanting to know about their families, villages and crops.

When inspecting a unit he does not make it a 'State Visit'. Every now and then, especially while reviewing troops, he stops. Looking into their eyes directly, he talks to them. In fact, it is from the answers he receives that he measures the efficiency of the unit. In his comments I found the word 'steady' used by him to describe a unit only when he was well satisfied. This was a big compliment to the unit concerned. He always considers a happy unit as the best unit. Inspecting a battalion on parade he watches them for their steadiness and turn out and, when marching past, for their bearing and self-reliance. I can always tell by watching him as to whether he is pleased with what he sees or not. During inspections I walk very close to him and listen to him. While he is talking to both officers and men, I make my own mental notes, which later, I discuss with him. He invariably confirms my impressions. Then I prepare the tour inspection notes. Working day and night, as I do, close to the Auk has enabled me to read his mind. Whenever it has been that the Auk has not been satisfied with a formation or unit commander he looks at me, and immediately I make a note of it. The case is then dealt with later.

Unlike most inspecting generals, the Auk is welcome wherever he goes. He knows most of the commanding officers and Subedar Majors by name.

The Auk likes to address the Viceroy's Commissioned Officers separately, seldom the officers by themselves. I have to write the speeches for him. He goes over them and makes any changes he wants to. Then he writes them in Roman Urdu script to be able to address the unit in their language. This may be while they are on parade or when they are gathered round him. He talks to them man to man, directly. This is where he scores, as the men feel he is one of them and that he understands.

Physically he keeps himself fit. At the age of over sixty and in an average temperature of 110°F he can walk most people off their feet. Even after lunch he seldom rests. The afternoons are occupied with conferences and indoor exercises. In the evening he dines in one unit mess or another.

The troops respect and love him. In a '*barakhana*' (a regimental feast) he sits on the floor with the men and shares their meal. He talks to the *Jawans* (troops) and listens to their problems, giving his full attention. One of his greatest assets is that he is completely at home with the troops, on duty or off duty, and feels part and parcel of them. In return the troops feel that he is genuinely interested in them. They trust him and know that he will not let them down. And he means what he says. Towards the troops he has a 'paternalistic' approach and treats them as his children. To the sepoys he is known as '*Sidah Sada Admi Hai*' (He is a straight-forward simple man.) His name is a legend in the Indian Army. He is their 'father and mother'. What he loves to see is a smile on the faces of the *Jawans* and considers it a sign of a happy unit. For him, this means that the unit is fit for war. In other words he uses affection as a weapon.

In a mess he becomes a Regimental Officer again, and mostly talks to the junior officers. He puts them at ease by his simple and friendly manner, which comes naturally to him. Once a newly joined officer had his arm in a sling; the Auk asked him how it happened. The young subaltern replied that he fell when trying to ride a bicycle backwards. On hearing this the Auk burst out laughing. Nothing escapes him. By the end of a day's inspection he has made a very fair assessment of the commanders and their formations.

He hates all forms of unnecessary ceremonial pomp and show. A Formation Commander was ticked off for getting the route lined by Army and Police personnel. He dislikes escorts and outriders and only allows a pilot to show the route.

The Auk seldom loses his temper. The only thing he is intolerant of is 'eyewash'. He is a straight-forward man. His genuine qualities make him an endearing personality. In fact it is right to say that the Auk is humane to a fault. One could say that he is too humane as he gives the benefit of the doubt to one and all when they do something wrong. He is firm as a rock but patient, kind and courteous. When he says 'no' he means it. Later if he sees good reason to change his mind he gives in. Many a time I managed to make him change his original stand, by giving him a different point of view.

Auk hates being idolized and detests publicity. He feels shy when correspondents question him about his work and accomplishments. Instead he begins to talk of his troops, as a father would mention the exploits and deeds of his sons. No wonder that he is known as the 'Father of the Army'. Young officers get very excited on seeing the 'Great Auk' for the first time. They call him 'The Auk' or 'Great Man – the Auk'. The Viceroy's Commissioned Officers revere him as they feel that he understands them and values their contributions in making the Army great. GHQ Officers affectionately call him 'The Chief' or the Auk. He has become a legend in his lifetime.

Whenever it has been that he has had to relieve someone from his duties, he has told him personally and in a forthright manner. He has great humility. He possesses a striking personality both forceful and charming and is even more popular than was Lord Roberts. There is nothing dominating or overbearing in his character at all. He just behaves as a normal human being and has a gift of making a man comfortable and at ease in his presence. His mental energy, enthusiasm, good temper and driving power are immense. How he has stood up to the strain of past years, I cannot imagine.

22nd May: We flew to Rawalpindi.

The Auk inspected the Royal Inniskilling Fusiliers. He is the Colonel of the Regiment. It was a magnificent parade. He addressed them later.

Later we left for Shinkiari to attend the GHQ Exercise 'Embrace' and stayed with Brigadier Kalwant Singh.* Like the Auk, Kalwant Singh is a 'First Punjabi'. Auk is very fond of him. He is a good officer though after a few drinks he becomes quarrelsome and loses his self-control. The first time I met Kalwant was at the Staff College, Quetta, where I was doing the course and he was an Instructor. One evening we were all dining with Lt-Col Gurdip Singh Dhillon,† a fine Sikh officer, when Kalwant told me that I had not officially 'called' on him. Because of this he said he could mar my career. It was such a ridiculous statement to make that we nearly came to blows. Gurdip intervened and saved the situation. Meeting him now, he is all milk and honey to me. He went out of his way to ensure that I was comfortable. Today the Auk was cross at me as I had forgotten to tell the ADC to look after our drivers and batmen and to see that they had been fed and housed properly.

The Auk enjoys living in camp and under the same conditions as the other officers. It gives him a chance to relax. When travelling by road he likes his baggage to be carried in the boot of his own car.

---

*Kalwant Singh became an Army Commander and was a great favourite of the Auk.

†Gurdip Singh Dhillon was a fellow student at Staff College, Quetta.

24th May: The Cabinet Mission so far has interviewed some fifty politicians. It is rumoured that the rift between the Congress and His Majesty's Government is closing. It is a battle of wits. Azad is conducting negotiations on behalf of the Congress. It seems as though some results may come out of the deliberations. The signs are there but we cannot be optimistic. There is still so much to be decided.

A strong rumour is going around that an Indian War Member is to be appointed. I think he will have to be 'educated' first. All are nervous about it, especially the British Officers.

27th May: We returned to Delhi today.

The Public Relations Directorate of GHQ is a very strong and effective organisation. It is headed by Brigadier Desmond Young, a veteran of the Desert, who had worked under the Auk previously, and is a great friend of his. Desmond is a great character, an excellent mixer, having good relations with the press both within the country and abroad. He knows most of them by their first names. It is right to say that GHQ never has any trouble with the press. His second-in-command, Colonel Majid Malik, was also in the Desert and had worked there under the Auk. Together they form a formidable team. Desmond is a man of good taste and enjoys parties. A large number of them he gives himself. Majid Malik had worked with various papers throughout India and finally with Reuters. He is a poet and a writer. He too has excellent relations with the press.

They have a fairly large staff, prominent among whom are Major Shams Arif, the Head of the Publicity Propaganda Broadcast Service to Indian personnel and Major Peter Goodwin of the Photographic Section. I have yet to see a better photographer than Peter. He is good both with stills and movies.

28th May: An internal defence exercise called 'Embrace' was held from 20th May to 28th May. The object of the exercise was to test the plan under Scheme 'Asylum' which caters for internal defence in case of an uprising. The exercise covered the testing of the signal communincations and the protection of the airfields, railways and vital points. A drill for the imposition of martial law if required was worked out. Communication and liaison with the Civil Authorities was thoroughly examined.

Wavell saw the Auk and gave him his appreciation of the present situation. The Auk said that it was becoming more and more obvious that the Congress wants the control of the Centre to themselves, to get rid of the British and deal at will with the Muslim and Indian States.

29th May: Colonel Lancaster, the British Military Attaché in Kabul, came for drinks. He has been in Afghanistan for twenty years and knows the country inside out. He is a dedicated man who believes in the policy of giving the Afghans artillery pieces to satisfy their ego and keep them happy, but only a few rounds of ammunition to keep them ineffective.

31st May: Sir Walter Monckton* came to stay. He is courting the Countess of Carlisle. The Viceroy had a lengthy meeting with the Secretary of State for India, Alexander and the Auk and discussed various actions to be taken in case of a breakdown in the negotiations. The C-in-C told Wavell that he was not very keen that the Home Department should have a look at the summary of evidence of the Indian National Army trials. However, he was overruled by the Viceroy.

Mountbatten called in the evening. He is flirting with the Congress leaders. I wonder why.

31st May: Auk was created a Field-Marshal. I received the signal and stepped into his office to announce his promotion. His initial reaction was 'Shahid, don't be funny'.

The *London Gazette* of 31st May notified:

'The King has been graciously pleased to approve the promotion to the rank of Field-Marshal of General Sir Claude John Eyre Auchinleck, GCB, GCIE, CSI, DSO, OBE, Indian Army, Colonel 4th Royal Inniskilling Fusiliers, Colonel 4th Bombay Grenadiers, Aide-de-Camp General to the King, with effect from June 1st, 1946.'

We wanted to celebrate the event but he forbade us to do so.

Stafford Cripps congratulated him but wrote in red ink. Amery's congratulations were genuine.

*Sir Walter Monckton (1891–1965) was created 1st Viscount Monckton of Bren-chley in 1957. A distinguished barrister, he was Attorney-General to King Edward VIII at the time of the Abdication. Though not then an MP, he was Solicitor-General in the Caretaker Government of 1945. He married Lady Carlisle in 1947 and was Conservative MP for Bristol West 1951–57.

June 1946

'We welcome that an attempt is being made by the leaders of the public opinion to make the Army feel that they are truly a National Force.'

The Auk.

2nd June: We left very early in the morning for UK to attend the Victory Parade celebrations.

4th June: This morning we arrived in UK, landing at Northolt. We are staying at the Dorchester Hotel.

5th June: The King called the Auk to Buckingham Palace to receive his Field-Marshal's baton. I think the Auk was greatly moved as he had achieved the ultimate goal to which a soldier can aspire. After the ceremony the King talked to him for quite a while.

Later the Auk was called by the Cabinet at which the Chiefs of Staff were present to give his views on the Breakdown Plan. The Auk told them that withdrawal to Muslim provinces was not militarily feasible. Finally the plan was rejected.

These days the Auk is flying the India Command Inter-Services flag. He designed this himself. It looks good. Flying this flag he went to the Aldwych to inspect the Indian Contingent that was to take part in the Victory parade.

8th June: The Indian Contingent is eight hundred strong. Every one of the participants is the recipient of a gallantry award, except its Commander, Brigadier Moochu Chaudhri, who is only an MBE. Originally Rajendra Singhji was to command the contingent. But General Sir Mosley Mayne used his influence and got Chaudhri selected.

General Sir Rob Lockhart,* who is also here, keeps an eye on the contingent. Brigadier Jimmy Green is in charge of the administration.

*General Sir Rob Lockhart (1893–1981) was Acting Governor North-West Frontier Province Jan–Aug 1947; C-in-C Indian Army Aug–Dec 1947; Director of Operations Malaya Dec 1951 – Feb 1952.

The contingent travelled in the *Mauretania* and brought their rations with them. On arrival in London they were lodged in a camp in Kensington Gardens behind the Albert Memorial. There were so many visitors and onlookers that a perimeter wire had to be erected to keep them away and afford some privacy. Sweeper Meherdin, who was awarded an IDSM in Italy for carrying ammunition to the forward areas, is a great attraction. Another attraction is the handsome cook, Piaro.

The members of the contingent are feasted constantly and are shown around the sights of London by retired British officers of their units. Many sight-seeing tours outside London are also arranged for them.

The King and Queen, along with the Princesses have visited the Indian Contingent in the camp. All the Field-Marshals who originally belonged to the Indian Army were present.

The Victory Parade was held today. It was a magnificent sight. The Indian Contingent looked most businesslike. They wore khaki Service Dress with no frills. They were cheered constantly. The Auk was very pleased with their bearing and turnout.

The Auk rode in a carrier, looking dignified and great. 'Look, there is the Auk,' was heard constantly. I was given a seat in the enclosure opposite the saluting base. From that position I could watch all the high and mighty. All eyes were on Churchill who made the victory possible. A number of those around me talked of Wavell, and the fact that he was missing.

9th June: We left for Berlin.

On our arrival we were received by the British Military Governor and the heads of the other Allied Governments.

Berlin is a sad sight. It is practically razed to the ground. There are very few houses standing intact. People are living in basements. I have never seen such devastation. The only thing which was still standing was the Stadium in which the Olympic Games of 1936 were held. I attended the games that year and had a glimpse of Hitler and of his popularity.

There are very few restaurants and shops open. The famous 'Tiergarten' is occupied by the Russians. They have mounted a tank on top of a high emplacement. In the garden itself there are enormous anti-aircraft gun sites on concrete pillar boxes, built by the Germans.

We visited Hitler's Chancellery building. The Great Hall was intact but the rest was destroyed. Files and papers were still littered around the floor. I picked up Hitler's writing pad as a souvenir.

Later we came to the famous bunker in the Chancellery gardens, descending the steps to the lowest storey. It had rooms with bunks. There was a military operations room which still had some torn maps hanging. Hitler spent his last days here. There was nothing special about the building, which is now just part of history. Potsdam was next on our itinerary. We visited the summer residence of the German Emperors there. This is now in the

Russian sector. Though their guard was not informed of the time of our arrival, they allowed us to go in. We had a picnic lunch in the beautiful grounds on the edge of a lake.

We left Berlin for India on 11th June via Istres, Luqa, Lydda and Basra and arrived in Delhi on the 14th.

While the Auk was away political activities in India had been stepped up. Gandhi has virtually given an ultimatum to Wavell to say that he must fix a time limit and then get out.

The Secretary of State and Cripps have been carrying on private negotiations with the Congress through Agatha Harrison,* Sudhir Ghosh and many others. Naturally this was disliked by Wavell who is basically a straightforward man. He does not believe in secret and confidential negotiations.

Patel has been very critical of the Quaid. He said that the Muslim League was out to wreck the negotiations. Wavell has assured him time and time again that this was not the case.

The League had accepted the Cabinet Mission Plan on 6th June. The resolution was passed 'in the hope that it would ultimately result in the establishment of complete sovereign Pakistan' [sic] and on the understanding that the Congress would also accept the plan.

Although the Quaid had called it a 'moth-eaten Pakistan', his prompt acceptance was a triumph for the Cabinet Mission. The Plan meant that all six provinces that were included would remain intact. In sections B and C the Muslims would be in the majority. The group would have all the power and the Union could do little without their approval.

Congress maintained that it should be optional for the individual provinces to join. Secondly, grouping would have to follow after the constitution had been finalized. Thirdly, provinces in B and C sections could later opt out if they wanted. Incidentally Rajagopalachari did not agree with the Congress and advocated acceptance.

On the 6th June Gandhi and the Congress High Command departed for Mussooree. They urged that the Interim Government be formed immediately.

On 10th June the Sikhs rejected the Plan and appointed a Committee of Action under Ex-Indian National Army Officers to fight the Plan. Major Short, who was their unofficial adviser, tried to assure the Sikhs that they could not be crushed. On the whole the minorities were not happy.

During our absence a plan for the expansion of the Army was issued under the orders of the C-in-C.

16th June: Wavell stopped negotiations and is now concentrating on the formation of an Interim Government.

Gandhi has disturbed all negotiations. This will have disastrous results.

---

*Agatha Harrison was a disciple of Gandhi and carried out private negotiations on his behalf.

Mistakes made by the Congress Party under the leadership of Gandhi have basically been due to the Gandhian doctrine of self-deception, the 'Inner Voice'. He has unwittingly contributed to the outcome. He has been prepared, despite his proclaimed dislike of violence, to risk bloodshed and anarchy. The 'modern-day saint' has shown his true colours. In spite of this, his personal popularity is enormous.

The Cabinet Plan for India has been rejected by the Congress. The three Cabinet Ministers and the Viceroy are going to give their 'award' on the future Government of the country. Everyone is sick of petty bargaining, strife and recriminations. The people want to know where they stand so that the country may be constructively governed and go ahead. The Congress feel that their political leaders have achieved nothing. They feel it is about time that new leaders took their place.

Wavell has said that whichever party was willing could form the Government. The Congress Party said they would be willing to form the Government if the Muslim nationalists could be included. However, the League maintains that they are the only body who are entitled to nominate the Muslim members for an Interim Government. In view of this stalemate the Viceroy, on his own, has issued an invitation to the following to form an interim Government:

Sardar Baldev Singh	Dr John Matthai
N. P. Engineer	Nawab Ismail Khan
Jawaharlal Nehru	Khawaja Nazimuddin
M. A. Jinnah	Abdur Rab Nishtar
Liaquat Ali Khan	Rajagopalachari
H. K. Mahatab	Rajendra Prasad
Vallabhai Patel	

Three more are to be added later. In all there are going to be sixteen.

17th June: Lord Wavell discussed the RIN Court Martial cases with the Auk. Both agreed that the decision should be postponed until the new Ministry takes over. The Viceroy wants the Indian troops back from overseas as soon as possible.

18th June: The Congress is likely to accept the short-term Plan.

In the middle of this turmoil Monty has arrived. He is staying with the Viceroy. We went to receive him at Palam Airport. When he got down from the aircraft both the Field-Marshals saluted simultaneously. Of course, the Auk was senior, but Monty, arriving as the Chief of the Imperial General Staff, perhaps, was under the impression that the Auk would salute first. I do not think there is much love lost between the two Field-Marshals who are diametrically opposite to each other in character and mental make-up.

It would be correct to say that Monty hates the Auk and cannot tolerate him. All this started from the days in the desert when he tried to belittle the Auk as much as possible.

Monty's first action was to take over the command twenty-four hours before the Auk had ordered him to do so. The Auk had no time for such ill-manners but completely ignored it. In fact the Auk had issued a message to the troops to serve Monty in the same spirit as they had shown under him.

Monty was afraid that the public would say that it was the Auk's Plan for the offensive which he was following. He said that when he took over the Command there were no plans for the advance at all. Instead, he maintained that the Auk wanted to retreat across the Nile.

As is well known, Monty is extremely ambitious and ruthless. He knows in his own heart-of-hearts that the Auk is a superior person and a better soldier than himself. The Auk was bred for battle. Monty was also afraid, at least at some stage or other, that Auk would be given a higher appointment. This could have been as Supreme Commander for Europe where Monty would have had to serve under him. He wanted to make sure that this would never happen. Auk's presence has always made Monty feel uneasy and inferior. In fact he has made a point of it to deny any credit to him.

He knows very well that Auk possesses a better intellect than him and has greater moral courage. This was exemplified by his not accepting the Iraq-Persia Command.

The Auk is an imposing personality. He is a born leader of men without unnecessarily imposing his authority, while Monty, at every stage, has to resort to insults and short temper to establish his. The ways followed by the two men are totally different.

Even Churchill, in spite of what he did to the Auk in the desert, respects him and regards him a better strategist than Rommel.

Field-Marshal Alan Brooke has a very high opinion of the Auk and has said that he is an able soldier, a man of splendid talent and strength of character. However, Alan Brooke maintains that, at times, the Auk has not picked his subordinates with care, and that his tolerance has extended too far.

Air Marshal Tedder considers him a clear thinker, a cheerful fighter, cool, honest, and full of guts. He is of the opinion that the Auk is head and shoulders above other soldiers.

All Monty could say was that the Auk's face is his fortune!

19th June: This morning Monty came to the C-in-C's Office for a fully fledged meeting.

The Auk has often told me that he loves the smell of a cigar, which he used to smoke himself. I enjoy smoking cigars and have his permission that when I go to his office I need not put it away. Before Monty's arrival, his Private Secretary appeared in my office. He looked at my cigar and said that the Chief of the Imperial General Staff did not like anyone smoking in his presence. I told him in no uncertain terms that I was not bound by the likes and dislikes of his boss. When Monty arrived I made certain that I had a cigar in my hand. I opened the door for him and showed him into the C-in-C's office. Not a word was said.

Monty discussed the future of British troops in India, their welfare and final repatriation. Monty had dinner with the Viceroy and we all joined them. He is reported to have said that the Auk was too much wrapped up in the Indian Army and was not paying enough attention to the welfare of the British troops.

20th June: This morning a group photograph of the Field-Marshals was taken, Wavell, Monty and the Auk. I had it autographed by them for myself. Monty was improperly dressed as usual. Later he met the Quaid. According to Monty the Quaid is reported to have said that if British troops are withdrawn there would be civil war.

I invited Nawab Ismail Khan and Khawaja Nazimuddin to lunch with the C-in-C so that they could explain the League's political stand. Khawaja Nazimuddin I have known for a long time. When I was at Aligarh Muslim University I often went to Calcutta to play in various tennis tournaments and stayed with him. Khawaja Sahib is an old Aligarian and plays tennis himself. Over the years our friendship has grown.

In 1942 I was posted to Calcutta for a short time and I met Shaheed Suhrawardy,* Mohammad Ali Bogra† and other Mulsim Leaders in his house. Khawaka Sahib used to come to us every Saturday for dinner and to play bridge. He enjoyed smoking a hookah.

Since my arrival in Delhi, Khawaja Sahib invariably stays with us. Sometimes he is accompanied by Khawaja Shahabuddin.‡ He is an undemanding guest and a welcome one. Whether we are in Delhi or away he just comes and stays. Khawaja Sahib is very fond of good food and over-eats at times. During one of his visits when we were in Simla, he fell sick after attending a dinner given in his honour. My orderly took him to the hospital and had him admitted and informed his relations.

Nawab Ismail Khan is not only a friend of my father but also of my father-in-law, Dr Ataullah Butt. He too invariably stays with us. He is very fond of music. His late wife was a great exponent of Indian music and had a melodious voice. When my wife was a little girl in Aligarh she taught her to sing. Whenever Nawab Ismail Khan is with us he insists that my wife sings for him the same songs which his late wife had taught her. He then sits with his head down, deep in thought, smoking cigarette after cigarette and listens. I suppose it brings back old memories! He is a great man.

*Shaheed Suhrawardy later became Prime Minister of Pakistan.

†Mohammad Ali Bogra also became Prime Minister of Pakistan.

‡Khawaja Shahabuddin, brother of Khawaja Nazimuddin, became the Governor of North-West Frontier Province in Pakistan.

The Auk gave a dinner in honour of Monty. Sir Ambrose Dundas, the Defence Secretary, wanted Monty's autograph on a plain piece of paper, but he would not do so. In fact he was very rude to him.

21st June: Thank God Monty has left. Everyone seems relieved at his departure. He was becoming a nuisance and had started indulging in Indian politics. Monty met Azad and asked him whether he could withdraw the British troops and officers from the Indian Army, and according to Monty, Azad said that they could not be spared. I am sure that if he had stayed longer he would have been a great embarrassment to Wavell and would have created many problems for him.

22nd June: Azad, as the Congress President, wrote to Wavell and assured him that no Muslim Nationalist would be included in the Interim Government but the rest of the Congress High Command objected and ultimately included three Muslim names.

The political activities are in full swing. The man who stands out among 'the three Magi' is Alexander. I am impressed by him. There is greatness in him. He is full of common sense as well as being shrewd and straightforward. He comes from peasant stock. He was rather critical of Quaid's attitude in the beginning but has gradually changed his opinion. He now openly says that the Congress attitude is the most deplorable that he has ever witnessed in his political career.

24th June: We flew to Poona and visited Karrackvasla, the future site of the Armed Forces Academy. Khizar and Baldev Singh have protested against this location for the academy; as most of the Army is recruited from the Punjab they feel it stands to reason that it should be located in the North. However, it is a beautiful site, alongside an enormous lake and airfield. As such all the three Services could be trained at one place.

Gandhi is now demanding an immediate transfer of power to the Hindus. He says they would in turn settle the political issues with the League. Such arrogance!

25th June: The Congress has asked for further clarification from the Cabinet Mission.

Maulana Abul Kamal Azad ranks extremely high among Congress Muslims. He joined the Congress very early on and never left it. He has a neat moustache, a beard and wears a fez cap. He is a great orator and has tremendous knowledge of the Holy Quran. Some of it he has translated. He is a man of the world and likes all good things in life. There are many among the Congress circles including Gandhi, Patel, Krishna Menon* and Aruna

---

*Krishna Menon, a communist, who later became the Defence Minister of India, was a great friend of Nehru.

Asif Ali who cannot stand him and oppose him at every stage. However, in Nehru he has a lukewarm supporter. Poor Azad is disappointed as he has worked very hard among the Congress circles for the acceptance of the plan. Though he is the President of the Congress, negotiations are taking place behind his back.

The Congress does not wish to form the Interim Government but has agreed to the setting-up of a Constituent Assembly and nothing else. For the rest they wish to go along with their own interpretation of the plan.

26th June: We returned from Poona.

Cabinet Mission thought that the Congress had accepted the plan and gave a full statement.

Azad told Wavell that he was prepared to work the plan but that Congress rejected the formation of the Interim Government. Gandhi is at the back of this decision. Quaid has said that he will form the Government. Gandhi says that he has no objection to it but that India's unity should be maintained by force. This is really an ambiguous statement!

It was decided by the Viceroy that further negotiations will be conducted after the formation of the Constituent Assembly. As a stop-gap measure it was announced that a 'Caretaker Government' will be formed which will be run by the secretatriat.

It is difficult to say whether the Cabinet Mission's visit was a success or a failure but it has achieved one vital objective. It has proved that the British are sincere in their negotiations and want to give Home Rule to India.

29th June: There was a lecture on the Atomic Bomb. In the afternoon the Cabinet Mission departed to the relief of all. Due to the fact that the mission had arrived with no definite plan it was to a large extent a failure. Gandhi contributed to the failure. Now he wants his disciple Sudhir Ghosh to proceed to UK to keep in touch with His Majesty Government. Apparently this has the approval of Pethick-Lawrence.

July 1946

'The value of the Universities is to be judged by what remains with the students when all that they have learnt is forgotten, whether they have inculcated a balance of mind and a capacity for meeting life's problems, boldly and squarely.'

The Auk.

1st July: We went to Lucknow via Cawnpore where we had lunch with Sir Padampath Sanghania. He is an industralist and an old friend of my father. Sir Padampath had collected a great many people including some women to meet the Auk. His house has a beautiful swimming pool fitted with a pump which produces waves in the water. He also has a spacious room to accommodate his elborate toy railway system. At Lucknow the C-in-C dined at 'Feroze Kothi', our ancestral home, which is next door to the Government House. It was a big occasion. The Auk was delighted to meet my mother and talked to her in Urdu. I had invited General Curtis,* the General Officer Commanding Lucknow District, as well. He is a tough soldier and is liked by all. I took Auk to see my old school, Colvin Taluqdar. The entire staff and students welcomed him and gave a first-class riding and physical training display. He seemed pleased with his visit and talked to the boys, trying to persuade them to join the Armed forces.

5th July: GHQ produced an appreciation of the strategic value of India to the British Empire (See Appendix III, p. 309).

6th July: The Congress Working Committee's actions were submitted for ratification to the All India Congress Committee at Bombay. The Socialist group has opposed it but it has been ratified. Nehru has said that the Congress is not committed to anything and may resort to another struggle. No one knows what the Congress is aiming at. They make so many contradictory statements.

*Major-General Alfred Curtis (1894–1971) was Commander of Lucknow District in 1946.

I have met Nehru before on several occasions. He is a good looking man with aristocratic features, and a Kashmiri complexion. He is known to be frugal and spends little on himself. On the *achkan* he invariably has a red rose. This makes him look very dressy. In Simla he is seen enjoying riding. To my way of thinking Nehru is not a realist. He is a dreamer who has conjured up an imaginary world around him. Even so he considers himself intellectually superior. He is an odd combination of English education and Hindu idealism. Hence his views and opinions are rather mixed up. Surprisingly, he thinks of himself as an authority on world affairs and is very fond of propounding his theories on the future of world organizations, international institutions, the effect of atomic power on human civilization, the reactions of the human being to social, psychological and scientific developments, etc. In fact he considers himself an oracle who can see into the future and, given a chance, could put the world in order. Nehru is very fond of giving lectures and advice to all and sundry. Tuker often says that it was time that he lectured less to other countries on putting their house in order and concentrated on cleaning up his own country. He feels that Nehru's policies of strategic segregation are a prelude to communist penetration.

Nehru's democracy is an elborate facade. He, basically, wants Brahmin supremacy over other castes; he is the mask of the Brahmins' resurgence. He is not a strict Hindu and hates religious organization and political parties structured on religious grounds. He did not even approve of India to be called 'Bharat'. Nehru is an enthusiastic speaker. He can address the masses and hold their attention and is loved by the Hindus. He talks of tolerance without meaning it. The only thing he really loves is power at any cost and he does not tolerate people, including Patel, who may challenge his position. He considers himself Gandhi's heir and takes his clues and lead from him. In his own heart of heart he hates Patel but cannot do without him. So he tolerates him. He wanted to bring in Jayaprakash Narayan[*] as his number two, but after some time found that he was a socialist and believed in violence as an instrument to get rid of the British.

George Fernandes[†] calls Nehru a hypocrite.

Nehru has always been very proud of his Kashmiri ancestry. Thus he is determined that Kashmir will be a part of India. On this issue he can see no reason. In fact he becomes quite irrational and is not even prepared to listen. To my mind Nehru is incapable of understanding political issues which may have far-reaching consequences. On the other side is Patel, the realist, who maintains that Kashmir will be a great drain on India. Patel sees no reason for supporting a state which has a predominantly Muslim population. But for Nehru, of course, it is a blind spot.

[*]Jayaprakash Narayan was a great Congressman who later turned against the Nehru family.

[†]George Fernandes was a South Indian who could not tolerate the Nehru family. He was responsible for the fall of the Indira Government and later became a Minister.

Nehru has a great command over the English language. He is a writer and a scholar. His main income is from the royalties on the sale of his books. Even the Russians pay him in Indian currency, which is contrary to their established practice of paying in roubles only. On the other hand Nehru has no head for figures. He has never raised any funds for the Congress himself, but relies on others to do so by dubious means from the black marketeers.

Nehru's daughter, Indira, is coming more and more into the limelight. It is said that Nehru is training her as his successor and that she has access to official papers. She lives with her father and acts as his hostess, though a poor one. To most people she is arrogant, conceited and spoilt. Her nose is always in the air. She gives the impression that she is above everyone and superior to them. This she has probably inherited from her father. In her childhood she was greatly pampered, which has made her overbearing. After her mother's death, and while her father was in prison, she was lonely and did not lead the normal life of a child. There were no parents to guide her and gradually she developed a personality which is full of complexes. Being Nehru's only child did not help the matter. But she is a determined personality and anyone who gets close to her father she cannot stand, including her talented and distinguished aunt, Mrs Vijaya Lakshmi Pandit. Mrs Pandit exercises her influence on Nehru in diverse ways. Over the years this must have made Indira feel very insecure.

At one stage Indira thought that her aunt was a rival as a successor to Nehru, even though it was obvious that Nehru was grooming his daughter for this purpose. On many occasions he was known to have taken Indira's side against his sister. Sadly Indira takes every opportunity to do her down. Anyhow the public calls her the 'Crown Princess'.

In 1942 she married a Parsi against the wishes of the family and in accordance with the Vedic* rites. She had threatened the family that if they did not agree to the marriage she would quit India where 'she had no roots'. The husband proved to be a playboy, and at one stage wanted to divorce Indira to marry a Muslim. Indira, I am told, had no objection.

Indira looks frustrated and shaky, but wants to loom larger than her father. She is bitter, gloomy and serious and seldom smiles. During the conversation her remarks are stinging and cutting. There is something very sinister about her that I cannot make out.

Mrs Pandit as a young girl fell in love with a Muslim, Syed Hussain, and wanted to marry him but the Nehru family as well as Gandhi tried their level best to prevent it and finally succeeded. She is a great freedom fighter, an eloquent speaker and a good negotiator. During 1945–46 she toured the United States of America to plead the cause of Indian Independence. She is to lead an Indian delegation to the United Nations General

*Veda is the general term for the ancient sacred literature of India, Vedism being an early Aryan religion of India.

Assembly along with Krishna Menon, who is the alternative delegate, and K. P. S. Menon.

7th July: The All-India Congress Committee (AICC), under the Presidentship of Abul Kalam Azad, accepted the Cabinet Mission plan in toto. Even Patel, the realist, supported it. There is a sigh of relief but one wonders for how long.

The All-India Congress Committee Meeting was held at Bombay and Nehru has been elected President of the Congress. He immediately delivered a long-winded speech sabotaging the Plan. I think that it is a serious blunder and may have far-reaching consequences.

8th–12th July: On 10th July Nehru took over the Presidentship of the Congress and called a Press Conference. He went back on what the All-India Congress Committee had already accepted. Nehru has demolished everything. This is bad news. There are bound to be reprecussions from other quarters. I am quite sure that in due course the Congress will regret the decision.

According to Nehru, 'Congress in accepting the Cabinet Mission long-term plan have agreed to go into the Constituent Assembly. They have agreed to nothing else . . . We have committed ourselves in no single matter to anybody . . . There will be no grouping'. The Quaid immediately retorted by saying that the League would reconsider its decision as well. He promptly withdrew acceptance of the long-term plan.

This was the last outside chance. It has been thrown away by the bad judgement, first of Gandhi and then of Nehru. The Constitution-making machinery could have been brought into operation if the Congress had not made such a grave error. The opportunity has been lost.

The Sikhs have started to arm themselves after the decision of the Congress, and the departure of the Cabinet Mission. Most of the arms are obtained from the dumps left behind by the American Armed Forces. These are mainly in Assam and East Bengal.

15th July: The Viceroy met the Auk and showed him the letters which he was going to send to Quaid and to Nehru, on the formation of the Interim Government.

16th July: We spent another very busy day. In the evening the King of Nepal came to see the Auk. The King was very simply dressed. He was courteous and dignified, and brought various presents for the Auk. He came to discuss the employment of Gurkha troops by His Majesty's Government.

19th July: The post-war Internal Defence Layout Plan 287 has come up for discussion. The troops earmarked for this purpose are:

Twelve Indian Infantry Battalions
Five British Independent Brigade Groups
One Indian Independent Brigade Group

Their location is as follows:

British Indep. Inf. Bde. Gp. Lucknow-Cawnpore
British Indep. Inf. Bde. Gp. Lahore-Sialkot-Jullundur
British Indep. Inf. Bde. Gp. Calcutta
British Indep. Inf. Bde. Gp. Bangalore
British Indep. Inf. Bde. Gp. Deolali
Indian Indep. Inf. Bde. Gp. Shillong

A tentative layout of the Internal Defence Battalions is being examined and is as follows:

Delhi	2 Bns	Ahmedabad	1 Bn
Agra	1 Bn	Bombay	1 Bn
Allahabad	1 Bn	Kamptee	2 Bns
Benares	1 Bn	Madras	2 Bns
Calcutta	1 Bn		

The C-in-C ordered that an examination be undertaken to ascertain what additional increase must be made to the Indian Armed Forces to enable them to carry out their roles if, for constitutional or other reasons, all British troops were withdrawn from India.

22nd–25th July: My old Professor, Colonel Haider Khan from Aligarh Muslim University, arrived in my office. He wanted to see the Commander-in-Chief in connection with the University Training Corps. I told the Auk that he had to see him and took him in. He was delighted to meet the grand old professor and promised to help all he could.

The Auk had visited Aligarh previously and had addressed the students of the University. His purpose was to encourage the students to join the forces and thus supply good leaders. In his address he had said that leadership needs to be assiduously 'brought out'.

More than 1000 ex-students of Aligarh were now serving as officers in the Indian Defence Forces. He considered that this record was a source of pride to the university and a proof of the excellent all-round training it imparts.

'The value of universities is to be judged by what remains in the students when all that they have learnt is forgotten. Whether they have inculcated a balance of mind and a capacity for meeting life's problems boldly and squarely.' This was part of the address he delivered to the students.

27th July: The League has finally rejected the Cabinet Mission's May Plan. It feels that it has been let down and may resort to other methods.

29th July: The Viceroy is very perturbed as he cannot get a decision from the Prime Minister on the policy to be adopted to solve the deadlock. The Viceroy then met the Auk and said that if His Majesty's Government did not like his handling of the situation, it is at liberty to find a replacement. He also told the Auk that the Prime Minister was trying to force him to accept Sir Maurice Gwyer* as his Political Adviser, but that he had flatly refused.

The League has passed a Resolution retracting its acceptance of the Cabinet Mission Plan. They have decided to observe a 'Direct Action Day' on 16th August.

Wavell said that he was sorry that the Muslim League refused the offer of the Cabinet Mission. He is of the opinion that Cripps and Pethick-Lawrence were basically dishonest and has no respect for them.

In fact the League's decision was due to the stupidity of the Mission who were known to be biased towards the Congress.

30th July: The C-in-C issued a policy note on the plan 288 – for the future expansion of the army. He went further and gave clear direction on the future of the armed forces. (See Appendix IV, p. 314) It is a masterly paper. It is revolutionary in its thoughts. I wonder whether it will sink in. It is a great step forward.

Brigadier A. A. Rudra, who is the Director of Morale but we call him the Director of 'Moral Rearmament', called. He has a team of three officers and who are known as the 'Three Fogies' – Colonels Mohammad Ali Noon†, Sheodatt Singh and Himmatsingji.‡ Their job is to assess the morale of the Indian officers and troops and report directly to the Auk.

Quaid gave a press conference on the 'Direct Action'. This may become a serious matter.

31st July: Elections to the Constituent Assembly have been complete. Congress won all except 90 seats. The League won all except five Muslim seats.

Wavell asked the Commander-in-Chief to prepare a note on the strategic implications of the inclusion of Pakistan in the British Commonwealth. In making this appreciation the Auk has assumed that firstly there will be two autonomous States – Hindustan and Pakistan; secondly, that Pakistan will consist of two parts, the western zone and the eastern zone; thirdly, that His

---

*Sir Maurice Gwyer (1878–1952) had been Chief Justice of India and President of the Federal Court 1937–43. He was Vice-Chancellor of Delhi University 1938–50.

†Colonel Mohammad Ali Noon was a cavalry officer and a great gentleman.

‡Colonels Sheodatt Singh and Himmatsingji were much respected by the Indian Commissioned Officers but did not go far in the Army.

Majesty's Government would leave Hindustan to its own devices and would take no responsibility for its defence; finally, that His Majesty's Government would agree to the inclusion of Pakistan in the British Commonwealth and lend her British sea, land and air forces to aid in her defence, in time of emergency.

The Commander-in-Chief considers that the vital Commonwealth strategic interests in the Indian Ocean are firstly the oil supplies from Persia and Iraq; secondly control of the Western entrance to the Indian Ocean and Red Sea; thirdly control of the Eastern entrance to the Indian Ocean, the Malacca Straits; fourthly ability to use their air routes across the sub-continent; fifthly the control of Ceylon for use as a port of call and as a Naval and Air base.

Auk maintains that, should India be unfriendly or influenced by Russia, the strategic position of the Commonwealth in the Indian Ocean will become untenable. At the same time Hindustan, outside the Commonwealth, might very well be tempted, in order to give effect to an inevitable urge, to conquer and absorb Pakistan, thus restoring the unity of India, and throw in her lot with Russia. Russia, with her taste for power politics and gangster methods, would be likely to take full advantage of any such tendency on the part of Hindustan. A Russian-influenced Hindustan might well constitute such a menace to the security of the Commonwealth as to cause its early dissolution.

The Commander-in-Chief then examined the influence of a British-controlled Pakistan on Hindustan. He said that in theory it might appear that Pakistan under British influence could act as a check to the hostile potentialities of an independent Hindustan. The Commander-in-Chief maintains that the future Hindustan would have the necessary resources and raw materials, industrial production, manpower and above all the requisite space to enable it to become a base for warlike operations against Pakistan if supported and equipped by hostile powers such as Russia. As the power and use of atomic weapons develops and other weapons improve, the dispersion of bases will become vital. Pakistan could never possess that depth, while India has it already. The conclusion he drew was that Pakistan could not provide the means by which the British Commonwealth could hope to influence an independent Hindustan and keep it free of hostile foreign influence and ensure security of our communications to the Indian Ocean.

The Commander-in-Chief then went on to examine the problems of the defence of Pakistan. He maintains that the probable reaction of an independent Hindustan to a Pakistan under British influence must be considered in depth. The separation of Hindustan from Pakistan, instead of eliminating the fundamental enmity of the Hindus for the Muslims, is likely to inflame it. Any attempt to establish an effective Pakistani zone in North-East India must include Calcutta. This is certain to be resisted by the Hindus. Hindustan without Calcutta and the control of Bay of Bengal is not a practical proposition.

The realization of this by the Hindus will inevitably lead to war between Hindustan and Pakistan. If this happens His Majesty's Government would be committed to fight for the retention of this zone by Pakistan. The actual defence of North-East Pakistan would be an extremely difficult problem as the sea communication would be vulnerable to attack from the bases in Hindustan.

The Commander-in-Chief was of the opinion that physically West Pakistan has both advantages and disadvantages from the defence point of view. The defence problems which West Pakistan will have to face are many and difficult. All the material for war will have to be provided from overseas through the only port, Karachi, which will be vulnerable to air, sea and land attack. Pakistan, with Kashmir as part of it, cannot be seriously threatened from the north though it will be vulnerable to air attacks. The desert of Rajputana and Sind similarly preclude any large attack by land, though large mobile armoured forces supplied by air can go through. However, Pakistan would be open to attack by land on a large scale from Hindustan. Its communication which run from north to south would also be vulnerable to air attacks.

The Commander-in-Chief then went on to consider the threat from the North-West. The aggressor in this case would be Russia, supported, possibly, by an unwilling and Sovietized, coerced Afghanistan. The problem of the defence of the north against Russia is an old one, but it will take on a new aspect, as a Muslim state will be taking over the commitment from a non-Muslim state, which is disliked and suspected and feared by Afghanistan. This situation may change. But in view of the well-known power of infiltration and seduction possessed by Soviet Russia, it would be unwise to rely on it as a permanent solution to the defence problem. Any invasion of Pakistan, instead of coming through the Khyber, is likely to take place from Kandahar against Quetta with Karachi as its objective. The Russians will develop their communications to Kandahar and in any case a fully supported mechanized and armoured forces could do the needful. If the British were to help Pakistan to defend itself they will be required to provide at least 50 squadrons of aircraft and ten divisions of troops against a determined Russian attack. In any case, were the Russians to control the Persian Gulf, then any supplies getting to Karachi would be in jeopardy.

The Commander-in-Chief said that the border between Hindustan and Pakistan could not be defined as it would not run along a river, or a mountain range. The communications running from the interior of Hindustan towards the frontier of Pakistan were good from Jullundur to Bhatinda, and to a lesser degree from Bhatinda to Kotri. India would have the advantage to choose the point of attack. The weight of the attack by land which Hindustan would be able to deliver would depend on the extent to which she has developed her industries and resources. It would also depend largely on the assistance she would receive from Russia. Hindustan, due to its depth, as a base for warlike operations at a big scale, will always be vastly superior to Pakistan. In fact it would be an efficient base for modern war which Pakistan could never be. If India attacks Pakistan and Pakistan is in the Commonwealth, then Britain would have to provide large air and land forces to ensure the integrity of Pakistan. But if Pakistan was to be attacked simultaneously by Russia and India, then the air and land forces which would have to be provided would be on an extremely large scale and through a single port – Karachi. In any case the Commonwealth no longer has the manpower to enter into a conflict of this size.

In conclusion, the Commander-in-Chief said that inclusion of Pakistan in the Commonwealth could be justified on the grounds that it would enable Britain to dominate and control an independent Hindustan so as to prevent her or her potential allies from disrupting our sea and air communication in the Indian Ocean. Secondly, it would help in maintaining the British influence in the Muslim countries of the Near and Middle East which would prevent the advance of Russia towards the Indian Ocean. However, the crucial point was that the British Commonwealth could not produce the forces which were required to defend Pakistan against a major power, or even India. Therefore the Commander-in-Chief advocated that the only way the British could keep their influence would be by keeping a united India. However, he admitted that Pakistan was the only country from where an attack on Russia could be mounted; at the same time it would hinder any hostile power dominating India. It was also an essential link in the Commonwealth air route.

A map was attached to the appreciation in which the boundary went from Jullundur straight up and no corridor had been provided to Kashmir as it was considered an essential part of Pakistan. I think his assessment is correct. History will show how right he was.

PART III

*The Still Serviceable Tractor**

See (p. 147)

August 1946

'An officer must be loyal to his service and to his country. He may hold whatever political opinions he likes but as long as he is serving he must not allow politics to affect his loyalty to his service or to the Government which is in power, even if he thinks that it is not the right form of Government!'

The Auk.

1st–3rd August: We went to Quetta to attend a model exercise preliminary to the War Office Exercise 'Evolution'. This is to be held at Camberley from 14th–17th August under the Chief of the Imperial General Staff.

The object of Exercise 'Evolution' was 'To take the basic principles of Modern War and, with that background to study the stage management and conduct of offensive land operations and to enunciate in broad outline a tactical doctrine for the armies of the Empire.'

India Command was to be asked to elucidate how the handling of Formations in each particular phase would have differed under conditions in their theatre, and to make any other comments on that phase with particular reference to Eastern conditions.

At Quetta the offensive operations in Burma from the beginning of the Japanese retreat from Imphal in 1944 up to and including the crossing of the Irrawaddy and the capture of Meiktila formed the basis of discussion. The following aspects were studied:

a) The build-up of an Army plan in an attack battle, and the handling of it at various levels.
b) The concentration of troops and organization of the battlefield and the preparation of the Fire Plan, Air Plan and the Plan for the control of movement.
c) The break-in battle.
d) The dog-fight battle.
e) The break-through.
f) The pursuit.
g) The opposed crossing of a major river obstacle.

At the same time the use of air power in support of land operations, and direct air support, was studied throughout the exercise.

Godwin-Austen came out the best, but Tuker was the only one who was really looking to the future. At the end of the Exercise he amused every one by saying that, though they had solved many problems, the greatest remained 'the crossing of miles of mud'.

In summing-up, the Commander-in-Chief reminded us of the magnificent achievements of the 14th Army. 'It might,' he said, 'be considered to have achieved the impossible'. The Auk mentioned that, before this campaign began, no experienced officer would have recommended the undertaking of any such campaign as the invasion of Burma from the north. Prior to 1943 it had been suggested that the Japanese should be left in Burma, and cut off from their bases by the employment of naval power in accordance with the British tradition of waging war. But the British had departed from that tradition by having abandoned the sea and plunged into Asia. He hoped that it would not happen again. However, at that time the Allies had not the resources for an amphibious operation, which such a course would have required.

Auk agreed with General Irwin that their ideas on the land forces of the future and their maintenance must be altered drastically. They must always look ahead. He said that new weapons were rapidly developing. As a result of this, important changes may well be put into effect within the next five years. He mentioned that the staff at GHQ would be asked to consider this problem in detail, and to put up proposals for a new model army. The Commander-in-Chief expressed his thanks to the Staff College for the good work done, the excellence of which was proved by the interest shown by those officers attending the discussion. He said that the models, notes and maps were particularly good. He was of the opinion that the discussion would be of great value during Exercise 'Evolution' and may prove that warfare in undeveloped countries may depend on modification of Western ideas, otherwise we would face the next war unprepared.

In the evening the Commander-in-Chief addressed the students in the Wavell Hall. (The main points of his speech are in Appendix V on p. 319)

Our return flight from Quetta was not without incident. When our DC-3 was flying over Khanpur in Bahawalpur State I noticed that one engine of the aircraft was misbehaving. I went to the cockpit and Paddy Greer, our pilot, said that he would have to land as soon as possible. Luckily there was an old unmanned airfield just below. I informed the Auk, who seemed quite unperturbed. Our plane was fully loaded. Travelling with us were Admiral Sir Geoffrey Miles*, the Flag Officer Commanding Royal Indian Navy, Generals Godwin-Austen,† Tuker, and several others. We made a safe landing in spite of the fact that there were cattle wandering all round. It was extremely hot and there was hardly any shade near the airfield. It was the month of Ramazan and I was fasting.

*Admiral Sir Geoffrey Miles (b 1890) was C-in-C Royal Indian Navy 1946–47.
†General Sir Alfred Godwin-Austen (1889–1963) was QMG, India Command New Delhi, 1945; Principal Administrative officer New Delhi 1945–46.

After I had made everyone sit in the shade of a lone tree close to the runway I went looking for the railway station. This was not very far away but at a good distance from the town itself. From there I rang the local Tehsildar. He arrived in the shortest possible time in a vintage car. He was a man of the old order, very proper and terribly polite. His car was short of petrol, which we filled with aviation spirit. Both car and owner seemed quite happy. All the officers huddled together in the car which made for the railway rest house. This was an ancient building, well maintained and extremely cool. There was no electricity, but coolies were produced for pulling the enormous ceiling punkhas. I commandeered all the food and beer which was available at the railway restaurant and had it brought to the rest house. Everyone helped themselves and were soon in good form.

Meanwhile the pilot had radioed a message to Delhi and asked for another aircraft to be sent. After lunch, Russell, who had a large paunch, decided to have a nap in the adjoining room. The others sat and chatted. Eventually the Auk peeped into the other room. There was Russell asleep and Auk suggested that his paunch should be measured. Whosoever guessed his girth correctly would be awarded a prize! A measuring tape was produced from somewhere and while the Pasha snored, we had great fun measuring his girth.

The plane from Delhi arrived at 4 pm. As luck would have it, it went out of action on landing. Another one had to be ordered.

By this time it was clear that we would have to stay the night at the rest house. We got some local policemen to mount a guard and man the compound wall. I decided that the ADC and myself would take turns doing the duties of the night orderly officer.

The Tehsildar knew that I was fasting and told me that he would provide the 'Iftari' (breaking of one's fast). At sunset some men arrived carrying enormous trays on their heads. I was told that it was the Iftari for me. Auk asked me whether they could join in. It was a real feast and everyone thoroughly enjoyed it.

A message came from His Highness the Amir of Bahawalpur who wanted to come and see us. We successfully put him off. Early the next morning the third plane arrived. By that time the other two were also serviceable. So having had a very pleasant night's rest we returned to Delhi.

5th August: Auk saw the Viceroy who told him that he intends to form an Interim Government.

6th August: Wavell asked Nehru to form an Interim Government. Nehru has accepted.

The League announced the 'Direct Action Day'.

7th August: We are leaving for United Kingdom to attend the Chief of the Imperial General Staff's Exercise. We shall return on 4th September. Our party includes Major-General Denys Reid, Nathu Singh, Cherry Jackson and my wife. Denys Reid is very good company as he has a tremendous sense of humour. Nathu Singh is going so that he can have a holiday at the expense of the Government of India!

On the day we were leaving the Auk said to my wife 'Begum Sahiba, most of the people in GHQ ask me to take them to United Kingdom. You never do.'

My wife replied that as our children were still small, she had never considered leaving them. When the Auk suggested they could be looked after by their grandparents, she reluctantly agreed to come. So we sent the children to Lucknow.

At the very last minute we had an SOS. The Viceroy requested the Auk to take a young girl with influential connections back to the United Kingdom with him. She had gone wild in the company of the Maharajas. Apparently, Wavell had received a message to the effect that she should be traced, retrieved, and put on the first plane back to United Kingdom. The message also stressed that Wavell must ensure she does not deplane en route and return to India.

Poor Wavell was very apologetic. Of course the Auk could not refuse. The girl was more or less forcibly brought and put on the plane. The Auk asked my wife to take charge of her and to ensure that during our journey she did not disappear. I took it upon myself to tell this girl, on the quiet, that she must behave herself. As a result we had no trouble with her. Basically she was a nice and likeable girl.

I had not time to get a passport for my wife. I told her to pin a 'WVS' badge on her sari. When we arrived at Mauripur (Karachi) a chap came to check the passports. He asked my wife for hers. She replied simply that she did not have one. His reply was prompt, 'Madam, if you had one I would have stamped it for you.'

Auk took us to Hamleys in Regent Street. He wanted to buy toys for my children. They were also holding an exhibition of models of Indian soldiers. That really made his day and he scrutinized each of them and checked them in detail.

The Auk was called in by the Chief-of-Staff and was shown a note by the Joint Intelligence Staff on the current situation in India. This said that the disturbances in India may lead to civil war in the near future. In which case the Indian Armed Forces could not be relied upon.

In reply the Commander-in-Chief said that the brief was on the gloomy side. To his way of thinking the situation was better than it had been two months ago. However, at present everything depended on Jinnah who, he felt, was not going to create widespread unrest.

The Commander-in-Chief was of the opinion that the left wing of the Congress Party was a dangerous organization. This may become stronger if an Interim Government is not immediately formed. It was also possible that it may set up a parallel Government of India and advocate a revolution.

As far as the Army was concerned, the Auk felt it had not been affected. However, it was on the cards that the Muslim troops may not take action against Muslims, or Hindu troops against Hindus. So far the Army was reliable.

The Indian Navy was recovering from the recent mutiny. However, the Indian Air Force was in the worst position. They had no background of tradition, were uneducated and undisciplined. As they were also politically conscious they may collapse. There were no signs of it for the present.

The Auk summed up the general situation as unpredictable and full of potential dangers. He felt that as long as the Indian Army remained loyal, he had sufficient forces to deal with any situation.

During our stay in the United Kingdom His Highness the Amir of Bahawalpur asked us to visit him at his house in Farnham. Having put him off visiting us the night our aircraft had made an emergency landing in Khanpur, we accepted his invitation.

Colonel Hashmi, his Minister-in-Waiting, was present. The Amir showed us his house and the paintings of his wives. We had lunch with him. He is a grand old man, cordial and affectionate. He lives in the past and tries to keep up the old order and traditions. He is a collector of manuscripts, paintings, and stamps. Incidentally he is allowed to issue stamps in the name of his State, which is a source of revenue for him. It is said that from his Palace in Bahawalpur he has had tunnels dug to the houses of his wives and uses a Baby Austin car to get round.

My wife and I were asked by Mr Foot* to lunch. He is an educationalist in India and was on leave in United Kingdom. The address was of a house in Berkeley Square. It was only on arrival that we found it was the Headquarters of 'Moral Rearmament'. Some call them the 'Oxford Groupers'. The house originally belonged to Lord Clive. The Groupers were there in force to entertain us; nonetheless it was dull company and we were happy when it ended. Probably they wanted us to join the Movement.

Nathu had not been in the United Kingdom since he left Sandhurst some twenty-odd years ago. When we arrived in London he decided to stay at a place which catered for poor overseas visitors.

When he visited us, I asked him how much was he paying for his board and lodging. It was one shilling and six pence per night. I thought he was pulling my leg but he again confirmed what he said.

Nathu was getting a very generous daily allowance and could easily have afforded to stay in a good hotel, but he decided to save every penny. I thought that he must be saving this allowance for shopping. On our return to India, I found that he had brought it all back.

*Arthur Edward Foot (1901–1968) was headmaster of the Doon School, Dehra Dun 1935–48; a member of the C-in-C's Indian National War Academy Committee 1945–46.

I invited him to lunch with the Auk. He asked Nathu whether he had comfortable accommodation. 'Yes' was the answer!

'Nathu has found a place where they pay him to stay,' I said with a smile. Though Nathu does appreciate a joke, he was furious!

'What shopping have you done?' I asked him later.

'Only a pair of tennis shoes for my wife,' he said.

'You could have bought a pair in India,' I said, 'Maybe she would have liked something better from here.'

'She doesn't know any better,' he said.

One day Nathu told us about the address book he has maintained since his days at Sandhurst. In it he has the address of the girls he befriended then.

Address book in hand, he went to visit one of them. At the correct house he asked to see 'Miss . . .'. No person of that name was there.

He had the shock of his life when the grey-haired grandmother in the family said that that was her maiden name. Nathu decided not to attempt to locate any more of his old heartthrobs.

The Auk went to Omagh in Northern Ireland and visited Crevenagh House where, in his youth, he spent many happy holidays. He was received with great rejoicing. He said, 'This is where I belong and that is why I am glad to be back here again to see you all'. He was deeply touched by the reception he received. Later he stayed with his relatives, Colonel and Mrs Darling.

The Auk wanted to visit the Royal Inniskilling Fusiliers at Klagenfurt. He is their Colonel Commandant. From Northolt we were to fly straight to Vienna, stay there a couple of days and then proceeded to Klagenfurt.

When we were flying over Munich, which was the Headquarters of the Americans, we were told that the weather was bad en route and we might not be able to keep within the space allowed for the corridor to Vienna.

We decided to land in Munich and spend the night there. The control tower was manned by the Americans. We got their permission to land but they radioed back that we should stay in the air till a proper reception was arranged, and a Guard of Honour for a Five-Star General provided.

With difficulty we managed to persuade them that we did not require VIP arrangements, or a Guard of Honour. We were only interested in spending a quiet night and were flying on the next morning.

However, by the time we landed they had a couple of cars ready with an escort to take us to a hotel in Munich. The American Theatre Commander was in the Bavarian Alps and they were trying to get in touch with him in spite of our request not to. We drove to the Four Seasons Hotel in Munich where I had stayed once before the war. This time it was in shambles, except for ten or twelve rooms which had been done up.

On entering the lobby, the receptionist told us that they had no rooms good enough for a Five-Star General. I told them that we required ordinary accommodation. Meanwhile a couple of Military Police jeeps and an enormous staff car drew up. An officer alighted with a message from the American Theatre Commander. We were told we must stay with him for the night at his Bavarian resort. The officer insisted that these were orders. We had no choice. The resort was close to a lake and we were made extremely comfortable. The Theatre Commander was very happy to have us with him and produced an excellent dinner.

Next morning we boarded the plane and left Munich for Vienna. At Vienna Airport a Guard of Honour and all the Military Governors were present.

We drove to the residence of General Steele,* the British Military Governor. It was close to Schonbrunn Castle, the summer residence of the Austrian Emperors. It was the property of the German aeroplane king, Heinkel.

Some thirty of us sat down to lunch at General Steele's house. The paintings on the walls of the dining room, the silver, the crockery and the cutlery on the table were very good. I had a feeling that I had seen all this before.

General Steele spotted me looking at it closely. 'I know what you are investigating,' he said. 'You may remember that all these things were on display at Schonbrunn. I have had them salvaged before the Russians could loot them. In other words I am only a custodian. When conditions return to normal, they will all go back.'

The following morning Auk insisted that we go and visit the famous Vienna Woods. I tried to persuade him not to do so, but he would not listen. I remembered reading that the woods had been hacked down by the Russians during the war and would not be worth a visit. When we got there I was proved right. The woods were no more.

Vienna was not the same Vienna as I had known in 1936, when there was music everywhere. At night we left for Klagenfurt by a special train. This was the Royal train and we were the only occupants. The coaches were formerly used by the Austrian Emperors. They were gold-plated, artistically decorated and luxuriously furnished. One coach was used as a sitting room, another as the dining room, the third one was the Royal suite, and the last one was for the Staff, which we occupied.

On arrival at Klagenfurt in the morning we left the Auk with the Inniskilling Fusiliers. The rest of us motored through Switzerland to Udine in Italy, where we were to emplane. We wanted to see some Swiss holiday resorts and have an easy day. We travelled in one of the enormous open Mercedes used by Hitler.

Soon we had a problem on our hands. On our way to Udine we had to negotiate a checkpost which was manned by the Russians. They had been

*General Sir James Steele (1894–1975) was Director of Staff Duties at the War Office 1943–45; C-in-C British Troops and High Commissioner, Austria 1946–47.

informed that the Commander-in-Chief was to go through, but had not been told that the group was divided into two. Then, of course, Tahirah was travelling without a passport. So we decided that the best way to negotiate the barrier would be to fly the Auk's Union Jack on our limousine. Our idea worked to perfection.

Having got through the Russian checkpost, we wondered what would happen when the Auk himself came by, but we promptly convinced ourselves that, as he would be escorted by Military Police, they would not dare stop him. That is what exactly happened.

At Udine the Auk joined us and we flew to Athens, where we spent the night. There was great rejoicing in the town. The Greeks were celebrating the return of their King and the restoration of the monarchy. The hotel we were staying at was in the centre of the town. Consequently we could hardly get any sleep and decided to join the celebrations.

When we arrived back in Delhi we carried with us very happy memories of the tour. Once again our minds were fresh to tackle the innumerable problems waiting for us.

It was decided by HMG that Top Secret information should no longer be passed to India. The Chief-of-Staff in UK decided to withdraw Top Secret papers from India. They also maintained that as the C-in-C's personal staff was Indian (that meant me) and handled all his correspondence, reliance would have to be placed on strictly personal letters to the C-in-C. They did not realise that I opened and read even those before putting them up to the C-in-C.

September 1946

'The object of the British is to hand over a peaceful India.'
The Auk.

During our absence there has been intense political activity. Wavell was making every effort to keep India sane.

Gandhi wrote a very unparliamentary letter to Wavell. In it he said that if a blood bath was necessary to achieve Independence, it would be welcomed.

He also wrote one to His Majesty's Government. In that he said the Viceroy had lost his nerve and should be dismissed. Gandhi is trying very hard to get the better of Wavell. On the other hand Wavell is convinced that Gandhi's saintliness is a political weapon. Behind it is an iron fist. So Gandhi is on the war path.

As a result of Nehru's various irresponsible and ill-conceived statements 'Direct Action Day', observed by the League, exploded into the 'Great Calcutta Killing'.

The civil authorities did not call in the troops in time and the curfew was not imposed early enough. It was only on the 17th that the troops began patrolling the streets and regaining control. On the 18th more troops, both Indian and British, which included the York and Lancaster, Green Howards and Worcestershire Regiments, were brought from Ranchi. On the 19th complete control was re-established. This was mainly due to the presence of the British troops. The public had full confidence in their impartiality.

The major killing was known to have been done by the Sikh taxi drivers.

Later the rioting spread to Dacca. Some 20,000 persons were killed. The Indian scavengers were employed in clearing up and were paid five rupees for each corpse removed.

Gandhi, the apostle of peace, kept away from the disturbances and made no effort to restore peace between the two communities. He always appears when conditions return to normal, and when law and order has been restored.

It is sad that all this is happening on the eve of Independence. Feelings are getting aroused. The Army stands alone between order and chaos. Wavell stands like a rock, unmoved and unbiased. He carries great responsibilities. He made a broadcast to the nation and appealed for sanity.

Sudhr Ghosh, Gandhi's emissary, whom Wavell calls a snake and who is financed by Tata, the great industrialists, has been to UK recently. I am sure he is negotiating with His Majesty's Government on behalf of Congress behind Wavell's back.

On the instruction of His Majesty's Government Wavell has worked out a Plan, called the 'Breakdown Plan'. This plan envisages giving South India (Bombay, Madras, Orissa and CP) immediate self-government, but retaining temporary authority in the rest of India. Wavell has always advocated a 'phased withdrawal'. However, the entire withdrawal from the whole of India is to be completed by 31st March, 1948. His Majesty's Government requires a military plan for the protection and evacuation of British personnel. Little do they realize that an emergency plan for the protection of the Europeans in the event of an anti-European outburst has always existed. Wavell already has a plan called 'Madhouse' and another called 'Bedlam' which caters for the withdrawal of British personnel and the Army, province by province, in case the Indian Army becomes unreliable or hostile.

2nd September: The Caretaker Council was dissolved and the Interim Government was sworn in. This was minus the League, though Wavell was very keen to have them in the Cabinet.

During the proceedings of the ceremony Nehru swore allegiance to the King. What a comedown! Nehru also said 'Jai Hind' (India be great).

The following have been included in the Cabinet: Baldev Singh, Rajagopalachari, Mathai, Shefat Ahmed, Bhabba, Patel, Nehru, Sarat Chandra Bose, Jagiwan Ram, Rajendra Prasad, Asif Ali and Ali Zahir. Two more Muslim Ministers will be added later. Now we shall see what kind of a show they make of running India. It is a critical time and the months ahead will not be easy. The killings that took place in Calcutta have been like a warning of things to come.

The Auk ceases to be the War Member. His role has been diluted, but he still has full authority over the forces. He is also an Adviser to the Defence Member. A Defence Members' Committee has been set up of which the Defence Member is the Chairman. The Commander-in-Chief, the Defence Secretary and the Financial Adviser are members.

5th September: Auk's first day in the office after the tour. A series of conferences were held in the morning. His Highness the Maharaja of Jaipur came to dinner. It is a pleasure to see Jai. As always he is full of life and bubbling with enthusiasm. His wife Aisha is a beautiful woman, who has great charm and dignity. They are in and out of our house constantly. He is a great Rajput, proud of his family connections with the great Moguls.

Lady Cripps has come to stay with Nehru. What a slap in Wavell's face. I suppose she is carrying some message from her husband.

12th September: The South-East Asia Command prepared a paper which considered the repercussion in their area to the possible launching of a 'Direct Action' campaign by Jinnah in India, with or without the declaration of Jehad (popular uprising). They doubted the possibility of such a campaign and especially that of the declaration of Jehad. However, they thought that there would be communal disturbances among the civilians.

They were of the opinion that, as far as the reaction among Muslim troops elsewhere in South-East Asia to the campaign was concerned, it was thought that it would be governed by the reaction of the Muslim troops in India.

The Director of Intelligence at GHQ prepared a very detailed paper on this subject and considered the various alternatives before the Quaid. He argued that Jinnah had not yet rejected the Constituent Assembly in so many words, and that there was a possibility that he may reconsider his decision. There was also the possibility that Jinnah has never really intended to have a separate Pakistan. He has used it as a propaganda weapon to win concessions from the Congress. Those who believe in this have based their conclusions on the arguments advanced by the Congress. These conclusions are, firstly, that Pakistan is a geographical absurdity; it is indefensible and economically poor, besides having large minority communities. Secondly, though 80 per cent of the Muslim elements in the Army are pro-Pakistan, only a small proportion are liable to respond to Jinnah's call, and an even smaller proportion can be counted on to revolt. Thirdly, the North-West Frontier Province, a potential Pakistan arsenal, is a Congress province. They will resist any call from Jinnah. Lastly, Direct Action will result in the arrest of Jinnah and other prominent Muslims, which will deprive the movement of both leadership and organization.

The paper went on to say that the organization for recruiting Congress volunteers is more advanced. This is because Congress has virtually monopolized the Indian National Army. It is now their chief potential weapon. Besides, the Congress militant wing, the Rashtrya Swayam Sewak Sangh (RSSS), with a strength of about half a million men, is an added force in their hands, and could be used against the League.

The paper said that Nehru had already stated that he intends to resist the Muslim League Direct Action. It may be assumed that the arrest of Jinnah would be his first move.

According to the paper the Muslims in the Congress Party would be problematical and may oppose all actions of Jinnah.

The paper concluded that Jehad was out of context but communal disturbances are likely to take place. The Direct Action called by Jinnah will amount to a Muslim revolt and may affect the Muslim personnel in the Armed Forces. The Muslim League has so far not attempted to approach the Indian Army. However, if it does so, the reliability of an important portion of the Indian Army and Indian Police in Northern India may well be affected. The Muslim personnel cannot be relied upon to use force against their co-religionists.

14th September: Nehru has sent a letter to the Commander-in-Chief saying that he is greatly interested in the problems of defence, especially in those which have a bearing on foreign policy. Along with the letter he sent a long note which he had written to the Defence Department for the C-in-C's comments before he placed it before the Cabinet. In the note Nehru said that he wanted to review the foreign policy and the future of the Indian Army. He started with his usual theme. 'Our first task is to attempt to transform the whole background of the Indian Army and make it feel that it is the National Army of India . . . It was impossible for this to be done in the past because the whole concept of the Indian Army was different, as the average soldier thought far more in terms of an external allegiance than of allegiance to his own country.' He further said that the Army consisted of a very fine body of men of whom any country could be proud. He maintained that it would be a great pity if communal feelings spread in the Army and that our policy should be to keep the Army away from communalism. He wanted the façade of the martial races done away with, and the Army made to feel that it was the National Army of India so that they realize that their service and their allegiance were primarily to their own country. Besides, they must be made to feel proud of their country and to believe in their great future and guard their country against aggression.

According to Nehru the public feels that the Armed Forces are theirs and they must come closer to them. At the same time the Forces should remain apart from politics. The Army should be nationalized as soon as possible. Though the process has started, it is too slow. Besides, the policy and control of the Army must be dictated from Delhi and not from London. He went on to say that the Army in the past has been mainly used for quelling domestic disorders and keeping the tribesmen of the North-West Frontier in check. He objected to the bombing of the civilian population in the tribal areas and said that some solution will have to be found in dealing with the frontier tribesmen.

He advocated the immediate withdrawal of British troops from India, stating that India must make her own arrangements for defence.

He further said that scientific research in all its forms should be the order of the day. The troops overseas should be called back immediately. He maintains that India wants to live in peace with its neighbours and has no fear of them.

The Commander-in-Chief is studying the note.

16th September: The Auk saw Wavell. They discussed the portfolio of the War Member. Both maintained that Baldev Singh should hold this portfolio as he is harmless. At this stage there is talk of the Quaid joining the Cabinet. This has terrified everyone. Wavell also said that Nehru had written to him complaining about the fact that while the Indian troops are being demobilized, Brithish troops are being retained. In the evening I took the Auk to see Maulana Abdul Haq and his impressive Urdu Library.

He is a very dignified old man who has dedicated his entire life to the promotion of Urdu.

17th September: The Commander-in-Chief has sent his comments on Nehru's letters to the War Member.

At the outset the Commander-in-Chief warned that the National outlook should not be made a reason for any slackening of discipline or obedience to properly constituted authority. He always advocated that the Armed Forces should be non-political and non-communal in character.

As far as the 'martial classes' are concerned, use of the term was forbidden several years ago. His policy has been to recruit as widely and as evenly as possible throughout the country. Units have been raised from classes where recruitment has not taken place previously. However, an exactly proportionate representation is not practical due to administrative and organizational factors which cannot be disregarded unless efficiency is made to suffer.

He welcomed the fact that an attempt is being made by the leaders of public opinion to make the Army feel that they are truly a 'National' Force.

The Commander-in-Chief welcomed Nehru's assurance that the attitude of the public towards the Armed Forces has recently changed. He said that he has always been working strenuously to achieve it in the past and in this connection has organized 'National Services Week' throughout the country.

The Commander-in-Chief maintained that nationalization is progressing satisfactorily. However, there is a dearth of suitable candidates for the grant of regular commissions in all the three Services. This has been causing him the gravest anxiety. However, it must be kept in mind that the policy of complete nationalization must not affect the efficiency and stability of the Armed Forces; therefore it must be done cautiously.

He said that the Armed Forces exist solely to carry out the policy of the Government that is in power. The officers must not allow their political views to influence them in any way in the execution of their duty. The Commander-in-Chief was of the opinion that the Police Force should be strengthened to deal with internal disorder. He said that the problems of the North-West Frontier Province are still unsolved. He said he would welcome the expansion of the Civil Armed Forces. However, under the present circumstances there is no alternative but to use the Air Force and Army to prevent the spread of lawlessness and unrest in the Frontier. The retention of British troops in India was a matter for the Government to decide. He said that attention was being paid to scientific research in the Defence Forces. He reassured Nehru that the troops from overseas were being withdrawn.

I think that the Commander-in-Chief was too mild in his reply. Nehru's letter gave the impression that nothing was being done in the Army. He was teaching the Auk how to run this mighty machine. There was not a single point in it on which the Commander-in-Chief had not taken action already. Nehru was just throwing his weight about to show that, though there was going to be a Defence Member, he, Nehru would be the one who would guide him. It was obvious to me that Nehru's letter was prepared by my old friend Colonel B. M. Kaul, who wanted to establish his bona fides with him. If Nehru had only taken the trouble of going through the various directives which the Auk had issued on nationalization, co-operation with the public, making the Army into a National Army, etc., the necessity of writing this note would not have arisen. Nehru did not care to remember that he was the one who had inflamed communal feelings and bitter resentment in the Army by pleading the cause of the Indian National Army. He forgot that the Army carries out the orders of the duly constituted Government and had, therefore, nothing to fear from it.

18th September: Nehru has written another letter. This time to Lord Wavell, complaining that the Governor-General's War Department had sent a telegram to the Secretary of State for India stating that the British troops should continue to remain in the country while the demobilization of the Indian troops was carried out. Nehru took great exception to the fact that he was not informed previously. At this stage the War Member had not taken up his assignment, and Wavell was right in having the telegram sent. Nehru maintained that, without reference to the Cabinet, such actions are constitutionally improper and discourteous. He said it would have far-reaching consequences, both political and financial. Nehru then went on to emphasize the fact that the British troops must leave immediately. There is no doubt that Nehru has started throwing his weight about. He is acting more as a Prime Minister than as Foreign Minister. In fact he is trying to run the Government of India. These are mean tactics to try and belittle Wavell and finally to get rid of him. The letter was sent by the Viceroy to the Commander-in-Chief to read.

26th September: The Auk called on the Viceroy who told him that Gandhi was unscrupulous. If it suited his purpose Gandhi would undoubtedly resort to violence. Once again he reiterated that Gandhi's mildness was only a cover-up. I found this very interesting, though not new.

To Auk service in the Forces is not merely a career but his very life. He has grown grey in the service of India for the pasty forty-three years. India is his home and the 1st Punjab Regimental Centre at Jhelum his Mecca. He is more Indian than British. His lasting achievement will always be the creation of a genuinely Indian Army.

It is seldom realized that his Command has rapidly expanded and administered and trained some two million men who fought in the war. Of these 63 per cent were Muslims. This has been no mean achievement. During this period the only person who was a source of trouble to him was Wingate who was allowed by Churchill to pick from all units for his special operations in Burma. The Auk believed that a fully trained unit is capable of taking part in all types of operations with specialized training. When Auk took over, Wingate had already created chaos and dislocation in the Indian Army. Being very close to Churchill, Wingate could get away with anything. He was a genius at his own style of fighting. He could not work or cooperate with any one else and had the knack of making enemies. Wingate believed that Burma could be won by his style of fighting alone and tried to convince Churchill accordingly.

In July, 1943, Wingate submitted a Report to Churchill. He was extremely critical of GHQ and the Indian Army. He called the Indian Army 'That System of Outdoor Relief'. Auk was furious and said that the type of operation which Wingate advocated would be of no purpose unless there was an Army to occupy the areas which had been captured and a follow-up course was most essential.

On 24th August, 1943, orders were issued that the C-in-C in India would be responsible for administration and supply, but not for operations. It is well known that when the resources to counterattack the Japs had been built up the Command was given to Mountbatten. Still the Auk's job in India remained vital to success. A new Command – South-East Asia Command – under Mountbatten, was created; Lt-General Joseph Stilwell,* Commander of the Chinese Army in North Burma (and known as 'Vinegar Joe'), was appointed his Second-in-Command.

On Auk devolved the responsibility of training the Army in jungle warfare and to channel the entire resources of the subcontinent towards the war effort. The forgotten 14th Army came into the limelight.

In retrospect, under the Auk, India's war record is great. It provided bases, troops and supplies to the Allied Forces. A great many war industries were set up under his orders. India's relations with the American and the Chinese Forces fell to him. The Auk had to do a great deal of semi-political work. He excelled in this. He supported SEAC Command ungrudgingly. Mountbatten is known to have said, 'No demand of his had ever been refused if it was humanly possible to meet.'

---

*General Joseph Stilwell (1883–1946) had commanded the Chinese 5th & 6th Armies in Burma in 1942; in 1945 he was appointed Commander of the US 10th Army in Okinawa.

October 1946

'In the Forces unity of thought and purpose is essential and in disunity lies disaster, not only for them but also for the country as a whole.'

The Auk.

1st October: According to statistics there are 80,000 British troops in India today, 1st October, 1946. They are to be reduced to 36,000 by 1st April, 1947, and to 23,000 by 1st April 1948. But in view of the general disorder in the country the reduction has been stopped. A new schedule is to be prepared.

2nd October: Today Gandhi is 78. The *Daily Dawn* wrote the following on Gandhi's birthday. 'The pile of non-violent literature he has produced during his fruitful political life has in turn produced such a pile of dead bodies and broken bones that we hesitate to wish him many happy returns of the fray.'

6th October: Auk has suggested to Baldev that Kaul should be appointed a Liaison Officer between the Defence Minister and the Commander-in-Chief. The background to it is that Kaul has gained the confidence of Nehru and is throwing his weight about. He has lost interest in his own job. The Auk thought it best to get rid of him. Kaul is impetuous and is spreading discontentment among the officers. Many Indian officers dislike him intensely.

Kaul is also making a fool of poor Himmatsinghji by pressurizing him to ask irrelevant questions in the Assembly, to which Himmatsinghji has been nominated as the representative of the Armed Forces.

8th October: We flew to Rampur to attend the marriage of Captain Murtaza Ali Kahn, affectionately known as 'Bachan'. He is the heir apparent of Rampur State and is getting married to Sakina, daughter of Raja Mohammed Mehdi of Pirpur.

Bachan's father, Nawab Raza Ali Khan, was with me in the Colvin Taluqdar School, Lucknow, so was his uncle Abdul Karim, who is a great friend of mine.

When Auk came back from the desert he was without a job and he stayed for some time with Raza Ali. When the Auk was appointed Commander-in-Chief he took Bachan as his ADC. At the time I came to Delhi, Bachan was still there but his father was insisting that he should come back to the State and look after its Armed Forces. Much to his disgust poor Bachan had to leave. He is a happy-go-lucky individual, a very good mixer and extremely popular with all. Even so it did not take long before father and son were not on speaking terms.

The marriage celebrations were held on the 8th and 11th. Half of the guests were invited on the first day and the other half on the second. Except for the Viceroy, everyone who was somebody in India was there.

The arrangements were excellent. Receptions, banquets, fireworks, flood lighting of the Khas Bagh Palace were all conducted in traditional style. The music at night, performed by the best musicians of India, was something not to be forgotten easily. Auk retired early but I listened to the music until the early hours of the morning. Raza Ali is a great authority on music and dancing. It is customary in Rampur that musicians parade in the streets before their performance.

9th October: We returned from Rampur. Baldev gave a talk on All-India Radio on the 'National outlook'. It was pretty feeble on the whole.

A paper has been prepared on the future Armed Forces of India for the consideration of the Cabinet. It is written from the viewpoint of an independent India. If the future Government of India chose Dominion status, it was visualised that certain problems would be simplified. It was hoped that the target of the reduction of the British troops would be completed by 1st April, 1947. It may have to be slowed down due to unforeseen events. It was stated that to build up Indian Forces for the future is a slow and complex process which takes time and requires careful planning and therefore it was necessary to get a clear directive from the Government of India.

It was emphasized that the basis of the planning of the post-war Armed Forces must take into account the geographical position and natural resources available. It was accepted that India will always occupy a key position in Asia. However strong a country may be, it could not alone expect to defend itself. The minimum requirement to ensure security was to maintain a highly efficient Field Army, a balanced Air Force and sufficient Navy to guard the coastline. However, financial considerations will present difficulty in maintaining a large force, but they must be big enough to stand the first shock of an attack by a major power such as Russia. Even during the short initial period early reinforcements and additional Air Force and Naval units would be required from elsewhere. At the same time India could be dependent on warlike stores and armaments from other countries until it builds its own industrial base.

So far the sea frontiers of India have been secured by the British Navy and the defence of North-West Frontier Province has been shared between Indian and British troops. Therefore the Navy will have to be built up and so will the Civil Armed Forces on the Frontier. As far as the internal defence is concerned, troops will have to be earmarked all the time for this important role.

The paper said that it was essential for any country to be prepared in the initial stages to protect itself, until help could arrive from its allies. The future major conflict would start very quickly and would be of devastating proportions. It was stated that in Russia there was such a preponderance of men and equipment that India could not resist and the possibility of an invasion through Baluchistan and a thrust to the Persian Gulf must be accepted. It was therefore essential that India's forces should be so organized that they were capable of rapid expansion. To achieve this in time forces must be properly balanced, self-contained and complete. However, the provision of officers and technical personnel will present a considerable problem. Besides, the cost of maintaining the Armed Forces is going to be high and especially the cost of buying new equipment.

It was also visualized that an independent India would wish to develop friendly relations and co-operation with the surrounding States for mutual benefits. To achieve this it may be essential to help them out with their defence needs.

10th October: Communal riots have started in Noakhali.

12th October: In the evening the Auk saw the Viceroy who showed him his reply to His Majesty's Government's comments on the 'Breakdown Plan'. He told the Viceroy that the Cabinet was pressing him hard for the release of all Indian National Army prisoners.

15th October: The League has decided to join the Interim Government. Gandhi and Nehru are upset. The League Cabinet Ministers are Liaquat, Nishtar, Chundrigar, Ghazanfar Ali Khan and Jogindra Nath Mandal. It is a great pity that Khawaja Nazimuddin and Nawab Ismail Khan have not been included. The Congress dropped Ali Zaheer, Shafat Ahmed and Bose. The Army Commanders came to lunch. In the evening there was an exhibition of paintings which the Commander-in-Chief opened.

19th October: It is seldom realized how much attention the Auk pays to the welfare of the troops. He is the driving force in ensuring that the men receive the amenities and comforts which mean so much to their contentment and morale. Troops' *Aramgahs* (rest houses) have been constructed all over India, together with excellent canteens, some of which are mobile. Leave camps are looked after by voluntary workers, men and women, who also help in running canteens at the railway stations and elsewhere. Radio sets have

Field-Marshal Sir Claude Auchinleck, Commander-in-Chief, India.

Mohammed Ali Jinnah – the Quaid.

The Quaid and the C-in-C at a party at the author's house.

General Akbar Khan, Sir Claude Auchinleck, the Quaid and Miss Jinnah.

Jinnah, Sir Claude, Admiral Jefford, Miss Jinnah and the author, at the author's house.

been provided for the troops on a massive scale. The ENSA and its Indian counterpart 'Fauji Dilkhush Sabha' are giving excellent shows in the garrison towns. Information rooms and libraries have been set up all over the country. A limited number of field libraries are also operating. More than half a million Penguin books are in circulation, along with many hundreds of thousands of magazines, periodicals and newspapers. Some reading material is especially published for the troops and officers, e.g. *Fauji Akhbar, Jang-Ki-Khabren, Contact, Weekly Commentary, Indian Army Digest, RIN Log, Journal of the Indian Air Force* and the *Indian Army Review*.

20th October: The Commander-in-Chief wrote the following letter to the Army Commanders:

At our recent Conference I discussed with you the excellent work which has been and is being done by the British officers of the Indian Army, particularly the old Regular officers and amongst them especially Commanding Officers of units. I realize very well how very difficult their present task is and that it is not likely to get easier in the future. I will be most grateful if you will take every opportunity of letting Commanding Officers know how much I appreciate the splendid way they are carrying on. They are doing a great service to the Army and to their country. The Commanding Officers of British units, too, are having not too easy a time, as I know from personal observation, though their difficulties are of a different kind. To them, too, I would like you to convey my warm appreciation of their unselfish and devoted efforts to make their units happy and efficient.

The riots in Noakhali have ended. Gandhi is going there. He always appears after the trouble has stopped. He is a source of concern to the authorities and has little influence in quelling the riots or any other disturbances. It is said that he is going to stay there till March.

23rd October: The Commander-in-Chief witnessed the Trooping of the Colour of the 4th Baluch on the occasion of the Centenary of the Battalion. It was commanded by Lt-Col Brian Montgomery, brother of Field-Marshal Lord Montgomery. Brian and myself were Instructors together at Staff College, Quetta. He is quite opposite to his famous brother, carefree and happy-go-lucky.

24th–26th October: Quetta was our next stop. The Auk inspected several units. The League joined the Government and took office on 26th October. They went in to prevent the Congress getting a hold of the country. Nehru said that the dual Government is a farce. The League's attitude has hardened and the Congress is now regretting their non-inclusion when they entered the Government. Wavell is trying to get the League to accept the long-term plan, and the Congress the grouping of the Provinces. The political leaders have been invited for a Conference in London.

28th October: During the last few days Pandit Nehru had been on a visit to the North-West Frontier Pronvince. This was against the advice of the Governor, Sir Olaf Caroe,* and the Viceroy. The main purpose of Nehru's visit was to boost the morale of the Congress and push their cause on the Frontier and to demonstrate to the tribesmen that a Hindu is 'boss'. This was resented by them and inflamed them. When he arrived at Peshawar Airport he was greeted by a large and hostile League demonstration. It was an ugly situation and he had to be taken out through a back door. Nehru then visited Miranshah and Razmak where again he received an extremely hostile reception from the tribal leaders. They were further enraged by his arrogance and by his ill temper. The tribesmen told him that they regarded the Hindus as their tenants and serfs and would have no dealing with him. At the same time Nehru called them 'pitiful pensioners', little realizing that the Congress were pouring in funds to win them over. He later visited the Khyber where the situation became alarming. Stones were thrown at his car and the Khyber Rifles had to open fire to disperse the crowd. Nehru was lucky to escape. He then visited Malakand and Dargai where stones were again thrown. Nehru, along with Ghaffar Khan and his brother, Doctor Khan Sahib, were injured. The crowd carried black flags and were out to demonstrate that he was an unwelcome guest. His decision to visit was impulsive and ill-timed. Even then, if he had taken with him the members of the other parties and adopted a non-party approach, it would have been better. He lost prestige while the League gained in popularity. He suspended Mehboob Khan, the Political Agent at Malakand. Nehru said that the demonstrations were engineered by the League. Wavell seems frustrated. Riots in Bengal and Bihar continue.

30th October: The Interim Government started functioning slowly. Wavell told Auk that he was very tired. He maintains that political negotiations were foreign to him and that he could not trust any one. He said that he was fed up with Cripps who had double-crossed him on each and every occasion. He said Cripps was carrying on private negotiations with Congress through Sudhir Ghosh. The Viceroy categorically said that the Mission created enormous problems for him and solved none. The Cabinet Mission gave the

*Sir Olaf Caroe (d. 1981) was Governor of North-West Frontier Province 1946–47; from 1939 to 1945 he was Secretary of the External Affairs Department in India.

impression to the Congress that His Majesty's Government was frightened of them. He said that had he been a little firmer towards the end of negotiations probably the Plan would have been accepted. Wavell sincerely believes that the Congress is dishonest. He has a very high opinion of the leaders of the League, their honesty, courage and dignity.

November 1946

*'Before we British officers go it is our bounden duty to
do all we can to ensure the continued well-being and
efficiency of our men, and of the Army we have loved so
well and served so long.'*

The Auk.

2nd November: The Auk has formed a Defence Science Board under Dr
D. S. Kothari, who is also the Defence Science Adviser to GHQ.

There has been widespread disturbance in Bengal and a great deal of
killing.

The Viceroy and the Auk have had a disagreement. Wavell considers that
British troops will have to stay until the country has a new constitution. The
Auk believes that they could leave after 1st January, 1947. He had given a
note to Baldev to this effect.

I think the Auk was forced to suggest this by Baldev himself. The Viceroy
also discussed the situation on the Frontier with him. The Auk maintains
that one of the reasons for its deterioration is that the Political Service is not
what it used to be.

3rd November: Nehru, Patel, Liaquat and Nishtar visited Patna to pacify
the various communities. Hussain Imam is doing excellent work for the
Muslims in this regard.

Noakhali district is burning again.

A great massacre of the Muslims has taken place in Gharmuktesar in
United Provinces. This was engineered by the Jats from Rohtak and Hissar.
It is a great pity. There are bound to be repercussions elsewhere. The UP
Congress Government has suppressed the news and the British Cabinet has
encouraged the policy of silence. Politically it suits them. Had the news been
splashed all over, the Opposition in Parliament might have exploited it, and
advocated the slowing down of the handing-over process.

4th November: I met Raj Kumari Amrit Kaur. She comes from Kapurthala
and was educated in the United Kingdom. She is a great pianist. Before the
Second World War there were three Indian beauties. She was one of them,

the other two were Maharani Indi of Kooch Behar and Princess Tai Rajwada. Raj Kumari is one of the founders of the Lady Irwin College in Delhi and at one time acted as secretary to Gandhi. She is outspoken and considers many Congressmen as rogues and rascals. She is always getting on the wrong side of the authorities.

7th November: Francis Tuker has prepared a Plan which will be implemented in the event of a complete breakdown of law and order in the Eastern Command. Secretly and by night he has moved stores, arms, ammunition and supplies through reliable units to certain selected points, which could be defended.

10th November: It was Sunday today. The Auk went out alone to Okhla to paint. This is his latest hobby. He is getting quite good at it. I have purchased a small car with civilian number plates for him which he uses on such occasions. He thinks that he will not be recognized in it!

12th–17th November: We left on a tour of Hyderabad and Sikandrabad. It was one of the happiest trips I ever made with the Commander-in-Chief. We stayed at the Residency. The Nizam invited us to tea at the King's Kothi. The Auk and myself drove in at the appointed time, but found no one to receive us except a small man in a Turkish fez and achkan. For a moment I thought I had made a mistake about the time. I got out of the car quickly and was about to ask whether there was anybody to receive us. Suddenly I heard the Auk say, 'How are you, Your Exalted Highness?'

We sat in the entrance passage of King's Kothi. The tea offered was rather poor. The cakes were stale. There were only the three of us. The Nizam is a great conversationalist and extremely well-informed. We discussed the internal and external problems of the subcontinent. When we were leaving he told the Auk that on his next visit to Hyderabad he must have lunch with him. I told the Auk later that he would have to make a special trip just to have lunch.

Azam Jah, heir apparent of the Nizam, gave us a lavish dinner with 23 courses. His dining room had a pond in the centre where swans swam.

The Auk took the salute at the parade of the State Forces. Azam Jah's ten-year-old son was also in uniform. It was an excellent parade and they marched as well as any regular Indian Army unit.

I went to see the historic Golcanda Fort and took a guide with me. Later the Auk asked me to show him around the fort. He was not prepared to have the guide accompany us or have an escort. At the main gate we found the famous Arab Legion mounting the guard. They were all over six feet tall. General and Lady Lockhart came with us. While conducting the party I lost the way. We landed in the Nizam's old arsenal which had countless matchlocks, old artillery pieces, mortars as well as solid shots piled up to the roof.

Auk was thrilled. We spent a long time examining them. The Nizam hates anything to be destroyed. He had stored these family treasures in a corner of the fort where no one could see them. It was with some difficulty that I managed to find the way out of the fort.

On behalf of the Nizam, Azam Jah gave a supper at the famous Sikandrabad Club for the Auk. There were some eight hundred guests. When I was leaving for Hyderabad my wife had asked me to look up a friend of hers who was practising medicine. I called at her parents' house and asked her whether she would care to come to the supper at the Club. She agreed. I had her collected, and she travelled with the Auk and myself to the Club. Azam Jah was there to receive us and keen to find out who she was. He was quite surprised to learn that she was one of his subjects. For the occasion the Nizam had allowed 600 bottles of champagne to be served with supper. By half past ten they had been consumed. When Azam Jah realized what had happened he immediately ordered the playing of 'God Save The King'. This indicated to the guests that the party was over.

I took the Auk to the Usmania University where he was received by Khalifa Abdul Hakim, my wife's uncle. The Auk was deeply impressed by what the University was doing for the Urdu language.

During the period we were away the Viceroy paid a visit to the Frontier. He went to Wana, Malakand, Dir, Swat and Peshawar. He was received with enthusiasm everywhere. What a contrast this was to Nehru's visit.

I think Nehru has begun to realize the gravity of the present situation. He knows it is getting out of control. The other day he said 'there appears to be a competition in murders and brutalities'.

On the 13th a press communique was issued on the establishment of an Armed Forces Nationalization Committee. They have to submit their report by June, 1947. (The members of the Committee and their terms of reference can be found in Appendix VI, p. 322)

Kaul is extremely happy on being appointed the Secretary of the Committee. He cannot contain himself. He is going round GHQ saying that he will now fix all the senior officers, including the Commander-in-Chief.

The riots at Gharmuktesar have ended. It has been such a tragedy. So many lives lost unnecessarily.

18th November: I took the Auk to the University of Jamia Millia, the head of which is Dr Zakir Hussain.* He is a dedicated man who has been instrumental in building up this great institution. We were greatly impressed by his simplicity and the sacrifices he has made.

20th November: We lunched with Khizer Hayat Tiwana, the Punjab Premier. He was very worked up on the proposed location of the Indian

*Dr Zakir Hussain later became President of India.

Military Academy. He, of course, wants it in the Punjab. The entry to the Academy should not be by competition. In this way he feels that none other than the *baboos* (clerks) will get in.

Wavell has issued invitations for a meeting of the Constituent Assembly which is to be held on 9th December. The Quaid has directed the Muslim Leaguers not to participate in it.

22nd November: The Commander-in-Chief wrote a policy note to all the Army Commanders on the promotion of Indian officers which is as follows:

> The policy regarding appointing Indian officers to high appointments in the Army was mentioned at the Army Commanders' Conference last month, and a draft letter on the subject was discussed. Please ensure that this policy is made known to all senior British officers in your command. For easy reference, the relevant paragraphs of this letter are reproduced below:
>
> It has been decreed, and in my opinion inevitably decreed, that we – the British officers – are to go. Before we go, it is our bounden duty to do all we can to ensure the continued well-being and efficiency of our men and of the Army we have loved so well and served so long. We can do this only if we give freely and fully of our knowledge and experience to those who are to replace us in the higher commands and appointments. By virtue of our training and long service we have this knowledge and experience and we must pass it on unselfishly and willingly to our Indian comrades who, through no fault of their own, have not perhaps had our opportunities. But this is not enough. If our young Indian officers are to be properly equipped to replace us in high commands and appointments, so as to be able to preserve the high standard of efficiency and man-management which we have always set ourselves, they must be given actual experience in the art of command and leadership. For this reason I have made up my mind that it is essential to provide the more senior of our Indian officers with the widest possible experience in the various duties which an officer may have to perform when he reaches the higher ranks of the Army. It will happen, therefore, that Indian officers may be given posts which, in the normal course of events, might have been reserved for officers of greater seniority. This does not mean that Indian officers will be appointed indiscriminately just because they are Indian. Far from it. So long as I am there, I will appoint no officer, British or Indian, to any post unless I am sure in my own mind that he is properly fitted for it.

For some reason or the other Baldev has fallen foul of Nehru. They are not on speaking terms with each other.

Mrs Sarojini Naidu* dined with us this evening. My first encounter with her was when I returned from Burma in 1941 and was staying for a couple of days with Sir Shankar Lall† in Delhi.

Mrs Naidu was a guest in the house as well. I was trying to book a telephone call in the house when I noticed Mrs Naidu approaching to use the telephone. I stood up and suggested she use it first.

'Young man, who are you?' she asked.

'Mrs Naidu, you would not know me, but I will tell you that I am married to Tahirah Butt.'

On hearing Tahirah's name Mrs Naidu put her arms round me and kissed me on both cheeks to my embarrassment. She had met my wife on many occasions when visiting the Lady Hardinge Medical College where Tahirah was studying. On making my acquaintance she told me how fond she was of Tahirah and would not stop talking and praising her.

Now Mrs Naidu is a constant visitor to our house and prefers to be alone with us. She sits on a *takhat* (wooden seat) with pillows all round her, completely at ease, listening to music or to poetry or talking to the children. Often she talks and we listen. Evenings spent in her company are a delight and an education. Mrs Sarojini Naidu comes from Hyderabad Deccan. She is very much a product of Muslim culture. Her way of talking and manners are typical Hyderabadian. I feel that she is one of those rare Hindus who do not differentiate between Hindus and Muslims. In fact she has a large number of friends from amongst the Muslim community, including the Quaid, of whom she is very fond.

At one stage Gandhi advised Nehru not to include Mrs Naidu in the Congress Working Committee. He believed she was likely to give their secrets away. I think she is more of a liberal in the political field. Possessing an extrovert personality, she loves holding court where she can really become a 'begum'.

Mrs Naidu is a great conversationalist, capable of holding her own in any company. She is cheerful by nature and very fond of giving nicknames to all and sundry. 'Mickey Mouse' is what she calls Gandhi and 'the Madras fox' is her name for Rajagopalachari.

25th November: Operational Instructions No. 4. which relates to scheme 'Gondola' were issued. These will become operative in case of an insurrection.

Originally a scheme called 'Asylum' had been prepared. This was to be put into force in case of a revolt against British rule. However, it was not

---

*Mrs Naidu was known as the 'Nightingale of India' and later became Governor of United Pronvices.

† Sir Shankar Lall (1901–51) was a rich millowner; managing director of the Delhi Cloth and General Mills Co.

feasible, as enough troops were not available for this purpose. Now 'Gondola' has replaced it.

The activities of the ex-Indian National Army personnel, and the availability of many unlicensed arms, is causing apprehension and is undermining the law and order situation in the country. It is feared that it may develop into an insurrection.

Under 'Gondola' certain bases, airfields and communication centres are to be held. These will be provisioned with special weapons which include tear and smoke bombs.

The warning system has been carefully worked out. When the code word 'Filbert' is issued, it will be a warning order for the issue of the code word 'Canker'. 'Canker' will mean that an open insurrection is imminent and the move to emergency stations is to begin. The code word 'Canker' is to be issued orally. The 'denial policy', to destroy and render useless certain installations, would them come into force and martial law would be declared.

26th November: Wavell sent an invitation to Nehru, Liaquat and Baldev to attend a Conference in London.

30th November: A very high-powered meeting of both civilians and the personnel of the Armed Forces was held to consider the 'Breakdown Plan'. At the start it was said that the British would have to clear out of India by the spring of 1948. The objects of the Breakdown Plan are:

a)   Withdraw with minimum of disorder.
b)   Maintain cohesion of Armed Forces.
c)   Administer shock and use political leaders to adopt saner outlook.
d)   Progressively reduce the British responsibility in India but at the same time, and at each stage, strengthen position in the remaining territory.

It was said that the accepted policy of His Majesty's Government was to hand over the control to India as soon as possible. Under no circumstances should the policy be delayed in implementation by the failure of Indian parties to come together. If this happens it may become necessary to take the following action:

a)   Dismiss/accept resignation of the members of the Interim Government.
b)   Establish a Caretaker Government.
c)   The Commander-in-Chief to remain in command of the Armed Forces.
d)   Withdraw Governor, Secretary of State services personnel and British troops within 4 months from Madras, Bombay, CP, Orissa.

e) The British officers and other ranks serving with the Indian Armed Forces would remain under the command and control of the Commander-in-Chief.

f) New Governor to be appointed on the recommendation of the ministers.

g) Similar programmes for withdrawal from remaining provinces would be implemented by the second quarter of 1948 when His Majesty's Government's political power in India would be demitted entirely, and the British troops and British personnel in the Indian Armed Forces would be withdrawn from India and British nationals given facilities for leaving India if they wish.

h) If, during, this period, a genuine Coalition Government was to be formed and if that Government requested the retention for a period of British officers in the Indian Armed Forces, it is hoped by His Majesty's Government that a satisfactory agreement might be reached.

The Commander-in-Chief was of the view:

a) That the Indian Army is the one disciplined force in which communal interests are subordinate to duty.

b) Indian officers and men must be expected to act in a way likely to put themselves right with the future rulers of the country. The Indian troops overseas are sure to desire repatriation. The Gurkhas are already beginning to show signs of disquiet owing to uncertainty as to their future.

c) Owing to Indianization the belief has been encouraged that his Majesty's Government could no longer govern India even if it wished to do so.

d) To keep the Army reliable an appeal to the Army spirit must be made. It must be emphasized that the British officers will continue serving for some time. It is vital that the existing organizations are not disturbed.

e) The effective announcement by His Majesty's Government of a phased withdrawal is likely to be very serious. This will create uncertainty, resulting in the deterioration of morale, and may lead to desertions with or without arms. Recruiting may come to a halt. Finally, it may be necessary to face the possibility of wholesale disintegration of the Army in India. In that event a programme of phased withdrawal would have to be hastened, and reliance placed solely on British troops for the collection and protection of European civilians. Therefore, a reduction in the number of British troops now in India cannot be accepted, for the present at any rate.

December 1946

'It is important that we should think rapidly and intensively so that we may not commit ourselves and our successors, to whom we owe the duty of planning progressively and with foresight, to a plan which will be obsolete in a few years time.'

The Auk.

1st December: The Cabinet has rejected the Wavell Plan. In spite of this they have asked him to come to the United Kingdom for discussions. He thinks that they are probably trying to force his resignation. Because of this he has resisted going until today. This morning Wavell left for UK and was accompanied by the Quaid, Liaquat, Nehru and Baldev Singh. Before leaving he asked the Commander-in-Chief to complete the planning of the 'Breakdown Plan'. Congress wants the immediate withdrawal of British troops but the Viceroy is insistent that until the new constitution comes into effect withdrawal is impossible.

3rd December: The London Conference has begun. Wavell gave his appreciation in note form to the Prime Minister.

9th December: The Constituent Assembly met today. The meeting was boycotted by the League.

9th–14th December: We left for Poona, Ahmednagar, Deolali, Lake Beale and Bombay to visit the famous 4th Indian Division. The Auk visited all the units of the Division and addressed their officers and Viceroy Commissioned Officers, and invariably had tea in the VCO's Mess. He also addressed many units on parade and presented gallantry awards. The Commander-in-Chief saw waterproofing and bridging (floating Bailey) demonstrations as well as a water crossing by a Battalion supported by tanks.

15th December: Lt-General Sir Frank Simpson,* the Vice Chief of the

*General Sir Frank Simpson (b. 1899) was Vice CIGS 1946–48; GOC-in-C Western Command UK 1948–51; Commandant Imperial Defence College 1952–54.

Imperial General Staff, has arrived with a large party which includes five Generals. Simpson is a fine man and a friend of the Auk. All of them are staying in the C-in-C's House. Simpson has served in the Bombay Sappers and Miners. He is well acquainted with the problems facing the Indian Army. I believe Monty and he do not get on well; Simpson forcefully puts across his point of view.

16th December: In the evening the Auk and Simpson had a private discussion. During the discussion the Auk did not mince his words. He told Simpson that at times Monty's instructions were contrary to the policies laid down by the Prime Minister. The Auk told him in no uncertain terms that to leave India quickly would be courting disaster and possibly end in civil war. He thought that it would take some three years to reorganize the Army before it could be handed over. Simpson told the Auk that Pethick-Lawrence was known in the War Office as 'Pathetic Lawrence', and that he does not keep the Chief-of-Staff in United Kingdom informed of the political developments in India. He also said that Wavell and Attlee were not getting on well together. Wavell was flustered by not getting a decision from the Prime Minister nor a firm date for handing over.

Both Auk and Simpson talked frankly. Simpson is now in the picture. They both have confidence in each other and the Auk often gets things done through him rather than approach Monty.

18th December: It is rumoured that the Prime Minister and Pethick-Lawrence have been seeing Mountbatten a great deal. I wonder why.

20th December: The Auk took the salute at the Passing-out Parade at the Military Academy, Dehra Dun. This is a great institution and well run. There is a great deal of emphasis on turning out well-mannered officers. To check up on this the Commandant invites them to his house for a meal. A story is going round that on one such occasion a cadet dropped his napkin and wanted to pick it up unnoticed. To the horror of the hostess he picked up the end of her dress to wipe his mouth!

22nd December: Today I met Morarji Desai.* He is a very courageous man. He is non-communal and gives protection to the Muslims in Bombay State. He never touches alcohol, meat, fish or even eggs. He does not have coffee or tea. It is said that he has had no sex life for the last so many years. His only pursuit is the attainment of power. It is said that Nehru's mind has been poisoned against him by Indira. They do not see eye to eye with each other.

---

*Morarji Desai later became Prime Minister of India.

23rd December: The Commander-in-Chief left for Bundi for Christmas. He was accompanied by Mrs Jackson. She wanted to take a friend of hers (the one who runs a shop) and told me to ask the Auk whether she could do so. I told her that her brother would never agree to such a request. The Auk would certainly lose his temper if I asked. But she insisted and I had to. The Auk told me to inform his sister that his aircraft was not a taxi.

27th December: Wavell saw the Auk and told him that he did not agree with the appreciation on the 'Breakdown Plan' produced by the Chief of the General Staff. He felt that they were on the wrong track. He also said that he had received no policy directive from His Majesty's Government and that his visit to the United Kingdom had been a waste of time.

The Congress is coming round to accepting that power will have to be transferred to two Central Governments. Both these Governments may have to remain in the Commonwealth. They have, much to their regret, accepted the emergence of Pakistan and know there is no way out. Menon has convinced Patel that the Interim Government is a façade, and the administration is on the verge of a breakdown.

30th December: Baldev wrote to the Auk:

> You will remember we discussed the question of release of Indian National Army prisoners a short while ago when a resolution on the subject came up for discussion in the Central Legislature. We were then able to have it postponed in deference to your wishes. But it is due to come up again in the ensuing session and in this connection I enclose a letter from Pandit Jawaharlal Nehru which is important. I would like to discuss it with you at our next meeting. Personally I agree with what Pandit Nehru says, as no popular Government can for long withstand the pressure of public opinion. I have carefully considered the reaction of releases on the Armed Forces and my view is that it will not be adverse at this stage. The issue would of course be different if it was for the reinstatement of Indian National Army personnel in the Army. There is no such suggestion. The releases, if ordered as a result of the usual review, will not affect the forces and [will] be appreciated throughout the country a very great deal. After talking the matter over with you, I will reply to Pandit Nehru.

Nehru's letter, which was enclosed, read as follows:

> I am writing to you especially about the Indian National Army men still in prison. I know that the Commander-in-Chief feels rather strongly about this matter, but I should like you and him to consider the broader aspects of this question. Indeed, I should have liked to discuss this with him and, perhaps, we might be able to fix up a meeting some time later for

this purpose. Quite apart from the merits of each individual involved, and I understand there are only a very few persons in prison now, we have to consider the consequences of either keeping them in prison or of discharging them. You will remember that the matter came up by a resolution before the Central Legislative Assembly. I feel that the time has definitely come for the Government of India to decide in favour of the release of Indian National Army prisoners and the payment of this forfeited balance of pay to the Indian National Army personnel. If Cabinet agrees to this course a recommendation to this effect might be sent to the Commander-in-Chief.

The Auk was furious.

January 1947

'I regret that in no circumstances can I agree to use my authority as C-in-C to remit the sentences on those men found guilty of the murder of their own countrymen and former comrades-in-arms.'

The Auk.

1st January: We dined with the Royal Scots Fusiliers. The Viceroy was also present. He was looking cheerful in spite of the very heavy burden which he is carrying. Wavell is a very great man. An ordinary individual would have cracked under the same pressure but he stands as a solid wall and works unperturbed. The politicians respect him though he is an engima to them. They also know too well that their threats and bluffs have no effect on him. At conferences and meetings he listens with no expression on his face. No one can make out what is passing through his mind. Occasionally he breaks the silence and asks a question. He is straight and honest. Even Gandhi, whom Wavell regards as an unscrupulous old hypocrite, cannot fool him. Wavell knows that Gandhi would not shrink from violence and that he prefers chaos to the partition of the subcontinent. It is because of this that Gandhi insists that the British must leave immediately. The more I see of Wavell the more I admire him.

Savory was given his Knighthood by the Viceroy. He knelt with his right knee on a velvet stool. The Viceroy tapped him on his right and then left shoulder and said 'Arise Sir Reginald'. He well deserved it and we are all delighted.

3rd January: On 1st November, 1946, the Honourable Member for Defence had announced that by 1st January, 1947, the British troops will be reduced to 62,936 and by 1st April, 1947, to 43,266. Now Baldev says that the Government of the day wants to retain them in view of the internal situation in the country. He further maintains that he has a right to use them in aid of the Civil Power, though he thinks that the Indian troops are quite capable of controlling disturbances. The Auk is against any reduction but His Majesty's Government wants them back as soon as possible.

6th January: The Auk wrote to Baldev on the release of INA prisoners:

I would like to make it clear that I am well aware of the difficult position in which the Interim Government may find itself in this connection and of the pressure which a certain section of public opinion may exert in order to secure the release of these men. I have given these factors full weight in my consideration of the question.

In my opinion, the effect on the rank and file – the 'Other Ranks' – of the Army of the premature release of these men might not in itself be very great though this would depend to a considerable extent on the publicity given to this condonation and to the extent to which it was used to make political capital against the late Government. In this connection, it must be realized that it is not only the men of the Army who may be affected, but also those of the Royal Indian Navy and the Royal Indian Air Force, neither of which forces are, for reasons which I need not go into, as stable or reliable as the Army.

The effect of this proposed condonation of crimes of brutality and violence on the Officers of the Army, and also on those of the other two Services, might, in my considered opinion, be serious. The Indian Officers of the Army, already uneasy and apprehensive lest the officers of the Indian National Army should be reinstated, would, I fear, regard this action as the thin end of the wedge and would become increasingly nervous of their future prospects. The senior British officers of the Army, on whom, to a very large extent, the continuance of the present excellent demeanour of the Army depends, would, I feel, regard this action as a betrayal of the principles to which they have throughout their service been taught to adhere and would, in consequence, be likely to lose faith in me as Commander-in-Chief. They would then be likely to ask themselves whether it was worth their while to continue to devote themselves whole-heartedly and selflessly, as they are now doing, to keeping the Army reliable and efficient, so that it may remain an instrument on which the Cabinet may rely to carry out its instructions in the event of serious internal trouble. These British officers have helped to a very great extent to make the Indian Army what it is today and I can not view with any equanimity any action which might seriously impair their morale in the troublous months which appear to lie ahead of us.

I regret that in no circumstances can I agree to use my authority as Commander-in-Chief to remit the sentences on those two men found guilty of murder of their own countrymen and former comrades-in-arms.

As regards the remainder, there would, in the ordinary course of events, be no question of their sentences being remitted or reduced as a result of a statutory review hardly one year after their conviction. In any other criminal case such clemency would never be considered unless some fresh mitigating circumstances had come to light meanwhile, and I could not, without doing violence to my principles and my conscience, consider taking any such executive action in the cases under consideration.

The final decision in this matter rests of course with the Governor-General in Council, but I would urge with all the earnestness at my command a firm stand against any agitation for the release of these convicts. It is my honest opinion that surrender to such pressure, which is, I believe, largely uninformed and emotional, is likely to make my task and the task of my subordinates in maintaining the discipline and reliability of the Armed Forces extremely difficult, if not impossible, and, moreover, to put Government itself in a position in which it will be unable to resist demands for the condonation of any crime, however obvious and non-political, which may have been committed before it took office. Such a situation so far as the Armed Forces are concerned can not be contemplated by me or by my advisers without the greatest anxiety.

The Auk discussed the release of the Indian National Army convicts with the Viceroy. It was decided that the time was not yet ripe. Another point which came up for discussion was the release of British officers and their replacement by Indian officers. This proposal was put up by Baldev Singh without consulting the Commander-in-Chief.

9th January: Wavell is upset that the 'Breakdown Plan' has been turned down by His Majesty's Government.

Baldev Singh saw the Viceroy about the release of the Indian National Army prisoners and the restoration of their pay. The Viceroy would have nothing to do with it and threatened that if it was carried out the British officers would leave the Army immediately. He wrote a letter to the Commander-in-Chief:

Baldev Singh came to see me this morning about the matter of the Indian National Army. He said that a resolution is likely to be moved in the Assembly early in February about the release of the Indian National Army men still under sentence, and that it will have the support of both the Congress and the Muslim League. He said that further demands were likely to be made for the restoration of payment to the Indian National Army men, and also for their reinstatement in the Army. A meeting in Calcutta would be held on January 23rd, at which the Indian National Army will put forward their demands.

Baldev Singh seemed to be inclined to give way over the release of prisoners and of the payment of arrears, not because he really thought they were justified himself, but to relieve political pressure. He agreed that re-instatement would be a serious matter, but said that might be pressed.

I warned him most forcibly indeed that any concession to the Indian National Army, even to the release of these prisoners, would be fatal for the Indian Army; that it would almost certainly make it impossible for the Commander-in-Chief, or any senior officer of the British Army, to remain responsible for the Indian Army, and I should find it impossible to accept responsibility for the security of India if the confidence of the Army was to be shaken in this way. I said that it seemed to me to be sheer madness to treat the Indian National Army as heroes, when most of them were the weakest element of the Army, men who had joined our enemies for the most part from fear of hardship and danger rather than from patriotism; if those who had stood firm to their oath, who were the greater part of the men captured, were to see the Indian National Army treated like this the effect would be fatal to the Indian Army.

Baldev said he would represent what I had said to the political leaders, but he held no great hope of being able to convince them. I am sure, however, that if we stand firm on this we shall gain our point. I trust therefore that you intend to maintain absolutely that you cannot consent in any circumstances to any further concessions of any kind to the Indian National Army. I am sure that all the senior officers of the Army will support you on this matter, and I shall of course do so.

It will be perhaps advisable that we should have a talk again, if so the sooner the better.

In the evening the Auk saw the Viceroy and told him that he had consulted the senior Army officers. He was determined that the Indian National Army prisoners would not be released. If the Congress insisted, the Auk said he would be prepared to hand in his own resignation.

The Secretary of the Armed Forces Nationalization Committee has issued the following questionnaire to certain officers to obtain their views:

1. Suggest ways and means by which the intake of officers in the Armed Forces can be increased immediately.
2. What should be the period of training for cadets being commissioned in the forces?
3. Should officers and other ranks who have been released and whose services might accelerate nationalization be recalled if they are willing?
4. Do you think it is advisable to retain such IECOs (Indian Emergency Commissioned Officers) as have been recommended for Regular or Short Services Commission but were rejected by the Selection Board?
5. Do you consider that suitable Indian State Forces officers should be attached to the Indian Armed Forces?
6. Has nationalization progressed satisfactorily so far? What attempts have been made to train Indian officers in the forces in all types of Regimental and Staff appointments?
7. Do you consider that the Commissioned Officers of the Indian Army, Royal Indian Air Force and Royal Indian Navy should continue to be

sent abroad for training? If so what type of training? What arrangements should be made so that such training could be giving in India in future and lastly give your views on any other aspect of the forces which may assist in rapid nationalization.

I received one as well.

11th January: We had a dinner party at our place. We invited the Auk as well, as he enjoys a relaxed evening.

Basically the Auk is a simple man with a zest for living, having unsophisticated habits and unadulterated joys. He enjoys the little pleasures life has to offer. He is informal and an extrovert, possessing the wonderful quality of putting people at ease whoever they may be. He gives the impression that he has all the time in the world for them. He inspires people, and is sometimes critical though never cruel.

Fishing and painting are his favourite pastimes. Horse races hold a great attraction for him though he puts no more than ten rupees each way on a race. When he has a winner he is overjoyed.

The Auk loves his Aberdeen terrier, and his two cranes called Mary and George. He does not care for shooting. I tried my best to get him interested but failed.

He is frugal and spends very little money on himself. He has no money of his own, but has saved a little. On tours I handle his funds. If he requires any he takes if from me.

Whenever he can he goes to the Church of the Redemption in Delhi.

The Auk is at his best when he is entertaining people or being entertained by others. He is the very spirit of a party and keeps everyone amused. He has a tremendous sense of humour and is capable of enjoying a good joke too. He has a twinkle in the eye and a hearty laugh. He enjoys the company of the young and old equally.

At the C-in-C's House there is a constant stream of guests. There is hardly a meal when someone or other is not present. Within the house there is no stuffed-shirt atmosphere. The Auk is great company at table. No one talks 'shop'. The parties are completely relaxed and are great fun.

Lady Cawthorn,* a close friend, was once late in coming to a dinner party. In a put-on fierce voice the Auk said, 'Kneel, thou unworthy woman; why are you late?' He then smacked her back with a Japanese sword. After she apologized, he said, 'Rise, have a drink and do not forget to put on your war medals.'

The Auk is very fond of a game of football which is played on a board supported by a small table. It has wooden footballers on rods. These are moved about to play the game with a ping-pong ball. Teams are drawn up

*Wife of Major-General Sir Walter Cawthorn (see footnote p. 38).

and as the game progresses the excitement grows. Sometimes the players even lift their side of the table to ease the ball sliding into the goal. At parties we have had great fun playing this, the Auk getting up to all the tricks.

Auk is fond of good food and enjoys the Indian dishes. At many a dinner my wife is asked by the Auk to have certain dishes prepared and sent to the house.

After Jessie's departure quite a few women in Delhi tried to get close to the Auk, and if possible marry him. His sister, Mrs Jackson, also tried her best to get him interested in someone. It seems the Auk has turned off any desire to get involved.

After the Army the Auk's other love is his old school, Wellington College.

The Auk for some time has been toying with the idea of establishing a club on the lines of the Services Club in the United Kingdom. To give it practical shape a provisional Committee has been formed.

13th January: The Viceroy asked the Commander-in-Chief for a draft Directive for a plan which the civil and military staff could jointly produce in case there was a breakdown of law and order in India. The Viceroy told Baldev Singh that there was no question of the removal of British troops from India until a constitution had been put in force.

14th January: Pandit Nehru came to lunch and discussed, once again, the release of the Indian National Army personnel. He has decided to ignore its consequences.

Incidentally, the GHQ High Command has evolved a code word for Nehru, which is Nero; for Baldev, it is Balmem.

15th January: The Commander-in-Chief saw the Viceroy and showed him the terms of reference of the Planning Committee on the withdrawal of British troops.

20th January: Today Attlee made his statement in the House of Commons regarding the transfer of power in India by June, 1948. The Viceroy saw the Auk and told him that Baldev Singh was adamant on the release of all Indian National Army prisoners, including those who were convicted for murder. Wavell said he would have nothing to do with it and believes that their release would mean the disintegration of the Army. The Auk has threatened to resign.

21st January: The Auk has given me a thundering Annual Confidential Report which I did not expect.

23rd January: A meeting of the Cabinet was held under the Viceroy to discuss the retention of British troops in India. On the previous day a telegram had been received from the Secretary of State to the effect that the British troops would remain until the final transfer of power. But if the Cabinet insisted on their withdrawal the Viceroy should not exercise his veto. He should say that he would refer the matter to His Majesty's Government. The Secretary of State also wanted the views of the Viceroy on the statement made by the Defence Member that Indian troops could control a communal emergency without the assistance of the British troops. The Secretary of State further said that British troops should be used as sparingly as possible for internal security duties.

At this meeting Baldev Singh was very vocal. He had been well primed by Nehru. He acted as his master's voice. He said that so far the British troops had been required to meet external aggression, to maintain internal security, and to provide a backing for the Indian Army. As there was no apprehension of any major conflict, Indian troops, without the backing of British troops, would be capable of handling any internal security situation. There were no grounds for the retention of British troops. Thereupon the Auk said that it would be unwise to attempt to do away with the British troops in view of the political situation and present communal tension. Baldev retorted that he was not prepared to take the advice of the Commander-in-Chief. He further said that by the withdrawal of British troops there would be a big saving in the defence expenditure.

Nehru maintained that the presence of British troops was completely opposed to any conception of an independent India. The Commander-in-Chief said that the presence of British troops was essential, as they provided a neutral element until such time as the composition of the Indian Army was such as to create confidence in all sections of the people that it would act fairly and impartially at all times. The minority communities invariably asked for the assistance of British troops. According to the Viceroy His Majesty's Government has the responsibility for law and order in this country until the new constitution is introduced. Baldev was of the opinion that a small body of British troops, in case of serious trouble, could do very little to save the life and property of 90,000 British inhabitants. Nehru placed great reliance on the Army remaining non-communal. In the end Wavell said that he would forward the views of the Cabinet to His Majesty's Government.

What an exercise in futility! They do not realize that a small, determined and impartial body can be very effective in case of trouble.

The Defence Member, on the instigation of Nehru, has written to the Viceroy to the effect that the Indian National Army men serving sentences should be released. He said they should be paid the forfeited amounts of pay and allowances for the period when they served as enemies. Little do most people realize that many were convicted of gross brutality and murder. Baldev said that the left wing of the Congress were making this into a major issue. He felt that if these demands were met it would have no unsettling effect on the Army.

The Commander-in-Chief told the Viceroy that such concessions would encourage further demands by the Indian National Army, including reinstatement. The Auk made it quite clear that if these demands were accepted it would be fatal for the morale of the Indian Army. At the same time it would make his own position impossible. The Auk further said that he had no doubt that if the demands were accepted it would lead the disintegration of the Forces.

After the defeat of the Unionist Party by the Muslim League, Khizar Hayat made a crucial error. On the advice of Baldev Singh he headed a Coalition Cabinet in the Punjab with the support of Congress Hindus, Sikhs and his own Unionists. The Government was supported by 18 Unionists of whom only 10 were Muslims, 51 members of the Congress Party who were all Hindus and 23 members of the Panthic Sikh Party. The Muslim League, the biggest single party in the House, with 78 Members, was ignored. A Cabinet of six ministers was formed, 3 Muslims, 2 Hindus and 1 Sikh. Sir Bertrand Glancy,* the Governor, accepted the new Government. This was an error on his part as he became a partisan. The Muslims were outraged and called it 'the unholy alliance'.

It would have been in the fitness of things if Glancy had taken over the administration himself under Section 93 of the Government of India Act.

Khizar has committed political suicide. His actions will probably result in a disaster.

Quaid's influence in the Punjab has increased. He has proved what he has been saying all along – that the Sikander-Baldev Pact was designed to separate the Sikhs from the Muslims and that Khizar was merely a tool in the game.

The Congress Ministers boasted that they possess the stick and will rule by it.

The Muslim League National Guard and the RSSS were today declared unlawful bodies. Raids have been carried out to unearth the arms. It is a provocative action and may develop into a civil disobedience movment.

Glancy, Khizar and his associates have totally misjudged the mood of the Muslims.

In the evening the King of Nepal came to see the Commander-in-Chief. The King was accompanied by a host of Generals, all attired in full regalia. Everyone was extremely polite. They discussed the future of the Gurkha units, but came to no decision. He also advocated the preservation of wild life on the border between Nepal and India. Wild life, he maintains, is being eliminated ruthlessly.

25th January: Nehru has asked the Union Powers Committee to the Constituent Assembly to produce a report on the Defence of India by 14th July. The Union Powers Committee is chaired by Nehru himself.

---

*Sir Bertrand Glancy (1882–1953) was Governor of the Punjab 1941–46.

27th January: There was a long meeting between the Viceroy and the Commander-in-Chief on the withdrawal of authority from India. No decision was taken.

28th January: Sir Sultan Ahmed* called. He told us that a story is going round Delhi that the 'higher ups' are keeping women in their houses and calling them their nieces! A foreign visitor to Delhi, who had heard of this, called on one of the big wigs. He was introduced to an attractive woman whom his host said was his niece. The visitor, who was on very friendly terms with his host, politely inquired, 'Is that what you call them in India?'

30th January: Asif Ali came to say farewell. He is leaving for the States and was full of himself. He wanted me to accompany him as his Military Adviser but I declined.

The Quaid has not been feeling well since he returned from United Kingdom.

In Eastern Command Tuker has organized military tattoos, demonstrations of fire power and visits to Army establishments for the benefit of the public. He hopes this wil bring the public close to the Armed Forces.

31st January: The whole day was spent at Kashmir House where a model discussion is being conducted on the future organization of the Indian Army. Mohammad Ali, the Finanacial Adviser, also attended. The Auk respects and trusts him.

A letter has been received from Monty to the effect that the Exercise 'Spearhead', to be held in Camberley, will only be attended by officers of the rank of Major-General and above. This will exclude any Indian officers from attending it. He went on to say that he was not sending Top Secret papers connected with the Exercise to India. He further said that he was very upset at Nehru's latest statement regarding India becoming a Republic. Under these circumstances it would not be possible for the Indian officers to attend the IDC in future where the Commandant will have to debar them from certain secret lectures.

*Sir Sultan Ahmed (1880–1963), a distinguished lawyer, was a Minister in the Central Government.

February 1947

'Indian forces constitute one of the most important factors towards the achievement of unity in India.'

The Auk.

1st February: Communal riots have broken out in the Punjab.

There is a food crisis. Rajendra Prasad, the Minister for Food, is in a fix, not knowing how to deal with it. He is a devout Hindu, interested in developing cow *ashrams* (old cows' homes) and visiting temples. It is said that he cannot stand having Muslim servants. Though he is a man of simple tastes, he is known to be a miser. He is Nehru's yes-man.

3rd February: The Legislative Assembly had its first session.

4th February: I met Rafi Ahmad Kidwai, affectionately known as 'Rafi'. In earlier days he was secretary to Motilal Nehru. He is held in great respect by the entire family.

Rafi was a great friend of my father, and had rented our house in Lucknow while he was a Minister in the UP Government. I called on him once and discovered that the house had been turned into what looked like a hostel. Boys of all ages seemed to be living here. When I asked him who they were, he said they were the best students from his constituency. As they were poor, he had taken it upon himself to educate them.

In fact he is a poor man himself. He keeps an informal open house. His devotees are known as 'Ruffians'. With them as with everyone else, he does not mince his words. In spite of this and his forthright ways, he is loved by many.

5th February: Sir C. P. Ramaswami Aiyer, the Dewan of Travancore, came to lunch. He is a shrewd politician and wants independence for his State. He is unpopular in the Congress circle and disliked by Patel and Nehru. They think he is inciting the Princes.

6th February: All the Congress members of the Cabinet wrote to the Viceroy and demanded the resignation of Muslim League Members. How arrogant they are! I think they are coming out in their true colours. Such actions are not conclusive to the betterment of relations.

8th February: There was a long Cabinet meeting to discuss the size of the post-war Indian Army. India can ill afford a large standing army. There are not enough funds to go round. Wavell sent a Directive for the Commander-in-Chief to work on.

Later in the day Wavell saw the Auk and told him that he, Wavell, had been sacked unceremoniously. The words he used were, 'I have been dismissed as if I were a cook.'

This decision was taken while Wavell was in the United Kingdom. Attlee did not have the decency to inform him then. He said that he was writing a stong letter to Attlee, telling him a few home truths.

What a shabby way of treating a great man who gave the best years of life to the service of the State. The more I have seen of Wavell the more I admire him. He has stood like a rock between order and chaos.

The Auk is very upset over this.

16th February: Wavell told the Auk that Mountbatten had been nominated to succeed him! This is a great surprise for everyone. What little I saw of Mountbatten during his various visits to meet the Auk, he struck me as being very smooth and excessively ambitious.

The political situation in Bengal and Punjab is going from bad to worse. Patel has threatened to withdraw the Congress members of the Cabinet if the League remained in the Interim Government.

17th February: Auk saw Wavell and discussed Mountbatten's appointment and its possible effects on the political negotiations.

18th February: The Assembly debated the release of the Indian National Army prisoners. The Congress members were very vocal while the League members kept quiet.

20th February: The British Cabinet has announced that Mountbatten will be next Governor-General of India.

The Prime Minister announced in the House of Commons that by June, 1948, power will be transferred to the Indians, and the British will withdraw. If by that date a Constitution is not forthcoming in accordance with the Cabinet Mission proposal, His Majesty's Government would have to consider 'to whom the power be handed over on the due date, whether as a whole to some form of Central Government for British India or in some areas to the existing Provincial Governments or in such other way as may seem most reasonable and in the best interest of the Indian people.'

By spelling it out it is quite clear that the subcontinent will be divided and the establishment of Pakistan will become a reality.

The truth has got home to the Congress that there is no alternative to Partition. They now realize their great mistake in not accepting the Cabinet Mission Plan. If it was offered to them now they would have agreed without hesitation. It has been a blunder and a great opportunity lost. The Indians would prefer chaos rather than agree to the establishment of Pakistan. The Socialists, under the leadership of Jaiprakash Narain, see it as a sinister move.

In actual fact the British have thrown the final responsibility for the solution on the Indian leaders themselves.

Wavell had been in the United Kingdom for the Conference from 2nd to 6th December. He stayed on in a fruitless attempt to help the Government to frame a policy. But the Government had no idea and no clear thinking.

Since the Cabinet Mission returned to the United Kingdom they did nothing except waste valuable time, with disastrous results. The solution His Majesty's Government thought of was 'a change in the bowling', a fresh start to avert disaster. If, on the other hand, they had given a clear-cut directive to Wavell, a solution would have been found by now. But, of course, the Labour Cabinet had no sympathy with Wavell. Cripps had also been critical of him, saying, 'Wavell was inarticulate and had difficulty in communicating'.

Partition is to take place seventeen months from now. I think the time is too short. There may be trouble. Wavell had suggested an orderly withdrawal by stages to be completed by April, 1948. It was actually his idea to fix a time limit for the handing over. But it is now said that it was Attlee's 'inspiration'.

My mind goes back to the famous words of Sir Syed Ahmed Khan: 'We are two nations and they both cannot sit on the same throne'. What he dreamt of will become a reality. He laid the basis of Pakistan.

21st–24th February: We visited Jaipur. It was a fascinating tour. I do not think I shall ever forget it. We stayed with Ayesha and Jai. They were excellent hosts. We had dinner with the Jaipurs in their little fortress overlooking the city. At dinner we were served from the famous gold service, an heirloom from the Moghul days. We were taken around the great palace in which old standards, sanads,* carpets and other relics are stored. These were given to Jai's ancestors by the Great Moghuls. Jai is very proud of his old connections with the Moghul Emperors.

25th February: All is not well between Patel and Nehru. Most of the time they are at loggerheads. It can be said that armed neutrality exists between them. Nehru allows him a free hand to sort out the party and keep them on the right path, but elsewhere he has to truck with him and holds him at arm's

---

*Title deeds given for lands awarded by the Moghul rulers.

length. Even his advice is not taken. In effect, Nehru tolerates Patel but does not trust him.

Patel comes from peasant stock and is very shrewd. He has tremendous organizational ability and is ruthless in his endeavours. The orders he gives are taken seriously. He is a natural party boss and is the Chairman of the Congress Central Party Board. As he is vindictive by nature, the party is frightened of him and consider him a dangerous enemy. He is often called the 'Bismarck of India'. Patel cannot stand Abul Kalam Azad or Rafi Ahmed Kidwai. He maintains that there is only one nationalist Muslim, who is 'Maulana' Nehru.

Patel has his favourites in the Civil Service hierarchy, the Chief being V. P. Menon to whom he has given a free hand. He fathers the civil servants and keeps them on his side by giving them concessions and privileges. However, many among them are enamoured of Nehru. This has resulted in a split among them.

Though in the Congress Party, Patel supports the RSSS and the Akali Sikhs. This he does to keep the pot simmering and to make Nehru's position difficult. It is known that he detests Muslims and speaks ill of the Quaid. Patel considers the Quaid a most tiresome man. Strangely enough he believes the Quaid is collaborating with the Russians!

26th–28th February: On the 26th Khizer calmed down and has removed the ban on League meetings.

It has been reported that Cariappa, who is at the Imperial Defence College, is talking out of turn. Cariappa said that he has been authorized by Nehru to say that the Congress expect to have all British officers out of the Indian Army in five to eight years. Until then India would retain only those who have sympathy with Indian aspirations. After Independence was accomplished, and provided the British Government gave no cause for offence, India would want a close alliance with Britain!

He also said that if His Majesty's Government wanted to maintain British troops as an Imperial Reserve in India, and was prepared to pay for them, the Indian Government would have no objection. He further said that, if he could help it, he would make English and not Urdu the language of the Army. The report went on to say that Cariappa has been talking as if he were the spokesman of the Congress.

29th February: At a Conference in London ways and means for devising a policy whereby the Indian Army could be handed over to more than one authority when power is transferred to India were discussed. It was stated at the outset that at present the composition and the organization of the Army was such that it could not be handed over to more than one authority without disruption. If disruption did occur and the Army was broken into communal elements it would affect the internal security of the subcontinent. It was stated that as soon as the Army takes on a communal complex the whole edifice of India may break down and civil war may follow. But, if it had to be done, it must be gradual and in accordance with an agreed plan.

Therefore it was essential that the military plan must be based on political developments which at the moment cannot be foreseen. However, it was desirable to plan for both the contingencies, that is – handing over to one central government or to two by June, 1948.

The plan should cover reorganization on communal lines. However, it should not be allowed to pre-judge the political situation, as the present Interim Government of India would not approve of such an action. For the moment it must remain organized as at present, until the situation is clearer.

It was stated that, as His Majesty's Government is responsible for the maintenance of law and order until the constitutional change takes place, it was essential to keep the British troops in the subcontinent.

Reorganization of the Indian Army should take place after the British troops have left the country and power been transferred.

However, the advantages of reorganizing the Army now will be that when it comes to partitioning the forces it will be, comparatively, an easier task. But during this period India would be left undefended and British troops would be placed in a dangerous position. At the same time it may bring about a crisis within the Indian Interim Government and break up the only stable element in India, the Army.

Another suggestion was to leave the Army organized as at present. When power was handed over it could be disbanded. Later the authority to whom the power had been transferred could re-raise their own forces. This course was considered a dangerous one.

It was decided to wait for the political situation to be clarified and then to plan accordingly. During this period the Army would be left organized as at present. However, it was admitted that this would leave insufficient time for the task of reorganizing the forces. Once the disruption of the Army started the defence of India would be reduced to a low level, and the position of the British troops would become progressively more difficult.

The Conference concluded that the Army should be kept as one Army for as long as possible. By doing so, the political object of His Majesty's Government would be assisted.

Liaquat's budget has been a bombshell to the Hindu businessmen and industrialists. A tax of 25 per cent was levied on business profits of more than a hundred thousand rupees. Liaquat also appointed an Income Tax Investigating Commission. Birla,* the great Hindu businessman, is very upset.

Patel believes that Liaquat has purposely done this to ruin the Hindu community. To my way of thinking this was a real strategic move by Liaquat.

---

*Birla supported the Congress and supplied them with funds.

PART IV

Government by
Hunches and Flashes

March 1947

'Mountbatten was already a partisan before he arrived.'
                                                    The Auk.

1st March: The Muslim League demonstrated their strength by holding several meetings in the North-West Frontier Province. As a result of this some arrests were made.

2nd March: There are rumours that Lord Ismay is being appointed as Military Adviser to Mountbatten. The Auk is upset and in a bad mood. He feels that Ismay may be used to override his authority.

The Auk sent the following letter to Scoones:*

> The recent announcement by His Majesty's Government has, as you will have realized, come as a considerable shock to very many people in this country who had thought, if they thought at all, that the process would be much more gradual. In fact, I think it would be true to say that a great number thought that it would never happen, or if it did, that it would come about so gradually as to be almost imperceptible.
>
> This announcement has brought a sharp realization of the very short time left for preparation and of the extreme urgency of the whole problem. It is too early yet to assess the effect on the country generally, but I do not see how it can fail to have an unsettling effect on the Indian officers and men of the Armed Forces and I am feeling considerable anxiety about this. The lack of definition in the announcement concerning the party or parties to whom responsibility is to be handed over is causing the greatest uneasiness in practically everyone's mind and this is readily understandable.
>
> There is a general feeling that the Viceroy has been rather shabbily treated and a strong feeling of regret in many quarters that he should be going. There is little comment, other than scurrilous, so far about his successor, who, in spite of his great record, is not really known to India or to the Indians, which may seem strange but is, I think, true.

*General Sir Geoffrey Scoones (1893–1975) was Director of Military Operations and Intelligence, Indiaa 1941–42; GOC 4 Corps, Burma 1942–44; GOC-in-C Central Command, India 1945–46.

3rd March: The unholy Unionist Government has tendered its resignation. The minorities are upset but the League is jubilant. The Sikhs are making wild speeches.

4th March: While waiting for the resignation to be accepted, Bhim Singh Sachar, the Finance Minister of the Punjab, allowed a political pro-Government march to take place in Lahore. Tara Singh shouted *'Pakistan Murdabad'* (Death to Pakistan) and brandishing his sword, said, *'Raj Karega Khalsa, Agi Rahe No Koi'*, meaning 'The pure (Sikhs) will rule and no resistance will remain'. This has infuriated the Muslims. As a result the Governor has taken over the administration of the Province under section 93 of the Government of India Act.

6th March: We flew to Bareilly and carried on to Rampur by car. I went out shooting with Abdul Karim, the Nawab's brother. He is a good shot. On one occasion the Nawab had invited the Secretary of the Political Department, Government of India, for a tiger shoot. The Nawab knew full well that there were no tigers in Rampur. So he asked Abdul Karim to buy a domesticated tiger. This was done. The tiger was put into a cage. The day of the shoot arrived, as did the guests. The cage with the tiger inside was placed a little way in where the jungle began. On the arrival of the beaters it was to be opened and the tiger was expected to go into the jungle. All went well until the moment when the door of the cage was opened. The tiger refused to come out. The poor animal was pushed out by sticks, and was ultimately shot by the guest. Later, to the utter horror of the Nawab, a brass ring was found dangling from the ear of the tiger.

The Hindu and Sikh leaders have formed a 'Council of Action' with Tara Singh as its President.

There were marches in several cities.

The Sikh procession of 4th March and the events in Bihar touched off the rioting in the Punjab. Both Hindus and Sikhs have suffered. There have been riots in Lahore, followed by some in Multan, Rawalpindi, and Attock. However, they were not a result of any far-reaching strategic motives. It was just mob fury. The Sikhs have retaliated in Amritsar where the Muslim Bazaar was burnt down. The administration took no action to control the mob which ransacked what they could for 24 hours.

In the House of Commons Churchill said that the Government of Nehru was a complete disaster and that the weakness in the administration followed from it. He said that Nehru was a bitter enemy of the British. He maintained that the fourteen months' time limit was fatal.

7th March: We returned to Delhi from our tour.

The Suffolks, the Wiltshires and a company of the Inniskillings were eventually called out in aid of the Civil Power in Amritsar. Some Sikh

Lord Wavell.

Major-General Sir Walter Cawthorn.

General Sir Reginald Savory.

The Nawab of Rampur and Sir Claude Auchinleck.

The author's house in Delhi – 12 Willingdon Crescent.

The C-in-C with his pet cranes, George and Mary.

A *Barakhana* at the C-in-C's house.

A game of football after dinner in the C-in-C's house.

Sir Claude Auchinleck taking the salute of the Indian contingent at the Victory parade in London.

refugees from the North have arrived in Rawalpindi. Rioting in the Punjab was expected but not of such severity. The Congress and other Hindu parties are loud in their criticism of the administration.

Jenkins* has said that there must be changes in the law. He has asked that the principle of minimum force should be abrogated. Jenkins is of the firm view that Baldev was at the root of the trouble and was inflaming the Sikhs. He has also advocated the imposition of Martial Law which, in reality, should have been done earlier. He has asked for more troops as the Police have become ineffective.

After the trouble in North Punjab the Sikhs believe that the Muslims want to turn them out of the whole province. They are determined to take revenge and massacre the Muslims in Amritsar. The Sikhs wish to stay as a coherent and undivided community. At one stage they were even prepared to expel the Hindus from their areas. As usual Gandhi, the angel of peace, did not visit the affected areas to restore peace.

The Police in Bihar staged a rebellion.

The Auk attended a meeting which was called by the Defence Member. Sir Gopalaswami Ayyanger† was also present. They discussed the problems connected with the nationalization of the officers' cadre. The Auk said that the present strength of the Indian Army was 22,000 officers and 600,000 men. Out of the 22,000 officers there were 13,500 British and the remainder were Indians. He estimated that the future strength of the Indian Army will be 8,500 officers and 220,000 men. However, there were not sufficient Indian officers of the right calibre to fill the officers' cadre of a completely nationalized Army. The major units, if immediate nationalization is to be carried out, will be commanded by officers of less than nine years' service. The Auk was not prepared to accept this. He emphasized that to look after and train men in peacetime calls for quality of judgement, wisdom, patience and above all a knowledge of human nature which can only come as a result of experience. He warned that, unless officers having these qualities were available to command troops, one was running a great risk, especially in the present circumstances when the disruptive and separatist forces were swaying public opinion.

He further stated that, even among the officers available, there were many who lacked character, personality, application and energy to make them fit for higher appointments. The present junior officers had no peacetime experience or background at all, though many of them have proved capable leaders in war. He said that the Selection Board which comprised senior Indian officers had stated, time and again, that the officers coming before

---

*Sir Evan Jenkins (b. 1896) joined the ICS in 1920; was Private Secretary to the Viceroy 1943–45; Governor of the Punjab 1946–47.

†Sir Gopalaswami Ayyanger assisted the Congress with his advice and was head of various committees.

them for Regular Commissions left much to be desired. However, the worst situation was in the technical services which had very few Indian officers. The officers required for such services had to undergo long training as they play a most important role in keeping up the efficiency of the Army. Inefficiency of these officers could bring disaster to the Army.

The Commander-in-Chief strongly advised the retention of British officers to tide the future Army over the period when they could produce their own.

11th March: The Sikhs and Hindus have decided to organize an 'Anti-Pakistan Day' throughout Punjab. The Viceroy took the salute at the 'George Cross Parade' in front of the Red Fort. It was a very impressive assembly. He presented six George Crosses of which five were posthumous. The sixth was presented to Captain Durrani of the Bahwalpur State Forces.

15th March: Auk wanted to hold a banquet for Wavell but he would not agree. Instead he accepted a quiet dinner. This was the smallest dinner party which was ever held in the house. There were only six of us, Wavell and his wife, Auk, Cherry, Tahirah and I.

Wavell was in very good form. I have seldom seen him so relaxed. He gave his views freely on various political leaders and what he thought of them. It was a hilarious party. After dinner we all sat round a low table and played games. One of the Auk's favourite games which we often play at the house is called 'slicing the flour'. A tumbler is packed hard with flour, turned upside down on a plate. The tumbler is removed. The packed flour then stands like a column. A lady's ring is placed on top of the column. Each individual in turn slices the column with a knife ensuring that the ring does not fall on the plate. He then lifts the plate and places it carefully before the next person. As the column gets thinner and narrower the excitement of the game increases. Ultimately, whoever drops the ring while carrying or slicing has to pick it up with his or her tongue. This results in their face being covered with flour to the amusement of everyone else.

As luck would have it, I was the victim! I put my tongue out and was fumbling for the ring when someone pushed my whole face into the plate! I must have been a sight. I looked round and there was old Wavell, laughing away and saying, 'Shahid, I have fixed you properly.' This was the other side of Wavell. He was a man full of humour, who could be life and soul of a party. It was one side of his character that few people knew about or even thought he possessed. During the evening he gave the impression that he did not have a care in the world, nor any burden on his shoulders. The party lasted well into the night. Lady Wavell, who is a dignified woman with tremendous strength of character, was charming as ever.

Incidentally Wavell has been recommended for an Earldom.

16th March: Evan Jenkins, the Governor of Punjab, submitted a report on the visit of Nehru to Lahore on the 14th. Jenkins said that Nehru did very little to pacify the public. In his talk with Jenkins, Nehru said that the Rawalpindi area should be handed over to the Military Commander. Jenkins told him that Martial Law was not imposed by proclamation and ordinance. It represented, in fact, a decision taken by the local Military Commander, when he felt that the civil administration had completely broken down. The Military Commander acts in the exercise of his recognized power under the common law. He has no statutory backing and is answerable afterwards for his actions.

The Governor said that Nehru wanted firm measures to be taken. Jenkins told Nehru firstly that in his opinion certain offences, such as attempted murder, kidnapping, robbery, dacoity, rape and arson should be made punishable by death. Secondly, the principle of 'minimum force' should also be abrogated. To this Nehru replied that he would support the amendment of the law.

Nehru then began to discuss the long-term problems facing Punjab. He said that some sort of partition was inevitable, but that it must be made within the framework of the present constitution. He thought that a Muslim area, a Central area and a Non-Muslim area should come into being.

Each area should be autonomous and should have its own ministers for certain purposes. Jenkins told him that the issue was a complicated one and full of pitfalls.

The following day Nehru again met Jenkins and discussed the amendents in the Criminal Law. He was of the view that forcible religious conversion should be punishable by death. Destruction of religious places and books should be similarly punished. Stabbing might be dealt with by a special system of collective fines. The Army should be given powers of search and arrest, and finally all should be disposed of by summary trials. Nehru was also of the view that any conspiracy should be dealt with ruthlessly. He suggested that a special search should be made for the Sikh women alleged to have been seized by the Muslims and that the village officials who have taken part in the disturbances should be suspended.

Jenkins told Nehru, in no uncertain terms, that if the necessary powers were given to his administration they would be able to handle the situation in a befitting manner.

Nehru went on to tell Jenkins that British officers were inclined to be hostile to the aspirations of Indian nationalism and were in some degree working against the Union of India. Jenkins disagreed with him and said that the British officers in the Punjab were, on the whole, in favour of a United Punjab and were not in favour of Pakistan. Jenkins maintained that Unionism was still the right answer. He felt that Nehru might have got that impression as a result of the non-introduction of the new All-India Services in the Punjab. This was partly due to the former premier, Khizer Hayat, who, while not believing in Pakistan, was naturally not anxious to identify himself too closely with the Centre.

Nehru also mentioned that he had seen Tara Singh and talked to him about a 'notional' Partition, which he thought was a workable solution. Jenkins did not agree and said that the only answer was the formation of a popular Ministry.

17th March: In the morning the Commander-in-Chief saw the Viceroy. This was his last official interview. The Auk was very depressed. He got on very well with Wavell and obviously regrets the change. We will all miss him. Truly Wavell is a great man. He is reliable, dignified and a man of his words.

Questions have been asked in the British Parliament as to why British troops and not Indian troops were used to restore order in Amritsar. The spokesman for the Government stated that so long as the British troops remained in India they must be available for any legitimate purposes for which the troops are required, including the maintenance of public order. The spokesman added that it was the normal winter arrangement to keep a Company of British troops at Amritsar. This Company was found by the Inniskilling Fusiliers. On 6th March one Company of 2nd Punjabis was added. On the 7th the situation had so gravely deteriorated that the Suffolks and Wiltshires also had to be moved to the city. The decision as to what troops had to be used rested with the local commanders. As these troops were easily available in the shortest possible time, they were called. Therefore there was no question of the British troops having been specially brought in for this purpose.

18th March: Auk received the following letter from Mountbatten:

My dear Claude,

God knows I did everything in my power to be allowed to go back to sea. Since, however, the King overruled me and I am to come to India I would like you to know that the feeling that I have such a true and wise friend in you makes all the difference to me. I hope we shall see lots of each other. Looking forward to seeing you.

Dickie

20th March: In a debate in the House of Commons A. V. Alexander, the Minister of Defence, said, 'Our forces in India have been drastically reduced. But until the transfer of authority to Indians by June '48 we have responsibilities which require the continued presence of the British forces. We are not therefore prepared to withdraw them.'

22nd March: Today was Wavell's last day as Viceroy. The Congress is jubilant at Wavell's departure. They systematically worked towards his unceremonious exit.

Wavell could never be a figurehead. He hated insincerity, double dealing and self-deception. He could not understand Gandhi, who was instrumental in Congress rejecting the 16th June statement. Wavell respected the Quaid and said of him that the Cabinet Mission, especially Cripps, treated him shabbily. Wavell told Nehru that he lacked statesmanship. Congress had mounted an anti-Wavell campaign. Gandhi had written to Attlee that Wavell did not understand politics and had lost his nerve. Sudhir Gosh and many others were constantly in the United Kingdom meeting Members of the Cabinet and Members of Parliament and insisting that a change was absolutely necessary to break the deadlock in the negotiations. Wavell, the strong, silent man, was a very shrewd judge of character. He carried out negotiations in a straightforward and honourable manner. He did not believe in underhand methods and intrigues. Every politician knew where he stood with him. Wavell saw through them and was not unduly impressed by their manifestoes and threats. The politicians could not bully him but respected him for his honesty and truthfulness. He was always neutral. He did not bend where principles were involved. He played fair by all and was not prepared to become a partisan. He performed his duties honestly without fear or favour. All this was disliked by the Congressmen who dubbed him as being pro-League.

It is true to say that he never received the understanding and support of the Labour Government, who somehow could not tolerate him. Members of the Government called him a defeatist. They themselves were novices at the Indian game and had no experience of playing Indian chess. They were dictated to by 'Father' Cripps who had been in India before. Cripps had cultivated his relations with Congress and was considered to be their spokesman in the United Kingdom. He was considered an authority on Indian Affairs. Cripps' main shortcoming was that he looked at the present situation in the knowledge of what he had learnt and summarized in 1942. He was a dishonest politician and led Pethick-Lawrence by the nose as he understood so little. On the other hand Alexander was a straightforward man but one who took a long time to understand Indian ways and politics.

At the end of the War the Labour Government started talking of giving Dominion status to the subcontinent. They had not done their homework properly. As a result, they did not have the faintest idea how to set about it. They started groping in the dark. They would not trust Wavell, the man on the spot, or the Auk for that matter, to produce a co-ordinated and a phased programme for handing over power. They were never able to give a clear-cut mandate or a final date of withdrawal to Wavell. They wanted Wavell to favour Congress. This he was not prepared to do. Whatever Wavell suggested they were quick to find fault with and put in cold storage. The Government created a very difficult and embarrassing position for the Governor-General. They carried out private negotiations behind his back and disguised many facts from him.

A Hindu stenographer on the staff of the Viceroy was a secret agent of the Congress. To discredit Wavell the information he obtained was passed on to Attlee. Attlee never informed Wavell of the leakage. However, Wavell came to know about it later and was disgusted.

The Congress was frightened of Wavell as they knew he was well aware of their underhand methods. It is an irony of fate that without giving him a policy directive they expected him to be in full agreement with the policy of His Majesty's Government which nobody knew, much less they themselves.

It is seldom realized how hard Wavell worked to bring about a political settlement. Though he did not succeed one cannot ignore the fact that he, and he alone, prepared the ground for the final settlement. He laid the foundation for the independence of the subcontinent. This no one can deny.

He would have patiently negotiated with those concerned and, if given time and support, would have pulled it off and sought justice for all. His Majesty's Government oscillated, drifted and wavered and finally succumbed to the pressure of the Congress. The decision to appoint Mountbatten resulted. Here again Cripps played the leading role. He brought Nehru and Mountbatten together and convinced the former that Mountbatten would support his party. Nehru had already met Mountbatten in Singapore and was on friendly terms with him.

Initially Cripps wanted the appointment for himself, but the British Parliament and public considered him ill-suited for the assignment. Even the name of Lord Ismay was considered for the Governor-Generalship and in this he was backed by Churchill.

Mountbatten on the other hand was young, presentable, popular, a member of the Royal Family, a successful commander and ambitious. Above all he was untried in the political field. As he was appointed by the Labour Government, it was presumed he would be prepared to toe their line. Attlee wanted a yes-man and found one. It was on 18th December that the Viceroyalty was offered to Mountbatten while Wavell was still in the United Kingdom. The Labour Government did not have the decency to inform Wavell of their decision. Even Mountbatten, who professed to be a great admirer of Wavell, did not bother to tell him. This was a dirty trick. It is said that Mountbatten wanted to come out earlier but before his official departure he wanted to see Wavell in London, to which Wavell did not agree in spite of Attlee's summons. The Labour Government could not afford to annoy Wavell further.

Before accepting the appointment, Mountbatten laid down his terms. These terms were agreed to in toto. He received a clear mandate. No Viceroy had ever been given such a free hand as Mountbatten. He has been created a Viscount.

It is now well known that when Wavell was being replaced, there was talk of replacing the Auk as well. Mountbatten supported the proposition. But

Lord Ismay intervened and said that the Auk was immensely popular in the Armed Forces and had great prestige in their eyes and should therefore stay. I suppose Mountbatten's objection was based on the fact that the Auk was very senior to him and always treated him as a youngster whenever he was in Delhi.

Mountbatten arrived at 3.15 pm at Palam and everyone was there to receive him. He brought a very impressive entourage which consisted of: General Lord Pug Ismay* (He was in the Indian Cavalry and ended up on the staff of Winston Churchill. He is an old friend of the Auk and is held in high esteem by him. He will act as Chief-of-Staff.) Sir Eric Mieville† (who used to be the Private Secretary to Lord Willingdon and was later on the staff of His Majesty the King), Erskine Crum‡ (to act as the Conference Secretary), Captain Brockman (his Personal Secretary) and Campbell Johnson (the Press Attaché). Mountbatten is also keeping Wavell's staff – Sir George Abell as Private Secretary and Ian Scott as the Assistant Private Secretary. He has also taken V. P. Menon on his staff, a man very close to Patel.

On the arrival of Mountbatten Francis Tuker remarked, 'We met the incoming Viceroy, sparkling as a new Rolls Royce. The still serviceable tractor trundles out of Delhi.' Before Wavell left he wrote to Attlee, 'I think that I am entitled to observe that so summary a dismissal of His Majesty's representative in India is hardly in keeping with the dignity of the appointment.' What a slap in the face of the Prime Minister! Attlee did not have the courage to sack him to his face, showed no gratitude and shunted him out without a word of thanks.

Wavell goes, unsung, into oblivion.

Mountbatten was received at the Durbar Hall of the Viceroy's House by Wavell with all pageantry and ceremony. He travelled in an open landau escorted by the Bodyguards. On dismounting he bowed his head to Wavell. Till now it was an established custom that the outgoing Viceroy departed from the soil of India before the arrival of the new incumbent. For the first time it was broken.

The Auk received a letter from Wavell thanking him for the excellent work done by the Army in re-establishing control in the Punjab.

*General Sir Hastings Ismay (1887–1965) was created Baron Ismay in 1947; joined 21st Cavalry (Frontier Force) 1907; Military Secretary to Lord Willingdon, Viceroy of India, 1931–33; Chief-of-Staff to Minister of Defence 1940–45; Deputy Secretary (Military) to War Cabinet 1940–45.

†Sir Eric Mieville (1896–1971), Private Secretary to the Viceroy of India 1931–36; Private Secretary to the Duke of York 1936; Assistant Private Secretary to the King 1937–45.

‡Lt-Gen Vernon Erskine Crum (1918–1971), became Commandant of the Guards Depot 1957–60; commanded 4th Guards Brigade 1963–65; GOC 4th Div BAOR 1967–69.

23rd March: We were invited to say goodbye to the Wavells.

Later we went to the airport to bid him farewell. Mountbatten was also there. I looked at Wavell and wished that I could read his mind and gauge his feelings. I am sure that, apart from whatever else he may have felt, he must have been sad to leave a task unfinished.

In the evening we attended the opening session of the Asian Relations Conference at the Purana Qilla Ground. This is Nehru's favourite baby and was inaugurated by him. Mrs Sirojini Naidu delivered the Presidential address. She is a brilliant speaker.

In the middle of all this unrest Nehru decided to hold an Inter-Relations Asian Conference. He could not have chosen a worse time. There is trouble even in Delhi. Instead of paying attention to restoring the internal peace and tranquillity among the various communities he decided to fiddle while India burnt. No wonder that he is called 'Nero'.

Nehru issued invitations to the Asian countries through a non-official body – 'The Indian Council of World Affairs' – so that it gave it a non-political outlook; at the same time it was meant to be a slap in the face for the Viceroy as it was being held without his approval and patronage. Nehru wanted to prove to the Asian countries that he was a law unto himself and was a world figure and could afford to ignore the Government. It was a stratagem to claim the cultural, moral and political leadership of Asia, and to impress on all countries that India had become important and he was its undisputed leader.

Delegates from 31 countries were invited which included those from the Russian Trans-Caucasian Republics. There were 51 delegates from India and observers from Britain, United State of America, Australia, etc. Many Hindu leaders were invited but no Muslim Leaguers. The League boycotted the conference as they were not made co-host and the *Daily Dawn* commented that 'Nehru is a Hindu imperialist and is engaged in perpetuating a fraud on the unsuspecting people of Asia'.

The site chosen was the Purana Qilla of Hindu mythology fame to impress on all that Hindu was the culture of India. A canopy was erected to accommodate 20,000 people and an enormous dais upon which 31 leaders of the delegations sat. It was all very impressive and quite spectacular. It was a big *Tamasha*. In other words, it was a sort of Victory Celebration.

Nehru, Mrs Naidu and Mrs Pandit were the soul of the conference. There were speeches by all delegates, film shows and exhibitions by the participant countries. Lavish dinners, lunches and tea parties were held. Money was no criterion. As usual it was funded by Birla.

Nobody knew as to which direction the conference was heading. There were discussions on Asian economic, racial and political problems and many others. Sometimes the delegates formed small committees. It was a free for all. Quarrels often broke out, especially between the Arabs and the Jews. No tangible results were emerging.

Nehru, except for ensuring that no anti-British speeches were made, could not direct or control the conference. Towards the end he suggested the establishment of a permanent Asian Organization with an HQ in Delhi. The small countries, being afraid of India's domination, shot it down. Finally it was agreed to establish a cultural organization of Asian countries of which the next meeting, two years hence, would be held in China. Before the conference closed, Gandhi addressed them.

Altogether it was a fiasco but as a drama it was superb.

Liaquat held a 'Pakistan Day' rally in Delhi. Quaid called upon Muslims to shed their last drop of blood for the struggle for Pakistan.

24th March: The swearing-in ceremony of Mountbatten took place in the Durbar Hall of the Viceroy's House. It was extremely colourful. The Durbar Hall was handsomely decorated. The trumpeters stood on the roof.

The Mountbattens came in a procession to the dais. Sir Patrick Spens,* the Chief Justice of India, adminstered the oaths.

Mountbatten was in the full regalia and Lady Mountbatten was dressed in ivory brocade and wore medals.

He has an aristocratic bearing; more so than the King himself. Everything around him was glittering as if he was trying to impress everyone with his 'royal presence'. It was not natural. Something was missing. In fact he looked arrogant and over-confident, in spite of his elegance. Though he is an impressive figure of a man, he seemed to lack grace. To me it seems as if he lacks magnanimity and benevolence. I could be wrong.

All political leaders, ruling Princes, civil and military officers were present, except for the Nawab of Bhopal and the Maharajah of Bikaner. Mountbatten delivered a short address after which we all moved to the north drawing room to be presented to their Excellencies.

Mountbatten's staff and the Congressmen have been spreading all sorts of fantastic stories about him and trying to build him up in the public eyes. It is said that he has been given plenipotentiary powers which are above that of His Majesty's Government. He will make all the decisions on the spot which would be implemented by the Government. He is going to be the boss. It is said that he has been given a clear mandate and all the necessary means available to succeed. In this he also has the blessing of the opposition in Parliament.

It is rumoured that Mountbatten did not wish to be saddled with the present assignment, but when His Majesty the King asked him he had no option but to accept.

Mountbatten said that he was forced to accept the Viceroyalty of India

*William Patrick Spens (1885–1973) was created 1st Baron Spens in 1959; Conservative MP for Ashford Division of Kent 1933–43; Chief Justice of India 1943–47; Chairman Arbitration Tribunal in India 1947–48; MP for S Kensington 1956–59.

by His Majesty the King. There can be no bigger untruth. It is common knowledge that he wanted it badly to enhance his political standing and he worked towards it. He established close contact with Nehru knowing that he would one day become the Prime Minister of India. It was the efforts of Krishna Menon which further cemented their friendship.

It is reported that Cripps wanted to come out as Mountbatten's Chief-of-Staff but Mountbatten refused and said that he was a 'cheeky, doddering old man, who has stupid and ludicrous ideas'. He, Cripps, considered himself an authority on India and wanted the Governor-Generalship.

According to common gossip Mountbatten has come to partition India as quickly as possible, irrespective of the consequences – sort out the Princes; take all possible measures to keep the two countries in the Commonwealth; ensure that Britain's strategic and mercantile interests in South Asia are not jeopardized and, finaly, keep the Indian leaders under pressure and give them no time to think.

It is also said that the unitary form of the Government and the Cabinet Mission Plan is out of date.

The Congress is jubilant over Mountbatten's appointment. He is using Krishna Menon as his contact man with Nehru, V. P. Menon with Patel and Sudhir Ghosh with Gandhi.

Delhi is a beehive of rumours and conjectures. Everyone has a story to tell. Each story is supposed to be coming from the horse's mouth.

25th March: Begum Rana Liaquat Ali was a great friend of Jessie Auchinleck. When Auk's divorce came through, Begum Liaquat persuaded her husband to cut off all social relations with the Auk. When I took over as the Private Secretary I got the Auk and Liaquat together for dinner at our house. I asked them to patch up their differences, which they did.

We dined with Iskandar Mirza. He is an attractive personality. He was a very successful Political Officer on the Frontier and was held in great esteem by the Governor, Sir George Cunningham. He loved playing the 'Frontier Game' and could twist the locals around his fingers and get away with it. The Pathans loved him for it. When he was the Deputy Commissioner in Peshawar, the Red Shirts decided to form a procession. Iskandar Mirza was told that they were not to do so. He evolved an ingenious method. He had some purgative mixed with their morning meal. As soon as the procession started, the men taking part in it felt the need to go to the toilet and gradually the procession petered out.

Iskandar comes and sits on my office table. Once he comes it is difficult to get rid of him. He loves to gossip.

Mountbatten is using all his charms to disarm Nehru.

26th March: The Commander-in-Chief attended the Army Commander's Conference.

In the opening address the Commander-in-Chief stated that planning had been going on for the composition and size of the future Army. The limiting factor was the financial resources likely to be available. It has been proposed to the Government that a smaller Army than was previously proposed will have to be accepted. He said that some units will have to remain on a cadre and certain training centres will have to be amalgamated. However, the reorganization of field formations must go ahead. Similarly the organization and the size of the Royal Indian Navy and Royal Indian Air Force were being replanned on a reduced scale.

The Commander-in-Chief went on to say that the appointment of the Principal Administrative Officers at GHQ had been abolished and will be replaced by the appointment of Chief of Inter-Services Administration (CISA), whose duties will be advisory and exploratory and not executive. His main task will be to advise on all administrative matters concerning the three Services and to explore further possible integration among them.

The Commander-in-Chief said that the problem and the process of nationalization was a complicated one and the time available for complete nationalization was limited and asked the Army Commanders to see that the plans, when approved, would be implemented by them in the same spirit as that in which they had been made at the Armed Forces Headquarters. The Commander-in-Chief went on to emphasize that a smooth handover depends largely on British officers. He could count on their loyalty and devotion to service. Moreover, he was sure that they would do their utmost to make the plans a success and he was making every effort to safeguard their interests.

It was considered and approved that the British troops may have to be used in aid of the Civil Power.

Major General L. G. Whistler* has been appointed Major-General British Troops in India. A Charter of his duties was issued.

Soon after the arrival of Mountbatten there was a point of disagreement between him and the Auk. The latter maintained that in order to uphold British prestige, British troops must be used to save lives. The Provinces were continuously demanding them for internal security duties. Mountbatten, however, was of the opinion that they must be sent away before the date of handing over. Behind this he had a sinister motive. He thought that their withdrawal would help in keeping both India and Pakistan in the Commonwealth as the two countries would not be too confident of their defence capabilities and probably bank on His Majesty's Government's assistance. Besides he was frightened of being blamed for any action the British troops may take in putting down disturbances.

Tara Singh has promised Ferozepore and Ludhiana Districts to His

---

*General Sir Lashmer Whistler (1898–1963) Major-General British Troops in India 1947–48; GOC-in-C Africa Command 1951–53.

Highness the Maharajah of Faridkot in return for his support to the cause of the Sikhs.

27th March: The Commander-in-Chief and the Army Commanders dined with the new Viceroy who asked them for their views on the present impasse. He also said that the present Muslim League High Command may break up as its members do not approve of Jinnah's authoritarian methods. He further said that he did not have the means to administer and that he has arrived too late to stop the migration and the massacre in the Punjab; all were surprised.

Henceforth the Viceroy's Executive Council is to be called the 'Cabinet'.

28th March: Mountbatten gave a garden party to the delegates of the Asian Relations Conference and to the Members of the Legislative Assembly in the Moghul Garden of the Viceroy's House. This was followed by an Hindu dance.

Nehru was all milk and honey to the Mountbattens. He did his best to show his familiarity with the new Viceroy to the guests. In fact it would be correct to say that the party was given for Mountbatten to meet the Congressmen.

The Viceroy has asked the Commander-in-Chief to give the breakdown of the various communities represented in the Army. I wonder why.

30th March: The internal situation is not too good. In Bengal the Police are in open rebellion. The Army has had to disarm them. Some were put behind bars; the rest were sent back to the barracks. The Eastern Command did a magnificent job of work. Gandhi has arrived in Delhi from Bihar obviously to measure up the new Viceroy.

31st March: Mountbatten called the Auk and tried 'to teach his grand-mother to suck eggs'. He thinks that he knows the Indian troops and the Indian Army inside out. He now wants them to be used constantly in aid of the Civil Power. Auk tried to convince him that it was fraught with danger as they could become partisan. With communal feelings running high they should be used sparingly.

Mountbatten would not listen. The Auk returned to the office in a bad temper and rang for me. He was banging the table with the clenched fist and kept saying 'I will not do it'. When his temper cooled he told me that Mountbatten wants him to sack me as he feels that a Muslim should not be his Private Secretary. The Auk said that he will not allow him to interfere in his affairs.

These are difficult times. The Army is being used for political ends and is keeping the Provincial Governments going. Rioting is taking place all over the country. On the slightest excuse the civil administration calls out the Army as they have lost confidence in the Police.

In his prayer meeting Gandhi said: 'Partition of India will be over my dead body'. Later Mountbatten met Gandhi.

Krishna Menon is forging ahead and is doing a great deal of running around between the Congress High Command and the Viceroy. He has offered his full support to the Viceroy.

Krishna Menon has had a chequered career. He moved to the United Kingdom in the early thirties and formed 'The India League'. At the time of the second Round Table Conference in London he met all the Indian delegates and tried to convince them of the good work he was doing for the liberation of India. On Sundays he was a regular speaker at Hyde Park Corner and led many processions as well. He was closely associated with the Communists in London and was a great admirer of Harold Laski,* and before that of Annie Besant.† He was known to change colours according to the season and time.

In London he lived in a hovel and behaved like a tramp. He had a mean and a hungry look, wore ill-fitting clothes, and never had a hair-cut. He made money by dishonest means, and was known to be a great intriguer, capable of provoking incidents or inventing them to suit his aims. It is said he has a diseased mind and no principles. All give him a wide berth, except Nehru. It was said that Edwina Mountbatten often met him and has befriended him.

In 1938 Menon toured Spain with Pandit Nehru. Nehru was impressed by him. So much so that he allowed him to handle his publications. Gradually he became Nehru's contact-man in the United Kingdom, as well as his adviser on British affairs.

When the Interim Government was formed Nehru brought him to India. In September, 1946, he sent Menon on a tour of European countries. This he did in the capacity of Personal Representative of the Vice President of the Interim Government, (Vice President was what Nehru was calling himself). In this trip Menon also wanted to visit Moscow, but it was opposed by Gandhi and Patel.

Menon drafted the preamble to the future Constitution of India for Nehru and presented it to him on 22nd January, 1947. In this he suggested that India become a Sovereign Independent Republic.

Menon is Nehru's blind spot. Strangely enough, and according to Menon, Nehru's relationship with Lady Mountbatten is sufficiently close to have raised many eyebrows.

When Mountbatten arrived there was disorder in the Punjab and, to a lesser degree, in the other Provinces, but the situation was by no means out

*Harold Laski (1893–1950) political scientist and university teacher of extreme left-wing views.

†Annie Besant (1847–1933) was an English theosophist and Indian political leader; founded the Central Hindu College at Benares 1898; organized the India Home Rule League; President, Indian National Congress, 1917.

of hand. Instead of restoring law and order, settling the administration and bringing the people back to sanity, he has plunged headlong into the political arena. This has given the impression that His Majesty's Government has cold feet and lost control over the situation. It is now being said that His Majesty's Government is on the run and cannot care less if the country plunges into disaster.

June, 1948, is the deadline. There is still plenty of time. A calmer atmosphere has to be created and tempers cooled to carry out negotiations in a realistic and businesslike manner. But in this charged atmosphere Mountbatten has added fuel to the fire. He is going 'full speed ahead'. I think he is panic-stricken.

Mountbatten should have tackled the Punjab first, before it became too late. Nehru wanted martial law in the Punjab but Messervy* and Jenkins objected to it. Auk was also in favour of doing so, but later withdrew his support due to non-availability of troops. British troops were not allowed to be used, lest a feeling developed that the British were trying to re-impose their authority and perpetuate their rule.

Great Britain has always boasted that it has given 'Law and Order' to India. This, they feel, is their most important mission in the subcontinent. The responsibility rests on their shoulders until they withdraw. Mountbatten has conveniently forgotten this role, and I am sure it will lead to disaster.

In Auk's opinion Mountbatten is quite the wrong choice for the Governor-Generalship and Viceroyalty of India for the following reasons:

1. He has an inflexible German mind.
2. His naval upbringing has made him ill-equipped for slow and patient negotiations.
3. He is a novice in politics and has no experience of the Indian scene or the complex Indian mind. Nothing happens here in a hurry because of the intricate inter-racial, religious and political currents.
4. He thinks that he knows India as a result of his various visits to Delhi and the very fact that he was the Supreme Allied Commander in South-East Asia. Incidentally, the Americans were indifferent to him and called his old command the 'Jackal Command'.
5. He was already a partisan before he arrived.
6. And lastly a member of the Royal Family can never become a politician because of a lack of such training.

To my mind his whole image and career has been built up because he is a member of the Royal Family. During the war his handling of the Dieppe

*General Sir Frank Messervy (1893–1974) commanded 7th Indian Division in Arakan and at Kohima 1944; Commanded 4th Corps, Burma, Tamu to Rangoon, 1944–45; GOC-in-C Northern Command, India, 1946–7; Commander-in-Chief Pakistan Army, 1947.

Raid came under severe criticism. His despatches as Supreme Allied Commander in South-East Asia were sketchy and often irrelevant. He went for slick solutions.

It is well known that he was jealous of Slim and was afraid that he might replace him if anything went wrong and finally he got him out of his way. He even got rid of Oliver Leese. He would not take any responsibility and was not prepared to risk his reputation which he was eagerly building. He often used to say that he would not fall at the last hurdle and no man would be allowed to stand in his way. He wanted his subordinates to carry the can for him. He forced General Christison* to do it for him on many an occasion.

In many ways Mountbatten has increased the Auk's problems, some of which he just ignores. He is of no help to him and seldom accepts his advice. The Auk calls him 'Pretty Dickie' and the senior brass at GHQ 'Tricky Dickie'.

---

*General Sir Philip Christison (b. 1893) commanded XXII and XV Indian Corps 1942–45; C-in-C Allied Land Forces South-East Asia 1945; Allied Commander Netherlands East Indies 1945–46.

April 1947

'As C-in-C in India, one of my responsibilities is the maintenance of law and order when so required by the civil authorities.'

The Auk.

1st April: Mountbatten had a meeting with the C-in-C, Nehru, Liaquat and Baldev. They discussed the motion on the Indian National Army which is coming before the National Assembly. It was a stormy session. The Auk was pressurized but he took a firm stand. He stated that the release of the Indian National Army men will undermine the discipline of the Armed Forces.

There is a feeling among the regular officers of the Army that they are not required any more and that in due course the officers of the Indian National Army will be replacing them. On several occasions the Auk has threatened to resign but it has not been accepted. Being C-in-C, he has great prestige in the Armed Forces. If he had gone, many of the British officers would have followed suit. No Government can afford to let that happen at this juncture. Incidentally, there is a belief in Congress circles that if Auk resigns he will be succeeded by Field-Marshal Sir William Slim. According to these circles Slim is pro-Muslim.

At the meeting it was finally decided that the Federal Court would act as an Adviser on the merit of each case of those who joined the ranks of the Indian National Army. A formula was evolved which said: 'Without creating a precedent, Justices of the Federal Court would review the cases and recommend whether there should be any alterations in the sentence.'

At his second interview with Mountbatten, Gandhi complained that the League Ministers in the Cabinet were not cooperating with their Congress counterparts. Gandhi suggested that if the League think that they could run the country by themselves they should be allowed to form the Government with Jinnah as Prime Minister. It was meant to be a jest, a wisecrack and a bait to see Quaid's reactions. It was meant to ridicule him and lower him in the eyes of his people. Gandhi knew full well that the offer will not be approved by the Congress High Command. He also knew that the Quaid will not accept it. What hypocrisy! In actual fact Gandhi did not mean a word of it. He just wanted to show Mountbatten how magnanimous he could be.

Gandhi is making every effort to be friends with Mountbatten and has fallen under his charm. Mountbatten calls him 'the modern saint' and addresses him as 'my dear friend'. Gandhi is quite unpredictable. Some say that he sleeps with naked young girls to test his vows of chastity.

A detailed paper has been issued by the G. S. Branch. It is on the reorganization of the Indian Army in 1947–48 and the experiments to be carried out by the 4th Indian Division. It states that past experience has shown that, between wars, there was a tendency for armies to work on theories evolved at the end of the last major war and consequently to be unprepared for the next war. It is quite possible that the next war will begin in entirely different circumstances.

It is stated that the Army in India is likely to be called to fight in the mountain and desert countries beyond the Western Frontier of India, in the Middle East, the Malayan Peninsula and in Burma. At the same time it must be prepared to support civil authorities in the exercise of their duties, both on the North-West Frontier Province and in India itself.

The present divisions have been thoroughly tested in the last war. They require a great deal of maintenance and a vast supply organization to keep them going. A detailed examination is to be carried out to see whether it is possible to produce a smaller self-contained formation than the Division, and to cut out some heavier elements.

The main object of this experiment is to try out a Division organized on the basis of self-contained brigades. Consequently it has been decided to include armoured regiments within the brigade. Besides it has to be accepted that the future organization will contain both light and heavy infantry battalions. This principle will equally apply to other arms. In future a greater reliance will have to be placed on air transportation, both for troop movement and for supplies. The building of forward airfields will become essential. The infantry will have to be organized on standard establishment capable of performing varied roles.

2nd April: The Viceroy asked all the Cabinet Ministers whether, in their opinion, law and order could be maintained if the police force had a non-partisan Army behind them. Everyone said it could. He then asked them whether they were of the same opinion as him that any solution for the transfer of power should be done in such a manner as to minimize the risk of strife and bloodshed. To this they replied in the affirmative as well. Thereupon he asked them whether the Indian Army could be sufficiently Indianized to stand on its own legs by June, 1948. Different views were expressed on this point. Most of them agreed that only a committee of experts could answer that question.

He then asked whether the Army could be divided along communal lines by June, 1948, and was told that it was out of the question. The League members thought that it was possible. However, all agreed once again that this question could only be answered by experts. The Auk informed Mountbatten that there was no hope of settlement in the Punjab and the Sikhs may take over the irrigation headworks.

A debate took place in the Assembly on the release of Indian National Army prisoners. This lasted three hours. Ultimately the resolution was withdrawn.

Gandhi saw Mountbatten again.

3rd–5th April: We left on a tour of Risalpur, Nowshera, Abbottabad and Tobe Camp.

The situation in Abbottabad is tense. The Deputy Commissioner, St John, anticipates further trouble and has not made up his mind what to do.

We saw a radio monitoring radar unit which is covering Central Asia. This is a 'Hush Hush' organization and not open to Indians. The Englishman in charge did not want me to see it so I told him to go to hell and stepped inside.

Mountbatten saw the Quaid. He told his staff that the Quaid was most frigid, haughty and in a disdainful frame of mind. Mountbatten has appointed a comittee comprising Ismay, Mieville and Abell to draw up a plan for the partition of India.

5th April: The Sikh community has distributed a pamphlet which contained the following:

O, Khalsaji! A critical condition has arisen for the *Panth* (community) which arose after the last great *Ghallughara* (general massacre of Sikhs). The Ghallughara which has occurred specially in Potohar and the Frontier is too painful for us to describe. It is not yet known what the future will bring. The time is extremely grave and the situation is extremely critical. Now for us matters have gone to the extent of 'the throne or the coffin'. In order to maintain the existence of the Panth at this juncture, every Sikh should do his duty to the Guru's Panth. In obedience to the Panth, lies the life of a Sikh. By dint of their strength the Muslims want to thrust Pakistan on Sikhs, Hindus and Christians and they have already shown to us a specimen of Pakistan storm. In their majority zones they have perpetrated such tyrannies as cannot be described. Thousands of Sikh and Hindu women and children have been murdered; *Keshas* (long hair) and beards of hundreds have been chopped off and an effort has been made to convert them to Islam; hundreds of women have been abducted. Whole villages have been burnt up. Hundreds of chaste women jumped into wells and have sacrificed their lives in many other ways in order to preserve their honour. The Panth which plumed itself on rescuing other girls, finds its own daughters in the hands of tyrants. Rest assured, as it is only a small specimen of Pakistan and more terrible incidents are yet to come. But,

Khalsaji, we are the Sikhs of that Guru who having had his four children slaughtered said, 'What if four have fallen? Thousands still survive'. We have to fight this tyrannical Pakistan and have to keep the Panth in high airs. This Panth has been prospering all the more after every Ghallughara and rest assured that even now the Panth will prosper. Be Alert; you should recover yourself.

Fifty lakhs of rupees are required at this time for fighting the Pakistan in which lies our death. Although our community is poor, it has been winning every *morcha* (stronghold) by dint of sacrifice in the name of the Tenth Guru. It is our vigorous appeal that money should be collected from every house, every *mohalla* (sector), every village and every city for achieving victory in the forthcoming clash. Collect one rupee, one per head, it is the religious duty of the Sikhs of that village or town to make up the deficiency. In this way 50 lakh rupees should be collected very soon. This sum should be collected up to the 15th Baisakh (Sikh calendar month).

This Baisakh should prove a re-birth of the Khalsa and should always serve to give encouragement to the Sikhs in history. Besides, the entire Sikh public is requested to offer prayers every day for 'Victory to the Panth'. Such a terrible conflict is approaching that even the sum of Rs.50 lakhs collected once cannot be sufficient. Hence all Sikhs are requested to give one-tenth of their income for this task. And in every house one handful of flour should be set apart for the Guru's fund at the time of kneading flour.

Note: For purposes of receiving this money, S. Baldev Singh, Defence Member, Government of India, Delhi and Sardar Bhag Singh (of Gurdaspur), Advocate, Teja Singh Hall, Amritsar have been appointed treasurers. Collected money should be sent to one of these three persons by hand or by money order.

It was signed among many others, by Kartar Singh and Baldev Singh, the Minister of Defence, who is acting as one of the treasurers for the fund. It is for certain that Baldev is inciting the Sikhs.

7th April: The Commander-in-Chief had a meeting with Baldev Singh and then with the Viceroy. During the meeting with the Auk, the Viceroy read out a letter he has received from Liaquat which says that the representation of the Muslims in the Armed Forces is inadequate. He suggests that the Army should be reorganized to make division easier between Pakistan and Hindustan. No attention was paid to Liaquat's request.

To my mind he was right. Many senior British officers, including General Tuker, had suggested such a course. Some had even suggested that the Army should be made into one-class units. Mountbatten has ruled this out.

In the history of the Indian Army such actions are on record. The Quaid is well acquainted with the problems of the Army. He has always advocated the case of the Army and urged the Government to change the fundamental principles of their policy towards nationalization. This resulted in the first batch of ten Indians being sent to Sandhurst in 1918, and also in the selection of eight units to be Indianized in 1923. The Quaid was a member of General Sir Andrew Skeen's* Army Nationalization and Indian Sandhurst Committee in 1925, and in this connection visited military establishments in the United Kingdom, France, Canada and United States of America. Again he was appointed a member of a sub-committee on Defence at the end of the First Round Table Conference in 1931. The Quaid in his deliberations insisted on fixing a time limit for the Indianization of the forces. In this Pandit Kunzru invariably supported the Quaid.

For the information of the Quaid and Liaquat, a group of us Muslim officers had prepared basic papers on the division of the Armed Forces (See Appendix VII, p. 324).

Jenkins told the Auk that Baldev Singh is of the opinion that the attack on non-Muslims was premeditated and organized. Muslim League leaders were inciting their followers to violence. No action was taken against them even when they launched their 'peaceful disobedience movement'. The trouble that arose ultimately resulted in the resignation of the late Coalition ministry. Baldev maintains that it was partly the fault of the administration which encouraged and then allowed the Muslims to resort to violence. He has said that the gulf which has been created between the two communities is unbridgeable. He even told Jenkins that he had written directly to His Majesty's Government on the subject.

Baldev also complained that under an ordinance recently issued the military authorities were given the same powers as the police. But the Deputy Commissioner, Rawalpindi, has now issued orders to the effect that military authorities would not interfere.

He further complained that large quantities of arms were being smuggled into Punjab from the Frontier and the tribal areas, and that non-Muslim military units should be used to unearth the unlicensed arms. He appreciated that non-Muslim elements were being recruited into the police. The police should also include Mazhabi Sikhs in their ranks. He complained that the Sikhs have been deprived of their kirpans (Sikh swords) by the police.

I believe that Baldev wants to run the Punjab himself and in this he has found the Governor a stumbling block.

The Commander-in-Chief has approved a tour of the National Cadet Corps Sub-Committee to the United Kingdom.

The Committee, of which the Hon Pandit H. N. Kunzru is the Chairman,

---

*General Sir Andrew Skeen (1873–1935) was GOC-in-C Southern Command India 1923–24, Chief of the General Staff, Indian Army, 1924–28.

was established in order to advise the Government of India on the formation of a National Cadet Corps. When formed, the NCC will, it is envisaged, consist of two divisions, a senior division for boys and a junior one for girls.

The aims of the Corps are to develop leadership, character and comradeship among India's youth and to stimulate an interest in the defence of the country.

8th April: The Commander-in-Chief had written a letter to Nehru thanking him for his speech on the Indian National Army resolution in the Assembly. The Auk received the following reply:

Thank you for your letter of the 7th. It was good of you to write to me in such a friendly way and I am grateful to you for it.

It is true I felt a little distressed at what I thought was your lack of faith in our adhering to our word. I did not think of this in any personal sense. And thus there was a sense of weariness at having to discuss the same thing over and over again and repeat the same arguments. As a soldier and a man of action you will appreciate this. I am myself too indifferent a politician to like long-drawn-out talks which end vaguely and without producing results. And yet circumstances have conspired to make me play a politician's role and to indulge in these very arguments.

Mountbatten has told Liaquat that the reorganization of the Army on the basis of India and Pakistan was not possible until the withdrawal of the British.

9th April: In the evening there was a Cabinet meeting. Nehru is trying to act as a Prime Minister but Liaquat is not having it.

10–12 April: Gandhi has changed his stand. He now says that his suggestion about the handing over of the Government to Jinnah was not acceptable to the Congress Working Committee; he was therefore handing over the future negotiations to them.

14th April: Gandhi has returned to Bihar. A joint statement by him and the Quaid was issued deploring violence.

Mountbatten discussed the splitting of the Army with the Auk. The Auk maintains that such a step, before 1 June, '48, will lead to a breakdown of the forces. The Army is the only stable element in the country and, in any case, unless a 'political decision' was forthcoming, he could do little.

Ismay has sent to the Auk a copy of a letter which the Viceroy had received from the Prime Minister before he left United Kingdom. In this were contained the guidelines which the Viceroy was to bear in mind when discussing the future of the subcontinent.

In the letter the Prime Minister had stated that it was the objective of His Majesty's Government 'to obtain a Unitary Government for British India and the Indian States, if possible within the British Commonwealth, through the medium of a Constituent Assembly, set up and run in accordance with the Cabinet Mission Plan'. If by 1 October it was found that no settlement was reached on the basis of the Unitary Government for British India, then the Viceroy should report and submit his recommendations on the steps to be taken for handing over power.

The Prime Minister went on to say that the Indian States 'should adjust their relations with the authorities to whom it is intended to hand over power in British India but as was explicitly stated by the Cabinet Mission, His Majesty's Government do not intend to hand over power and obligations under paramountcy to any successor Government'. The Viceroy should therefore try to enter into negotiations with the individual States for adjusting their relations with the Crown.

The Prime Minister states that the date fixed for the transfer of power is a flexible one but the Viceroy should aim at 1 June, 1948. He goes on: 'While the Interim Government would not have the same powers as a Dominion Government, His Majesty's Government would treat the Interim Government with the same consultation and consideration as a Dominion Government, and give it the greatest possible freedom in the day-to-day exercise of the administration of the country.'

Therefore the keynote of the administration should be the closest co-operation with the Indians and 'you will impress upon the leaders the great importance of avoiding any breach in the continuity of the Indian Army and of maintaining the organization of defence on an all-India basis, and stress the need for continued collaboration in the security of the Indian Ocean.'

15th April: Mountbatten is holding a Governors' conference and is due to present 'Plan Balkan', which means the division of the subcontinent. The Governors maintain that the division is imminent and a quick decision to the effect must be taken.

Mountbatten had his first meeting with Jinnah. It is said that he wanted to get on the right side of the Congress and hatch a plan before he saw the leader of the Muslim Community.

Mountbatten is reported to have said that the Auk lacks political sense!! I think it applies more to Mountbatten himself.

16th April: The Commander-in-Chief saw the Viceroy at dinner. The Viceroy told him that Liaquat had complained of the inadequate representation of Muslims in the Armed Forces and that they should be reorganized in such a manner that they could be readily split up between Hindustan and Pakistan. For its implementation the Commander-in-Chief should be directly responsible to the Viceroy and not to the Defence Member. Mountbatten told Liaquat that he was attempting to pre-judge the issue and there was no question of a complete partition of India. However, it was a subject which could be dealt with by the Defence Committee. Detailed examination may be carried out by a sub-committee. Mountbatten further told the C-in-C that Baldev was the treasurer of a fund which the Sikhs were collecting for buying arms. We knew that already.

17th April: The police in Bengal have mutinied. The Army was called out to disarm them. The Army is becoming a 'Super Police Force'.

We attended a party at Feridkot House where all the Sikhs rulers were present. According to Savory they are planning a Civil War in order to establish 'Sikhistan'.

19th April: In the evening Mountbatten came to see the Auk. He was of the view that the emergence of Pakistan cannot be avoided. I informed the Quaid accordingly.

20th April: The Auk gave his views on Liaquat's letter to the Defence Member. The Auk said that the Armed Forces of India, as they stood, could not split up into two parts and into two self-contained armies. The proposal would involve the rebuilding of forces and the providing of essential components which do not exist in duplicate. He said that Pakistan includes all the important land frontiers of India and the forces required to defend it would be virtually the same as those now required to defend the subcontinent. The reorganization which will have to be carried out will take several years, during which period the Armed Forces will remain ineffective. Any talk of division will demoralize the Army and the troops will not take orders from officers other than those which belong to their own community. At the same time the hold of the British officers will become loose and they would prefer to leave the country. There was also a danger of the troops getting politically minded. The Auk maintained that it was a complicated situation as the troops were in the process of coming back from overseas and being demobbed. Besides, there was the question of accommodation in their new location. In the end, he mentioned that if the Armed Forces were to remain effective to deal with the unsettled condition in the subcontinent they must stand as they are.

On receiving the letter Baldev prepared a paper for the Cabinet on the lines advocated by the Auk. He praised the Armed Forces and condemned Liaquat's suggestion. He also said that the nationalization of the Armed Forces must be given top priority. (The paper and comments are at Appendix VIII, p. 330). His Majesty's Government, to meet the defence requirement of Britain, was keen to keep the Indian Army intact. It may also be maintained that it would be a crime to divide the Army.

24th April: Mountbatten has asked the Commander-in-Chief to give his opinion on the strategic implications of setting up an independent Pakistan. The C-in-C has sent him a paper which is based on purely military and strategical aspects; these are the only angles from which the problem is viewed. He has also enclosed a note written by the Deputy Chief of Staff setting out a view which might well be taken by the advocates of Pakistan. (The paper is at Appendix IX, p. 334.)

Master Tara Singh and Kartar Singh Gyani have threatened Mountbatten that if their demands are not met they will fight to achieve it. Will Mountbatten have the courage to arrest them?

25th April: Today was another crucial day. In the morning Mountbatten circulated Liaquat's paper to the Defence Committee. This had Auchinleck's and Baldev Singh's comments on it. The Committee was held in the evening. The papers were of such great secrecy that at the end of the meeting they were withdrawn.

It was a lengthy meeting. Baldev stuck to his guns, but Liaquat insisted that the Plan for the division of the Armed Forces must be prepared and the forces reorganized in case the establishment of Pakistan was agreed to. The Auk at the outset stressed that his views projected the practical difficulties and was in no way to influence a political decision which must be taken first. Until then there was no basis on which he could plan. Then the split was examined along with Menon's Plan which spelled out the 'Heads of Agreement' on the division of the subcontinent. Finally Mountbatten said that by June, 1948, the division of the forces and nationalization were possible and they should act accordingly and draw a broad outline plan only. He approved the formation of an 'Expert Committee' to make the necessary recommendations and all concerned, including the C-in-C, were to give evidence before it. In other words the decision to divide the forces was accepted in principle but no action was to be taken until a political decision was arrived at.

It was decided to hold up nationalization.

Mountbatten also mentioned that he is responsible for law and order, and in the last resort has the British troops to fall back on. (The Minutes of the Meeting are at Appendix X, p. 340.)

26th April: The Earl of Listowel* has replaced Pethick-Lawrence as Secretary of State for India.

Mountbatten has decided to send Ismay and Abell to London with the proposed Partition Plan. The Auk gave an At Home to meet the Mountbattens.

---

*William Hare, 5th Earl of Listowel (b. 1906) was Secretary of State for India from April to August, 1947; Minister of State for Colonial Affairs 1948–50; Governor-General of Ghana 1957–60.

28th April: Against the advice of all concerned, Mountbatten has left on a tour of the North-West Frontier Province. He wants to judge the mood of the Pathans. I hope that the tour will go well, but, considering what they did to Nehru, I am sceptical. Besides, the Pathans now are aware of the fact that he is a friend of Nehru.

Rajendra Prasad has been elected as the President of the Constituent Assembly which has been boycotted by the Muslim League.

Conditions in Punjab are bad.

The Auk has been convinced that there is no alternative but to split the Armed Forces. I had to work very hard on him. I well understood how he felt.

His Majesty's Government has approved the use of British troops in aid of the Civil Power in India until June, 1948.

29th April: Mohammad Ali called to see the Auk.

We left for United Kingdom to attend the Exercise 'Spearhead'.

May 1947

'The recent announcement of HMG has come as a considerable shock to very many people in this country who had thought, if they thought at all, that the process would be much more gradual.'

The Auk.

29th April–31st May: We were in the United Kingdom to attend the Chief of the Imperial General Staff's Exercise 'Spearhead'. We stayed at Claridge's and established our office in the India Office. I had an office to myself.

Ismay is going round selling Mountbatten's Plan but the Minister of Defence, A. V. Alexander, is a hard nut to crack, as he now understands India.

The Auk had a long session with the Chiefs of Staff. As directed by Mountbatten he gave his views on the partition of the Armed Forces.

The Chiefs of Staff in the United Kingdom are well aware of the fact that the situation in India is politically and administratively bad. It is known that there is no likelihood of Pakistan and India ever agreeing to any machinery for co-operation in the centre. They feel that it has therefore become imperative that a Partition Plan is produced by His Majesty's Government as soon as possible. The size and the extent of Pakistan is to be settled by the Indians themselves.

The Chiefs of Staff wish to ensure that the States remain in the Commonwealth. This, they feel, will greatly enhance British prestige and give them many strategic advantages. Pakistan and some native States, including Travancore, have already declared that they would like to remain within the Commonwealth. Hindustan intends to become a Sovereign State and would like to be known as 'The Republic of India'. Incidentally, this is Nehru's trump card. He will use it to pressurize His Majesty's Government which is determined to keep India in the Commonwealth.

The Chiefs of Staffs are keen to keep Pakistan in the Commonwealth. The reasons are many. In case of war with Russia, they could have strategic bases and other facilities in the North-West of the subcontinent. Besides, it will allow them the use of the Muslim's manpower and the good will and support of the other Muslim States. It will also ensure the independence and integrity of Afghanistan. At the same time it will have a stabilizing effect on India and keep her on the right path.

However, they thought that Pakistan's inclusion in the Commonwealth might antagonize India. In case of a war between the two countries Britain might find herself in a compromising position. Therefore it is essential that the Plan should cater for the granting of Dominion status to both simultaneously.

The Chiefs of Staff are keen to safeguard their communications with the Far East both by air and sea. In case of war they are keen to have the use of ports, airfields and supply bases in the subcontinent.

During our stay in England many events of great significance have taken place in India. We have been kept informed.

On 1st May Mountbatten was reported to have said that Suhrawardy wants an Independent State of Bengal with its own Armed Forces but within the Commonwealth. Suhrawardy is also reported to have said that, until the granting of Independence, a Central Defence Council could control and run the unified forces of the three Dominions.

Mountbatten considers the proposition feasible and has sent the proposal to His Majesty's Government. He has named it 'Operation Balkan'. Later, when he told Nehru about the matter, the latter was very upset and has begun losing confidence in Mountbatten. Krishna Menon came to the rescue and interceded. The proposition has been dropped.

Mountbatten is very keen to get a firm date for the transfer of power out of His Majesty's Government. He had hoped that this would bring things to a head.

In their announcement of 20th February, 1947, HMG had clearly announced their intention that power could be transferred to more than one authority. Mountbatten maintains that this does not preclude subsequent negotiations for a united India. He has still not grasped the mood of the Muslims.

At no stage did Mountbatten consult the Auk when he was preparing the Plan. He seems to have no confidence in the Commander-in-Chief and is doing his level best to keep him in the dark. This annoys the Auk immensely. However, nothing can be kept secret in Delhi. Information trickles down to us in some form or the other. The Army alone is the stabilizing factor and has kept steadfast, in spite of being under great strain. It is the Auk who provides the firm base. He will have to shoulder all the responsibilities if anything goes wrong.

In my mind I am sure that Mountbatten will make a mess of the Plan. He is obsessed with the notion that 'he has come, he has seen and he is prepared to plunge in irrespective of the consequences'. Just divide and get out as quickly as possible.

It is expected that both India and Pakistan will become Dominions and stay in the Commonwealth. Mountbatten thinks that the division could be completed by the end of the year. His Majesty's Government has ended its age-old treaties with the States. The Princes have been let down. It is their death knell. Some States have asked for new weapons to replace their old ones, but this has been rejected.

On 2nd May the plan was sent to HMG.

On 3rd May a Committee was formed to explore the possibilities of splitting the Army. This was under the chairmanship of Major-General S. F. Irwin, Deputy Chief of the General Staff.

As I thought, Mountbatten's visit to the Frontier was a fiasco. It is said that he took a great risk in facing the angry Pathans. In actual fact they were brought, under the orders of the Governor, Sir Olaf Caroe, to make their wishes known to the Viceroy, so that he could see for himself that all Pathans were in favour of the Muslim League. It was no hostile demonstration but a most friendly one. They even gave him a cheer at the end.

It is said that there was a meeting between the Quaid and Gandhi on 6th May. On the 8th Gandhi suddenly left for Calcutta. He wants a united India.

Mountbatten has been reported to have said that the Quaid wants him to be the 'Prime Minister's representative' over the two Governors-General with powers on the distribution of assets.

On 22nd May Quaid demanded a corridor to connect one wing of Pakistan with the other. He also wants to retain all the British officers in the future Army of Pakistan. India on the other hand only wants some.

Nehru is in full cry, making wild speeches like a dictator. He is threatening to take action against all and sundry but specially the Princes and the Muslim League.

The Hindus are no less militant than the Sikhs. They want to ensure that Pakistan, if established, should not survive. The RSSS has become very active throughout the country. Gandhi has proclaimed that the British should leave India immediately and let the political parties settle their differences. In other words he is advocating a civil war.

There is a feeling in Congress circles that the establishment of Pakistan would be temporary. In due course it will return to the fold. Gandhi has said, 'Let the whole nation be in flames. We will not concede one inch of Pakistan.'

All over the country the Press is acting in a most irresponsible manner. It is maligning the Armed Forces at the instigation of the Congress. *Amrita Bazar Patrika* is most vocal. The Muslim League papers are also sceptical of GHQ. They maintain that GHQ is following the dictates of the Congress. They also feel that GHQ is controlled by Baldev Singh, which is not a fact.

The Sikhs are working hard for 'Sikhistan'. The Maharajah of Patiala is not satisfied with the decision of the Congress. In this decision it was stated that no areas with a non-Muslim majority should be part of Pakistan. The Maharajah wants half of Punjab. There are only 12 out of 29 districts which have a non-Muslim majority. Patiala is reported to have told Mountbatten that the Sikhs will have no option but to fight. Mountbatten told him that it was his, Mountbatten's, responsibility to keep law and order. He would not tolerate any communal disorder and would not hesitate to use aircraft or machine-guns to restore sanity.

The Quaid and Liaquat had many discussions with Baldev Singh and other Sikh leaders. They have also had discussions with the Sikh Princes to try and come to an understanding. Quaid was prepared to concede a homeland to the Sikhs within Pakistan where they could be autonomous in the day-to-day administration of the State. He has offered them practically everything under the sun. But they are already committed to cast their lot with the Hindus and no reason or persuasion has any effect. The Hindus have done their job well in inciting and exploiting the Sikhs, leading them to the eventual destruction of their identity. As a result the constant stubbornness of the Sikhs has hardened the Muslim attitude towards them. The Sikhs are simple people who act before they think.

Listowel is of the opinion that the Sikhs have exaggerated ideas as they are only 4 million in Punjab out of a population of 28 million. However, their demands may be left to the Boundary Commission.

The Sikhs are now advocating mass emigration of their community to East Punjab as they do not want to be split into two halves.

Baldev has been advocating that the Punjab should be partitioned on the basis of Sikh landed property, their shrines and interests. Such a vague demand can only come from Baldev. He has circulated a letter, along with a map, which shows the Sikh province consisting of Ambala, Jullundur and Lahore Divisions, and Lyallpur or Montgomery.

It is well-known that in Punjab the Sikhs, assisted by the Hindus, are preparing for a communal war.

The Maharajah of Patiala is supplying arms, ammunition and explosives and has also sent some of his troops in mufti to Amritsar. The Maharajah of Faridkot has also joined in. He has been promised the district of Ferozepore. Nabha is supplying arms, while Kapurthala provides the funds. Even Alwar, Dholpur, Bikaner and Bharatpur have supplied arms.

They are also procuring arms by wagonloads from the dumps abandoned by the United States of America in Assam and elsewhere. The US forces were supposed to destroy them before leaving the country. Army intelligence has unearthed these activities. The Auk has reported this to Mountbatten but he has taken no action. The Auk is furious. The Army has a most effective intelligence set-up which is more efficient than that of the civil.

The weapons are being collected in the *gurdwaras* (temples) all over the country and in the Sikh States. The Sikh rulers are giving the instigators training in their use and have recruited Indian National Army personnel for this purpose.

The Police are ineffective and helpless.

Jenkins has told Mountbatten that the Sikhs are preparing a war of revenge.

As a result of this Mountbatten has warned Baldev that he knows about the intention of the Sikhs. With the assistance of the Hindu businessmen they are contemplating an attack on the Muslim villages. This, he said, will not be tolerated.

In reply Baldev told Mountbatten that the Sikhs are active, as they are jittery and want to safeguard their position, but they would cease doing anything unlawful as soon as the Army appeared in strength.

In spite of the warning Mountbatten gave, it had no effect on them. They have sent a delegation to the United Kingdom to plead and pursue their cause. Major Short is doing his best for them.

Jenkins told Mountbatten that it will require four years to split the Punjab peacefully.

Mountbatten is expecting a flare-up in the north. He is trying his best to avoid it and has suggested to His Majesty's Government that very strong measures should be taken against the fanatics, even if it means wiping them out. He said that in the long run it will save many massacres. He believes that such actions will be endorsed by the Coalition Interim Government. He has asked His Majesty's Government to give their approval.

On the 7th Mountbatten left for Simla. On the 8th both Nehru and Krishna Menon went to stay with him.

On 10th May the Partition Plan was returned to Mountbatten. This had been prepared in six weeks and Ismay had taken it to London to get it duly approved by the British Cabinet. It envisaged handing over the authority to Provinces, or such association of Provinces which decide to group together in the interim period, before power is transferred. It also recommended an independent State of NWFP.

Mountbatten showed the Plan to Nehru. Nehru was very angry and totally rejected it. The Plan was immediately withdrawn which resulted in much confusion in the British Cabinet.

Mountbatten even refused a ministerial visitation to India which His Majesty's Government suggested. Thereupon the Plan was re-hashed between Mountbatten and Nehru, and Menon produced the revised draft for the approval of His Majesty's Government. It was finalized on 11th May and sent to London that very day. He accepted Congress demands. HMG was about to give them approval but someone pointed out that they also owe an allegiance to Muslims. Mountbatten was very upset and asked permission to visit London and discuss it with the Government.

Previously Mountbatten had announced that he would be meeting the Quaid, Liaquat, Nehru, Patel and Baldev on 17th May to show them the Plan for the transfer of power. The meeting was postponed. This upset the Muslim League who became convinced that Mountbatten had become a partisan and was in the process of hatching a plot.

In order to get Nehru's approval to the Plan, Mountbatten is reported to have convinced him that Pakistan was not a viable proposition and the division of the subcontinent was a temporary phase. In the not too distant future Pakistan would return to the Indian fold.

Mountbatten argued that Pakistan was economically unworkable, strategically unsound, and undefensible. Politically it would also be divided, leading to chaos and disintegration. He further said that the whole experiment would be short-lived provided no Muslims were banished from India. On the other hand free and democratic India under the Congress would grow from strength to strength. It would become a great power and be in a position to absorb Pakistan.

Mountbatten himself was convinced that Pakistan would be undone and so was Gandhi. Even Attlee believed this. Birla maintained that it was 'nonviable'.

The fact is that Nehru is getting on in years and is tired of waiting for power. He does not wish to take part in another struggle against the British. He is prepared to accept what was finally offered. The British want to find a way out before further communal disorder, and partition is the answer. They are convinced, however, that it is temporary and that later the two will come together.

The Quaid had included all the six Provinces as part of Pakistan, these being North-West Frontier, Punjab, Sind, Baluchistan, Bengal and Assam. But Mountbatten promised Nehru that the Punjab and Bengal would be partitioned on the basis of the contiguous majority areas and he would ensure that Jinnah accepted it. In the North-West Frontier Province, where a Congress Government rules, a referendum would be held to ascertain the wishes of the people and also in the Assam Muslim areas which were contiguous to Bengal.

At all costs Nehru wanted Kashmir to be part of India. Mountbatten gave his word that a corridor would be provided to connect Kashmir with India and the term 'other factors' would be used initially to give the latitude to the Boundary Commission to do the needful. The deal was clinched between them. Mountbatten also promised him that the Ferozepore Headworks will be part of India.

Nehru even dreamed that through Kashmir a route could be established to the North-West Frontier Province which, if the referendum went in his favour, would become part of India. This was really some planning! Some vision! He even talks of an independent State of NWFP.

Mountbatten conceded to Nehru that Hyderabad would not be allowed to become an Independent State and His Majesty's Government will give no assistance to them in this respect.

And finally that His Majesty's Government and the Commonwealth will give all possible assistance to India in preference to Pakistan and would give her the 'most favoured nation treatment'.

Mountbatten returned to Delhi from Simla on 14th May. On the following day he was summoned to London and left on 18th May. He was accompanied by Menon.

Before Mountbatten departed for the United Kingdom he had obtained Nehru's approval of his becoming the Governor-General of both Dominions. Mountbatten wanted the same assurance from the Quaid. Quaid told him that he wanted two separate Governors-General. He said that Mountbatten could stay as a super Governor-General. If this was not possible as a representative of the Crown, as a supreme arbitrator who would have the responsibility and power over the division of assets between the two Dominions.

Mountbatten said flatly that he would never agree to such an arrangement. His pride was hurt and he started losing interest in Pakistan. He told his staff that he will not stay as Governor-General of one Dominion but Jinnah must not know.

Consequently Nehru is very happy as he is now in a position to use Mountbatten as he wants. He is a clever manipulator and an astute politician. To achieve his end he has cultivated Edwina Mountbatten and is on very intimate terms with her. There are all sorts of conjectures about their relationship.

Nehru believes that all women are in love with him and the names of many have been associated with him. Mridula Sarabhai, a rich Gujrati, pursued him relentlessly but after the initial romance he lost interest in her. She is outspoken and tough and is constantly worried about Nehru's security. She was appointed the General Secretary of the Congress Working Committee in 1946.

Padmaja Naidu is in love with Nehru and wants to marry him. She makes no bones about it. She invariably stays in his house in the adjoining bedroom. Indira dislikes her trips with her father. When Nehru transferred his attention to Edwina Mountbatten, Padmaja took it as an insult and refused to meet him. Publicly she says that Nehru is not a 'one-woman man'.

The name of another woman, Shardha Mata, a scholar of Indian scripture and mythology, was associated with him but the romance did not last long.

As far as Nehru's relationship with Edwina is concerned Mountbatten seems quite happy about it. This friendship suits him very well. Nehru is in and out of the Viceroy's House to meet Edwina. She has hypnotized and captivated him. Krishna Menon says that it is more than that. God knows! Edwina has Jewish blood in her. She has great charm, compassion and nervous energy. She is constantly on the move, visiting hospitals and welfare organizations. Edwina often says that Nehru is a lonely man and needs a woman in his life. I suppose she has decided to be the one. It is said that she writes adolescent and juvenile letters to Nehru and he does likewise. However, her relationship with Nehru has been of immense help to Congress.

In reality she tried to charm and enamour all the political leaders in turn and successfully too. The only one with whom she could not make any headway was the Quaid. Even Gandhi calls her 'an angel of mercy' and addresses her as 'my dear friend'.

On our return to Delhi we found the Army in good shape. Units are returning from overseas and some personnel are being sent to their homes on leave. At the moment there is little communal feeling among them. But once they come in touch with their kith and kin in the cities and villages it is bound to affect them. There has been no case of disobedience in the Armed Forces so far, except that a State Force unit in Gwalior refused to go on parade. There were a few minor incidents in some of the Ordnance depots and Army factories.

At this stage the troops are basically interested in the benefits which are going to be given to them before they are demobilized. Few want to serve in the post-war Army. There is a delay in the publication of the post-war terms of pay and allowance. Some troops on return from overseas could not be sent on leave as they were needed in the units which were on internal security duties. As they are returning after winning a war they are not keen on such duties. Sikh troops on return are being contacted by their leaders who are persuading them to defy the orders of their officers. Congress is determined to establish control over the Armed Forces. Gradually it is getting difficult to keep the Army together. Rumours, to lower the prestige of the forces and cause dissatisfaction among the troops, are being circulated.

Many Indian officers are hobnobbing with politicians and scheming to get on their right side to get quick promotion. Lt-Colonel B. M. Kaul, who was my contemporary at Sandhurst, is the leader of the gang. He is not only cultivating Nehru but also Jai Parkash Narain and Krishna Menon. He wants to have a finger in all the pies. He loves intrigues and is over-ambitious. The residences of Sir Sri Ram and his brother Shankar Lall are being used by the politicians as 'contact points' with the officers of the Armed Forces.

A tribute must be paid to the British officers in the various Indian units. They are putting up a magnificent show and are trying their best to be completely impartial. I think it is correct to say that they are largely responsible for keeping the Indian Army sane. Of course, there are many Indian officers who are also non-political, dedicated to their profession and who are performing their duties impartially. All the senior officers are still British.

The Nationalization Committee submitted its report in 12th May but, due to the impending constitutional changes, it was out of date.

The Adjutant-General, Lt. General R. A. Savory, has issued a personal memorandum to senior officers by name, on 'Communal Harmony Within Units'. It was the result of an investigation to determine the possible effect on the Indian soldier of events likely to test his military loyalty on a strictly non-communal basis.

In this memorandum Savory has advocated maximum possible harmony in a mixed unit and impartiality when called out in aid of the civil power. He maintains that their unblemished conduct will make a healthy impression on the civil population and they will gain their confidence.

He further wants the troops to exercise maximum restraint when on leave in their villages. He hopes they will not get involved in local politics and, whenever possible, will act in bringing about reconciliation among the different communities.

It is said that on 31st May Mountbatten threatened the Quaid that if he did not agree to his plan he would ensure that the boundary in Punjab would be drawn in favour of the Sikhs. The referendum in NWFP will be held under the Provincial Government. He also said that he will hold a referendum in Baluchistan.

June 1947

*'I am sure that under the new arrangements the divided
Indian Army will keep up the great name they have won
for themselves throughout the world.'*

The Auk.

1st June: On return from United Kingdom there is so much to do. The most important task is to catch up with the political currents. Everybody is on edge and talking in whispers. The Auk has not yet seen the details of the Partition Plan.

2nd June: Today has been a crucial day. Mountbatten spelt out the Partition Plan to the leaders. Among those present were Nehru, Patel, Kirpalani,* Baldev, the Quaid and Nishter. Gandhi was called in afterwards.

The Congress and the Sikhs accepted the Plan immediately and in writing. They were already aware of its contents. The Quaid gave his approval verbally.

The Plan is unofficially known as 'The Menon Plan', as everyone knows he drafted it. Any form of a Unitary Government is now out of date, as is the Cabinet Mission Plan. It is said that the disorder and riots in the country brought about a change in the Plan. At the same time Congress has accepted the fact that the 'stubborn Muslims' must be severed completely from Mother India. The Congress was prepared to pay the price, provided Pakistan was not permitted to extend too much. Previously Mountbatten had said that the truncated Pakistan was not in the interest of the Sikhs. But the present Plan is worse. Now the Sikhs will be divided into two which I am sure will lead to bloodshed.

Ambitious civil servants among the Muslims are secretly rejoicing as they feel that, due to the lack of administrative experience in the League hierarchy, they, the civil servants will get an opportunity to rule the country.

Mountbatten wants to appoint Menon as a Governor of a province.

Nehru wants Sir Olaf Caroe, Governor of NWFP, to be removed as he considers him to be taking the side of the League.

*Kirpalani became the President of the Indian National Congress.

Nehru is adamant that Bharat should continue to be called India as he considers himself the successor to the British Raj, while Pakistan, in his words was no more than 'some provinces which may be allowed to opt out of the union of India'. He is against using the term 'division of India'. He claims that his Government should inherit all that the British in India possessed. This obviously means that India will be regarded as a continuing entity from which various provinces have seceded. I am sure that it has the blessing of Mountbatten.

Apparently Mountbatten has prepared a thirty-page paper on the 'Administrative Consequences of Partition'.

Later in the day the League formally accepted the Plan. A story is said to have originated from Mountbatten where he is supposed to have said to Quaid that if he did not accept the Plan he could go to 'hell'. I think that it is complete fabrication. Mountbatten would not dare insult the Quaid in these words. He is frightened of him. The story has probably been circulated to appease Congress and to demonstrate that Mountbatten was all-powerful.

Tuker has asked Ismay to tell Mountbatten that an impartial force, possibly all Gurkhas, be initiated to deal with the disorder which will arise with the partition. Ismay has replied that he knows Nehru will never agree to such a suggestion.

3rd June: In the Durbar Hall of the Viceroy's House, Mountbatten announced the full Partition Plan and thus made it public. The salient points are:

1. Division of the subcontinent into India and Pakistan.
2. Pakistan is to be truncated – on the basis of 'contiguous areas' of population.
3. Referendum in North-West Frontier Province and Assam.
4. Establishment of two Constituent Assemblies if the existing one is not accepted.
5. Division of Armed Forces and assets.
6. Establishment of a Boundary Commission in Punjab and Bengal to demarcate the boundaries on the basis of the contiguous majority areas of Muslims and non-Muslims which will also take into account 'the other factors'.
7. Anticipated date for handing over to be some date in 1947.
8. Independence for the Indian States, but these were advised to accede to one or the other Dominion.
9. Grant of Dominion status to India and Pakistan.

At the same time a Paper on the 'Administrative Consequences of Pakistan' was circulated.

The Partition Plan was simultaneously made public by Attlee in the House of Commons. Mountbatten spoke on the All-India Radio network. He was followed by Nehru, Quaid and Baldev. The Quaid's talk was masterly and in simple language which could be understood by the common man. He ended it with the words *'Pakistan Zindabad'* (Long Live Pakistan). It was the first time that this term was heard over the radio. It was good to hear it. Nehru talked of the great struggle and Baldev had a word of praise for the Armed Forces.

The Police have mutinied in Calcutta.

Having made the Sikhs act as he wanted, Nehru is pleading their cause with the Secretary of State for India. This he is doing with the approval of Mountbatten. Nehru does not want the notional boundary to be treated as an administrative boundary. He insists that the final decision must be left to the Boundary Commission, who should take 'other factors' into consideration. Nehru also wants the North-West Frontier Province to be given independent status.

The British Cabinet has acted so quickly that it has shaken the very foundations of the country. They never consulted the Auk about the partition of the forces. He has been caught in a dilemma, due to the very short time available for doing so. Until now this very important issue has not been considered seriously. This was a grave mistake. Tuker had suggested a long time ago that a plan be prepared in case of such an eventuality arising.

It is not an easy task to bring about a partition of the forces in the middle of political chaos and disorder in the country. Besides, the Auk is facing the after-effects of the Indian National Army trials, the continuous demand for nationalization, and all other problems that follow the end of a war. There are problems such as demobilization, rehabilitation, terms and benefits for the men going out of the service, the reduction and reorganization of the forces for the peacetime Army and the repatriation of the British troops. The troops are getting restive as they have been continuously employed in keeping law and order in the country. At present this is not a palatable job, especially when anti-British feelings are running high and the Congress are encouraging the traitors.

The Auk, the Air C-in-C and F.O.C. RIN and the Principal Staff Officers categorically said that partition of the forces cannot be done in the time available. Mountbatten has overruled them and said that it had to be done, irrespective of the consequences. The Auk's stand is that he wants to hand over a properly organized and efficient Army to each of the Dominions. He believes in an orderly withdrawal and maintains that hasty actions will lead to chaos and anarchy. This will have far-reaching consequences.

Mountbatten is already committed in the eyes of the Muslims to the cause of the Hindus. The Auk is adjudged the only impartial authority but finds himself helpless without the support of the Viceroy.

At the moment law and order depend on the reliability and efficiency of the Army. It is the Auk, and he alone, who holds it together. Otherwise there would be civil war. The Army trusts him and has faith in him. He has so far maintained its morale as a fighting force reasonably unaffected by political or racial loyalties. But for how long can he hold the Army together? Douglas Kay said in the *Daily Mail*, 'If there is anyone who could hold India together, it is the Auk'.

The Auk has the wisdom and the patience of a statesman. As far as possible he has kept out of the politics of the subcontinent. At times he has considered resigning from his job. It is not that he lacks the moral courage to do so, but that he has too great a respect for the Crown. He is too loyal a subject to create further problems for His Majesty's Government. On a few occasions he has stood up to Mountbatten and got his way but invariably he is dictated to by him. Sometimes the Auk has tried to put Mountbatten on the right lines but was unsuccessful as the latter was flowing fast with the tide of events. There was no holding him back.

Mountbatten has the full support of the Cabinet and the Crown. Under these circumstances the Auk can do little. The Cabinet consider the Auk as being old-fashioned and not keeping up with the trends in the country. In actual fact he knows the situation better than the Viceroy or any British minister or civil servant. Mountbatten has considered getting rid of the Auk but due to his great popularity with the Armed Forces he could not afford to do so. Hence he has decided to pressurize him as much as possible. There is no love lost between the two.

4th June: Mountbatten held a Press Conference. Some three hundred journalists from all over the world were present. A Sikh journalist asked him whether he realized that he had divided his community into two halves with most of their assets being in the land which is to be known as Pakistan. Mountbatten replied that the division of the Punjab was at the request of the Sikh community and he had informed their leaders of the consequences. Then the journalist asked him whether it would entail a transfer of population and Mountbatten replied in the negative.

Later, to the utter astonishment of all present, Mountbatten announced 15th August as the date for the transfer of power. It was a bombshell! I wonder what brought this last-minute change? Does he realize its consequences? Why this hurry? Why this shock treatment? What is at the back of it all? Has he got cold feet and is losing control or is he not prepared to shoulder the responsibilities? Why is he bulldozing everything and leaving no time for an organized handover? Does he not realize that things done in such a desperate hurry can lead to chaos, confusion and shambles? Has he not the foresight or has he been caught in a torrent of forces beyond his control? Is he trying to show to the world that he has succeeded in finding a solution and has managed to keep the two States in the Commonwealth? Is he thinking that he should give the political leaders no more time in case they change their minds and have second thoughts?

The pace is unrealistic. I think he is prepared to accept bloodshed and human miseries. Everyone can see the tragedy looming. Strangely enough, Mountbatten does not see it. Maybe he could not care less. One has a feeling that he wants to please his bosses in the United Kingdom and get out before a greater mess is created. Then he can blame all the politicians for the disaster.

So many questions come to my minid. Why this panic? Why this total surrender? Has Mountbatten become chicken-hearted? He says, 'It was dictated by my experience since I arrived in India.' In reality he is a novice in politics and does not know that this is India, where things do not happen in a hurry.

It was obvious to all that, as soon as the principle of partition was decided, the Army and the Police will be needed to prevent disorder. The Intelligence agencies had already warned against this danger. At least one year would be needed to reconstitute the independent armies and the police forces of the two Dominions and get them functioning as separate and effective entities. The Army Commanders want the date postponed. Even some thinking politicians would have agreed. Mountbatten has refused.

I can foresee the result. The trouble-makers will start arming themselves, the British officers will lose interest, the administration will become ineffective, and general confusion will prevail.

Two States are to be born in 77 days from now. There is no such parallel in history. This is sheer irresponsibility. It will lead to the most stupendous explosion. Mountbatten will never live it down.

Wavell as Viceroy would never have agreed to a change of the date. Mountbatten is impetuous and a hustler and gives decisions on the spot. He possesses incurable optimism and is over-sensitive to criticism which hurts his vanity. This is his weakest point. He is not prepared to listen. Thank God that he will not be able to say 'This mad Pakistan idea' any more.

There is communal trouble everywhere. It is likely to accelerate. What form it will ultimately take cannot be predicted. Jenkins, the Governor of Punjab, has sent hair-raising reports of the disorders which may follow. Mountbatten is paying no attention to them. Communal emotions and tension are rising and this will ultimately affect the Army on which Mountbatten is relying. He expects the Auk to keep it under control. There is a limit.

Mountbatten is making things very difficult for the British officers. They are losing control and want to quit. There is already tension between Muslim, Hindu and Sikh officers. The Muslims do not feel safe now in Bharat and vice versa. All hopes are centred on the British troops keeping law and order. I wonder if they will be used!

Mountbatten has also issued a tear-off calendar indicating the days left for the partition. This really is a juvenile act!

The announcement of the Plan has put GHQ in top gear. The task before them is a nightmare. Auk has slipped up but the fault also lies with Mountbatten. He never really took Auk into his confidence, nor did he give him any information in advance. However, the Auk is going to try his level best to reconstitute the two Armed Forces as it may well be his last service to the Army in India and the greatest.

There are many officers who still think that the British are not going to quit, and that the Plan is some sort of a trap. Colonel Thaper,* who is commanding the 1st Punjab, asked me whether the British were really leaving, or was the present announcement part of a cover plan to prolong their stay.

The Sikhs have accepted the Plan by and large. God knows why they are satisfied. They are the worst hit. All their rich agricultural land and property is in West Punjab which will be Pakistan. They have little in India. It serves them right for casting their lot with the Congress. As I have always felt, they act first and then think. They could have had a semi-independent state of their own if they had played their cards well.

When Mountbatten announced his Plan, the Sikhs promptly perfected their Plan for revenge. They are now encouraged by the fact that the Boundary Commission, when demarcating the line, will take 'other factors' into account. The introduction of these two words was purposely left vague to accommodate any future demands of the Congress and the Sikhs and to raise their hopes regarding the settlement of any subsequent problem that may arise. This was a dirty and dishonest trick. The accepted basis for partition was 'predominantly' by area populated by a community. It has raised their hopes that the future boundary may run along the River Chenab. British politicians and Major Short's ill-advised utterances have also given false hopes to the Sikhs. Short had been introduced to Mountbatten by Cripps as the authority on Sikh affairs.

Fooled and deceived by the Congress, the Sikhs are left with no option but to take the law into their own hands. Led by their warrior class and assisted by their leaders, they have organized themselves into *jathas* (groups). They have adopted force and terror tactics. They are now preparing their followers physically and psychologically for the brutalities to be inflicted on the Muslims. The Congress High Command is encouraging them and calls them the 'sword arm of the Congress'. In reality they want the Sikhs to destroy themselves as a separate effective community which may at some stage become a source of trouble to them. At the same time this would weaken Pakistan by creating problems connected with the migration of population. The Sikhs were the first to start the mass migration, going into the areas that would be part of Bharat.

Mountbatten at no stage encouraged the Sikhs to come to a settlement with the Muslim League which would have partially avoided the massacre.

*Thaper became the head of the Indian Army.

In fact he encouraged them to stay with the Congress to earn their goodwill. When the Sikhs became violent he arrested none.

Quaid was satisfied with a truncated Pakistan which he preferred to any fettered and unwieldy block.

Initially Gandhi was against Partition but later advised the Congress to accept the Plan. Nehru wanted power at any cost and as quickly as possible. Patel was the realist and was prepared for the Partition lest the British had an excuse for prolonging their rule. However, every Hindu hoped and prayed that Pakistan would not become economically viable, would remain politically weak and strategically unsound and finally collapse and be compelled to re-unite with India.

The Hindu officers of the Armed Forces make no bones about it. They say that India is very strong militarily and could dismember Pakistan whenever they want.

The Communists are very sorry at the division.

Attlee has been shouting from the rooftops that the Plan is a great success.

Lord Beaverbrook has said that 'the Plan is too late to save the massacre'.

Mountbatten addressed the members of the State Negotiating Committee. The Princes are in a pathetic condition and completely demoralized. He told them that the paramountcy would lapse and they would be free to determine their own future. This is their end and all their treaties with His Majesty's Government have gone by the board. They were told to behave, toe his line and forget the past or face the consequences. Bhopal resigned as the Chancellor of the Chamber of Princes.

The Daily Tribune commented on the Plan thus: 'Our motherland is to be dismembered . . . the Plan offers no permanent solution . . . today is the saddest day in our history . . . the Frontier Province could be joined to India through Kashmir . . . HMG would have taken a different line if we had proclaimed to remain in the Commonwealth right from the start'. It further called the Quaid 'the Fuhrer' and the League 'Jinnahites' and that 'they will have nothing but a truncated mutilated and moth-eaten Pakistan.' And finally 'the Sikhs will appeal to cold steel'.

Apparently it is said that Kiran Shankor Roy, the leader of the Congress Party in Bengal, told Suherwardy that the Congress High Command was not in favour of an independent Bengal. Thereupon Suherwardy suggested that Calcutta should get the status of a free port and be placed under the joint control of the two Dominions.

In the Viceregal circle there is a feeling that after partition the two states will have stronger bonds between them and work together like one unit. They will have a common Governor-General, a joint defence policy, a joint economic policy and will co-operate in all other matters. Of course they will both stay as members of the Commonwealth which will make all easy. What wishful thinking! What ignorance! Mountbatten should have studied the history of the subcontinent.

5th June: Mountbatten discussed with the leaders the administrative consequences of Partition.

When Mountbatten returned from the United Kingdom he told the Quaid that the appointment of a supreme arbitrator was considered by His Majesty's Government. They were of the opinion that it was unconstitutional and unworkable.

Mountbatten has told his staff that he cannot stay as Governor-General of India alone; he even mentioned that he will be ineffective as Chairman of any Committee of the two Dominions after 15th August.

6th June: The Auk has sent a paper on the splitting of the Armed Forces to His Majesty's Government. In this he stated that it would take some three years to split the Army. During this period a central authority would have to be maintained and all British officers retained. This was considered by the Committee in London at which Savory represented India. No decision was taken.

The Auk asked whether I would like to take up the appointment of the Military Attaché in Washington. I replied that at this juncture it was difficult for me to leave the subcontinent as I had my old mother and the family to look after. The Auk insisted that if I changed my mind I could come back. Whereupon I agreed, but rather reluctantly. My name was submitted by the C-in-C to Pandit Nehru, the Minister for Foreign Affairs, for approval. This was supposed to be only a formality. Nehru wrote on the file that he could not agree to my appointment. He said that Kaul should be sent instead. The Auk was very angry indeed. He said that he was going to make an issue of this case, but that if his advice was not taken he was quite prepared to resign. I told him that, in the first instance, I was not keen to go and, secondly, my case was too small to be made into an issue. The Auk maintained that the selection he made as C-in-C was final and should not, under any circumstances, have been questioned.

Later Asif Ali, who had been appointed Indian Ambassador to the USA, approached me to say that he was prepared to put in my nomination as his Military Secretary and would write to Nehru as well. I told him that I was not interested.

8th June: Everything is moving so fast that it is difficult to keep track of things. Everyone is in a spin. There is no time to relax.

Gandhi has condemned the British in no uncertain terms. He said that they would be responsible for any calamity which takes places in the subcontinent. Jai Parkash Narain, the socialist, has made up with Nehru and is speaking the same language. Mountbatten is in a carefree and happy mood. States like Travancore, Hyderabad and Kashmir are very concerned about their future. Communal disturbances in the Punjab continue. The Meo tribesmen in Gurgaon are up in arms against the Congress. There was a proper battle and troops had to be sent to restore order.

Nehru has upset the British officers by accusing them of being unable to control the rioting, yet they did it successfully during the civil disobedience movement against the British. Of course the answer is that they are not now sure of the support and backing of the Provincial Governments. There has been mass killing of the Muslims in Garhmuktesar in United Provinces.

The press is clamouring for rapid nationalization of the Armed Forces. At this stage there is a great deal of speculation as to who would become the C-in-C of the two Dominions. The Muslims are hoping that General Sir Francis Tuker would become the C-in-C of the Pakistan Army. However, the Auk has selected General Sir Frank Messervy. He is an able commander but wants to retire and look after his growing family. Tuker on the other hand is a visionary, a planner of the highest order, a soldier of great distinction, a man with convictions and above all he is very fond of Muslim officers and men. I wish that he had been appointed C-in-C. I told the Auk how I felt.

The maintenance of law and order throughout the subcontinent is becoming a problem. There is a great demand for British troops from the provinces.

9th June: There was meeting after meeting. General Whistler called. In order to get away from everything, even for a short while and to keep sane, the Auk and I went out fishing in the afternoon.

The Khaksars* demonstrated outside the Imperial Hotel where the Quaid was holding a meeting. They created some trouble.

10th June: The Meo Rebellion against the Hindu oppressors is taking a serious turn. The Meos are demanding that the British troops should be sent to keep law and order.

The Armed Forces Nationalization Committee has submitted its findings. It was examined by the C-in-C Committee, and the Branches and Directorates have been asked to examine its implications and submit a report.

The Committee has highlighted the great shortage of experienced officers on the staff and in the technical corps and services and pointed out that it would take many years to train them and suggest ways and means of doing so.

Nawab Ismail Khan agreed with the findings but said in his note of dissent:

> The revised plans submitted to the Committee by the Chiefs of the three Services (Army, Navy and Air Force) were prepared by them after

*The Khaksars were a militant Muslim organization.

the announcement was made by Mr Attlee, the British Prime Minister, in the House of Commons, in February of this year that it was the definite intention of His Majesty's Government to transfer power completely to responsible Indian hands by June, 1948. The authors of the plans, in outlining their scheme of nationalization, have assumed that the Armed Forces will remain as they are under the control of some kind of Central Government. They have not taken another equally vital and important part of this announcement into consideration in which it is stated explicitly that, if the conditions obtaining in the country continue, transfer of power will be made to more than one Indian Sovereign State, which clearly indicates partition of the country and, in consequence, involves the division of the Armed Forces. These plans therefore must be recast and modified to accomplish the division of the Armed Forces in as smooth and efficient a manner as the circumstances permit. It is proposed in these schemes that a certain number of suitable Indian officers should be selected for the highest commands and senior staff appointments advancing progressively through intermediate appointments. In giving effect to this proposal I trust that a sufficient number of Muslim officers will also be put through this special training in order to fit them to hold these high appointments in the Armed Forces of their State. As has been remarked in the preamble of this report a decision on the question of partition of India appears to be imminent. I would therefore urge upon the Government to direct the Chiefs of the three Services to apply their minds seriously to this task of the division of Armed Forces. The division of the Armed Forces cannot, in my opinion, retard nationalization, as some of my colleagues apprehend. I may add that as far as the replacement of the non-Indian element in the Armed Forces by Indian personnel is concerned, I am in full agreement with their views.

In the context of the present situation the note was an exercise in futility. Had it been produced earlier it would have served a useful purpose. Now it is not a question of 'nationalization' but 'super-nationalization'. Some officers, including myself, were asked to reply to a questionnaire which was issued by the committee. Not knowing the postwar size and strength of the Army and the finances available, it could hardly be tackled. I said so in my reply, and also said that nationalization must not be at the expense of efficiency. Knowing the limitations of Kaul, its Secretary, one did not expect a realistic and a purposeful approach. Sam Manekshaw* wanted to glamorize the Army and put them in the uniforms of the Middle Ages.

11th June: A Committee of the Cabinet has been set up to examine the Memorandum – 'The Administrative Consequences of Partition'.

---

*Sam Manekshaw, a Parsi, was later created a Field-Marshal in the Indian Army.

Mountbatten is the Chairman with Patel, Rajendra Prasad, Liaquat and Nishter as its members.

The Viceroy has set up a Partition Council to divide the personnel, assets and liabilities between the two Dominions.

The Partition Council has appointed a Steering Committee with H. M. Patel and Mohammad Ali as its members. A Partition Secretariat has been established. To assist its working ten Expert Committees have been formed, each dealing with a group of subjects. There are also Departmental Committees to assist the Expert Committees.

The most important Expert Committee is the 'Armed Forces Reconstruction Committee'. This is under the Auk with C-in-C Navy and Air Force, Chief of the General Staff and G. S. Bhalja (Additional Defence Secretary) as its members. There are four sub-committees – Army, Navy, Air Force and one dealing with the financial aspect of the divisions.

The Auk has been designated as the future Supreme Commander and will work under the Joint Defence Council. This will be chaired by Mountbatten. It will have no operational control over the forces of the two Dominions except the Boundary Force.

The Supreme Commander will be responsible to the two Dominions through the Joint Defence Council. He will be responsible for ensuring the correct division of the Armed Forces' assets between the two. This will be completed by 1st April, 1948. In the case of British troops in India, he will be directly responsible to His Majesty's Goverment.

The transfer of troops will be carried out in two stages. The first stage will cater for the move of the Muslim majority units to Pakistan and the second for combing the mixed units for Muslim personnel.

Demobilization has been stopped.

It must be mentioned here that the Quaid is not in favour of the communal division of the forces. He maintains that the basis should be 'citizenship' and the individuals left to opt as they wish, except that a Muslim from Pakistan would not be allowed to serve in India and vice versa. Some senior officers of both Dominions are going round advocating that the Armed Forces should not be partitioned and their joint control is a practical proposition. What imagination!

Here, in all fairness to the Auk, it must be mentioned that he was initially opposed to the partition of the forces, but once the 'political decision' was taken he has wholeheartedly accepted the task assigned to him. The division of assets will not be an easy assignment. Pakistan is due one third of the stores, that is some 170,000 tons. Besides there are 16 Ordnance Factories in India to be divided, two of them are lying packed in crates. There are several workshops, laboratories, etc. to be divided as well.

All the Armed Forces Headquarters are in Delhi and will naturally be dominated and influenced by Indian thinking.

The Auk prepared a paper for the Armed Forces Reconstitution Committee and the Joint Defence Council on the employment and retention of British officers in the two Dominions. In this connection he sent the following letter to Ismay:

I cannot stress too strongly my conviction that the success of any Plan for the division of the Indian Armed Forces depends on the willing cooperation of the British officers now serving with them, the great majority of whom it will be essential to retain during the process of reconstitution. The goodwill of British officers is more likely to be secured if the Partition Committee – on behalf of the future Governments of Hindustan and Pakistan – openly state that the services of British officers are essential to the success of reconstitution, notwithstanding the 'Quit India' cry of the past, and request them to remain in positions of command and on the staff during the period of reconstitution of the Armed Forces. I hope that this may be done, as I am not at all certain in my own mind that the requisite number of British officers will wish to stay on, and I am most strongly opposed to the application of any form of compulsion to them.

In the afternoon the Auk saw the Viceroy and tried to persuade him to allow the employment of the British troops in aid of the Civil Power. The Auk pointed out that, at a previous meeting, Mountbatten had stated that they could be used as the last reserve.

Mountbatten did not agree and thinks that it might give the impression that His Majesty's Government is trying to re-establish its authority and prolong British rule.

12th June: Mountbatten had a small dinner party around the swimming pool at Viceregal lodge. My wife and I were invited among others. He looked agitated. I asked one of his staff the reason and was told that Mountbatten wants to stay as Governor-General of both the Dominions, failing which he would resign. The wife of the American Military Attaché who was in the party asked Mountbatten, 'How is the Partition getting on?' There was pin-drop silence and he only smiled in reply.

Edwina Mountbatten asked me to look at some Persian carpets which were in the house. She intends buying them. After dinner I was paraded into the house to give my opinion. I do not know who could have told her that I knew something about carpets. Frankly I do not know what Nehru finds in her.

There was a Cabinet Meeting and I am told that it was a stormy one. The League took exception to the appointments being made by Nehru in the Diplomatic Corps. Nehru said that he would not tolerate any interference by the League in the working of his Ministry.

14th June: Congress endorsed the 3rd June Plan. Azad is very disappointed, while Patel is happy at the amputation of the 'diseased limb'. The Congress on the whole feel that a part of *'Akhand Bharat'** has been taken away from them. The Sikhs want a 'Sikh State' and the Frontier Congressmen a 'Pakistan State'. The Auk saw Mountbatten later.

16th June: A new Policy has been evolved by the C-in-C which deals with the evacuation of the British personnel from the subcontinent under the worst possible conditions. These are when both the Dominions may find themselves unable to maintain law and order. It is proposed to recommend to His Majesty's Government that the British troops should be retained after Partition, until 1st January, 1948, as an insurance to cover the initial stages of reconstitution, as well as to ensure the safety of British lives. They should also be retained to meet any trouble on the Frontier. Besides, their presence will act as a stabilizing factor until the reconstitution is completed. In case the Dominions do not make a request for their retention, then His Majesty's Government must remain firm about their staying on. In this case the British forces will take their orders from the C-in-C only, and an all-British chain of command would be established, including an 'all-British' signal communication system. However, the British troops would not be employed for putting down communal disturbances. This was submitted to the Viceroy.

There are rumours that the present Government would be divided into two, one for India and the other for Pakistan, so that they could further the interest of their countries.

18th June: Ismay wrote back to the Auk that Mountbatten does not agree with the C-in-C's 'New Policy' and ordered that the evacuation of the British forces should be carried out as speedily as possible after 15th August. This should be done unless the Dominions requested their retention. He said that a handful of British troops could do little. However, Mountbatten ignored the fact that there was the equivalent of three British Divisions in India. He was guided by Nehru's statement: 'I would sooner have every village in India put to flame than to keep the British troops after 15th August.'

19th June: Mountbatten has ordered that the British High Commissioner in India should be kept informed of all matters secretly and special information to HMG should be channelled through him. No classified information is to be supplied to India until the negotiations on the defence of the subcontinent are completed. To my mind these are pressure tactics to ensure that the two countries stay in the Commonwealth.

Under Nehru's instructions Mountbatten left for Kashmir to pressurize

*Greater India.

the Maharajah to throw in his lot with India. Pandit Kak,* the Prime Minister of Kashmir, is very upset and disturbed by this visit.

The Auk saw Baldev Singh. Incidentally Baldev Singh is a big industrialist in his own right but has little influence in the Sikh community. However, the Sikhs use him to achieve their ends. It is said that a visitor to his house wanted to telephone a friend and asked for the directory. Baldev Singh was the 'Director' of several companies but not being well versed in the English language thought that probably a Director's wife was called a Directory. He promptly replied that the Directory had gone to the village!

Lord Ismay called on the Auk to pacify him. He was furious at Mountbatten's comments on his 'New Policy'.

At the weekly conference the C-in-C said that the Armed Forces Reconstitution Committee (AFRC) and its three sub-committees are being formed. The Army sub-committee will be under Major-General S. R. Irwin, the Naval under Commodore Jefford† and the Air under AVM Perry-Keene.‡ The C-in-C said that the 'work must be tackled with resolution and impartiality and the sooner the better'. The reconstitution will be on a territorial basis.

The C-in-C wants the 5000 Polish refugees to be removed from India. He also said that no orders will be passed by GHQ which would affect adversely the successor Governments.

The C-in-C remarked that the Armed Forces were becoming a target of attack in the Press and that the Director of Information and Morale, Brigadier Rudra, must contradict false reports.

He also said the Partition of the Armed Forces was in the offing. He was preparing a plan accordingly, so that it would be carried out impartially, logically and without rancour. Everyone must ensure that welfare, morale and discipline is not impaired.

The plans for accelerated nationalization were suspended.

20th June: Repeated efforts are being made by Mountbatten's staff to ascertain from the Quaid whether he would accept a common Governor-General. Ismay saw Liaquat but could not get an answer.

The C-in-C wrote the following letter to Ismay:

My dear Ismay,
   Thank you for your letter of the 18th June about the withdrawal of the British Forces from India.

---

*Pandit Kak wanted Kashmir to join Pakistan and was hated by Nehru.

†Vice-Admiral James Jefford (1914–76) became Flag Officer commanding Royal Pakistan Navy on the inception of Pakistan in 1947; Vice-Admiral Royal Pakistan Navy 1953.

‡Air-Vice Marshal Allan Perry-Keene (b. 1898) was Air Officer i/c Air Administration, Air HQ, India, 1946; Air Commander Royal Pakistan Air Force, 1947–49.

My paper COS (44) 29B was submitted to the Viceroy in response to a request from him for my view on this subject. The paper represents my opinion as the Viceroy's adviser on all military matters and was naturally written from the general military point of view. As Commander-in-Chief in India, one of my responsibilities is the maintenance of law and order when so required by the civil authorities.

I adhere to the advice I gave in the paper under reference but realize of course that the Viceroy has every right to disregard it for overriding political considerations. That is solely his responsibility and it is not my business to comment on his decision. It is my duty to accept it and I do accept it.

I have no data at my disposal to confirm your statement in the third paragraph of your letter that the number of British nationals desiring to leave India is likely to be relatively small and that they can be got away in the next two months. If this is so, then so much the better, as my responsibility in this matter would be considerably lightened.

I am afraid I cannot agree with your opinion that the 'handful of British troops' that might remain in this country could do very little to safeguard British lives as a whole. My considered opinion, in which my advisers support me, is that even small forces of British troops at, say, Calcutta, Bombay, Delhi and Karachi might make all the difference should the tide of feeling in the country take an anti-British or anti-European turn. I agree that they could do little to protect individual Europeans in country districts, but the bulk of Europeans are concentrated in the larger seaports and towns.

I request that this opinion may be recorded and conveyed to His Majesty's Government in the representations that the Viceroy is going to make on the subject, as I feel that it would give His Majesty's Goverment a wrong impression if we were to say that they could do very little. It all depends on circumstances prevailing at the time, of course, but the above is my opinion given as military adviser to the Viceroy.

I must, in justice to myself and in pursuance of my duty as military adviser to the Viceroy, point out that on the withdrawal of British troops the instrument on which the civil authorities will be able to rely for the protection of British and European lives against mob violence will be the Indian Army. That Army will soon be involved in the process of reconstitution during which the majority of its units will not be capable of rendering armed assistance to the civil power even if the Indian officers and men composing them were willing to carry out these duties for the protection of Europeans, which I cannot in any way guarantee.

In order to carry out the reconstitution of the Army in an orderly and logical way, the very large number of units now distributed in small detachments all over Northern India on internal security duties will have to be recalled to undergo reconstitution. Also for the next six months and more there will be a continuous movement and cross-transfer of units between Pakistan and 'India' which will virtually immobilize the units involved for the time being .

Moreover, I cannot state with any certainty that, during this process of reconstitution, the Army will retain its cohesion or remain a reliable instrument for use to aid the civil power in the event of widespread disturbances.

I have dwelt on this aspect of the situation at some length as I wish to make it clear to the Viceroy, and through him to His Majesty's Government, that if I am to remain, as I understand is proposed, in central control of the Armed Forces during the process of their constitution, I can no longer be responsible in grave emergency for the protection of British lives and property should these be threatened, once the British forces have been withdrawn.

I hope that no such need will arise, but it may, and, should this happen, it is essential that the position, in respect of the Indian Armed Forces and as it affects myself and my subordinate commanders, should be clearly understood by His Majesty's Government.

I should very much like to discuss the whole question with you before the Viceroy returns to Delhi.

Yours sincerely,

Claude Auchinleck

P.S. We talked of this last night but should you wish to discuss the matter further I am at your disposal – as always!

23rd June: In the middle of the upheaval Field-Marshal Lord Montgomery dropped in out of the sky! There is enough to do without having him around. He has increased the worries of the Auk. Montgomery has no idea of the present situation in India and that he is visiting a country which is undergoing great change, in fact passing through very difficult times.

Monty and the Auk discussed the withdrawal of British troops from India. Shipping is the real bottleneck. It was decided that their withdrawal should be phased over a period of six months from the date of transfer of power. The use of British troops for internal security duties was also discussed. Mountbatten has been pressurized from all quarters that they must be available. But he would rather see a bloodbath than make use of them. In this Mountbatten wants Monty to support him, who, not knowing anything about the seriousness of the situation, has agreed.

They all seem to be frightened and think that the heavens would fall in if British troops are used. It is not a question of the reimposition of British rule in India but of saving human lives. The British have always stood by the downtrodden and invariably taken up their cause and come to their assistance. But at the present moment massacres are taking place while British troops sit and watch. It is quite contrary to the British way of thinking, and the British character. They will never live it down. History will catch up with them and the events of 1857 will fade into oblivion.

Mountbatten, and Mountbatten alone, will have the blood of all these innocent people on his hands. He will have to pay for it some day. His actions will lead to a black page in the history of the British Empire.

Mountbatten is not going to use British troops as part of the boundary force. This, I am positive, both Dominions would welcome. What a tragedy. I also blame Monty for agreeing with Mountbatten and not consulting the Auk or getting his views on the subject.

Monty has succeeded in getting the agreement signed by His Majesty's Government on the use of the Gurkha troops.

The Quaid saw Mountbatten. The latter again stressed the desirability of having a common Governor-General. If not then the question was who should be the Governor-General of Pakistan. Quaid told him that he would let him know.

Kak, the Prime Minister of Kashmir, dined with us. He told me that he is in favour of Kashmir joining Pakistan but Mountbatten is applying pressure on the Maharajah to accede to India.

There was a case of stone-throwing at Nehru's car when he toured Malakand some time ago. Because of this Mahbub Ali, the then Political Agent, had been suspended. Mr Justice Clarke was appointed to enquire into the case and exonerated Mahbub Ali. He came to tell Auk all about it. At the same time he has torn Abdul Ghaffar Khan to shreds and exposed him as a dealer in false coins. Even Dr Khan Sahib does not come off much better.

The Governor of North-West Frontier Province is of the opinion that the orders of suspension against Mahbub Ali should be withdrawn and that he should be reinstated. He said that if any other charges are made against him it will look very like a case of victimization. A possible line could be to let him retire after reinstatement but this will not please Pandit Nehru. The Governor blames the External Affairs Department of trying to have Mahbub Ali Khan on another charge, that of having connived at the forcible conversion of certain Hindus in his village. The Governor said that a magisterial enquiry was conducted and the allegations were proved completely false. He was of the opinion that the Ministry has been vindictive.

The Governor went on to say that most of the trouble started when Nehru took over tribal affairs. This he followed with his ill-conceived visit to the Frontier. All friction and tension started from this date. He said that the tribes will never accept a Hindu.

Nehru was deeply interested in getting Mahbub Ali convicted by fair or foul means. But as Mahbub belonged to the Political Service, which is subject to the rule-making control of the Secretary of State, he could not achieve his end. The whole case remains undecided.

The Quaid has told Mountbatten in no uncertain terms that he must have a Pakistan Army ready by 15th August. There must be an operational C-in-C by that date as well, who could take his orders from the Government of Pakistan. Thereupon the Viceroy said that for administrative matters both armies should continue to be under the Field-Marshal.

Mountbatten has been saying that the Quaid has no faith in the C-in-C. This is to malign him and to give the impression that he, Mountbatten, is the only one who is trusted by all the communities. The Auk admires the Quaid for his tenacity, character and his forthright ways, though he maintains that at times the Quaid could be difficult.

The Punjab Legislative Assembly had a meeting where all the Muslim members voted against the partition of the Punjab while the Sikhs and Hindus were for it.

24th June: The terms of retirement which have been given to the British officers and to the Governors are considered extravagant by all.

The Quaid and Mountbatten met and discussed the withdrawal of British troops which is to begin on 15th August. The Quaid was anxious that the withdrawal should not be a hasty one, especially in view of the fact that trouble could erupt at any time. Quaid wants the British officers to serve in the Pakistan Army until they could be replaced by the Pakistanis. Mountbatten said that this depended on the terms and conditions which Pakistan would offer to them.

Mountbatten has suggested to His Majesty's Government that General Whistler's designation should be changed from that of 'Adviser' to the present C-in-C to one of Commander. He asked His Majesty's Government to lay down clear-cut rules as to the employment and use of British troops in the event of widespread disturbances threatening British life and property.

Monty at this stage has complicated many issues concerning the employment of British troops by taking unilateral actions and not letting them go through the normal channels. Ismay is furious.

Monty did not give a clear picture of his various talks with the leaders and it was feared that he might have committed His Majesty's Government in some respect which would disturb the plan of withdrawal. Monty said that he found Nehru easy to deal with, while the Quaid was tense, distrusted the Hindus and did not like the C-in-C. He also mentioned that Mountbatten was in the pocket of Nehru.

The Auk has told Monty in no uncertain terms that, while he agreed to General Whistler becoming the GOC British troops in India, the responsibility for implementing the decision rested with him and not with the Chief of the Imperial General Staff. The Auk has to decide on the size of the staff, the exact power of command, etc. and suggested that no executive action should be taken by CIGS until officially requested by the Government of India. Monty as usual is throwing his weight about and making things difficult.

25th June: Thank goodness Monty has left today. He has a knack of creating problems out of nothing. He hates any one who has served in the Indian Army. Auk thinks that he is a 'silly man'. Even Ismay thinks likewise. We all have heaved a sigh of relief.

Trivedi,* the ex-Defence Secretary, has arrived to assist the AFRC in its deliberations. He is trusted by Auk but I think that he plays a double role. Choudhry Mohammad Ali came to clear some points with the Auk.

The Quaid met the Viceroy and told him that he must be utterly ruthless in suppressing the trouble in Lahore and Amritsar.

Nehru has suggested that Martial Law should be declared in Lahore, Amritsar and other areas, and the whole operation should be handed over to the military. The troops should be ordered to shoot at sight and the Police withdrawn.

After a discussion with General Bruce,† the GOC, the Governor of Punjab came to the conclusion that he was against the introduction of Martial Law. He maintains that the trouble in Lahore and Amritsar is not rioting but continuous and widespread cloak-and-dagger activities. General Bruce is of the opinion that the imposition of Martial Law would make no difference as it could not be operated without the police. This was very inadequate. Besides, if Martial Law is declared, then it is imperative that the troops must be effective immediately; otherwise they may land themselves in a very difficult situation. He, therefore, maintains that Martial Law is not the answer. He said that they have improved their intelligence set-up and may within reasonable time get information about the organizations behind the outrages. Then pressure must be brought to bear on the people who are supporting the destructive elements and, if need be, they should be imprisoned.

26th June: There was a Cabinet meeting. Nehru attacked Mountbatten for not keeping law and order in the country. He wants the Governors and senior civil servants concerned to be sacked.

Baldev has ordered that there will be no move of machinery, stores and equipment during the reconstitution of the armies. This is bad. I think he is full of evil intentions.

A questionnaire has been issued to officers asking them which Dominion they would like to serve.

Orders have been issued that India Command Joint Operation instructions No. 2 'Madhouse' is to be destroyed.

---

*Trivedi was a civil servant and later became Governor of Orissa.

†Major-General John Geoffrey Bruce (1896–1942) was Deputy Director of Military Operations India 1941–42; Deputy CGS, Indian Army 1942–46; GOC Lahore District 1946–47.

The British troops are to start moving out on 15th August.

The Punjab Boundary Commission has been constituted.

27th June: The committee of the Cabinet, which was previously called the Partition Committee, is now to be known as the Partition Council. Mountbatten is the Chairman. The members are Patel, Rajendra Prashad, the Quaid and Liaquat. Rajagopalachari and Nishter are alternate members. Trivedi has been inducted in the Council. The first key plan for the partition of the Army has been prepared by a committee consisting of Arthur Smith, Wood, Irwin and Savory.

The C-in-C ordered that minutes of his weekly conference should also be sent to the Principal Staff Officer at the India Office and to the Army Commanders.

28th June: His Highness Jodhpur, an Honorary Air Marshal in the RIAF, called. Last time I met him, along with the Nawab of Bophal, was at an evening reception which I gave in their honour when I was an Instructor in Quetta. They both came early in the evening but did not leave till very late. We had to produce supper for them. Jodhpur is a blue-blooded Rajput and a great gentleman, but will some day drink himself to death. This will be in keeping with his family tradition.

It had been decided to ask Sir Cyril Radcliffe* to be the Head of the Punjab and Bengal Boundary Commissions. I think that it is a great mistake, as he can be influenced by Mountbatten. It would have been far better to have selected a man who came from a country outside the Commonwealth. I told the Quaid so but he said that he had already agreed to the nomination.

29th June: Altaf Hussain,† the Editor of *Dawn*, has been writing some very good articles but they are not relished by Mountbatten. Ismay told Auk that Mountbatten has received a very rude letter from the Quaid.

30th June: The Partition Council met under the chairmanship of the Viceroy to consider the reconstitution of the Armed Forces. Patel and Rajendra Prashad represented the Congress and the Quaid and Liaquat the League. Baldev and the C-in-C were also present. Trivedi, the Governor of Orissa, was also present as a consultant.

The Partition Council laid down the general principles which would govern the reconstitution of the Armed Forces. They were:

---

*Cyril John, 1st Viscount Radcliffe (1899–1977) was raised to the peerage as a Baron 1949; created Viscount 1962; Director-General Ministry of Information 1941–45; Punjab and Bengal Boundary Commissions 1947.

†Altaf Hussain was a brilliant journalist and later became a Minister of the Government of Pakistan.

a) India and Pakistan will have the operational control of their forces from 15th August onward, which will be predominantly composed of non-Muslims and Muslims respectively and which, after 15th August, will be reconstituted predominantly on a territorial basis.

b) The Heads of the three Services should be appointed as soon as possible, and would be directly responsible to their own Head of State.

c) All the existing Armed Forces of India will remain under a single administrative control until sorted out into two distinct forces and the two Governments are in a position to administer them.

d) Until this is achieved they will remain under the administrative control of the present C-in-C in India who in his turn will be under the Joint Defence Council. The Council will consist of Governor-General or Governors-General, the two Defence Ministers and the Supreme Commander. However, the Defence Ministers may be accompanied to the meeting by one other Minister and experts.

e) In order to avoid confusion the existing C-in-C will be entitled 'Supreme Commander' with effect from 15th August until his work is completed. He will have no responsibility for law and order, nor will he have any operational control over any unit save those in transit from one Dominion to another, nor will he have any power to move troops within the borders of either Dominions.

f) The Partition of the Forces will be in two stages. The first one will be more or less rough and ready division of the existing Forces on a communal basis and the Plan should be prepared forthwith. The next phase will be to comb out the units themselves on the basis of voluntary transfers. However, there will be an exception – the Muslims from Pakistan now serving in the Indian Armed Forces will not have the option to join the Armed Forces of the Indian Union and similarly a non-Muslim from the rest of India now serving in the Armed forces would not have the option to join the Armed Forces of Pakistan.

Every effort will be made to complete the reconstitution of units and provide each Dominion with its own administrative and maintenance services for its own Armed Forces by 1st April, 1948, after which no central administrative control will exist. However, the two Governments may agree to share some administrative or training establishment. As soon as the central administrative control is dispensed with the Government will be free to organize their forces as they think best.

The Partition Council decided to set up an Armed Forces Reconstitution Committee under the Chairmanship of the C-in-C.

Violence has broken out in Punjab.

Patel is adamant that out of the eight printing presses with the Govenment of India none should be given to Pakistan, as they are required by him.

Nehru wants Corfield,* the Political Secretary, to be sacked and disgraced as he considers him an enemy of India. Nehru has taken away the State Department from him, and has placed it under V. P. Menon with Patel as its Minister. Mountbatten, Gandhi and Nehru are contemplating a visit to Kashmir.

*Sir Conrad Laurence Corfield (1893–1980) joined the ICS 1920; Resident for the Punjab States 1941–45; Political Adviser to the Viceroy as Crown Representative 1945–47.

July 1947

'A proper reorganization of the Army will take years.'
The Auk.

1st July: I have had a great deal of time to study Mountbatten. My observations are that Mountbatten is a human dynamo with unbounded energy, optimism and courage. He is a good organizer and has the German streak of being thorough in him. At times he can be quite ruthless as well. He possesses a sharp mind and is quick to spot the cracks in any discussion. He gets the best out of his staff by making them feel that they are his partners. He picks their brains and the ideas they produce he calls his 'intuitions' and 'flashes'. He believes that one man can do all the planning. By this he means himself. Often he is two steps ahead of his staff. On many occasions Ismay is known to have disagreed with him but to no effect. The Auk's opinion does not count; it is brushed aside. Ismay is used to calm him down. For his conferences he checks the minutes meticulously and changes them invariably when it does not suit him. His records of interviews are not always circulated among his staff. When a draft is to be prepared he changes it many times. He does not realize what he really wants until his staff sets it up. He seldom drafts himself; probably he cannot do it. His staff says that he is not clear in his own thoughts.

However, Mountbatten is egoistic and impetuous. These traits of his character often lead him astray. He does not stand on formalities when it suits his purpose, and is capable of charming and humouring people. This is often overdone. Mountbatten excels in the art of public speaking. In fact because of his mastery over words he is capable of making a speech without saying anything concrete. He is trying to follow in the footsteps of Lord Curzon. Perhaps he has his eye on higher appointments. He never lets people forget that he belongs to Royalty and uses these connections to impress all those around, especially the Princes. He often works on his family tree, filling it in and keeping it up-to-date.

Mountbatten has many sides to him. He is conceited and cannot tolerate criticism. In fact he pays little attention to other people's opinion. He lacks sincerity of purpose and because of this all his actions seem artificial. Ambition is one of the salient features of Mountbatten's character. I am sure that his personality and character has been deeply affected and bruised by the treatment meted out to his father which he calls a 'disgraceful episode'. He wants revenge and has become vindictive which has affected his judgement.

Somewhere looms an inferiority complex which he tries to camouflage by over-stating the first person. He often uses terms such as 'I will succeed . . . I have the power to succeed . . . I shall not be defeated . . . I can settle all and do not need any assistance . . . I am making history . . . I have the trust of the common man . . . I have a personal relationship with all . . . an understanding with the leaders and have their trust . . . and if need be I can bully them . . . I alone decide . . . I cannot be wrong . . . What I say goes with all . . . God is on my side . . . No one knows more than myself about India as I had Indian troops under my command in SEAC . . . The time limit was my idea . . . Wavell had lost contact with the Indian leaders and had no communications with them . . . The only thing I inherited from Wavell was the plan Madhouse . . . One fifth of humanity is in my hand and I am the most powerful man on earth . . . Lady Wavell looks like my wife's maid . . . The Army has taken a liking to me.'

Mountbatten wants the Union Jack to be part of the Pakistan flag but the Quaid would not have it.

As the situation worsens Mountbatten is getting frightened and panicky. His on-the-spot decisions are often dangerous and instead of solving a problem create new ones. He is now relying on his 'flashes', 'intuitions' and 'hunches' which he says he gets at night. In fact this has become a joke. At the beginning of the day's work people ask one another, 'What is the hunch or flash today?' God protect us from them. If the Partition is to be based on hunches and flashes, disaster is inevitable.

Mountbatten often says that he has been saddled with an 'idiotic Indian Government' where nothing happens and that he is sitting on a bomb and on a volcano which is about to explode. It is touch and go and the only way to avoid it is by partitioning the subcontinent at top speed.

The tactics and philosophy Mountbatten uses in dealing with the leaders and the Princes are crude and unvarnished. He believes in giving no time to others to think, analyse or absorb. He banks on solid threats, bluffs, blatant lies and dishonest tactics.

Mountbatten believes in a high sense of drama, in theatrical and dramatic gestures. Every meeting and conference, every talk and interview, is pre-planned and rehearsed beforehand, and the actors primed. He is a master of conferences which are brilliantly stage-managed but they achieve little. Manipulation is the order of the day. The media, too, is directed and controlled to suit his policies. Foreign and Congress journalists are taken into his confidence and won over to sing his praises. A team of able constitutional lawyers from United Kingdom has been imported to help him: firstly, to develop certain inter-Dominion organizations which he hopes will keep the Dominions together; secondly, to evolve a working relationship between the Princes and the Dominions; and lastly, to work out a system for handing over power.

Edwina and Pamela Mountbatten are wandering all over the country trying to mobilize opinion in favour of Dickie. Edwina is the real power behind the throne and eggs Mountbatten on.

I feel that Mountbatten's relationship with Edwina is rather a shallow one. It obviously suits both of them. He has a working arrangement with her.

As August draws near everything is drawing to a close. The curtain is due to fall. The situation is going from bad to worse everywhere, but especially in the Punjab. Mountbatten is taking little notice of this matter, though he has been constantly warned by Jenkins. General Curtis, Commander of the Lucknow Area, has taken a tough line with the rioters. Due to the stupidity of the Nawab there is trouble in Rampur State as well.

The Commander-in-Chief has written to Ismay to say that after 15th August British troops may be employed operationally to protect British lives and property. This will also include other Europeans but they must not be used in communal disturbances unless British lives are in danger. He also said that Jinnah may well appeal for the use of British troops on the North-West Frontier on the principle of one Dominion helping the other. If such a request is received it should be referred to His Majesty's Government.

The Auk is personally against the use of British troops on the Frontier as they are not trained for Frontier operations. If they have to be used they should only protect the 'bases' and release the Pakistani troops for operations in the forward areas. It should also be made clear to the Native States that, on the ceasing of the paramountcy, they will have no right to call for the assistance of British troops.

The Auk further emphasized that he should be recognized as the 'Supreme Commander' of British Forces in India so long as they are here and that the GOC British troops in India should be under his control and not under the War Office.

2nd July: Quaid has decided to become the Governor-General of Pakistan.

Mountbatten saw the Quaid and used all possible arguments to induce him to accept the principle of a common Governor-General who would ensure the fair division of assets and stores, and an equitable boundary between the two Dominions. He said that Pakistan would be a weak country and would need all assistance to safeguard its boundaries. Mountbatten said that Pakistan stands to lose a great deal if it does not accept a common Governor-General. This was Pakistan's only hope for survival. The Quaid replied by saying that he is prepared to accept Mountbatten as a Super Governor-General, though no such precedence exists in this world.

Mountbatten also said that the Quaid should become the Prime Minister of Pakistan. In this way he could have all the power in his hands. Quaid said that this did not worry him. The Nawab of Bhopal also tried to persuade the Quaid to accept Mountbatten as the common Governor-General. Mountbatten further said that the tribes on the North-West Frontier would split and it will be impossible for Jinnah to control them. Besides, Pakistan will be at the mercy of India and if he was around it would not be so. He would appoint a number of Inter-Dominion Committees to sort out all problems between the two Dominions. He would also establish a Defence Council for the overall defence of the subcontinent. The Viceroy's Lodge in Simla would be made into neutral territory where all Inter-Dominion committees could be held. Mountbatten finally said that the East Pakistanis would not approve of his appointment as a Governor-General.

Quaid was not prepared to risk the destiny of Pakistan by naming a man sold to the cause of the Congress as its first Governor-General of two Dominions, and who had already damaged the cause of Pakistan in many respects.

If Mountbatten was appointed a common Governor-General, where would he function from? It would obviously be Delhi and if so it could be reasonably assumed that he would be dictated to by the Hindus. He would obviously take the advice of the leaders of a bigger country. Would he oscillate between the two capitals and establish an office in Karachi, or would a shuttle service of couriers be established? However, Mountbatten maintains that the Quaid as Prime Minister could officiate as Governor-General during his absence and he would only visit by his consent. What effect would this have on the public if they knew that they were being dictated to from Delhi and, instead of the Quaid, it was Mountbatten guiding their destiny? The nation would lose faith in their leader. The Quaid maintains that the only way he could sell the presence of British officers in Pakistan to the public is by himself becoming the Governor-General. Pakistan was being born out of the suffering of the Muslims, it was being created from nothing and it therefore required a leadership in which the public had confidence. Superhuman efforts would be required from all, which would only be forthcoming if Quaid himself took the leadership. It is a question of survival and not of vanity, as some say. However, there are many Muslims who advise Quaid to give Mountbatten a chance and accept him at his word. They feel Mountbatten may change his colours, which to my mind is very doubtful.

Mountbatten has been hurt. He has received a rude shock from which he may never recover. He has taken the matter personally.

He has reported the conversation to His Majesty's Government and said that the Quaid's decision was a bombshell to him, to HMG and to the Chiefs-of-Staff, as it has upset their political plans and military requirements.

Mountbatten has been openly saying that he has tried every trick on

Jinnah but they do not work and that he has failed to make him see reason. Jinnah wants to run Pakistan but he insists that he (Mountbatten) must stay in India. Jinnah was furious when Nehru decided to call his country India and not Bharat as it would entitle him to be the sole inheritor of everything that was British India.

Mountbatten calls Jinnah a bastard, a dolt, a clot, a psychopathic and hopeless case, a one-man band, an evil genius, a fool, a cold and repressed person; the only advice that Jinnah listens to is Jinnah himself. He is counting on the support of the Conservative Party and Churchill. Incidentally, it is said that Churchill has told Mountbatten not to harm the interests of the Muslims in the subcontinent as they have never plotted against the British. Mountbatten has admitted that the Muslims wanted the British to remain in India, as, under them, no harm could come to them.

Mountbatten has adopted a posture of being hurt with the Quaid. He at last realizes that the Quaid has the key to the solution of the Indian problems.

4th July: All the members of the Cabinet were made to resign. They were then asked to carry on until the passing of the Indian Independence Bill by the Parliament.

The States were asked to join one or the other Dominion.

Nehru is still harping on the Indian National Army as if there is nothing else to do.

Mountbatten had his staff meeting at which the question of him accepting the Governor-Generalship of India alone was discussed. It was said that in the case of Mountbatten not staying on, the C-in-C and the British officers would resign as well, which would lead to disintegration, riots and bloodshed. This was hypothetical. But if Mountbatten stayed on, the Joint Defence Council, of which he was the Chairman, could act as a stabilizing factor.

However, Ismay maintained that it would be impossible for Mountbatten to act impartially in matters dealing with Partition. Therefore it would be morally undignified and wrong for him to stay on. Even Lady Mountbatten wants her husband to quit. Thereupon Mountbatten has asked for the advice of His Majesty's Government and a note has been sent to United Kingdom through Ismay. It may well be that HMG will force him to stay on as Governor-General of India in the hope that she would stay in the Commonwealth.

Liaquat wrote officially to Mountbatten to inform him that the Quaid will be the Governor-General of Pakistan and that the League hopes that Mountbatten will stay on in India.

Mountbatten has asked His Majesty's Government if he may be allowed to use British troops in an emergency to save British and European lives after 14th August.

Civil disorder and riots and watching native women and children being butchered is having a very demoralizing effect on the British troops as they have been forbidden to interfere.

The Khan of Kalat is very active, hob-nobbing with all, especially with Mountbatten. The Khan has asked him to return the 'leased areas' in Baluchistan, which include Nushki, Bolan, Nasirabad and Quetta. He is working hard to secure independence for the Kalat State.

5th July: The C-in-C wrote the following to the Viceroy:

PERSONAL AND SECRET

Dear Lord Mountbatten,

I was asked by Your Excellency at a recent meeting of the Partition Council to prepare a Plan in case of possible clashes or disturbances in the neighbourhood of the boundaries between the two Dominions after the 15th August.

I recommend that the Joint Defence Council should have the authority of both the INDIA and PAKISTAN Governments to declare any affected districts to be 'disturbed areas'.

When this has been done, the Supreme Commander, acting on the request of the Joint Defence Council, will specially appoint a (BRITISH) commander, with an adequate Headquarters who will have MILITARY control over the area and of such troops and air forces as are considered by him to be necessary. These troops etc. should be allotted by the Commanders-in-Chief of the two Dominions, at the request of the Joint Defence Council.

The British Commander, so appointed, will be responsible to the Joint Defence Council, through the Supreme Commander, who, for this purpose, will temporarily have operational control.

The above procedure would be similar to arrangements I would make for the disturbances on the boundary before 15th August, and will apply both in the PUNJAB and BENGAL.

Yours sincerely,

H.E. THE VICEROY   C. J. AUCHINLECK

7th July: At a meeting Mountbatten said that previously his staff was of the opinion that he should not stay as the Governor-General of India alone. Now they maintain that he should accept India's offer.

The C-in-C, who was present, stated that there will be adverse Muslim comments on his staying on. However, if possible he must stay in some capacity or the other, so that British ties with the subcontinent remain.

India has asked Mountbatten to be their Governor-General. This is not for love of him or his so-called popularity, as he believes, but to make use of him towards their selfish and materialistic ends. Congress always talked in terms of the 'cursed British' and 'cursed British rule'. Now that there is a change of heart, Mountbatten has become their beloved hero. Congress wants him to fulfil the promises which he had made to Nehru when he stayed with him in Simla on 10th May this year. Congress want him to fix the future boundary as far as possible to the west, giving the Indians a corridor to Kashmir and ensuring its accession to India. Lastly, Congress wants him to finish the Princely States once and for all.

The referendum in Sylhet and North-West Frontier Province has started.

Ismay left for London to apprise His Majesty's Government of the present developments and to find out whether Mountbatten should stay as Governor-General of India.

9th July: Ismay met all concerned in the United Kingdom. His Majesty's Government has decided that Mountbatten must complete his task. They were of the view that by his accepting the Governor-Generalship of India it was certain that India will stay in the Commonwealth. Even the King asked him to stay on. To the great surprise of his staff, he told them that he would stay on as the Governor-General of India.

In my opinion he has lost face and is likely to become hostile towards Pakistan. I am convinced that a Hindu Governor-General of India would prove to be more cooperative than Mountbatten will probably be, knowing him as I do.

11th July: Everybody recognizes that the most dangerous period will be between 15th July to about 15th October. The Governor of Punjab agrees. He said that there is common talk among the Sikhs that they intend to make trouble when the Boundary Commission gives its Award. In the meantime they do not wish the Government of East Punjab to leave Lahore until its fate has been decided.

Mountbatten has urged all the Governors not to ask for troops. This would interfere with the reconstitution of the Armed Forces. The Governor of Punjab has reported that communal feelings are unbelievably high. There is confusion everywhere and everything is leading towards a climax. The Sikhs are uneasy. They believe that they will be expropriated and possibly massacred in Western Punjab, and that they would be smothered by Congress and the Hindus in general in Eastern Punjab. So the Sikhs are preparing for a rising immediately after the transfer of power unless the Boundary Commission gives a favourable award.

The civil services in Punjab are no longer effective and have practically disintegrated.

According to Jenkins the meeting of the Partition Committee resembles 'a peace conference with a new war in sight'. He maintains that within the available time a proper partition cannot be accomplished.

The Governor complains that the Chairman of the Boundary Commission does not arrive until 14th July. Because of this it is very difficult to visualize how the Chairman will be able to submit his report by 15th August, as they will have to issue a long questionnnaire to those concerned which will take weeks to answer.

Edwina Mountbatten has written two letters to the Auk. The first one is marked 'Personal' and was in her own hand-writing. At the end of the letter she says 'When you write informally I cannot believe that it is necessary to be so formal in addressing me and I shall set you a good example. "Yours ever, Edwina Mountbatten".'

The second letter is in reply to her pleading the cases of certain Indian National Army officers. The Auk gave her the full picture and his views on the subject. In reply to that she writes that in sending him Mrs Kiani's* letter she did not wish to plead her case but wanted some material on which she could base her reply to her.

Every now and then Edwina writes such letters to the C-in-C.

I met Rajagopalachari. He is a simple man and greatly respected through-out India. He is considered as the spokesman of the South. He is a mystic, a philosopher and an author. He has a razor-sharp intellect and rare moral courage. He is dry and logical and is not afraid of being unpopular. Among the Congress circles they are afraid of him. He does not hesitate to disgree with his Congress colleagues when his conscience tells him they are wrong. He takes a long-term view of situations and has made many efforts to bring the Muslims and Hindus together. Coming from South India he is not communal. He listens to people very attentively and no one can make out what he is thinking behind his dark glasses. He does not care for Indira and says that she has nothing of the father in her. He believes that 'a life-time of criticism and opposition does not befit people for the task to govern'.

12th July: Mountbatten wants to get on the right side of the Quaid and offered him a GCMG. Quaid told him that the Muslims have already passed a resolution rejecting all British honours. Therefore he is not in a position to accept one. He would not have accepted in any case.

Mountbatten says that he will raise the point again with him. According to Mountbatten the Quaid has said that by not accepting a common Governor-General, the GCMG, the flag etc., the British Government may have thought it a rebuff. It was not intended as such. They will find Pakistan a loyal and a permanent member of the Commonwealth.

15th July: The Viceroy has asked His Majesty's Government to be allowed to make a public statement to the effect that British troops will not be used

---

*Mrs Kiani was the wife of an Indian officer who joined the Indian National Army and was under trial.

Three Field-Marshals: Montgomery, Wavell, Auchinleck.

A reception at the C-in-C's house; left to right: Admiral Miles, General Godwin-Austen, the C-in-C, Sir Walter Monkton.

The C-in-C with Their Highnesses of Jodhpur, Bhopal and Jaipur.

The C-in-C with Lord Mountbatten and Field-Marshal Slim.

Lord Pethick-Lawrence with Lord Mountbatten.

The Auk's farewell to India.

operationally and will not be available to intervene in internal disorder after 15th August. The Viceroy considers that British and European civilians should have this information. This would also remove any suspicion that the British intend to reimpose their authority.

16th July: There has been some discussion on the proposal submitted by the C-in-C. This suggests that the Joint Defence Council should have the authority of the two Dominion Governments to declare any affected district as a 'Disturbed Area'. When this happens the Supreme Commander would appoint a British military commander to control the area. It is said that the Joint Defence Council has been established for the specific purpose of dividing the defence services. It will have no operational responsibility after 15th August.

If agreed upon this will place the Viceroy, the C-in-C and the British Commander in an impossible position, as they would have no effective means to exercise their responsibility and still would be criticised by everyone. It has also been suggested that the two Governments will be placing their troops at the disposal of the British Commander; however, the aggrieved Government may withdraw them if they so desire. An awkward situation may arise if some units decide to mutiny, which might involve the use of British troops to suppress them.

17th July: There was a meeting of the Partition Council. It was held under the chairmanship of Mountbatten and was attended by the Quaid, Liaquat Ali, Patel, Rajendra Prashad, H. M. Patel, Mohammad Ali and the C-in-C. At the instigation of Mountbatten the Council decided to establish a Punjab Boundary Force and the following directive was issued –

a)   That they would deal with the disturbances on the boundaries on or after 15th August in accordance with the guide lines as indicated by the C-in-C.
b)   That Military control would be exercised by Major-General Rees* who will be assisted by two advisers, a Muslim and a Sikh.
c)   That the zones of operations will be defined and approved by the Partition Council.
d)   That the troops will be in position by 8th August.
e)   That there should be no change in the law governing the use of troops in aid of the Civil Power after 15th August, for such period as these forces are employed.

*Major-General Thomas (Pete) Rees (d. 1959) commanded the 10th Indian Division in Iraq and N. Africa 1942; 19th Indian Division Burma 1944–45; 4th Indian Division 1945–47; Punjab Boundary Force Aug–Sept, 1947; Head of Military Emergency Staff to Emergency Committee of Cabinet, Delhi, Sept–Dec, 1947.

f)   That the troops would be drawn, as far as possible, equally from both the Dominions and will be units of mixed composition. It was realized that the reconstitution may be delayed.

g)   That the troops employed on these duties will be directly under the Supreme Commander, who will be directed by the Joint Defence Council.

h)   And if any Air support was required the AOC-in-C will decide in consultation with General Rees.

The participants were told that Nehru did not wish the British troops included as part of the Boundary Force.

In the evening the Auk went to see the Quaid and assured him that all possible steps were being taken to ensure the partitioning of the forces in due time.

Major-General L. G. Whistler, the Commander of the British troops in India, has been going round all the British formations and units and talking to them. The British troops are getting impatient and want to be repatriated to United Kingdom and demobilized. There is considerable uneasiness among them. They realize that it is the end of the Empire and therefore they are no longer interested in the subcontinent.

18th July: An Investiture Ceremony was held at the Viceroy's House. This was followed by a banquet to commemorate the Silver Wedding Anniversary of the Mountbattens. It could well be said that it was the last great social function of the British Raj. Everyone was there. Before dinner I had to leave on an errand for the C-in-C. I met the Quaid in the corridor of the house. He was walking alone, in a stately manner, though half-an-hour late. Knowing that he was very particular about timings, I could not help but ask him why he was late. Thereupon he replied, 'My boy, do you think I would come to this damn man's party in time? I purposely came late to show him that I despise him.'

19th July: A circular letter from the Branch office of the Lahore RSSS has been issued and reads as follows:*

Pakistan stunt no doubt started at a mad man's cry . . . Relying on its impracticability and unworkability it was ignored or ridiculed but it appealed to masses and individuals . . . with this background Pakistan appealed to ordinary Muslims and no doubt it gained a momentum which is now manifest . . . Unless Pakistan is virtually nullified and Muslims find it harmful they will not leave it . . . They must realize that their structure is costly to maintain, otherwise they will not give up this mad cry . . . On the

*This letter is in the original wording and has not been corrected.

other hand if they have to depend on India or outside resources for their subsistance they will clamour for strong support in the centre at the cost of other provinces. Therefore if the most paying tracts in Punjab Rechna and Bari Doab canals colonies areas are excluded for Pakistan, the object would be achieved. The problem therefore is to so arrange things that the District of Lahore Sheikhupura Lyallpore Montgomery and part of Multan have to fall in with India . . . With this in view the present problem is to so organize the change and migration of population as to reduce the excess of Muslims and to get most efficient results in those Tehsils (districts) which bring in the most revenue and those whose excess is smaller will have to be tackled first. If small pockets are left they would automatically fall in granted that the schemes exist by which a certain number of Muslims can be replaced by non-Muslims. The silent extinction of the evil of Pakistan can be planned.

The best way to change the population must be worked out. The proposition is to remove a certain number of Muslims from certain areas and to replace them by non-Muslims. The Post War Settlement of demobilised personnel, colonization of Thal and Haveli areas and establishment of industrial centres are the means which can be used in pursuance of the object.

The silent change-over of population will open everybody's eyes and the Pakistanis will automatically find they have lost the battle. If then you offer them Pakistan you can be sure that they won't take it.

20th July: Mountbatten was in Lahore today and held a meeting with the Governor, the Army Commander and the Commander of the Boundary force. Messervy advocated that in the districts of Sialkot, Gujranwala, Sheikhupura, Lyallpur, Montgomery, Lahore, Amritsar, Gurdaspur, Hoshiarpur, Jullunder and Ferozepore special military measures were required. He said that for this purpose five brigades and one Armoured Regiment had been earmarked. The Command will be operative from 1st August. Messervy considers that it would be preferable to have the Ordinances cover all eleven districts rather than to declare Martial Law in some. In any case there were not sufficient officers to carry out Martial Law duties. The Punjab Public Safety Act, the Punjab Disturbed Areas Act and the Governor-General's Ordnance on special powers for the Armed Forces were the measures which would have to be continued in the operational areas. However, Mountbatten felt that in spite of this Martial Law may have to be declared if the situation gets out of hand.

I feel that the positioning of the Boundary Force has come too late. I wonder whether it will be able to exercise any effective contol. General Rees is a very capable Commander but this task is beyond him. Political forces will come into play and he will be pressurized from all directions, and even maligned.

The Cabinet has been reconstituted in two groups representing the two Dominions. Each is responsible for its own affairs but those subjects common to both are to be referred to the Viceroy. There are now two Provisional Governments. The Defence Department has also been split.

British officers of the Indian Army want the silver and the property divided and their share sent to United Kingdom. The Auk does not approve of this action and there has been a row over it.

The Auk has received a letter from Mountbatten enclosing one from Nehru on the release of Indian National Army prisoners. Mountbatten wants his views and some material from the Auk for a reply. Nehru has the same old argument. He says that the matter was referred to the Federal Court Judges but that he is unaware of their recommendations. Nehru considers the men of the Indian National Army as political prisoners. The C-in-C maintains that they are not. Nehru wants the Indian National Army prisoners to be released before day of Independence; otherwise there will be a feeling among the people that Independence was only a facade. If they are not released, the question may be later raised in the Constituent Assembly.

Nehru further said that the Pakistan Government intends to release them. The C-in-C maintains that no such intention has been assured.

21st July: Mountbatten has received a signal from His Majesty's Government to the effect that British troops will not be used to put down disturbances except in exceptional cases and that they should be withdrawn from India. However, the Auk feels that in view of the grave political situation they should not be withdrawn. General Rees wants them for the Boundary Force.

A joint statement by the leaders of the Muslims and Hindus has been issued to the effect that the minorities will be protected. The leaders admit that they could not visualize the magnitude of the disorder and they are now thoroughly disillusioned.

Baldev has asked Major Short to fly out to India and use his influence to get the boundary line drawn as much to the West as possible. The Sikhs are out of control in the rural areas. The only way to restrain them would be by the use of horsed cavalry which is practically non-existent.

22nd July: Lord Ismay has come back from United Kingdom having obtained full approval of His Majesty's Government to the line of action suggested by Mountbatten.

The Boundary Commission has been set up and has started its deliberations. It is a very difficult task, if not an impossible one.

For some time past I had been trying to persuade the Auk to give a reception for the Press. Delhi is full of foreign correspondents and they are very keen to meet the Auk. It is obvious that he cannot give them individual interviews. He is shy and avoids meeting journalists. However, with my persuasion he has agreed.

The local correspondents wanted to drag him into the political issues, while the foreign pressmen were appreciative of his great role. Auk gave them convincing replies, as well as the background material on the division of the forces.

It was a good Press Conference. Everyone was impressed by his sincerity of purpose, which came through so clearly.

In certain quarters people are speculating that Pakistan will not be capable of controlling and running the North-West Frontier Province. Some well-wishers maintain that the leaders of Pakistan should endeavour to make friends with Afghanistan. To despise Pakistan, the Congress has started flirting with Afghanistan. The Afghans have been told that the Durand Line* is not the logical boundary. General Sir Francis Tuker once suggested to me that the best way to control the Frontier would be to withdraw all the garrisons from the Tribal Areas and replace them by strong Frontier Militias. I have passed the message to Quaid-e-Azam.

23rd July: The transfer of the units will start immediately. In order to avoid a sudden reduction of troops it was proposed to interchange battalions between India and West Pakistan on a one-for-one basis.

The boundary between Western Pakistan and the Indian Union has been assumed to be in accordance with the 3rd June announcement. The battalions in areas where disturbances may occur will be moved last.

24th July: The Punjab Boundary Force has been positioned. I think that it is too small a force to be effective and will not be able to control the rural areas. The Sikhs have decided to ignore it and put their plan of vengeance into operation. British troops have not been included in the Boundary Force in spite of the Auk's recommendations. Auk is of the view that once the two Dominions are established the Boundary Force will have no status or meaning and cannot be relied upon. He maintains that British troops would have been most effective and, at the same time, impartial. The Sikhs are out to secure the Ferozepore Headworks and get the general boundary pushed as far west as possible.

Major-General Joe Lentaigne† has suggested that to avoid bloodshed a 25-mile strip of territory on either side of the notional boundary be evacuated and policed by British and Gurkhas troops. No one has taken any notice of the suggestion, though Mountbatten is furious.

---

*Named after Sir Henry Morton Durand (1850–1924) Indian civil servant and diplomat who in 1893 led a mission to the Amir of Afghanistan whereby the Durand Line between British and Afghan areas of influence was demarcated.

†Major-General Walter David Alexander (Joe) Lentaigne (1899–1955) was Director of Military Operations and DQMG, GHQ India, 1947; Commandant, Indian Staff College, 1948–55.

Tuker has refused a boundary force for Assam and Bengal and says that he is quite capable of controlling any disorder.

In London Ismay had meetings with the Chiefs of Staff. On his return he said that they hope to send out a delegation to discuss matters of mutual defence interests with the two Dominions soon after the transfer of power. The delegation will also hold discussions with the Joint Defence Council.

A report has been received that if Nankana Sahib (the second largest of the Sikh shrines) is not included in East Punjab the Sikhs will start trouble on a big scale. They intend to act on or about 7th August. Before that date they will organize and hold public meetings and stir up communal feelings. For this reason they have collected large quantities of arms. The Muslims are likely to react. God help us all in these troubled times.

Mountbatten has been saying that the Quaid is his friend and has full faith in him. There is no remorse in his utterances. Is he being naive or does he possess such an inflated ego that it makes him believe what he wants to hear? Everyone knows that there is no love lost between them. Mountbatten makes out that everybody is wonderful and everyone is his friend. He is going ahead like a bull in a china shop. I wonder where he will land us.

The other day someone asked Mountbatten whether he has seen Tuker's paper on the arrangements to be made should it come to partition. He replied in the negative. It goes to show he is obviously not interested in other people's ideas.

There have been riots in Dehra Dun, Meerut, Pilibhit, Alwar, and Bharatpur. Many Muslims are being massacred.

25th July: Mountbatten addressed the Princes, overawed them and gave them hell. They listened to all he had to say and are most depressed. They have no future. Many have signed the Instrument of Accession. Those who did not were told to face the consequences.

There was the interesting episode of a certain Chief Minister. As the Ruler of the State was abroad, the Chief Minister was representing him when he went to meet Mountbatten. After gazing for a long while into the glass paper-weight on his table, Mountbatten said he could see the Ruler's face in it. Then, much to the surprise of the Chief Minister, he told him that the Ruler was saying that the Minister should sign the Instrument of Accession.

There are 560 Princely States, occupying half the area of India and having 25 per cent of the population. Some of the States are museum pieces but others are progressive. They have survived as a result of British patronage. His Majesty's Government held that 'their affection and loyalty are important assets for Britain'. In 1858 Queen Victoria had proclaimed, 'We shall respect the rights, dignity and honour of the Native Princes as our own'. The Viceroy of India was the Governor-General of British India but, as far as the

States were concerned, he was the representative of the Crown to whom the States owed allegiance.

The Maharajahs of Jodhpur and Jailsalmir want to opt for Pakistan. They were warned against doing so by Mountbatten. Hyderabad, 'the most Faithful Ally of the British Crown', has signed a standstill agreement. Kashmir is a very tricky case. Kak, the Prime Minister, wants to join Pakistan. Sir Conrad Corfield, the Political Secretary, maintains that His Majesty's Government had let down the States and has not honoured its treaty commitments. He has been pleading their cause forcefully, much to the dislike of Mountbatten. When he found out that he was not making any headway he resigned and is leaving for the United Kingdom. Patiala has succeeded the Nawab of Bhopal as the Chancellor of the Chamber of Princes.

27th July: Patel is using the big stick to keep the Rulers of the Indian States under control. Short has arrived and is staying with Baldev. He is attached to Mountbatten's staff and is their unofficial adviser on Sikh affairs. There is no love lost between Baldev and the Auk. He is conspiring against the Auk nowadays.

28th July: There was a reception at the Viceroy's House for the Ruling Princes. Those who had not signed the Instrument of Accession were taken individually to Mountbatten's study and received a dressing down. What shabby treatment to those who stood firm and supported the Crown for two centuries.

Mountbatten gave an interview to the Khan of Kalat. It is reported that he praised the Viceroy sky high and said he was the saviour of the subcontinent. According to Mountbatten the Khan is thankful to him for obtaining from the Pakistan Government the recognition that Kalat was an Independent Sovereign State in treaty relations with the British Government! Kalat is saying that he had a meeting with Jinnah who had said that he wished to be his friend and would draw a suitable treaty or agreement with them. However, he maintained that the bone of contention between them was the lease territories. It is said that Mountbatten persuaded Kalat to obtain legal opinion as it appears that the Pakistan Government would inherit the leases in the same way as they would inherit the Anglo-Afghan treaty of 1921. Kalat is reported to have said that he does not want a Pathan AGG in Baluchistan and requested that Sir Geoffrey Prior* should stay on. However, if he is not available then he should be replaced by another Englishman if Mr Jinnah wants peace. He further told Mountbatten that all the Baluchis love and trust him (Mountbatten) in a way they have never trusted anyone else.

---

*Sir Geoffrey Prior (1896–1972) joined the Indian Political Service in 1923; was Political Resident Persian Gulf 1939–46; Governor of Baluchistan 1946–49.

29th July: Reggie Savory buttonholed by Mountbatten. The Viceroy told him that the Auk was getting himself into bad odour with Nehru and the Congress, and has been branded as pro-Pakistani. Mountbatten also said he is having trouble in trying to persuade Nehru of the Auk's integrity. Mountbatten stressed that he had implicit faith in Auk and asked Savory to try to stop the Auk dabbling in politics.

Savory maintains that Baldev was behind all this. It was definitely a move to get rid of the Auk, and a serious attempt to prevent him becoming the Supreme Commander. Savory also said that the Auk is too big a man to be messed about though it would not take much effort to make Auk go. The Auk is a disillusioned man, sick of intrigues and the continued hatred with which he is surrounded. Savory told me that the interview with Auk was the most awkward moment in his life. He was very angry with Mountbatten and said that the latter did not have the guts to tell the Auk himself. He said that it was a great pity that the Auk's integrity was being questioned after forty years of service. Savory maintains that Mountbatten is trying to please his future bosses who have already started kicking him around. That is why they had wanted him as Governor-General. He is fast losing his prestige. Savory told the Auk about Mountbatten. The Auk was furious. He resented Mountbatten's action in speaking to one of his subordinates and not to him direct. Auk told Savory that if he did not receive the support which he was entitled to expect, he would resign.

Farikdot has offered Savory the post of C-in-C of the Khalistan Army on any terms and conditions which he may dictate. He seemed amused when he told me about it.

Gandhi has been speaking about the ills of a military dictatorship. I wonder why. Does he think that the Auk may assume the powers of a military dictator?

30th July: The Auk sent a letter to Baldev Singh demanding an apology from him. He had accused Walmsley,* AOC-in-C, of dishonestly removing aircraft and stores from India to Pakistan and in general being pro-Pakistan. Auk said that Baldev was becoming impossible and intolerable.

The Sikhs want Nankana Sahib, their holy shrine, to be given the same sort of status as the Vatican enjoys.

31st July: Gandhi is on a visit to the North-West Frontier Province and Kashmir. We know his purpose. It is to persuade the Maharajah to join the Indian Union.

---

*Air Marshal Sir Hugh Walmsley (b. 1898) joined the RFC in 1916, was Senior Air Staff Officer HQ Bomber Command 1944–45; AOC-in-C, Air HQ, India 1946–47; Deputy Chief of the Air 1048–50.

'Kipper' Cariappa says that the Army will not tolerate a *Dhoti Prasad** as the C-in-C. He and Muchu Chaudhry are at loggerheads. Muchu says that Cariappa has a disease called 'Kipperitis' and does not stick to anything for long.

Met Govind Ballabh Pant.† He comes from Almora and is known as the 'Tiger of Kumaon'. He is straightforward and tows Nehru's line.

Mountbatten has lost his balance and has become unhinged. He has lost all sympathy for Pakistan which is quite understandable. As he is bitter about not being accepted as a common Governor-General he will probably resort to vengeance.

---

*A man who wears a loincloth instead of trousers.
†Pant was a very successful Chief Minister of United Provinces.

PART V

The Unprecedented Upheaval

August 1947

'Military plans must be based on political developments.'

The Auk.

1st August: His Majesty's Government and the Chief of Staff in the United Kingdom are very worried about the defence of the subcontinent and that of the Indian Ocean. They want some sort of agreement between His Majesty's Government and India and Pakistan in this respect. They are hoping that both countries will stay in the Commonwealth and help Britain in time of emergency. They had wanted one Union Government of India and feel that any division will seriously weaken the security of the subcontinent.

His Majesty's Government and the Chief of Staff maintain that the Indian subcontinent has long claimed the moral leadership of South-East Asian countries. To discharge its duties to this effect external assistance must be ensured. It was therefore accepted that His Majesty's Government will provide advice and technical assistance in the reorganization of land, sea and air forces of both the Dominions. Britain will also be prepared to come to their assistance with additional forces if a major threat to their security develops. To fulfil this objective, planning on a Commonwealth basis was essential if they were to act together. It was suggested that a centralized system of Commonwealth defence should be encouraged to establish coordination, liaison, etc. The system should be flexible and provide discussion on vital problems and be so framed as to cope with varying outlooks and allow a central direction of efforts.

While the reconstruction of the two Forces is being carried out the situation is fraught with danger. The United Kingdom is prepared to aid the Dominions in tiding them over this period.

The Chief of Staff suggested that the continent of India should continue to be the main support area in war and that His Majesty's Government should have the use of strategic airfields, Naval and Air bases. However, the two Dominions will have to take primary responsibility for their own defence and accept the obligation to participate actively in the event of a threat developing in any neighbouring territory. In return the United Kingdom will give them all possible assistance and advice.

For some time the Auk and Baldev have not been seeing eye to eye on matters connected with the reconstruction of the Forces, particularly on the division of the assets. Baldev expects him to favour India, which the Auk has not been prepared to do. However, Baldev has acknowledged his error and normal relations have now been restored. Baldev told the Auk in confidence that he was not getting on with Nehru and Patel in the Cabinet and is soliciting Auk's help.

Kalat has been saying that he has met the Quaid on several occasions but has made no headway in the negotiations. He says there is no spirit of give and take. He has been saying that Quetta and all the ceded areas belong to Kalat State. According to him on the termination of the treaty with the British Government these areas must revert to the State. However, he is prepared to come to a reasonable settlement with Pakistan in respect of such problems as Defence and Communications. According to him Quaid-e-Azam has not been in a mood to admit his rights.

2nd August: For the first time, orders are issued in the name of the Supreme Commander. These pertain to the release and issue of controlled stores to the armies of India and Pakistan. It was mentioned that the existing stocks of equipment are being divided between India and Pakistan and it is hoped that by the end of 1947 the respective armies will be notified of their stock balances. All future demands will now be routed to the Supreme Command Headquarters through the two Dominions' Army Headquarters. However, the demands of the Punjab Boundary Forces will be submitted direct to the Supreme Commander, and also that of the British troops.

The Congress Government in the NWFP has refused to resign in spite of the fact that they have lost popular support.

3rd August: Sometime ago I had met the Quaid and told him that the officers of the Armed Forces were anxious to get a glimpse of him. Most of them had never met the 'Great Founder of their country', and they were frightened of him. He pondered over my suggestion and then said:

'What do you suggest?'

I told him that if he cared to come to our house one evening I would arrange a get-together. To my utter astonishment he agreed and even gave me a date, but said that he may be a little late as he had to attend a meeting of the Muslim League Committee of Action.

We had invited the Auk, the Naval and Air C-in-Cs, principal staff officers, some civil servants apart from all the senior Muslim officers of the Defence Forces, also some Hindu officers. For a while Tahirah and I waited at the entrance for the Quaid, but as they were held up at the meeting we joined our guests on the back lawn of our house, where everyone had assembled.

A little later the Quaid arrived. As Tahirah and I were not there to receive him, he walked through the house on to the lawn. We apologized for not being at the entrance to receive him. He said that he was sorry at being late. I asked him whether he would like the guests to be introduced to him, to which he agreed.

To my surprise the Quaid was in a talkative mood. He had something to say to each person who was introduced to him. The officers gathered around him to ask all sorts of questions. He answered them in his characteristic manner – slowly, clearly and convincingly. It is always a pleasure to hear him explain his point of view. He meant what he said. He did not pretend to be what he was not. He did not mince his words. He put the problem which he will have to face squarely. I was with him most of the time. The only time he became solemn when someone asked him about the prospect of promotion in Pakistan. I could see from the look of Quaid's face that he did not like the question. In his typical style, he looked him over from head to foot before giving an answer.

'You Mussulmans, either you are up in the sky or down in the dumps. You cannot adopt a steady course. All the promotions will come in good time, but there will be no mad rush.'

To another question he replied, 'Pakistan's elected Government will be that of civilians and anyone who thinks contrary to democratic principles should not opt for Pakistan.'

He also said that all would have to work hard to build the new nation and guard and preserve the identity of the Islamic State and that our task was not easy.

He was full of praise for the Muslim minority in India, especially that of the United Province which he said spearheaded the Pakistan Movement and which supplied the leadership which played a great role in the establishment of Pakistan. He paid great tribute to the late Sir Syed Ahmed Khan who, he said, was the founder of the two nations theory.

He said that the ideology of Pakistan must be preserved and under no circumstances must our tradition be forgotten. He laid great stress on acquiring knowledge and establishing a sound system of education. He said that we wanted to live in peace with India.

It was a memorable evening and a very relaxed one at that. For Tahirah and I it was a great honour to have him at our house. He met our children and even kissed them which was a unique gesture on his part. He looked very frail, but otherwise he was in good form. It was a great day in our life.

His final words to all were, 'Now it is for you to build Pakistan as the greatest Muslim state in the world.'

The Congress did not approve of my inviting the Quaid to my house.

4th August: Jenkins says that when the Hindus mention that ruthless action must be taken to restore law and order they mean that every Muslim should be killed.

5th August: Trevidi has been ordered to visit Punjab and submit a report on the present situation. Bhopal dined with the C-in-C. He is finding himself alone among the Princes. He talked about the future and the tragedies which lie ahead. Mountbatten told the Quaid, Liaquat and Patel that the Sikh leaders are implicated in sabotaging the Partition Plan. He told them, however, that he has taken no action against them.

6th August: The Joint Defence Council held its last meeting in its present form.

General Gracey* called on the Auk. He thinks that my present job has gone to my head. As Gracey has been appointed Chief of Staff to the Pakistan Army, I thought that this time was as good as any to have a talk with him over this matter.

I told him that his assessment of me is completely wrong. My present job is not an easy one as I have to deal with all sorts of people. In any case if the Auk, who is my boss, is satisfied with my handling of the people who come to see him, that was all that matters. Gracey could not say anything to that and kept quiet. I think I made myself clear.

On several occasions the Auk has asked me what job I want and what he can do for me. I have always told him the same thing which is that I have never asked for an assignment, nor have I ever manipulated my career. I told him that our family motto is 'work and wait'. In my belief it is God Almighty alone who is the Giver. I hesitate to ask even from Him as He already knows what is the best for us. I think the Auk understands the sort of man I am. The rank that I hold in this appointment is what I achieved in 1942. It is now August, 1947.

This evening the Indian officers invited their Pakistani counterparts to a party at the Imperial Delhi Gymkhana. Everybody was there including Pandit Nehru who was looking very off-colour and had little to say for himself. However, the Indian officers were making themselves very agreeable to the Pakistani officers. Cariappa as usual was talking in a strain which was far from reality. The going was heavy and the atmosphere charged with uncertainty. Cariappa presented a silver trophy to Aga Mohammad Raza,† the senior Pakistani officer present, as a parting gift. Then all sang 'Auld Lang Syne'. Cariappa said in his speech, 'I say au revoir deliberately and with it I associate the honest and sincere wishes of every one of us here, and all those with the Services outside, that we shall meet each other frequently as the best of friends in the same spirit of good comradeship that we have had the good fortune to enjoy all these years. We have worked together so

---

*General Sir Douglas Gracey (1894–1964) commanded 20th Indian Division 1942–46; Commander 1st Indian Corps 1946–47; Chief of Staff Pakistan Army 1947–48; C-in-C Pakistan Army, 1948–51.

†Aga Mohammad Raza was a senior Muslim officer who later held many diplomatic assignments.

long on the same team. We hope we shall continue to work together in the same spirit for the defence of the two Dominions against external aggression. Comrades-in-arms, during all our life in the various Services we have lived together, worked together, played together and fought together in the various battlefields on which our magnificent Armed Forces have fought with the highest degree of fellowship and comradeship. May this spirit continue even after we are separated.'

Brigadier A. M. Raza replied that he was:

deeply touched by the true spirit of comradeship and genuine feelings of brotherhood evinced and expressed by General Cariappa. I assure everyone of the innate desire of all who are in this distinguished gathering and particularly of my brothers-in-arms. The Armed Forces of Pakistan will always uphold their traditions under which they served shoulder to shoulder with the Indian Armed Forces and will continue to do so whenever required, not only in the interest of our own people, namely the inhabitants of this subcontinent, but also for universal security which is the aim and object of humanity that has suffered the unprecedented horrors of two devastating world wars within a few decades.

At the Joint Defence Council, Ismay mentioned that on his last visit to the United Kingdom he met Mr A. V. Alexander, the Defence Minister, and the British Chief of Staff and gave a résumé of his talks with them. In his opening remarks Ismay said that the Chief of Staff was anxious to hold a discussion with the Indian and Pakistan Governments on long-term defence arrangements. The object was to ensure that the necessary assistance is given to both by the United Kingdom and the rest of the Commonwealth in the event of either of the new Dominions being victims of aggression. He further went on to say that the Chief of Staff maintains that the subcontinent of India has a dominating geographical position and its security affects all the countries in South-East Asia and all other countries which are dependent on sea communication through the Indian Ocean. He said that the security of both India and Pakistan has been prejudiced for the moment but it is a temporary phase. It was the desire of the United Kingdom and other members of the Commonwealth to be in a position to come to their rescue in case of aggression. He said that all the experience of the United Kingdom in defence organization and training would be available to both the Dominions.

Ismay said that the Chief of Staff stressed the point that the mutual arrangements which they contemplated would not in any sense represent a commitment either to India or Pakistan or necessarily to His Majesty's Government. It is not a treaty. The Dominions will decide what they wish to do. However, plans must be prepared beforehand. Ismay said that the Chief of Staff realizes that the two Dominions are not yet in a position to discuss the situation. Nonetheless they would be prepared to send a high-ranking military delegation to the subcontinent whenever the Dominions are ready and in the first instance they would discuss it with the Joint Defence Council. In conclusion Ismay said that the Chiefs of Staff were anxious to establish a system of liaison staff to be stationed in Delhi and Karachi so that they could keep in constant touch.

7th August: The Quaid has left for Karachi. We will miss him and his guidance. His presence in Delhi had a choking effect on the Congress and discouraged them from their ill designs. They are very happy that he has left. Many people are of the opinion that the Quaid should have stayed on, formed the future Government and the Secretariat and got the decisions of the Partition Council implemented in front of him. It is feared that Mountbatten will now have a free hand. He dominates all except the Quaid.

9th August: Everyone is talking about the impending Boundary award. On many occasions Radcliffe, supported by his secretary, Beaumont, had said that the Muslim Majority Tehsils of Ferozepore which include the canal headworks, Zehra and Moga, will form part of Pakistan. This has agitated the Hindus and Sikhs. It is said that yesterday Radcliffe had finalized the Award. He has now submitted it to Mountbatten, who is trying to keep it a closely guarded secret. Many of its salient points have already leaked out through the staff of the Boundary Commission and through his own staff. A copy of the Award, unwittingly, and unknown to Mountbatten, has been sent by George Able to the Secretary of the Governor of Punjab and is known to many. It is common talk that Mountbatten is busy changing it – giving India a corridor to Kashmir through Gurdaspur as well as the Ferozepore Head-works. The Muslims are very jittery.

Radcliffe originally said that he would require one to two years to establish the boundary line but Mountbatten has over-ruled him. He wants him to base it on the 'rule of thumb'.

There is continuous consultation between the Congress, the Sikhs, the Princes and Mountbatten. Something is cooking.

Nobody knows the date of the announcement of the Award. It is up to Mountbatten. It is said that he is terrified to announce it before the Independence celebrations as disturbances may ensue on a large scale which would be his responsibility and that of His Majesty's Government to handle and control. This he is not prepared to face.

It is said that he wants the Independence celebrations to go according to plan and administer the bitter pill afterwards. He is afraid that the injured party may boycott the celebrations.

The Governor of the Punjab has been asked by Mountbatten for advice as to the date of the announcement.

It is also said that the Viceroy will not be issuing the Award in the form of a communique from the Viceroy's House. It will be published as a

Gazette Extraordinary under the instructions of the Boundary Commission. Mountbatten wants to give the impression to the world that he had nothing to do with it.

The Supreme Commander will derive his authority from the Joint Defence Council, and will be responsible for implementing the decisions of the Armed Forces Reconstitution Committee and will issue the necessary instructions to the Commanders of the two Dominion Armed Forces.

The Supreme Commander will have no responsibility for law and order nor will he have operational control over any unit save those in transit from one dominion to another.

Rioting by the Sikhs has started. This is in accordance with their plan. Jenkins is very worried and says that the situation in the boundary areas is extremely serious and has asked for Army reinforcements. The C-in-C says that the Army is already committed elsewhere and could not possibly provide any reinforcements, but he will try his level best to raise some men. However, he will provide some tactical reconnaissance aircraft in the near future.

Ismay is concerned about the loyalty of the Sikhs in the Army. The Viceroy himself is doubtful about the loyalty of the Sikhs in his Boydguard and has issued orders that they will not attend the 15th August parade. To pacify the Sikhs of the Bodyguard he has made it known to them that he had nothing to do with the award of the Boundary Commission.

Today I met Shaheed Suhrawardy at a party in the Imperial Hotel. He said that he had been offered the post of Pakistan's roving ambassador abroad by the Quaid. He said he would like me to accompany him as his Military Adivser. According to him the Quaid has agreed to my appointment. I was nonplussed and made no comments.

Gandhi has issued a statement that he will go to Pakistan and will live and work there for the benefit of the poor. What hypocrisy!

10th August: As the time for Partition gets closer everybody seems to be in a spin. Some are preparing for the coming celebrations while others are more concerned with avoiding the impending bloodbath.

The Quaid wants the British officers to serve in the Pakistan Army for the time being and lay the foundations of a strong Army. In India the British are not wanted and are mistrusted. It is said that the Supreme Commander's Headquarters will not be able to function, and that a showdown is inevitable between them and the Indian Government. It is common talk among the Indian officers that they are going to make things very difficult for Pakistan both economically and financially, and that they will not allow the defence stores to be divided.

The life and property of Muslim officers in Delhi are no longer safe. Many have left their houses and found accommodation in Army messes.

11th August: A report has been received from the Punjab Boundary Force which says that:

a) The arrangement for splitting the Punjab is proceeding rapidly.

b) The refugee problem, mainly from Eastern Punjab to Western Punjab, is becoming increasingly difficult and there is a continuous demand for escorts from the Punjab Boundary Force.

c) The disturbances are producing an average of anything between two to five hundred killings a day. Raids are organized and usually carried out by well-armed gangs of Sikhs. As the sources of intelligence have dried up, the information invariably arrives too late for action to be taken.

d) It is only the presence of troops which is holding back the uncontrolled massacre of the Muslims in East Punjab. There is no Government in Eastern Punjab to help and assist.

e) The railway authorities want aircraft to fly up and down the railway line to avoid sabotage attempts to the tracks.

f) Derailment of trains is a common occurrence. The Maharajah of Faridkot himself is known to be organizing the operations. His people escape into his territory and cannot be traced.

g) The police in Lahore and Amritsar have become completely unreliable. On arrival in Amritsar to take over their duties, the non-Muslim police disarmed the Muslim members of the police force. This created considerable alarm, with the result that the police force has been greatly reduced. There are more calls for the troops of the Punjab Boundary Force.

Quaid has been elected President of Pakistan's Constituent Assembly.

Very alarming reports are being received from the Governor of Punjab. He says that neither the railways nor the main roads are safe for traffic. Raids in the villages are quite impossible to control. He has asked for more troops.

General Messervy has also reported that the situation in Punjab is really bad. The Sikhs are operating large numbers of gangs and timely information about their movement is impossible. The situation in Amritsar is fast deteriorating as a result of the disarming of the Muslim Police by the Hindu Superintendent of Police. Steps are being taken to evacuate small villages but the moves have been interrupted by Sikh patrols mounted on horses. The situation in Lahore is also deteriorating. Messervy is of the opinion that the postponement of the Boundary Commission Award is causing uncertainty and immense bloodshed. He also mentioned that the civilian British officials are pulling out very soon.

The Auk has decided to visit Lahore. He is a very harassed man.

13th August: The Auk did not approve of what happened at the Residency in Lucknow. It came to his notice that General 'Tiger' Curtis took a body of sappers there at night, hauled down the Union Jack and demolished the stand on which the flagpole stood and left no trace of its location. The flag, as is well known, was not even lowered at night. It is now being sent to His Majesty the King, to be placed in the museum at Windsor Castle.

We left for Karachi via Lahore to attend the Independence celebrations. We flew over East Punjab and came in very low to watch the columns of refugees proceeding to Pakistan. We saw areas in East Punjab that were burning. These were obviously Muslim areas. Smoke covered the country-side. It presented a grim picture of a battleground.

At Lahore we met Jenkins, the Governor, Pete Rees, the Commander of the Boundary Force, and an officer whom I have never met before, a full Colonel – Ayub Khan.* He and Colonel Brar are acting as advisers to Rees. Ayub Khan asked me to introduce him to the C-in-C, which I did. Jenkins and Rees gave their views on the prevailing condition. They did not mince their words and painted a very gloomy picture. They said that the Sikhs were behaving with 'pre-medieval ferocity', and felt the worst had still to come. At the end of the conference the C-in-C prepared the following notes:

My conclusions are set out in the following paragraphs and represent my personal opinion based on my conversations at Lahore and intelligence reports received in the last week or ten days.

Amritsar and vicinity. The strife here was started by the Sikhs who have formed armed bands of considerable strength which are carrying out raids on Muslim or preponderantly Muslim villages. Three or four such raids have been occurring nightly. These bands are well-organized and often include mounted men who are used as scouts to reconnoitre for a favour-able opportunity.

One such band is reliably reported to have killed 200 Muslims in one village a few days ago. The connivance of one of the Sikh States is strongly suspected.

There are also Muslim bands organized for the same purpose, but these are fewer in number, smaller in size and less well-organized, apparently.

The Army has had some successful encounters with some of these bands and has caused considerable casualties in some instances where bands have been caught red-handed. The difficulty is always, of course, to catch the offenders in the act as lethal weapons cannot be used against apparently peaceful villagers unless they obstruct or attack the troops, as has happened in some cases.

Constant and continuous patrolling is being carried out, but the area is large and the troops are few in relation to it. There is no remedy for this, unless the troops are permanently posted in villages as armed police and this is neither practicable nor desirable.

In Amritsar City the casualties (predominantly Muslim apparently) were high and largely due to the emasculation of the City Police Force by the disarming by a new Superintendent of Police of the Muslim members of it. This has since been rectified and the official replaced. Several

*Ayub Khan later became the President of Pakistan.

houses were burning in Amritsar City as I flew over it and four or five villages within ten or fifteen miles of the city were apparently completely destroyed by fire and still burning. The Army is occupying the City in some strength.

Lahore. The aggression here is chiefly by Muslims, said to be in retaliation for the massacring of Muslims in Amritsar. The most disturbing feature here is the defection of the Police, particularly the special Police, who are predominantly Muslim. There is very strong evidence that the Police are taking little notice of the orders of their officers (all the remaining European officers left yesterday) and that they have actually joined hands with the rioters in certain instances.

But for the presence of the Army there would by now be a complete holocaust in the City. Local Muslim leaders are trying to persuade the Muslim soldiers to follow the bad example of the Police – so far without apparent success.

Muslim League National Guards also appear to be acting in the furtherance of disorder.

It is estimated that as many as one tenth of the houses in Lahore City may have been destroyed by fire, or say about 15 per cent of the total area of the City. Destruction to this extent was not readily apparent as I flew over the City but shells of burnt-out houses are not always easy to distinguish in a crowded city like Lahore. A large number of houses were still burning and a thick pall of smoke hung over the City. There were also many houses on fire in the neighbouring suburbs and villages. The roads and streets were practically deserted.

The civilian casualties in the Force Area up to the 13th were estimated to be about 1500 killed and wounded, all due to communal strife. The troops in their clashes with riotous mobs are believed to have killed or wounded over 200 Muslims and non-Muslims in the proportion of 1:2.

In some instances mobs of *jathas** have resisted the troops and fought back. The troops have captured mortars, tommy guns and rifles, and the Sikh bands are armed with light machine-guns.

Ex-Indian National Army personnel are known to have been involved in the East Punjab and are said to have been recruited by the Police in the same area.

Communications. The usual police arrangements for the protection of the railways have completely broken down and the only safeguard now is patrolling by troops, but these are too few to provide adequate protection.

Railway personnel are afraid to leave their houses to go to work, so a breakdown or at least a severe curtailment of railway services seems inevitable unless there is an immediate cessation of communal strife. Such

*A body of Sikhs.

a breakdown will naturally restrict the mobility of the Army and its power to move reserves rapidly to danger areas and will also largely put a stop to the process of reconstitution of the Armed Forces.

Boundary Commission. The delay in announcing the award of the Boundary Commission is having a most disturbing and harmful effect. It is realized, of course, that the announcement may add fresh fuel to the fire, but, lacking an announcement, the wildest rumours are current and are being spread by mischief-makers, of whom there is no lack.

General. The position is thoroughly bad and is getting worse, particularly as the trouble has now spread to Sialkot and Gujranwala, where trains have been attacked.

Large-scale uncontrolled evacuation of Muslims is going on from Amritsar District.

Trains were held up three miles from Wazirabad, casualties estimated 100 killed, 200 wounded, by stabbing.

Trains were derailed at Sialkot and attacked by mob of 3000 which was dispersed by troops opening fire.

North-Western Railway has stopped running trains except Mails, Expresses and Military Mails. No goods trains are running as train crews are not reporting for duty.

Conclusion. Two more brigades (one from India and one from Pakistan) and one mixed armoured squadron are being sent to reinforce the Punjab Boundary Force, but no amount of troops can stop the indiscriminate butchery which appears to be going on on both sides.

General Rees and his Brigade Commanders are doing all they can and so far the troops have been completely impartial and extremely well-disciplined, in spite of baseless and mischievous stories to the contrary which are being spread, in some cases by people in responsible positions. Such stories do the greatest possible harm and may well result in the troops ceasing to be impartial, in which event the situation, bad as it is now, would become truly terrible.

So far as Lahore is concerned Muslim League leaders are said to claim that after 15th August they will be able to control the situation and stop the butchery and burning now going on. I hope that this is true and that the same may apply to the East Punjab Districts, because the Army is now stretched to its fullest extent and it is going to be most difficult, if not impossible, to find any more troops.

We arrived in Karachi thoroughly depressed after witnessing the carnage of the Muslims which was taking place in East Punjab. I immediately went to Quaid and Liaquat and told them of the happenings and the gruesome sights I had witnessed.

Apparently the Quaid, on entering the Government House in Karachi for the first time as Governor-General, had said to his ADC:

Do you know, I never expected to see Pakistan in my lifetime. We have to be very grateful to Almighty God for this great gift.

Karachi is in a festive mood but there is inadequate accommodation for the hundreds of correspondents and visitors who have gathered to see the State of Pakistan being born. My brother-in-law, Colonel Majid Malik, Director of Public Relations in GHQ India, is now the Principal Information Officer to the Government of Pakistan; he is being greatly harassed. All the correspondents expect the impossible. There is no Government of Pakistan but it is being created overnight. There are no Government offices, no Ministries, and no office furniture or stationery. Typewriters are a luxury. It is utter chaos but there is a will to organize all as soon as possible. The Viceroy expected that by 13th August Karachi would emerge as a fully fledged working state capital and would be in a position to receive him, the King's representative.

We are staying at the old Governor's House which is now the Governor-General's residence.

The first function was the banquet at the Governor-General's House where some fifty guests were invited. The atmosphere was tense. Quaid-e-Azam made a short speech. I think it was the only time when he proposed a toast to His Majesty the King. On the contrary Mountbatten, after conveying the good wishes of the King, indulged in a long oration which was not in keeping with such an occasion. Among other things he mentioned that people often wonder why he brought the date of the transfer of power forward. He drew a childish simile by saying that the best way to teach a youngster to cycle was to take him on top of a hill, put him on the seat and then push him down the hill. By the time he arrived on the flat ground below he would have learnt to cycle. Thereupon somebody whispered that there was also the danger that he might break his neck!

After the banquet, which lasted longer than anticipated, there was a reception outside in the garden. It was attended by over a thousand guests. Quaid-e-Azam was quiet and aloof. I went to him and stood close by him without saying a word. He looked at me and smiled. I am sure that he understood that I had come to wish him well and to tell him that all my prayers were with him in the great task that lay before him. I felt proud of such a leader.

He looked every inch the Father of the Nation and the Founder of the ideological State of Pakistan. However, physically he looked frail, tired and pre-occupied. Somehow I could sense that he wanted the reception terminated as soon as possible. Mountbatten did not seem in a mood to go, trying his level best to charm the guests and to convince them that he was a friend and wellwisher of Pakistan. Obviously Quaid-e-Azam could not leave until the representative of the King had left.

I was not far from the Quaid when he called his ADC and told him to tell Mountbatten to go home and that he has had enough of him. The poor ADC did not know what to do. He came to me for advice. I told him to go and tell Mountbatten exactly what the Quaid had said. To give him moral support I told him that I would accompany him. We walked up to Mountbatten and gave him the message verbatim. He was taken aback and said, 'Of course, I should have realised how late it was and that Mr Jinnah was getting tired.' He walked up to the Quaid, apologized and left! What a day it had been.

14th August: This morning there was so much happening, in the middle of which Mountbatten tried to pull a fast one. He had it conveyed to the Quaid that, according to Intelligence sources in Delhi, a plot has been unearthed. A bomb would be thrown at the carriage carrying the Quaid during his State drive through Karachi. He asked the Quaid to cancel the drive. Quaid refused to do so, whereupon Mountbatten suggested that they travel in a closed car. Once again the Quaid declined.

Mountbatten is obviously scared to death. When I heard about it I expressed the opinion that no one would dare do so on such an occasion. It was a false alarm, fabricated by Mountbatten and his staff to convey the impression that Pakistan will not be a bed of roses for the Quaid.

All along the route there was great enthusiasm and wild cheering. It was a sight for sore eyes and very difficult to describe. A dream was coming true and a State was being born. The name of the Quaid-e-Azam was on everyone's lips as well as their thanks to the Almighty.

On their return Mountbatten told his staff that Jinnah was tense and pathetic and held his knees and broke down. He also said that Miss Jinnah is a 'funny woman'.

All thinking people realize the gravity of the task ahead, and of the challenges which Pakistan may have to face if India takes up a hostile stand towards Pakistan.

In the Assembly the Quaid looked most dignified and graceful. On the other hand Mountbatten looked uncomfortable and was overdoing his role. It was not a long ceremony. Mountbatten read out the King's message and then delivered his address. It was followed by a reply by the Quaid. When the ceremony was over everyone was congratulating each other. Edwina Mountbatten was trying to get on to the right side of the Pakistani women, kissing them and showering congratulations all round. Soon after the ceremony the Mountbattens left for Delhi to the relief of all. Some people observed that they were happy to get rid of Mountbatten, calling him 'the evil genius'. Little do they realize that he is still the Head of the Joint Defence Council and as such could do immense damage to Pakistan. He is still responsible for getting the assets and stores divided between the two Dominions.

We flew back to Delhi very tired. The celebrations here are due to start.

The Northern Command from Rawalpindi has issued a Directive on the reconstitution and organization of the Pakistan Command.

HQs Northern Command are to be abolished at midnight 14th–15th August and redesignated as Army Headquarters Pakistan. Many changes are to take place. Certain areas and sub-areas will be disbanded and others established. Everything will be completed within one month.

On our return we found Delhi in a festive mood. The Constitutional Assembly was called late in the night. Independence was proclaimed and Mountbatten was invited to become the Governor-General of India. Dr Rajendra Prasad, President of the Constituent Assembly, and Nehru, conveyed the message to Mountbatten and obtained his acceptance. There were great scenes of rejoicing in the Assembly. Conch shells were sounded and *Hindustan Hamara* (India is ours) by Mohammad Iqbal was sung. Nehru made his famous speech: 'Long years ago we made a tryst with destiny . . .'

The ceremony had to take place today as, according to the astrologers, 15th August is an inauspicious day.

15th August: This morning Mountbatten was sworn in as the Governor-General of India at Government House. The ceremony was followed by Mountbatten's speech to all the legislatures, praising the Congress, Patel and Nehru in the most flattering language. This sort of language had never been used by a Governor-General before. Rajendra Prasad spoke after him.

The invitations to attend the ceremony were in three languages, English, Hindi and Urdu. Later the Indian National Flag was unfurled and a salute of 31 guns fired. Edwina Mountbatten went to Roshan Ara Garden to give away sweets to the children. In the afternoon the Congress flag was unfurled at a ceremony in Princess Park. The British troops lined the route. As there was no law and order at these functions, the public was out of control. The parade was wrecked completely. Mountbatten's carriage, along with the Bodyguard, was mobbed. It could hardly be called a 'ceremony', it was a '*tamasha*'.* There was no discipline and no organization to control the public. Mountbatten's return journey was equally boisterous and Nehru had to be hoisted on top of the carriage. He was screaming, shouting and shaking his fist at the unruly crowd.

In the evening a banquet was given at the Governor-General's House. This was followed by a late evening reception in the Moghul gardens.

I was walking through the Moghul gardens when I noticed a man sitting on a stone bench, with his head bent, smoking a cigarette. The outline looked familiar so I walked up to him. To my surprise I found it was Nawab Ismail Khan in deep meditation. I asked him when he was leaving for Pakistan. Very quickly he said that he would stay in India and look after the people who stood by him and voted for him. He felt that such people needed

*An uncontrolled show.

him more now than ever before. He could not let them down. He maintained
that some Muslim leaders must stay behind for there were still too many
Muslims in India who were not able to dream of going to Pakistan.

The simplicity of his statement left me dumbfounded and I admired him
all the more. Here is a great man with no self-interest.

Independence was celebrated in various provincial headquarters, but
there was confusion everywhere. Some Pakistani units wanted to hoist the
Pakistan flag while still in India but were forbidden.

Mountbatten has been created an Earl.

Thus the great day of 15th August ended.

Gandhi has asked Mountbatten to turn the Governor-General's House
into a hospital.

The Auk, as the last Commander-in-Chief of the Indian Army, issued his
last order.

From now on the Auk will have to swallow the bitter pill of holding
responsibility without power.

On this occasion Savory said:

Sad to see the approaching end of an Empire. Sad not so much because of
our departure but because of what we are leaving behind us which looks
like bloodshed and anarchy now raging in Punjab and elsewhere. Is this to
be the culmination of the British rule in India and the fulfilment of our
great mission? The end of Nehru's Government which will be remembered for wrecking the law and order which the British had tried their
level best to bring about in the subcontinent. The lack of cooperation
between the Muslim and Hindu members of the Cabinet who were often
not on talking terms and finally the slaughter of Hindu businessmen by
the Liaquat's budget of February 1947 and by the establishment of a tax
evasion Enquiry Commission.

The Hindus had the power to keep the subcontinent under one government as long as they decentralized the power to the Provinces. They lost
three great opportunities of keeping India together: the first when they
refused to form Coalition Ministries in the provinces in 1937, the second
when they refused Cripps's offer of the steps to be taken towards self-
government in 1942 and finally when they rejected the Cabinet Mission Plan
in 1946. They regret it now. They had no statesman among them. Whenever
they conceded anything to the Muslims it was grudgingly given and was
always too late. They lacked foresight and the essence of responsibility and
greatness. Their brain could be termed as a brain of the professional middle-
class. The Congress High Command was arrogant and lived in a world of
make-believe and was not prepared to face the reality of the situation, which
helped indirectly in bringing about the establishment of Pakistan. They now
maintain that this was a by-product of their effort to free India.

By their short-sighted policies they antagonized the Muslims, who gradually came to believe they were out to destroy them as a community and that there was no racial, cultural or linguistic unity between them and they could not live together. Their approach to human problems is totally different to that of the Muslims. They have a split personality. Their actions are different to what they practise and they have developed an inferiority complex which is understandable as they were ruled by the Muslims for many centuries. On the other hand, though the Muslims were destroyed by the British, they did not suffer from any anti-British sickness. After 1857 the Hindus received all the encouragement and support from the rulers but they slandered the British, maligned them and blackmailed them, but at the same time gained every advantage from their presence.

The Auk told me that Mountbatten had offered the C-in-C-ship of India to Bill Slim knowing full well that he would not accept it. There is no love lost between the two. Auk said that Bill Slim has written a rude letter to Mountbatten to the effect that he is not prepared to serve the Hindus.

The London *Times* wrote an editorial under the heading 'The End of an Era'. *The Times* was happy that the two States had decided to join the British Commonwealth. It said that Pakistan had emerged as the leading State of the Muslim's World since the collapse of the Turkish Empire. The gap has now been fulfilled and Karachi will become the centre of Muslim cohesion, and a rallying point for Muslim thoughts and aspirations. As far as India was concerned, *The Times* went on to say, the caste system forbade the rise in India of a community such as the Western World expects and that these barriers will have to be removed. The Indian States, in response to the Viceroy's appeal, have associated with the Dominions but the case of Kashmir and Hyderabad is still to be decided. It went on to say that the Joint Defence Council under Lord Mountbatten's chairmanship is evidence of the fact that in the face of a common danger the subcontinent of India will still be one. It further said that Mountbatten has given the assemblies at Delhi and Karachi the British traditions.

Sudhir Ghosh, who had been appointed Public Relations Officer, Government of India, at India House, London, wrote to *The Times* to the effect that the past was dead and that they face the future with faith in the destiny of India. He wrote: 'We shake hands with British people for as we fought them we also learnt to understand and respect the good that is England.' He further went on to say that Mahatma Gandhi is a true friend and a lover of the British. He gave credit to Gandhi and said it was he who made it possible for their British connections to end in comparative peace and free from hatred and bitterness. At the same time he said that Gandhi would not take any part in the Independence celebrations, because his slogan is 'Love and forgive, love and create, love and be free.'

Another correspondent wrote, 'India has never seen anything worse than this present orgy which has already sullied the name of the Sikhs.'

The Quaid reviewed a Parade of the Armed Forces in front of the Governor-General's House in Karachi. Later he greeted the citizens of Pakistan as follows:

It is with feelings of the greatest happiness that I send you my greetings. August 15 is the birthday of the independent and sovereign State of Pakistan. It marks the fulfilment of the destiny of the Muslim nation which has made great sacrifices in the past few years to have its own homeland.

At this supreme moment my thoughts are with those valiant fighters in our cause who readily sacrificed all they had including their lives to make Pakistan possible. Let me assure them that Pakistan will remain grateful to them and cherish the memory of those who are no more. The creation of the new State has placed a tremendous responsiblility on the citizens of Pakistan. It gives them an opportunity to demonstrate to the World how a nation containing many elements can live in peace and amity, and work for the betterment of all its citizens irrespective of caste or creed. Our object should be peace within and peace without. We want to live peacefully and maintain cordial friendly relations with our immediate neighbours and with the world at large. We have no aggressive designs against anybody. We stand by the United Nations charter and will gladly make our full contribution to the peace and prosperity of the world.

Muslims of India have shown to the world that they are a united nation and their cause is just and righteous which cannot be denied. Let us on this day humbly thank God for His bounty and pray that we might be able to prove that we are worthy of it.

This day marks the end of a poignant phase in our national history and it should also be the beginning of a new and noble era.

Let us impress the minorities by our words, deeds and thoughts that as long as they fulfil their duties and obligations as loyal citizens of Pakistan they have nothing to fear. To the freedom-loving tribes on our borders and the States beyond our borders we send out greetings and assure them that Pakistan will respect their status and will extend to them its most friendly cooperation in preserving peace. We have no ambitions beyond the desire to live honourably and let others live honourably.

Today is the Jumat-Ul-Wida, the last Friday of the Holy month of Ramazan, and it is a day of rejoicing for all of us wherever they may be in this subcontinent or throughout the world. Let the Muslims congregate in their thousand in all the mosques and bow in all humility before the Almighty to thank Him for His eternal kindness and generosity and seeking His assistance and guidance in the task of making Pakistan into a great State and themselves into its worthy citizens.

Finally, let me tell you fellow citizens that Pakistan is a land of great potential resources but to build it up into a country worthy of the Muslim nation, we shall require every ounce of our energy that we possess. I am confident that it will come from all wholeheartedly.

PAKISTAN ZINDABAD

16th August: There was a meeting of the Joint Defence Council under the chairmanship of Mountbatten. It was attended by Nehru, Patel, Baldev and Liaquat.

The Auk was there as well and gave his views on what he had seen in the last few days and on the discussion he had had with Jenkins and Rees. These were more or less according to the notes he had prepared after his visit to Lahore. He emphasized that the delay in announcing the award of the Boundary Commission had resulted in the wildest rumours, even to the extent, for example, that Lahore will be part of India. This has given fresh impetus to the killings by the Sikhs. The award should have been announced on 9th August, as Jenkins had suggested earlier.

At the meeting Patel said that rioting at Rawalpindi started a chain reaction. He admitted, though, that Tara Singh had recently made indiscreet and inflammable speeches, which had added fuel to the fire. Liaquat openly said that the whole thing had been carefully engineered by the Sikhs, under the guidance of Baldev. Without the active cooperation of the Sikh leaders he could not visualize any improvement in the situation.

Baldev, as usual, denied all knowledge and said he was in no way connected with it. However, he would use his good offices to make them see reason.

Nehru sat depressed and in a daze. He asked whether there was a military escort on every train. If so, why did the massacres take place? He was told that the gangs got on to the train with their arms concealed. Once on, they then attacked suddenly. Sometimes they put one man on the train to pull the communication cord at the spot where the rest of the gang was already waiting. The train escorts could do little.

Mountbatten tried to humour everyone and admitted that he hoped he had not made too big a mistake by not announcing the award on 9th August. He said that the storm was not unexpected, but its extent could not have been anticipated. He said he now realized that if he had rounded up the Sikh trouble-makers, including Tara Singh, he would not have had to face this day.

At the end of the meeting it was decided that the leaders would meet in Ambala the next day to find ways and means of controlling the fury.

My designation is now 'Private Secretary to the Supreme Commander'. I told the Auk that it was advisable that I should give up the present job and go over to Pakistan where I had volunteered to serve in spite of my home being in India. The Auk is very reluctant to let me go and wants me to stay as long as he is in the subcontinent. Thereupon I told him that it was in his own interest that I relinquish the present assignment otherwise he would be censured by the Congress for keeping a Pakistani in such a key position. With the greatest difficulty I have managed to convince him, and suggested that he should get a British Private Sectretary. In the end he agreed and his nephew, Lt-Col Jackson, has been selected to relieve me.

The award has been shown to the leaders. It is a black day for Pakistan. All the rumours were true about Mountbatten amending the findings, and that he has destroyed the proof. What he did not realize was that, by mistake, a copy was sent to the Secretary of the Governor of the Punjab which Jenkins gave to his successor, Sir Francis Mudie,* who handed it over to Liaquat. This has horrified Mountbatten.

The amendments Mountbatten made were common knowledge. The Canal Headworks at Ferozepore have been awarded to India on the instigation of his great friend, the Maharajah of Bikaner who, on the 11th, sent his Prime Minister, Sirdar Pannikar, and his Chief Engineer, Kanwar Sain, to see him and were given a long interview. It has convinced the Muslims that Mountbatten altered the award. It is also rumoured that Bikaner threatened to join Pakistan if the Headworks were not given to India. Finally, Nehru was instrumental in getting the award altered. A corridor has been provided to Kashmir. Mountbatten says that he received the award on 13th August and signed it on the 15th. Everyone knows this is not correct. The late announcement has caused havoc because of the uncertainty of which areas would finally belong where. Mountbatten wanted the bloodbath to happen when the two Governments had been established, so that the reponsibility would not be his. However, Mountbatten told the Auk that he hoped that he (Mountbatten) had not made a wrong decision in not announcing the award on 9th August.

The award goes against 'the majority population principle' laid down for the guidance of the Boundary Commission. It follows the natural boundary near Gurdaspur which leaves the Muslim majority areas in India. This goes to prove that the so-called 'other factors' here come into play. There is no doubt now why they were introduced.

Mountbatten denies that he altered the award, but everyone realizes that this was his parting kick to Pakistan.

The creation of a corridor is a present to Nehru for agreeing to the partition of the subcontinent. To cover up and dispel doubts, both the Sikh and Hindu leaders are condemning the award. As a result the Muslim leaders are bewildered.

The award is final and irrevocable. It will add another dimension to the bloodbath.

Incidentally, Jenkins, the Governor of Punjab, would not allow Radcliffe

---

*Sir Francis Mudie (1890–1976) entered the ICS in 1914; was Acting Governor of Bihar 1943–44; Home Member, Viceroy's Executive Council 1944–45; Governor of Sind 1946–47; of W. Punjab 1947–49.

to stay at Government House. I hear that Radcliffe's own Secretary is not too happy over the award either.

17th August: The Award was published today.

A meeting of the Joint Defence Council has been held in Ambala. Both the Prime Ministers were there. Arthur Smith represented the Auk. Pete Rees told the meeting that without the Punjab Boundary Force the slaughter would have been far greater. He hoped that the force will stay on until the two Governments take control.

Liaquat and Nehru have been doing their best to bring people to sanity. They have issued many orders. In West Punjab these were carried out but, due to a weak administration in the East, they could not be implemented. The forces unleashed against them are too strong. The Sikhs are burning the country from Lahore to Jullundur and turning it into a battlefield.

Percy Howard wrote in *The Sunday Express*, 'It was really the movement of the Sikh community out of the new Pakistan which sparked off the great killings in the Punjab and they acted like savages.'

18th August: The Pakistan *Times* reported, 'In the Punjab the notional division had been unfair but the final award has gone much further and hacked off some of our richest tracts of land. The blow has been the hardest in Gurdaspur where the two Muslim Tehsils of Gurdaspur and Batala with a Muslim majority have been thrown into Hindustan along with the Pathankot Tehsil, taking away from Pakistan the rich Muslim industrial area of Batala. A part of Lahore has been broken off. Radcliffe has gone to the trouble of drawing a village to village boundary but the Ajnala Tehsil of Amritsar District with a 60 per cent Muslim majority and contiguous to the district of Lahore has been completely forgotten. The Tehsils of Zehra and Ferozepore with a clear Muslim majority have been dismissed with talk of "disruption of communication".'

19th August: The Auk is very worried as reports pour in from all over the subcontinent on the communal disturbances. There has been a rebellion in Rampur against the Nawab who has been pro-Congress all along. On one occasion at our house Liaquat was angry with Zaidi, the Chief Minister of Rampur, for playing a leading role in undermining the struggle for Pakistan. Liaquat had told him that when the time came he, Liaquat, would have no objection to the State joining the Indian Union, but he should not do it prematurely as this would jeopardize the fate of the Indian Muslims.

The Punjab, especially Amritsar, is bad. Sikh personnel of the Indian National Army have formed a private army for the slaughter of the Muslims. They, as their aspirations were not fulfilled, have been enraged by the terms of the Award. They want to ensure the elimination of Muslims from the Sikh areas of the Punjab. The Indian Government is incapable of controlling

The Auk with the author and his children.

The Auk with Ayub Khan on the way to review the parade of the 1st Punjab Regiment.

The Auk with the author's younger daughter Chootu during a visit to Pakistan.

The Auk, the author and his wife at the Auk's 90th birthday party at the Hurlingham Club.

DEAR SHANAZ

THANK YOU VERY MUCH
FOR YOUR LETTER AND
THE PICTURES. I LIKE
THE MOTOR CAR VERY
MUCH AND THE FLAG
TOO✱ TO MORROW I WILL
TRY TO GET SOME 🪑🪑🪑
🪑 AND 🪑🪑 AND
🪺🪺 AND 🪴🪴 for the NEW
HOUSE. IF WE CAN NOT FIND

THEM IN THE SHOPS
WE SHALL HAVE TO
MAKE THEM
                    LOVE FROM CHIEF

A letter from the Auk to one of the author's children.

the Sikhs. There is virtually no Ministry in East Punjab; in fact they are collaborating with the attackers and the looters. The Delhi administration has broken down as well.

Trains to Pakistan are being looted each day and its occupants slaughtered. It is a battleground. People have gone mad. At Amritsar a man was caught carrying powdered chillies which he confessed were used for blinding the Muslims. British troops equivalent to three divisions are still in the subcontinent but only as spectators. People want them to restore law and order.

We all knew that carnage was in the offing. So did Mountbatten. Events are out of his control and he is flowing with the tide. There is even communal tension within the Punjab Boundary Force, and there is a likelihood that the troops may be shooting at each other. The situation is explosive. Both the Dominions are blaming the Boundary Force. Poor Pete Rees, as Commander of the Force, is doing his level best under the circumstances.

The Auk has told Mountbatten that any attempt to replace the Boundary Force by Dominion-controlled forces, forbidden to cross the common boundary, would be likely to end in disaster, and possibly in an open clash. He said that he had no wish to retain operational control of this critical area a moment longer than necessary.

In the history of the subcontinent this will be recorded as the greatest exodus. The killings are on a massive scale. Great Britain will never live this down. Is all that is happening Mountbatten's parting shot, or is it due to his slow-wittedness? Has he performed a 'physical miracle'? History will tell. Whatever the Auk has prophesied has come true.

20th August: A meeting was held of the Joint Defence Council where the Army was blamed for not keeping law and order in Punjab.

Another meeting, that of the Supreme Commanders' Committee, was held. It is quite obvious that the decisions taken by it are not being implemented. India is only interested in disbanding the Boundary Force and winding up Supreme Headquarters. India maintains that it has no powers and no machinery to implement the decisions. All this is being done to ensure that the assets and stores are not divided.

The Auk maintained that if the original timetable had been adhered to, which was that the division take place by April, 1948, it might have been possible to reconstitute the forces and avoid bloodshed. In any case Mountbatten did not agree and saw no reason why the Supreme Headquarters could not deliver the goods. In fact, if the original timetable had been followed, there would have been no need to appoint a Supreme Commander. Mountbatten was very keen to have somebody in that position as a scapegoat in case things started going wrong.

Pakistan is interested in getting its share of ordnance stores and India determined that it should not and the only way India can achieve their end is by getting rid of the Supreme Commander's Headquarters – in other words the Auk. They have, therefore, started a slanderous campaign against him in the Press and are making his task most difficult. Even Mountbatten is not giving the necessary support and backing to the Auk in this difficult task.

British authority ended on the night of 14th–15th August, and the Boundary Force is to end on the night of 1st–2nd September. I wonder what will happen after the disappearance of the Boundary Force. A civil war? Is it meant to be? Is it a part of a Plan that the two Dominions will always be at loggerheads? Is it the price Pakistan is paying for not having Mountbatten as a common Governor-General of both the Dominions? What a mess the Labour Government is making. Is this the peaceful transfer of power they advocated? Wavell would never have allowed it to happen this way. If there had been another Governor-General he would have resigned by now, ashamed over what is happening, but not Mountbatten. Does he wish to see the destruction of Pakistan? In fact he is ensuring that even Kashmir goes to India.

The Auk is disgusted and fed up. He is a broken man. On occasions he opens his heart to me. From the beginning Mountbatten's theme has been 'I have come, I have seen and I have partitioned, whatever the consequences!' He hardly ever consults the Auk. The British Empire which tried to build India over centuries can never live down this great tragedy.

The Auk also wrote to Mountbatten and said that in East Punjab every effort should be made by the leaders to stop the killing, so that reprisals may not start in West Punjab. If this continued, anarchy is bound to follow, adversely affecting the discipline and impartiality of the troops.

21st August: Jackson, my successor, has arrived. I have prepared my handing-over notes for him. I have also put down 'likes and dislikes of the Supreme Commander', as a point to be discussed with Jackson. When the Auk saw the whole list he commented that he himself would like to have a list of his likes and dislikes for reference!

22nd August: A meeting of the Indian Cabinet was held to consider the situation in the East Punjab. Nehru said that fresh outbreaks of violence in certain areas has taken place in spite of the fact that Master Tara Singh and Giani Kartar Singh* are undertaking a tour of the rural areas.

Nehru complained that the manner in which the Boundary Force is functioning is not altogether satisfactory and the command of this force does not inspire confidence in the people. He suggested that the Boundary Force in these areas be put under the Commander of the respective communities.

23rd August: Menon is going to London as the Indian High Commissioner. This is not to Gandhi's liking. Menon is bound to induct his old communist

---

*Leaders of the Sikh community.

friends in the Embassy, which I am sure will not be appreciated by His Majesty's Government.

25th August: Joint Defence Council. The Boundary Force came under heavy criticism. Everyone wants its dissolution.

The *Times* Special Correspondent in the Punjab has written a harrowing article under the heading: 'Massacres in Punjab – Muslims butchered by armed mobs of Sikhs – breakdown of civil administration.' (See Appendix XI, p. 344.)

This evening the Auk gave a large supper party to bid me farewell. He spoke a few words which were very touching and presented me with an inscribed silver salver. He also gave me the 'Union Jack' which flew over the C-in-C's House as a memento.

The Auk told me that my son, Hassan, must go to Wellington, his old school in United Kingdom. He said that he had already written to the school and that Hassan's name had been registered. While there he would like Hassan to live in the same dormitory where he lived.

26th August: Most of the day I have spent packing. Tahirah is away in Simla. I went to say goodbye to my many friends and associates. Cariappa tried to persuade me to stay on in the Indian Army. He is a well-meaning individual. Rajindra Singhji came to my office to say goodbye. He too wanted me to change my mind and stay on in India.

27th August: The *Hindustan Times* has written a very damaging article. It said that the British officers of the Boundary Force did not rise to the occasion. Perhaps they did not have any interest in their jobs now that India has been lost to the Empire. It said that the manner in which the British civilians and officers have reacted to the situation was not satisfactory. The article went on to say that the West Punjab Government was freely distributing arms among the villages. Muslim officers were working zealously for the evacuation of Muslims from Amritsar, whereas non-Muslim officers are not given similar freedom in Lahore. The article did not say anything about the massacre which was taking place in East Punjab. In fact the paper completely overlooked it.

It stated that it was generally agreed that the choice of General Rees as the Commander of the Boundary Force was not a happy one.

The Auk protested to Mountbatten about this article. To pacify the Auk, Mountbatten said that, after obtaining Nehru's permission, he would send for Devadas Gandhi and Sahney, who represented the *Hindustan Times* and *Indian News Chronicle* respectively. He said he would tell them that the Government did not wish the officers to be attacked in the Press and specially British officers who have volunteered to remain.

Mountbatten also said that Baldev Singh has again put forward a scheme for the separation of the Boundary Force.

I flew from Palam to Chaklala in an air force plane. As I got into the plane I had a guilty conscience that I should not have left my job as the Private Secretary to the Supreme Commander and should have stayed with him during the turmoil. In that capacity I could have been of some use to my countrymen in getting them evacuated from Delhi. Not that an individual could have changed the trend of events, but perhaps I could have influenced them to some extent. I felt as if I was escaping. I am quite sure that my residence would have become a refugee camp as I could not have possibly denied protection to many of my friends. It was a sad feeling.

The way things are shaping out it may become difficult to travel between the two countries. I hope and pray this does not happen. I have too much at stake with my mother and other relations still in Lucknow. There has been no communal friction in the city till now, and I hope there never will be.

Until now, in this diary, I have recorded the events that took place in the subcontinent, during the two years of my posting in Delhi.

Now that I go to Pakistan, to begin life as a Pakistani, I have been wondering whether I should continue writing and recording.

I have come to the conclusion that some day I may publish my diaries as a book, for in it there will be certain facts brought to light of which few people have knowledge. These facts emerged through my close association with the Auk. Even though I will no longer be a member of his staff, I will certainly keep in touch with him, and follow his activities during the remainder of the time that he is Supreme Commander.

PART VI

Dismissal

August 1947

'I have no hesitation whatever in affirming that the present Indian Cabinet are implacably determined to do all in their power to prevent the establishment of the Dominion of Pakistan on a firm basis.'

The Auk.

27th August: On my arrival in Rawalpindi I have been posted to the 'Staff Duties' Branch of GHQ. My job is to trace and locate Pakistani units and Pakistani elements in Indian units which are spread all over India and to get them to Pakistan as soon as possible. This is not an easy task.

28th August: The partitioning of the Indian Army is going at a great speed. Things are not looking too good. The Punjab is in a very bad way. The Sikhs continue protesting against their area being divided between Hindustan and Pakistan. They are going round in organized gangs of about 500 strong, burning and killing. Practically no trains are getting through to Pakistan from Delhi. Many of them have been held up and looted and Muslim passengers hacked to pieces. The ghastly atrocities are difficult to record. It is not easy to see where this will end. The Army can do little. All this is within a fortnight of India's freedom. Nothing much appears in the Indian Press which is severely muzzled under the new regime.

29th August: This morning we heard that another Muslim train from Bharat has been looted and burnt. Millions are on the move. Some refugee columns are twenty-five miles long. General Key,* the Commander of Lahore Area, is doing his best. Trains are arriving in Rawalpindi full of the injured and dead.

Major-General J. B. Dalison† gave us a harrowing account of his train journey from Delhi. He said the train he was travelling in had no escort and

---

*Major-General Berthold Wells Key (b. 1895) commanded 11th Indian Division 1942; commanded Rawalpindi District 1946; commanded Lahore District 1947.

†Major-General John Bernard Dalison (1898–1964) was DAG (India) 1944–45; DQMG (India) 1947; AG (Pakistan) 1947.

was attacked by 500 Nihang Sikhs dressed in dark blue and yellow uniforms. They were well organized. They broke open the window and dragged his bearer out of the compartment, hacking him into pieces in front of his eyes. All the Muslims were taken out and murdered and the train looted. He said it was a most appalling sight. Dalison said that the Sikh community had only one object. This was the elimination of local Muslims from East Punjab. The Government machinery in the province no longer operates and everyone is prophesying a civil war. He also said that their leader informed him that he had orders not to harm the British 'this time'.

September 1947

1st–2nd (Night) September: The Boundary Force has been wound up. This was the unhappiest command ever created. Its creation was the result of one of Mountbatten's 'hunches'. The job was stupendous. They tried their best but failed.

2nd September: Patel has said that anarchy looks like spreading throughout India and that he is powerless. General Rob Lockhart is advocating that the Auk should take over the country, declare Martial Law and run it till sanity returns. It is too late already.

Patiala is keen to extend the boundary of his State.

4th September: The Indians are determined that the division of assets and stores should not take place. No decisions are forthcoming and there is little movement of stores. Everything seems to be at a standstill. Patel and his henchman, Bhalja, have said that they will not allow any machinery to be despatched to Pakistan. India is in possession of everything. Why should they give it up? They are determined to undo Pakistan.

India wants the Supreme Headquarters to be wound up. A campaign has been mounted in the Press against the Auk to force him to resign. He is now considered to be a champion of Pakistan. V. P. Menon says that the object of the exercise is to force the issue with the Auk and give him notice to quit. In other words they are resorting to skull-cracking.

The Auk returned from Simla. He had told my wife that the Indian administration is facing a breakdown. He said the Indians would like to detract public attention from their failure to control the situation by turning it against the Supreme Commander and his staff. By doing so they are insinuating that the Supreme Commander is responsible for all the present ills.

The Auk maintains that India and Pakistan are drifting towards war.

Mountbatten is in Simla. V. P. Menon has asked him to return to Delhi and take over the country. He said if that is not done within twenty-four hours India would be lost. He told Mountbatten that this request had the blessing of both Nehru and Patel.

In UP Pant has controlled the disturbances. This happened after General (Tiger) Curtis threatened that he would impose Martial Law if the Sikhs were not forbidden to carry their *kirpans* and the civil authorities were not given wide powers to deal with the situation. His bluff worked and law and order has returned.

5th September: Mountbatten returned to Delhi along with Ismay. He has immediately formed a Cabinet Emergency Committee to control the disturbances. The situation in Delhi is extremely critical. Muslims are being hunted and butchered in the streets, and the bodies lie rotting. Arson and looting are the order of the day. Conditions in the refugee camps are appalling. It is a real disgrace. The Muslim policemen have been disarmed. A handful of troops of doubtful reliability are supposed to protect the lives and the property of the refugees. I am told they watch the destruction and have become partisans. There is utter chaos and the Government has lost its balance. The city transport has been suspended, the telephone and telegraph system has broken down as there are no operators to attend to it. There are no clerks in the offices. The appeals for protection are being ignored.

6th September: Royal Scots Fusiliers were called to Delhi to quell the disturbances. This was conveniently labelled by the Congress as a move to 'protect British lives'. One company was also sent to Palam Airport. Aircraft carrying Muslims were not allowed to land.

7th September: No planes were allowed to land at Willingdon Airport as it was unsafe and a massacre was in progress.

Even Nehru has asked for a British Guard on his house! What a come-down! These are the very troops he has been trying to send away. Delhi is totally out of the control of Nehru and company. Obviously the Indians have no idea of how to tackle the situation.

8th September: Even though I wrote to the Auk the other day, I spoke to him on the telephone this morning and asked him to get my family down from Simla. The situation in Northern India is bad. The Sikhs in Simla have been slaughtering the Muslims according to a pre-arranged plan. The civil administration in East Punjab is practically non-existent. There too the Muslims are being slaughtered according to a concerted plan. Anarchy prevails in many areas.

The Supreme Commander has written to Nehru bringing three incidents to his notice which took place on 7th September in Delhi. These involved British officers. Nehru wrote back deploring the incidents and said that they should not be tolerated. He said that the British officers and men were perfectly entitled to resist any such interference and were rightly bitter about the incident. He also saw no objection to the British Guard being posted on the Messes and Quarters.

9th September: The Auk had a clash with Mountbatten, who issued orders to General Wood and Air Marshal Walmsley to attend a meeting of his Emergency Committee over the Auk's head.

Panic in Delhi has been reduced due to the arrival of another British battalion.

10th September: The Auk sent his ADC and a platoon of infantry to bring Tahirah and the children from Simla. Colonel Altaf Qadir along with his family and other officers joined my family for safety. They passed through armed crowds and jeeps loaded with armed men, and saw Muslims being shot and their property burnt. At Kalka the caravan was joined by Col. Ayub Khan who was evacuating his family.

The Auk had sent his aircraft to Ambala, which brought Tahirah and the children to Delhi. Flying over the city my wife said she saw many buildings burning.

The Auk was happy on their arrival and put them up in his own house. 'Thank God that you have arrived safely,' he said to Tahirah. Soon after, General Rajindra Singh, the Area Commander, called on my wife. He told her that he was ashamed to mention that he had no control over his troops and that they had become hooligans. He also said that he had asked for South Indian units which he knew were not communal-minded. Two battalions of Madrassis were on their way. With their arrival he hopes to restore law and order.

Cariappa also called on her and expressed similar sentiments.

The Auk sent quite a few of his photographs and a host of papers to me here at Rawalpindi. F/Lt. Salauddin, one of the ADCs, has a good collection of the Auk's photographs too.

The Auk had a meeting at which the three Deputy Supreme Commanders – Navy, Army and Air Force – and the Commanders of the three Services from both the Dominions were present. He says that the likely date of the closure of his office will be 1st April, 1948. He maintains, however, that certain joint organizations, for example ordnance factories, will not be split by that date and perhaps might never be. He is going to recommend to the Joint Defence Council that they run under some Joint Inter-Governmental Committee after Supreme Commanders' HQ closes.

The Auk says that his HQ takes orders from the Joint Defence Council and not from either Dominion. The sole object of his HQ is to ensure rapid and efficient reconstitution of the Armed Forces and he is not prepared to accept any further responsibilities.

He referred to the attacks appearing in the Press against his HQ and against himself. This was highly undesirable and was part of a plan to malign him.

He went on to say that there appeared to be an idea that he wished to delay the nationalization of the forces of the two Dominions in order to prolong the stay of the British officers in the subcontinent. This was entirely incorrect. The reconstitution and nationalization were inter-related and any action taken during reconstitution must be in consultation with his HQ.

11th September: Delhi is in the grip of panic and nothing is working. The Sikhs are at the bottom of all the trouble and are asserting themselves to retain their identity in trying to carve out a pure Sikh province for themselves.

The Indian officers are getting communal-minded.

12th September: There is great rejoicing in East Punjab over the killings of the Muslims.

13th September: The Sikhs have sworn to kill every Muslim in India as a revenge for the killings in Rawalpindi. The Muslims in Delhi are terrified. Small parties of Sikhs come around the bungalows occupied by British officers. They are looking for Muslim servants, who are usually protected by their masters. Muslim families have been shifted to Central Army Messes. There are reports of starvation in the refugee camp.

A horrific incident occurred when armed Sikhs entered the lounge of the Grand Hotel in Simla in broad daylight to slaughter Muslim women and children under the very eyes of other hotel guests. No news was allowed to leak out, and no action was taken against the culprits. This is the doing of the 'Hindu Inner Circle' who want to ensure that no British officer should witness the killings lest it became known outside the country.

I have always maintained that Gandhi has double standards. He is now advising the Muslims to 'stay and risk death rather than run away to Pakistan'.

The Auk wrote to General Rees and congratulated him on his excellent work while in command on the Punjab Boundary Force. He said that the Force had been formed as a neutral body to help the civil authorities in the event of trouble over the Award of the Boundary Commission. He further said that the Force would have been quite adequate for this purpose, but the situation it had to face was a completely different one. The massacre, arson and disorder which started in Amritsar, even before the Boundary Commission had made its award, had nothing to do with boundary or anything connected with it. The whole movement was undoubtedly planned long beforehand. Soon this gave rise to inevitable repercussions in West Punjab with the result that the Force had to face problems beyond their power. The complete breakdown of the civil administration and the total failure of the police force placed a burden on them beyond their capabilities. Still, no amount of praise was enough for the way it was tackled. And he hoped that some day people will acknowledge their debt to the Punjab Boundary Force. All that the Force did was in the interest of humanity and security.

The Auk wrote the following letter to Mountbatten:

PERSONAL & PRIVATE
SUPREME COMMANDER'S HQ
DELHI, 13th September, 1947

My Dear Dickie,

I have been thinking over our talk yesterday afternoon and, even at the risk of wasting your time and of interfering in what is not my business, I feel I must tell you of my fears about the present situation. I see in today's newspaper that the ban placed on 'kirpans' has been virtually withdrawn. I feel that the general public, here and all over India, can place one interpretation only on this action, which is that the Government does not really mean or wish to grasp this problem of asserting its authority over the forces of disorder. The inference is that it is afraid to deal with the Sikhs as they should be dealt with. As we agreed yesterday, everyone is unanimous in placing the blame for the actual shedding of blood on them, whether it was planned by them or someone else. They are the physical users of force against the defenceless in Delhi and this force was used after careful and extended reconnaissance – there is no doubt as to this.

My original proposal to you for really decisive action, such as would have been hailed all over India and throughout the World as a proof that this India Government were determined to rule and be masters in their own house, may not have been wholly practicable, but the present policy of half-measures and appeasement of the Sikhs on religious grounds is in my opinion worse than useless, and is fraught with the gravest danger for the future. At least I cannot help thinking that it is. I do not question the sincerity of the leaders and I think many people of reason and experience are prepared to believe in their good faith. All the same, although their policy and actions as reported in the Press may look all right, the immense majority of the people, Indian or European, do not believe in its reality or effectiveness. I am sure that not one single Muslim in Delhi today believes in the smallest degree in the good faith or intentions of this Government, and I think this is a terribly dangerous state of affairs, not only for the present, but for the future and from the widest point of view, not merely the local.

Whether the Government can now do anything to restore confidence I do not know. I am sure, however, that confidence can only be restored by decisive action to prove the goodwill of the Government and not by long speeches or half-measures which deceive no one. Least of all the instigators and perpetrators of these horrors!

Two more small points if you can spare the time to read on. First – although it is stated in today's papers that food, etc., has been distributed to the Muslim refugees – nothing whatever had reached those in the Purana Qila by 4 p.m. yesterday when I visited the place, though while I was there a very belated party arrived to instal water points to ensure a reasonable supply readily available. Food had been supplied – not much I am afraid – by the efforts (quite improper!!) of my QMG and of various humane people, Indian and European, who had bought up supplies in the market and sent it in to be resold to the refugees, many of whom have no money.

Secondly, my DMS – Treffry Thompson* – of whom I have the highest opinion, warns against too indiscriminate and uncontrolled inoculation against cholera. The inoculation is effective only for two or three months, and we may well have to face large outbreaks all through the cold weather, while the supply of vaccine is by no means unlimited. He advocates close watchfulness, the holding in readiness of vaccine reserves and inoculation when it is apparent that the risk is real. I agree with him.

Forgive this long screed – it is meant only to help. Don't bother to answer it.

Yours,
CLAUDE AUCHINLECK

P.S.

I have just had some inside information on the Sikh intentions.

If my information is true, and I see no cause to doubt it, then the Sikh plans are much what I have always thought they would be. Briefly, they intend to make Simla the capital of a Sikh State, in which there will be very few if any Muslims and possibly not many Hindus either. Today Simla is completely under the thumb of the Sikhs and the Maharaja of Faridkot is in this business right up to his neck. He personally warned British ladies in Simla that it was time they got out, as their turn might be coming soon. He told poor old Miss Hotz to get rid of all her Muslim servants overnight from Wildflower Hall – which she managed to do, though there were six corpses on the road outside her gate next morning. I am pretty sure myself that Patiala is in it all too, though he has been more discreet.

They think they are well on top of this Delhi Government and I dare say they are right. Certainly they are arrogant and ubiquitous. One theory – very widely held – is that the Sikhs intend, possibly with the aid of Sikh units of the old Indian Army and the troops of Sikh States, to march on Lahore and retake it as well as the rich lands of Montgomery and

---

*Major-General Sir Treffry Owen Thompson (1888–1979) was Director of Medical Services to Allied Land Forces South-East Asia 1944–45; DMS to Supreme Allied Command SE Asia 1945; DMS in India 1946–47.

Lyallpur, from which the Sikh landholders and farmers have withdrawn by order of the Sikh leaders, not under Muslim pressure at all. The idea seems to be to concentrate the Sikhs as far as possible in the Eastern Punjab so as to have concentrated power there. The Muslims of Lahore and the border districts are in a very jumpy state and firmly believe in the coming Sikh 'invasion'.

The theory is that the Indian Government would not sponsor any such aggression but would make a show of trying to hold the Sikhs back without actually doing very much. If the attempt failed they would disown them and say 'we did our best to hold you back – now you have had it.' They (the Hindus) would then set about the Sikhs properly and destroy their cohesion. If the attempt succeeded, it is probable that the India Government would back them up and use the chance to destroy the Pakistan Government and so bring Pakistan to an end, substituting a Brahmin 'Raj' for the whole of India including Pakistan. This may sound fantastic to you, but I assure you that it is quite possible, though I do not go so far as to say it is probable.

It is yet one more indication of how unsuitable a place this is becoming for the British officer, unless he be a completely unscrupulous adventurer!

I must ask you not to show this letter to anyone or to divulge the contents of it as having come from me, though you can at your discretion pass the information on for what it is worth as having come from a usually reliable source!! I enclose a copy of an intelligence report I received after writing the above, which, though not from an altogether neutral source, is, in my opinion, reasonably fair and correct so far as my knowledge goes.

16th September: Ambrose Dundas says that the Government of Nepal is keen for the employment of three battalions of the Gurkhas by the Pakistan Army.

18th September: India is increasing pressure on Hyderabad and Junagarh. Three sloops have been sent to frighten them into submission.

19th September: Field-Marshal Auchinleck wrote to General Scoones:

... Things have happened here and in the Punjab which would have been unbelievable a few weeks ago. The refugee problem is really colossal and to find a solution for it seems almost impossible. In short, the idea that the coming of Partition and the grant of Dominion autonomy would cause communal feeling to die down has proved entirely false. Communal feeling today, from the highest to the lowest, is, in my opinion, as bitter as it possibly could be and any idea of real cooperation between the two Dominions on any subject is almost unthinkable at present. One can only hope that reason will prevail and that matters will now begin to improve in this respect. But there is no sign of it at present. Our position as a neutral body trying to partition the Armed Forces to the equal advantage of both Dominions is not, as you will realize, exactly an easy one.

There is no doubt, I fear, that the Army has become infected with the communal virus.

We expect not more than about 3,000 British officers out of a rough total of 9,000 to volunteer to remain on during Reconstitution. With the Army at its present size, over 40,000 men, there are not enough officers, even counting the British officers, to go round. As you know, moreover, the quality of such officers as there are are nothing like high enough to enable us to find sufficient officers of the requisite experience and knowledge to fill the high command and staff appointments. This has been pointed out by me at frequent intervals. I do not think, however, that facts such as this make much impression on people who are determined to nationalize the officer cadres as quickly as possible, which appears to be the case so far as the Indian Government is concerned. In Pakistan the authorities seem to be much more reasonable and they are refusing to listen to the clamour of certain interested dominion officers that national-ization should be speeded up regardless of efficiency. In fact they have taken the line that they do not intend to promote Dominion officers too soon or too quickly and they have given Frank Messervy a very free hand in this matter. I think myself they are very wise in the course they are pursuing but whether they will be able to resist the pressure of interested people for very long I do not know. I do think, however, that they are certain to ask for the services of quite a number of British officers even after reconstitution has been completed. I do not myself think that India will ask for the services of many British officers after this date, if she asks for any at all. Personally I doubt if she will ask for any except possibly for a few technicians, who will probably be asked to adopt Dominion nationality.

20th September: The Auk rang me today to say that he would bring my family along with him to Pindi.

While my wife was in Delhi, General Dudley Russell,* the GOC East Punjab, had suggested that she could travel by train across the border. The Auk gave him a piece of his mind and told him that he was talking nonsense. No journey was safe. This is as much as Russell knew of the prevailing situation!!

23rd September: The Auk brought my family and servants with him in his aircraft to Rawalpindi. 'Can I have a receipt for the goods delivered?' he asked me with a smile.

*Lieutenant General Sir Dudley Russell (1896–1978) was Chief British Adviser to the Indian Army 1948–54.

My baggage also arrived intact through the good offices of Pete Rees.

For a long time the Auk sat with me in the hotel room and surveyed the entire political situation of the subcontinent. He told me that he had been let down by His Majesty's Government. He said categorically that Mountbatten, as Chairman of the Joint Defence Council, was no longer impartial and his (the Auk's) position was becoming untenable. I told the Auk that he should relinquish his appointment otherwise Mountbatten would push him around further and make a scapegoat of him. The Auk was a very sad man carrying within him a deep sense of failure.

26th September: Mountbatten has dismissed the Auk and wrote to him thus:

STRICTLY PERSONAL

Government House,
NEW DELHI
26 September, 1947

My Dear Claude,

This is probably the most difficult letter that I have ever had to write in my life, because although it will end with a piece of news which gives me the greatest pleasure to break to you, the proposition that I now feel bound to put to you distresses me very much and I only hope it will not give you pain.

As you know, I have always held the view that it was absolutely essential iin the interests both of India and of England that you should remain at the military helm, not only until the transfer of power, but also until the reconstitution of the Armed Forces had been substantially completed. You have proved a tower of strength: and I do not know what I should have done without you. I have, as you know, always tried to fight your battles with the greatest vigour against all criticism, from whichever quarter it may have come.

I admit that I was anxious as to what your position would be after the transfer of power; but when the Joint Defence Council accepted my proposal to make you Supreme Commander in charge of a Supreme Headquarters, I hoped that we had succeeded in devising an arrangement which would satisfy the desire of both the new Dominions to have forces under their own operational control, with effect from the 15th August, and which, at the same time, would ensure central administrative control over all the forces in the subcontinent of India during the process of reconstitution. I had hoped, in particular, that your own position was safeguarded by the fact that you were not to have any operational control, and that, even in the administrative field, you would be carrying out the directions of the Joint Defence Council.

Alas, my hopes were very soon shaken. Scarcely had the new set-up come into force when a volume of criticism started, not only in the papers (which I managed to get stopped) but in the Cabinet itself. I am sure you have been aware of this criticism but I doubt whether you realize its extent or its persistency. The complaint of the Indian leaders is that the previous Commander-in-Chief in India and his subordinate Commanders-in-Chief have merely been converted into a Supreme Commander, with three very senior Deputy Supreme Commanders and Supreme Headquarters containing senior staff officers, which towers over their own Navy, Army and Air Force commanders. They say that this is a derogation of their sovereignty and is impeding the autonomous development of their Armed Forces, and so on and so forth.

I am well aware that you did not ask for the title of Supreme Commander, and I plead guilty to having selected it but I was anxious that your status after 15th August should be in no way diminished.

It is not, however, only the title to which exception is taken. There is no doubt in my mind that Indian Ministers resent the fact that at the head of the Supreme Headquarters there should be a man of your very high rank and great personal prestige and reputation – so immeasurably superior in these respects to their own Commander-in-Chief. I should be a poor friend if I did not admit that this resentment, which was initially directed against your position, has inevitably turned against yourself. One of the most balanced and level-headed Ministers complained recently that you seemed to regard yourself as the champion of Pakistan's interests; such is the reward of strict impartiality! It is only fair to add that Pandit Nehru himself has no personal bias in this matter and sympathizes with the difficulties of your position.

I have argued the case with the Indian leaders at great length. I have pointed out that you have no operational command over the Armed Forces of either Dominion, and that Lockhart, Elmhirst* and Hall† are responsible solely to the Indian Cabinet. I have explained that everything that you do in the administrative field is subject to the approval of the Joint Defence Council. I have emphasized that you are responsible to His Majesty's Government for all the British officers now serving in India, as well as for the British troops who are awaiting withdrawal. I have reminded them of your unparalleled services to India and to the Indian Army, and of the deep personal regard which they entertained for you in the past.

*Air Marshal Sir Thomas Elmhirst (1895–1983) was Chief of Inter-Service Administration in India 1947; first C-in-C Indian Air Force 1947–50; Governor of Guernsey, 1953–58.

†Rear-Admiral John Hall (1896–1964) was Senior Naval Staff Officer, India Office, and RIN Liaison Oficer 1944–46; Flag Officer Commanding (later Commander-in-Chief) RIN 1947–48.

I am sorry to say that I have completely failed to convince them – the heated arguments at Tuesday's meeting of the Defence Council may have been the last straw – and the point has now been reached when I can no longer prevent them from putting up an official proposal to the Joint Defence Council that the Supreme Headquarters should be abolished and replaced by an organization with a less high-sounding title and headed by less high-ranking officers.

The discussion of a proposal of this kind in the Joint Defence Council would be absolutely deplorable. It is possible that the Pakistan representatives would oppose the proposal out of cussedness, but not, I fear, out of any sincere desire to support you. It is only a short while ago that they were pressing for your removal on the grounds of your alleged anti-Moslem sentiments during the Gurgaon disturbances. But whatever line Pakistan might take, I myself would find it a most difficult case to argue.

There is of course the point of your special personal responsibility to His Majesty's Government for British officers in India; but it seems to me that, now that the Joint Defence Council have approved your paper suggesting that all who wish to stay on should enter into new contracts with the two Dominion Governments, your personal responsibilities will have been substantially discharged. In any case I myself would find it very difficult to argue that a Supreme Commander, with the rank of Field-Marshal, and three Deputy Supreme Commanders with the rank of Air Marshal or its equivalent, are essential to look after their interests. We all know how much they look to you personally but it would be a terrible reflection on other senior officers if none could be found to take your place.

But, above all, my dear Claude, I should simply hate to contemplate a discussion in which your great name became the subject of bitter controversy, and in the course of which imputations might be made which, though palpably unjustified, could not but cast a slur on your reputation and prestige. This must be avoided at almost any cost and I see only one way out of the dilemma.

You have often told me, with characteristic unselfishness, that you would willingly and indeed gladly fade out of the picture if I were at any time to tell you that this would help me personally or the general situation in this country. Bitter though it is for me to say so, I sincerely believe that the moment has arrived for me to take advantage of your selfless offer: and my suggestion is that you should yourself write a letter to me as Chairman of the Joint Defence Council proposing the winding up of Supreme Headquarters as soon as the major units have been transferred to their respective Dominions and its replacement by an organization with a less high-sounding title and headed by much less high-ranking officers.

I would not dream of suggesting the exact terms of such a letter to you, but should you be willing to fall in with my suggestion, the attached rough draft might be helpful.

Having seen this coming for some time – although hoping against hope that I could get the clamour to die down – I took the opportunity of Listowel's presence out here to discuss the matter with him. I do not need to assure you that I repeated to him what I told the Cabinet in London, namely that I regarded you as the greatest Commander-in-Chief that India has ever had. I explained the volume of criticism that was now being unjustly directed against you, and I emphasized your special responsibilities to His Majesty's Government for all British officers in India and for the British troops still in this country. I concluded by warning him that the position might even be reached when the feeling of nationalism and the desire to be complete masters of their own house would reach a point at which it was impossible for any living Englishman to retain the title of Supreme Commander.

Having now no secret channels of communication to the Prime Minister and in view of the frightful difficulty of explaining a complicated story like this in a telegram I asked Listowel to explain the position that might arise to Attlee, and through him to the Chiefs of Staff, and to obtain his contingent approval to my acting at my discretion if I felt the time had come. The Prime Minister's approval has now arrived. In other words, His Majesty's Government have given their approval to any arrangement that I may think advisble.

I have felt so guilty in our recent talks at being unable to put the case fairly and squarely before you: but I was so terribly anxious to keep you by my side that I hoped against hope that things would blow over.

I have been keeping back from you till now a matter which I have only recently received the Prime Minister's permission to disclose to you.

In the final Indian Honours List which I was instructed to send in on the eve of the transfer of power on the 14th August, I need hardly tell you that your name appears in a class by itself at the top of the list. I asked the Prime Minister to recommend your name to the King for a Peerage, and I am immeasurably gratified and thrilled to be able to inform you that the Prime Minister wishes me to obtain your consent to putting your name forward to His Majesty for a barony.

I know you are not the sort of person who would wish to seek an honour of this sort for yourself, but please bear in mind that this honour will have its effect on all those British officers who have looked to you so long. It will make them feel that there is no question of your being pushed out, but that the rearrangement of the headquarters was a natural event, and that your sterling services have been recognised by the King.

My original intention was that your peerage, if you decided to accept it, would appear in the next New Year's Honours List, since, at the time of recommending it, I imagined that you would be at your post until the Spring of next year. If that, alas, is not to be the case, I should like to see your peerage announced by itself, simultaneously with the announcement of your resignation: and I much hope that you will allow me to send an immediate telegram to the Prime Minister to this effect.

Yours ever
Dickie

P.S. Pug has tendered me advice to release him within the next month or so for he too feels that as an 'impartial' official he will soon be subject to similar criticism.

His Excellency
    Field-Marshal Sir Claude Auchinleck,
        GCB, GCIE, CSI, DSO, OBE.

Mountbatten enclosed the draft of the letter, which follows:

DRAFT OF A SUGGESTED LETTER FROM THE SUPREME COMMANDER TO THE GOVERNOR-GENERAL OF INDIA (IN HIS CAPACITY AS CHAIRMAN OF THE JOINT DEFENCE COUNCIL)

I have been reviewing the position of Supreme Headquarters in connection with the reconstitution of the Armed Forces. It will be remembered that originally the target date was April, 1948. I am glad to say that, in spite of the setbacks which we have naturally received through the troubles in the Punjab, this date can be advanced to the end of February or early March, 1948.

Between now and that date there will not only be a progressive reduction in the headquarters, but I have come to the conclusion that there will be a point at which a radical step-down could be made in the whole set-up. This date I suggest should be in October. On this day, I consider, that the Supreme Commander and the three Deputy Supreme Commanders of the Navy, Army and Air Force could be released without loss of efficiency and their work continued on a lower level by the existing Principal Staff Officers. At this moment I consider it will be proper to abolish Supreme Headquarters in its present form and replace it by an organization which might be called 'the Joint Administrative Headquarters of the Armed Forces'.

I would suggest that the senior of the existing Principal Staff Officers should take charge of the Headquarters under the title of 'General Officer in Charge Joint Administration', with a Commodore Royal Navy and Air Commodore to look after the interest of these two Services.

It will be noticed that by this arrangement the Commanders of the three Services of the two Dominions will all be senior in rank to the senior officers of their respective services in the Joint Administrative Headquarters.

I would suggest that the G.O. i/c Joint Administration should take the place of the Supreme Commander in the Joint Defence Council, and that he should be responsible to His Majesty's Government for the British troops awaiting withdrawal.

So the Congress has succeeded in getting rid of the Auk. But the way it has been done is shabby and not in keeping with the great office he holds. First, Mountbatten obtained the permission of His Majesty's Government for Auk's removal. He then faced him with a *fait accompli*. The least Mountbatten could have done was to have discussed the issue with the Auk in the first instance. I am certain the Auk would have put in his papers immediately. Mountbatten did not have the moral courage to do so. The Auk on many occasions had volunteered to resign, but for him to leave now under a stigma of being dubbed as the champion of Pakistan's interest, and to question his impartiality and integrity is, to say the least, a degrading and a dirty trick beyond all comprehension.

Mountbatten has praised the Auk sky high and said that the Auk has proved to be a tower of strength to him, and that he does not know what he could have done without him. It is all very well to say it now. The truth is that, in most of the decisions, Mountbatten never consulted him. If he had, he would not have made such a mess of things.

Mountbatten is trying to convince the Auk that what he is doing is in Auk's interests. He is safeguarding the Auk's prestige and reputation. In fact the Auk is too great a man to care for such trivialities.

In a nutshell the Indian leaders have decided not to honour their pledge of dividing the assets and stores. They were finding the Auk a stumbling block in their designs. So they have got rid of him. Mountbatten has become a tool in the hands of the Congressmen.

On a previous occasion the Auk had been offered a barony but had refused. Mountbatten has offered it again. The Auk had said that he cannot be bought. He maintained that he had received the highest rank which the Army could offer and is not interested in any other honours. I think that if the offer had come from His Majesty the King, the Auk would have accepted it dutifully. Mountbatten did not know the Auk.

The same day Ismay wrote to the Auk:

Dickie has shown me his letter to you. At first I was very unhappy; but, on further reflection of all the forces at work in this sorry situation, and of all the unpleasant possibilities that face us, I have come to the conclusion that Dickie's proposal is the happiest solution of an absolute impasse.

I feel as strongly as I have ever felt anything in my life that you in a big way, and I in much smaller way, are now in completely impossible positions by reason of our lack of power. I simply could not bear the thought of the possibility that mud should be cast on you in the last months of an Indian career which has been longer than that of any previous C-in-C – not excluding Bobs of Kandahar – and certainly not less glorious than any of them.

I have seen the possibility coming for some time – as indeed I know that you have from various things you have let drop. And it has frequently been on the tip of my tongue to raise it. But somehow or another I thought that you would do so – if you so wished; and I refrained. I only hope to God that on this – as on many fundamental things – your feelings will be the same as mine; and I long to come and have a yarn with you whenever you wish. As to the peerage, I doubt whether this will give you much of a thrill. But I beg you to accept it, as it will give so much real pleasure to your legion of friends, and to the wonderful Army that you created – but which has now alas been disrupted. One day we will spend an hour or so on the crossbenches, but it will be many years before I make my maiden speech. How about you? My thoughts are much with you, old friend, and I want to see you.

28th September: The Auk sent a situation report for the information of the Cabinet and Chiefs of Staff in the United Kingdom.

It said that Mountbatten's personal popularity in India was immense. However, in Pakistan he was looked upon with suspicion. Soon after the rejoicing, there were signs that there was trouble ahead. The Auk said that 'Pakistan Government removed themselves from Delhi with almost indecent haste and proceeded to establish themselves as far away as possible at Karachi. . . . There was little doubt in my mind at the time that they would have done better to have formed their Government at Delhi in the first instance and functioned from there for the first few months.' 'There is now open enmity between the two Dominions and in the opinion of many they are on the verge of actual conflict.'

As far as the plan of the partition of the Armed Forces was concerned, the Auk said that it was hoped that initially the two Dominions would share a number of training and other establishments but this has proved completely in vain. He went on to say that the Armed Forces Reconstruction Committee functioned to start with extremely well. However, on one of the main issues, that is the ratio in which the moveable assets of the former Armed Forces of India are to be divided, difference of opinion arose. These included the reserves and working stock of all classes of stores, arms, ammunitions and equipment. These assets were worked out on the basis of the strength after reconstruction and the result was 64 per cent to India and 36 per cent to Pakistan. However, the Indian Government is apparently 'determined to contest it to the last ditch. Meanwhile the whole work of the division of these stores, etc. is held up'. He maintained that the Armed Forces Reconstitution Committee must continue to function as there were still major points of policy to be decided.

The Auk said that the Joint Defence Council has been supervising the work of the Armed Forces Reconstitution Committee and the general division of Armed Forces and their movable assets. 'Pakistan's representation on the Council has undoubtedly suffered from the fact that her Government was at Karachi and not in Delhi and this has resulted on more than one occasion in my having to suggest or present the case of Pakistan which is understandable as it has undoubtedly increased the already strong and carefully fostered conviction of the members of the Indian Cabinet and their subordinate officials that I and the officers of the Supreme Commanders HQ are biased in favour of Pakistan.' In future the Joint Defence Council will meet alternately in Delhi and Karachi, and when the Joint Defence Council cannot agree on any matter it will be referred for decision to the Partition Council composed solely of representatives of both Governments or to a tribunal presided over by Sir Patrick Spens, the former Chief Justice of India.

In the second half of the Report the Auk describes the political situation. He says:

My opinions are based on close personal observation, on reports received from my subordinate commanders and officers, both on my own headquarters and in the Armed Forces of the two Dominions, as well as from discussions and conversations with Indians of varying status and opinions.

In my considered opinion, there is no doubt that today the communal feeling and tension between the two Dominions of India and Pakistan is so great that there is a real risk of their becoming involved in open war with each other at short notice. I sincerely hope this will not occur.

I have no hesitation whatever in affirming that the present Indian Cabinet are implacably determined to do all in their power to prevent the establishment of the Dominion of Pakistan on a firm basis. In this I am supported by the unanimous opinion of my senior officers, and indeed, by all responsible British officers cognizant of the situation. No one was originally more strongly opposed to partition than myself, if only for military and strategical reasons, but since His Majesty's Government made their decision and I was entrusted with the task of dividing the former Indian Armed Forces between the two Dominions, I and my officers have worked wholeheartedly and impartially to effect this. There can be no question as to the truth of this statement.

Before the transfer of power on 15th August, the representatives of the new India forbore to show their hand and displayed generally a spirit of reasonableness and an apparent desire to cooperate. The meetings of the Armed Forces Reconstitution Committee were conducted in an encouraging spirit of cooperation and of give and take.

Since 15th August, however, the situation has steadily deteriorated and the Indian leaders, Cabinet ministers, civil officials and others have persistently tried to obstruct the work of partition of the Armed Forces. I and my officers have been continuously and virulently accused of being pro-Pakistan and partial, whereas the truth is that we have merely tried to do our duty impartially and without fear, favour or affection. That we have done this is universally acknowledged by all fair-minded people. This campaign continues and grows stronger and more vicious every day. The Governor-General, Lord Mountbatten, is subjected to strong and unceasing pressure to abolish my Headquarters, so that the one impartial body remaining in this country shall be removed.

The attitude of Pakistan has been reasonable and cooperative throughout. This is natural in the circumstances, as Pakistan has practically nothing of her own and must obtain most of what she wants from the reserves of stores, etc. now lying in India . . .

There is no doubt the civil administration in the East Punjab (India) has almost completely broken down and that law and order have practically ceased to exist. In the West Punjab (Pakistan) conditions in this respect are better, but the administration is terribly weak there also.

The Sikhs have throughout taken the major part in the orgy of murder, loot and rape which has been going on for weeks past and is still going on in the East Punjab. This campaign was deliberately conceived, planned and executed under some central direction. This is common knowledge and there is ample evidence to prove it.

It is not clear whether the plan originated with the Sikhs or whether they acted as agents under the bidding of some more sinister and obscure leadership. In Delhi the same happened. The Sikhs led the massacre, to effect which systematic reconnaissance had been carried out for weeks beforehand. The result is that, today, in my opinion, few think that the Indian Government is now able to control the Sikhs.

In the early days of the Delhi massacres I urged the Governor-General to try to persuade the Indian Government, in their own interest as well as in that of humanity, to take some really decisive action against the Sikhs and prove to the world that they were the rulers. The Government, however, took no such decisive action. The weak and hesitant action taken in respect of the wearing of kirpans only made the situation worse and exposed the weakness of the Government.

It is commonly believed that the rulers of the Sikh States of the Eastern Punjab have been behind the campaign of extermination, for such it is, in the East Punjab. They certainly do not appear to have done anything to stop it, in spite of their protestations.

Today there is an organized system of information and control which enables Muslim refugee trains to be attacked with impunity. A few days ago 1,500 helpless refugees are said to have been massacred in one such train alone at Amritsar, the escort, including the British officer in command, being killed or wounded. On the other hand military trains carrying troops and stores in the furtherance of Reconstitution are unmolested.

Delhi is quiet now, but there is no guarantee that the killings will not start again at any moment. The country around Delhi is in a thoroughly disturbed state though and no Muslim can move about freely without risk of his life.

On the other side, too, in Pakistan, there have been equally horrible occurrences, though the general impression is that these are more spontaneous and less organized than those in the East Punjab.

In the last week or so at least five British officers have been killed in India in carrying out their duty in attempting to protect refugees or in putting down disorder.

I have tried to explain earlier in this Report that the obstructive tactics of the Indian Government have already made Reconstitution largely inoperative, now that the actual movement of major units of the Army and the division of the Navy and Air Force are practically complete . . .

In the event of open hostilities between the Armed Forces of the two Dominions, by no means an impossible contingency, it will be essential to order all British officers and Other Ranks serving with these Armed Forces to desist at once from any form of activity connected with their command and administration. Arrangements have been made to effect this at short notice and Commanders concerned have been informed. Both Governments have been officially made aware of this position through the Joint Defence Council.

General Savory, who originally belonged to a Sikh unit and was much admired by them, prepared a paper and the Auk said 'I agree with all you say in this really first-class paper, which puts the whole situation most clearly and concisely.'

This paper formed the basis of a talk on the Sikh problem which Savory was called on to give to the Chiefs of Staff in London, on 8th October, 1947.

The Sikhs would have been prepared to enter Pakistan had it not been for the March riots. These made it impossible. The Sikhs, as part of Pakistan, would have retained a measure of political identity. But, as part of Hindustan, they feared economic absorption by the Hindus; also religious absorption. In short, they feared (probably correctly) virtual extinction as a political force; and survival only as a rapidly dwindling religious sect of Hinduism.

They were therefore in a cleft stick. Their leaders were divided. They played their political cards, before 15th August, very badly. So badly, in fact, that there were many people in high positions who thought that they were exhausted as a major political factor and could be ignored.

The partition of the Punjab and the March riots gave the Sikhs the necessary impetus for taking what they considered to be the only action remaining to them for survival, i.e. force. This is in complete accordance with Sikh tradition, particularly when directed against the Muslim.

The Sikh action was well planned, well directed and well carried out. There has been in all their actions clear evidence that their long connection with the Indian Army has served them well.

Their large colony in Montgomery moved, on orders, into the East Punjab, giving up the rich lands which they had personally made cultivable out of the desert during the past generation. It would not have been difficult for them to have remained where they were. Their convoy was not a mere 'refugee column'. It was an organized movement, carried out with military precautions, tactical and administrative, and it moved in good order with few casualties.

This move helps the Sikhs to concentrate in their original homeland, where they will be more powerful than ever.

Meanwhile, the rising has gone on and achieved much success. Such success indeed that its influence is now felt distinctly in Delhi and Simla.

It is possible that the Sikhs themselves have been surprised at their success.

In the East Punjab they are a law unto themselves. They ignore the orders of the Provincial Government. They also ignore, when it suits them, the orders of the Central Government, which is supine with regard to the Sikhs, whom it obviously fears.

In fact the Central Government have lost control of the Sikhs and a situation is now arising in which they will have to decide whether to re-impose their will on them, which will mean the use of force and will alienate the Sikh soldier of the Indian Army, or whether it would not be wiser to recognize what is a *fait accompli* and grant the Sikhs a measure of autonomy within the Union of India, on condition that they extend no further east, and settle down to the peaceful administration of their territory.

There is a risk in either course, but it would seem that the latter is the lesser of the two evils. There is, however, a danger that the Sikhs, having tasted success may later try to extend further eastward. It is not without significance that there has recently been a recrudescence of trouble in the Gurgaon District and in the States of Alwar and Bharatpur. The Jats have many similarities with the Sikhs and a Sikh/Jat movement is by no means impossible. It has in fact been canvassed actively during the past year.

The position of the Central Government is not a happy one. They have already begun to lose control. In the geographical sense their position is possibly even less happy. Delhi is dominated today by the Sikhs. Tomorrow it may be on the very border of the Sikh State. Can it stay where it is? Can it stay at all?

So far the rise of the Sikhs has been considered only in relation to its effect on Hindustan. What about Pakistan?

In the first place, the Muslim is the traditional enemy of the Sikh. Today the Muslim is no longer this. He is the 'actual' enemy.

Secondly, the Sikh State of the eighteenth and nineteenth centuries extended right across the Punjab to the mountains on the North-West Frontier. The Sikhs remember this.

Thirdly, the Sikh colonies around Montgomery, the Sikh shrine at Nankana Sahib, the old Sikh capital at Lahore, are all not only very tempting baits but are within comparatively easy reach.

The hatred of the Muslim, the memories of the old Sikh Raj (only three generations ago) and the desire to regain the fertile areas so recently evacuated, are all strong incentives. The strongest, in my opinion, is the desire (possibly the determination) to get back the Montgomery colonies. The rest supply the moral impetus. The combination is indeed strong.

The canals which irrigate the Montgomery colonies have their headworks on the Sutlej, the very border. The Sikhs are now in a position, therefore, to stop all irrigation of those lands; and in their present temper they will undoubtedly do so.

The Sikh shrine at Nankana Sahib is very near to the canal headworks at Balloki. One will lead to the other – a religious goal with an economic result, a strong combination. This would bring the Sikhs to the Chenab.

Further north are the headworks on the Chenab of the system which irrigates the area. (It is a curious coincidence that these headworks are near Chilianwala.*)

In short, the Sikhs already have a hold in the fertile area around Montgomery (I am told that in evacuating this area they destroyed the distribution system irrigating their farms), and the other systems are not beyond striking distance, even if the objective merely be to deny, by destroying their headworks, the irrigation system now watering another of the remaining fertile areas of Pakistan. The possibility is real. The effect on the economy of Pakistan would be great.

The Sikhs therefore are a threat, not only to Hindustan, but also to Pakistan, and they are in a mood to take action. They are in a mood to take precipitate action; and this might possibly be their undoing.

30th September: Here in Rawalpindi Tahirah and Lady Messervy, along with other ladies, have formed an organization which is receiving the refugees at the railway station and taking them to the camps where they are being looked after by the Army and Civil authorities.

---

*Scene of a famous battle between the Sikhs and the British on 13th January, 1849.

October 1947

'Mountbatten made many false steps. Kashmir was a lasting disgrace and tragedy. . . . He has a good deal to answer for. . . . His knowledge of India and Indians was practically nil. Also he had some odd advisers.'

The Auk.

3rd October: The situation in East Punjab is shocking. There is wholesale slaughter of the refugees both on the line of march and in the trains.

The refugee camps in Delhi are in a deplorable state and cholera is fast spreading among the occupants. The Muslims are frightened for their lives. Nehru blames the Hindu Mahasaba and the Rashtrya Swayam Sevan Sangh* (RSSS) for the slaughter of the Muslims. He says that they have penetrated the ranks of the junior civil servants who have been shouting 'India for Hindus' and 'Down with democratic principles'. Nehru maintains that the RSSS have joined hands with Sikhs and have incited them.

The Quaid has said that the stand Nehru has taken about the events was a fiction and designed to act as an excuse for the complete lack of control. The Quaid maintains that Nehru is incapable of suppressing the Sikhs. His only aim is the destruction of Pakistan. He says that Nehru is impractical, vain and unbalanced, that at the moment he is only a figurehead and that he has lost much ground in favour of Patel who holds the real power. Patel is truly mixed up with the RSSS and will not allow them to be suppressed. Incidentally Ismay is of the same view and believes that the Sikhs are at the root of all the trouble. Tara Singh and the Sikh princes are organizing, arming and financing them. He is of the opinion that it is quite possible that the Sikhs may start guerrilla warfare on the boundary between India and Pakistan, and will certainly be backed by the Congress.

5th October: Auk wrote a letter to General Scoones at the India Office marked 'Personal and Top Secret'.

It said:

I send herewith for your personal information only a copy of a note I propose to submit to the Joint Defence Council on the winding-up of

*A Hindu militant party.

my Headquarters. . . . As you know there has been a violent animosity towards my Headquarters, the Joint Defence Council and indeed any form of joint activity, which may help to secure anything for Pakistan at the expense of India, in the minds of the Indian Government, and they have put every possible pressure on Mountbatten to get rid of me and my Headquarters. We are quite willing and anxious to go, as you will readily understand, but we cannot quit leaving all the British officers out here without a head or without an organization to look after them and their families.

The Auk, after consultation with Geoffrey Miles, Arthur Smith and Walmsley suggested that he wind up the Headquarters by 31st December. He went on to say:

Whether the Indian leaders will oppose the date being as late as 31st December I do not know but I shall do my best to stick to it as I am sure it is right. Pakistan has no desire to see us go as they know very well that in us lies their only hope of getting anything out of India . . .

The Chief of the Imperial General Staff is, I know, particularly ill-informed as to the situation out here and I expect you realize this too.

The Indian Government, he said, are showing a tendency to by-pass and ignore Rob Lockhart and his British staff officers, and take backstairs advice from Cariappa, etc. They were likely to have no British in any high position after 31st December. He said Pakistan on the other hand wished to keep the British officers in command and high staff appointments for some time to come.

Even in Pakistan there was some opposition to the retention of British officers in high command and this is supported by ultra-nationalist politicians, though frowned on at present by Jinnah and Liaquat, who want to keep the British officers for some time yet . . .

The Liaquat Government is by no means firm in its seat, as there is a strong and rapidly growing opposition to it. I can see no real alternative to Liaquat Ali as Prime Minister.

Regarding the Gurkhas the Auk said there were no signs of any progress towards holding the Katmandu tripartite conference and His Majesty's Government must put a screw on the Government of India.

He further said that the relations between the two Dominion Governments were bad as ever if not worse.

Regarding the Indian annexation of Junagarh the Auk said:

The expedition to Kathiawar in connection with this idiotic affair was ill-advised. I did all I could to stop really provocative action but even this action is almost certain to have serious repercussions in Pakistan and, with tempers as high as they are now, may bring the risk of open conflict between the two much nearer. The whole business is just sheer lunacy.

By this time the Auk has lost the little remaining confidence he had in Mountbatten. It is obvious that he is not going to trust him a moment longer. Hence he submitted his views through a safe channel without Mountbatten's knowledge. He even went to the extent of telling Scoones not to let it be known that he had seen the draft.

6th October: Field-Marshal Auchinleck wrote to Admiral Mountbatten:

I enclose a draft of a note which I have prepared for the Joint Defence Council on the subject of the premature (in relation to the original date of 1st April, 1948) closing down of Supreme Commander's Headquarters.

This note has been prepared by me after the most careful consideration of all the factors involved and in the closest consultation with my three Deputies, who are in unanimous and complete agreement with its contents and with the recommendations made in it.

I personally am convinced that it would not be right or safe to close down my Headquarters earlier than December 31st, though I and my principal advisers would be very willing to do so.

I am well aware, of course, of the pressure which is being put upon you by your Government to effect the removal of myself and my Headquarters. I and my advisers are well aware of the reasons for this pressure. I would, however, remind you that my Headquarters serves not only India but also Pakistan, through the medium of the Joint Defence Council, of which you are the independent Chairman. Therefore, before any action can be taken in this matter, the prior Agreement of the Government of Pakistan is necessary. So far as I am aware, the Government of Pakistan has not yet been consulted as to what it considers should be the date for the closing down of my Headquarters.

In conclusion, I would remind you that there is another aspect, which is rapidly increasing in importance with the deterioration of the general situation out here, and that is my responsibility to His Majesty's Government in the United Kingdom for British officers and other ranks still in this country.

I shall be grateful for your comments on the draft note so that it may be sent without undue delay to the Secretary of the Joint Defence Council to be placed on the agenda for the next meeting.

In his note the Auk recommended:

a)   That the Supreme Commander and his Headquarters should disappear on 30th November, being replaced by a Commander British Forces, India and Pakistan, who would be responsible only for the control and repatriation of the British forces and individual British officers, other ranks and their families in India and Pakistan, excluding such officers and other ranks as might remain in the Services of the two Dominions, under terms to be arranged.

b)   That the existing Military Movement Control Directorate should remain as part of the Headquarters of the Commander British Forces in India and Pakistan until it is closed down.

c)   That the Armed Forces Reconstitution Committee should be dissolved on 30th November, 1947.

d)   That Headquarters British Forces in India and Pakistan should cease on 31st December, 1947.

e)   That as soon as possible after 31st December, 1947, all British Forces and individual British officers and other ranks due for repatriation should be concentrated at Deolali and Kalyan in India, or at Karachi in Pakistan, under the control of two British commanders, who should be responsible respectively, in direct communication with His Majesty's Government in the United Kingdom and the Defence Ministries of India and Pakistan as the case might be, for their welfare and embarkation in accordance with a pre-arranged programme.

7th October: Ismay is reported to have said that Mountbatten had intended to imprison all the Sikh leaders before 15th August, but at the last moment he lost his nerve and changed his decision. Ismay also said that Mountbatten was not impartial and was placed in such circumstances that he had to back India. On many occasions Ismay had disagreed with Mountbatten and wanted to quit, but the Auk persuaded him to stay. Ismay is reported to have said that by now even Churchill had strong anti-Mountbatten feelings. Ismay also says Mountbatten's mission is a failure.

Thereafter Ismay tried his best to dissociate himself from Mountbatten before too much damage was done. Ismay backed Savory for the appointment of Administrative General which, though much talked about, never came into existence. Incidentally the Auk had told me that in the normal circumstances Savory would have succeeded him as C-in-C.

The Auk wrote to Mountbatten and said, 'I gather from Arthur Smith who has told me of his talk with you that you are quite clear as to my powers in respect of the postings of British officers attached to the forces of the two Dominions.' And he enclosed the Charter as agreed by the Partition Council. Mountbatten had questioned his powers to transfer officers from one Dominion to the other.

A proper campaign in the Indian Press has started to get rid of the Auk.

9th October: The Auk saw the Quaid in Karachi and put him in the picture. On his return to Delhi the next day he wrote and thanked him.

Lord Ismay gave his personal view of the happenings in the subcontinent to the Chiefs of Staff in the United Kingdom. He said that the storm which broke out in August was still raging. It was not unexpected but its extent was not anticipated by anyone in authority. He said that, as the date of the transfer of power drew nearer, the Sikhs began the trouble. The intelligence organization had practically ceased to exist and everything was conveyed by rumours. The Governor of the Punjab had reported a Sikh plot to paralyse train movements to Pakistan. The Viceroy, after consultation with Nehru, Patel and Jinnah, decided to round up the Sikh leaders, including Tara Singh, on the eve of the transfer of power. Later, for reasons best known to Mountbatten, this decision, on the advice of Nehru, was cancelled. All along Mr Jinnah maintained that if the original decision had been implemented the trouble would not have taken place.

Ismay further said that it was hoped that the Punjab Boundary Force would be able to control any trouble. It was also visualized that the Muslim and non-Muslim officers of the two Armies would remain on friendly terms as had been demonstrated and advocated on many occasions. On 17th August Nehru and Liaquat had met at Ambala. The situation improved and confidence was established. This was short-lived. In East Pakistan decisions were not implemented as no administrations existed. Besides, there were stronger forces at work undermining the authorities.

Ismay went on to say that on 5th September he returned to Delhi where the situation was critical in the extreme and in the days which followed got worse. He reported that the Muslims were being butchered. Those who were left were sent to camps where the conditions defied descriptions. There was no food, no water, no sanitary arrangements and no security. The dead lay in the streets with the dying. There were no hospital arrangements. Arson and looting were the order of the day. The Muslim members of the Delhi Police had been disarmed. Even the troops used were of doubtful reliability. Everyone wanted guards to protect them. There was no public transport and Delhi was in chaos. The Government of India for all practical purposes did not exist. Nobody cared to comply with their orders. On the return of Mountbatten to Delhi a Cabinet Emergency Committee was set up to handle the situation.

There has been wholesale slaughter of refugees in the trains or on the line of march.

In order to protect Mountbatten Ismay made a lame excuse. He said that the intelligence sources had dried up so the Governor-General did not know what was happening. Everyone knew what was to come. It was written on the wall. It did not require an intelligence organization to tell the Government what was coming. In the countries of the East attention has to be paid to the rumours going round as they are invariably in the nature of a forewarning of the events to come. The fact was that Mountbatten had decided to take no action. He had become an instrument in the hands of the Indian leaders and other trouble-makers.

Ismay said that Nehru, by not accepting his own incompetence, had laid all the blame on the Hindu Mahasabha and the Rashtrya Swayam Sevan Sangh who, he said, were prepared to overthrow even the present Government. According to Nehru they wanted India for the Hindus and their slogan was 'Down with democratic principles'. The Congress, as everyone knew, was a mighty organization and had a great following. It still remained or decided to remain ineffective as others were doing the job for it. Nehru also said that the RSSS, together with the Sikhs, were responsible for organizing the Delhi massacre.

Ismay said the Sikhs were at the root of the trouble as they were highly organized prior to the transfer of power. The only person who could control them was Tara Singh. He was helped by a terrorist organization which was exceedingly well-armed. It had considerable support from the Sikh rulers who helped plan movements and actions. The Sikh supreme religious authorities played an important part. Ismay maintained that Sardar Patel could control them. Until this was done, there was no hope for peace. The Sikhs were strong and confident and if they are to be brought to order, strong action will have to be taken against them.

Ismay said that Nehru has lost a lot of ground while Liaquat had gained. He was of the view that the Sikhs would have to be contained in their new home in East Punjab, otherwise they would either turn towards Delhi or Lahore. Most probably it would be Lahore. In that event guerrilla warfare may ensue, and the Sikhs, backed by India, may invade Pakistan.

Ismay had painted a very correct picture which was in keeping with the Auk's views communicated earlier to His Majesty's Government and the Chiefs of Staff.

13th October: The Auk submitted a paper to the Joint Defence Council stating that both the Joint Defence Council and the Armed Forces Reconstruction Committee were finding their task difficult owing to the differences of opinion between the two Dominions and he could not discharge the responsibility laid upon him by the Partition Council. He said that the division of movable assets had hardly begun and cannot be completed by 1st April, 1948, and that of the Ordnance Factories and Bombay Dockyard much later, if ever.

Auk said that his Headquarters have been made ineffective and they should be closed down on 30th November. The repatriation of the units still abroad could be arranged by the Dominions themselves.

The Auk recommended that an organization to replace the Supreme HQ be created to handle the repatriation of the British officers and personnel and that the military Movement Directorate be centrally controlled.

16th October: A momentous meeting of the Joint Defence Council was held at Lahore where Field-Marshal Auchinleck's Paper of 13th October on the closing down of the Supreme Headquarters was considered. It was chaired by Mountbatten and was attended by Baldev Singh, Gopalaswami Ayyanger,* and Liaquat Ali Khan. At the outset Liaquat said that he did not agree with the proposal as the task allotted to the Supreme Headquarters had not been completed, while Mountbatten maintained that the only task left was the division of the assets which will take many months to complete. He suggested the formation of a small organization to handle the remaining work and the enlargement of the Joint Defence Council by the inclusion of the two Commanders-in-Chief of the Dominion Forces and the Commander of the British Forces in the subcontinent. The two Cs-in-C would set up Inter-Dominion Committees of their own representatives to arrange the division of the assets. Thereupon Liaquat said that the two Cs-in-C were under their own Defence Ministers and would not be in a position to perform this difficult task, as it was essential to have neutral machinery for this purpose. Mountbatten did not agree. He said that it was a thankless job for any individual or organization and if he had realized this fact earlier he would have dissolved the Joint Defence Council on 15th August. Liaquat reiterated that the establishment of a neutral organization was vital to carry out the division of the assets impartially.

The Auk made it clear that he was not running away or shirking the responsibilities assigned to him. His task had been made impossible by the continuous accusation by India as to his partiality which he was not prepared to tolerate. He was bitter. Liaquat maintained that the answer was not to wind up the Headquarters but to make it effective by giving it full cooperation and support. Mountbatten again did not agree and said that the reason for its being ineffective was that it was a neutral agency. Besides, the conditions in Delhi were such that it made the operation of the Headquarters impossible. Thereupon Liaquat suggested they move to Karachi.

Mountbatten treated the division and movement of stores as a minor matter. Liaquat was adamant that it was not so, and said that once the Supreme Headquarters was closed Pakistan would not receive its share of the stores. Thereupon Baldev pledged that he would be responsible for delivering them to Pakistan. To get rid of the Auk he would have pledged heaven itself.

Mountbatten then tried to implicate the Quaid, saying that he had already agreed to the dissolution of the Headquarters. This was incorrect.

Gopalaswami Ayyanger very strongly advocated the closure of the Headquarters.

It was the end of the Supreme Commander's Headquarters as desired by India and an important step towards retaining all the stores.

*Gopalaswami Ayyanger was the Chief Minister of Kashmir for some time.

21st October: Field-Marshal Auchinleck wrote to General Scoones:

> The HQ will close down on November 30th. . . . As you will see from my proposals, it is my intention that I should be succeeded by a Commander, British Forces in India and Pakistan, who would take over completely and discharge, in exactly the same way as I have been doing, my responsibilities in respect of British units in this country and British officers and other ranks serving with the Dominion forces. This is absolutely essential and must be maintained, whatever Mountbatten or the Indian Government may say.
>
> When my proposals for a successor HQ have been agreed to by His Majesty's Government, which is, of course, necessary, I propose to recommend to the Chiefs of Staff that I should be succeeded by Arthur Smith.
>
> The appointment of Arthur Smith is likely to be unpopular with the Indian Government because they resent his impartiality and outspokenness. They have already tried to persuade Mountbatten that he should not be appointed. As, however, he will have nothing whatever to do with reconstitution of the Armed Forces of the two Dominions except in so far as his responsibility for the welfare and fair treatment of their British officers is concerned, the matter is really no concern whatever of the Government of India or of the Government of Pakistan. As a matter of fact, I think Pakistan would welcome Arthur Smith, but, as I say, it is no concern of theirs. I am entirely against bowing to the wishes or prejudices of the Indian Government in this matter. They are the people who have made the present position impossible and they are the people who would like to get control over the British officers and other ranks who will still remain after I go. It is for His Majesty's Government to say who is to command the British Forces in this country and it is for me, I think, to recommend whom I consider suitable. So I shall recommend Arthur Smith, and if you agree with me I rely on you to support me in this.

Mountbatten and the Indian Government are getting worked up over Kashmir.

In order to understand the politics of Kashmir it is necessary to go into the background of the whole affair.

Hari Singh, the Maharajah, was a playboy (the famous Mr A of a notorious case in Europe). He took no interest in the affairs of the State. He seldom moved out of the palace and never visited his far-flung territories. The only time he moved out was to visit Bombay or Calcutta to enjoy himself and meet his women friends. He was frightened of his Muslim population, especially the Poonchis, who had, on many occasions in the early '30s, rebelled against him. There was systematic persecution of the Muslims in the Vale of Kashmir.

In the spring of 1947 the Muslims in Poonch refused to pay their taxes. The State Troops were sent in. This was followed by an order that the Muslims would not be allowed to celebrate Pakistan Day on 15th August. The tempo was further increased with the infiltration of members of the Rashtrya Sewam Sangh, the Indian National Army and the Akali Sikhs who ran amuck in the State.

The Muslim population of certain areas was disarmed. This created panic and taxes were levied on every hearth, every window and every cow, buffalo and sheep and even on every wife.

Hari Singh was under the influence of his 'Kitchen Cabinet' and his Brahmin priests.

Ram Chandra Kak, a Kashmiri Brahmin, took over the Prime Minister-ship from Sir Gopalaswami Ayyanger, ICS. He wanted to introduce reforms in the State but Hari Singh resisted and thereafter they fell apart and there was no love lost between them. On no occasion was his advice accepted. Kak, who was a constant visitor to see the Auk in Delhi, was a man of strong character. Western in outlook, he spoke fluent English and had married an Englishwoman. He was a man of the world. Nehru thought him too clever and hated him.

Kak was a realist and openly advocated that Kashmir should join Pakistan. He maintained that the State would get a fair deal and would be saved from turmoil. However, Hari's priests were more powerful than Kak, and induced their master to carry out private negotiations with the Indian leaders and there was constant coming and going between Srinagar and Delhi by trusted emissaries.

Some Ruling Princes from East Punjab and the President of the Indian National Congress, Acharya J. B. Kirpalani, visited Kashmir in order to persuade the Maharaja to join India. This was followed by a visit from Gandhi on 1st August to clinch the deal. Before his departure from Delhi the 'Apostle of Truth' announced that his tour was absolutely non-political and was being undertaken to fulfil a previous promise to visit the State. In reality it was to pressurize the Maharajah to accede to India and to remove Kak.

Hari Singh also started negotiations with the Sikh mountain states on the Eastern border to allow him to build a road which would bypass Gurdaspur and give him direct access to Delhi.

Kak kept warning Hari Singh that the people of Kashmir would rise against him if he ceded to India.

The British Resident, Wilfred Webb,* maintained that it was logical for Kashmir to cede to Pakistan and that it was in the best interests of the State. He was of the opinion that Kashmir would not be an easy meal for Pakistan

---

*Lt-Colonel Wilfred Francis Webb (1897–1973) was Political Agent Malwa and Bhopal States, Central India 1941–45; Resident in Kashmir 1945–47.

to swallow altogether, and thus they would respect its integrity, status and importance. At the same time Kashmir's economy depended on Pakistan's support. Pakistan could not possibly deny this to their co-religionists.

Kak gave a strong warning to the Maharajah that the Muslim population could not be kept under control for long. It would ultimately rise in support of brother Muslims who were being massacred in India. He also said that there was a danger of the Muslim tribesmen descending from the mountains in Kashmir if there was any sign of accession to India. Only Pakistan could prevent them from entering the State. If trouble broke out then Hari Singh himself would not last for a day.

The outcome of the warning was that Hari Singh locked himself in the Palace, ignored Kak's advice and carried out private negotiations. At the same time he started cashing his assets in Kashmir and transferring them to India and the United Kingdom. He also started negotiations with Vickers for buying a Viking for his safe passage out of the State.

By his advice to the Maharajah to cede to Pakistan, Kak had burnt his boats as far as Nehru was concerned. Everyone knew he would not last long.

Both Mountbatten and Nehru visited Kashmir and tried their level best to persuade the Maharajah to accede to India. The stumbling block was Kak and the Muslim majority in the State.

In August he was dismissed and when he tried to escape incognito was arrested. He was replaced by a palace underling. Hari Singh did not join the Indian Constituent Assembly as he wanted complete independence for the State. He had no wish to surrender his ruling powers to a democratic India, where he knew he would become a nonentity.

In June he was assured by Mountbatten, with the approval of Patel, Minister of States, that he was free to act as his people might wish, and was advised to ascertain their wishes and act accordingly. He was also told that the Government of India will have no objection if he decided to join Pakistan. This was said for public consumption. All the while secret negotiations were continuing for accession to India.

In September Gopalaswami Ayyanger, who was Prime Minister of Kashmir 1937–43, was made Minister without Portfolio and was put in charge of Kashmir Affairs. He was known to be anti-Muslim. Everyone realized that India meant business.

Patel is a realist and had told Nehru time and again that he should let Kashmir join Pakistan as it was of no value or advantage to India. The main reason was that the greater part of its population was Muslim. Nehru was a sentimentalist and a Kashmiri. When it came to accession of Kashmir no reason was good enough and he accepted no advice.

Nehru was also hoping that by Kashmir acceding to India a direct land connection would be established with the North-West Frontier Province. This province had a Congress Government and may become part of India.

In September Ismay visited Kashmir and confirmed that secret negotiations were being carried out between Mountbatten/Nehru and the Maharajah and probably an agreement had been reached.

Hari Singh's Government did not take heed to the events. His Muslim subjects, the Poonchis, rebelled. The Kashmir army was sent to restore order but joined them instead. The tales of atrocities in India had inflamed their feelings.

As long as there was hope that wise counsel would prevail and the Maharajah would respect the wishes of his people, the tribesmen were held back from entering Kashmir. Once it was known that Hari Singh was likely to accede to India, they could not be held back any more and started infiltrating into Kashmir.

In the first half of October when Mountbatten and Nehru further increased their pressure on the Maharajah to accede to India some tribesmen entered Kashmir. On 22nd October more tribesmen crossed into Kashmir. This helped the Maharajah to make up his mind.

The will of the people was never ascertained and on 24th October Hari Singh asked for military assistance from India.

The next day the Indian Defence Committee of the Cabinet met under the Chairmanship of Mountbatten. Rob Lockhart read out a signal from Gracey that the tribesmen had entered Kashmir in force. The Committee ordered the Indian Chiefs of Staff, General Lockhart, Admiral Hall and Air-Marshal Elmhirst, to prepare plans for the invasion of Kashmir immediately. The troops were to be moved by air and some officers were flown in advance to Srinagar to work out the details and arrange reception. The fire was lit.

On 26th October Menon arrived in Srinagar and returned to Delhi the same day. Hari Singh wrote to Mountbatten through him and ceded the State to India. The Indian Cabinet accepted the accession and the invasion was legalized.

Hari Singh wrote:

My dear Lord Mountbatten,

I have to inform your Excellency that a grave emergency has arisen in my State and I request immediate assistance of your Government. As Your Excellency is aware the State of Jammu and Kashmir has not acceded to either Dominion of India or Pakistan. Geographically the State is contiguous to both the dominions. It has vital economic and cultural links with both of them. Besides my State has a common boundary with the Soviet Republic of China. In their external relations the Dominion of India and Pakistan cannot ignore this fact. I wanted to take time to decide to which Dominion I should accede or whether it is not in the best interest of both the Dominions and of my State to stand independent, of course with friendly and cordial relations with both.

I accordingly approached the Dominions of India and Pakistan to enter into a Standstill Agreement with my State. The Pakistan Government accepted this Agreement. The Dominion of India desired further discussion with the Representative of my Government. I could not arrange this in view of the development indicated below. In fact the Pakistan Government under the Standstill Agreement are operating the Post and Telegraph Systems inside the State. Though we have the Standstill Agreement with the Pakistan Government, that Government permitted steady and increasing strangulation of supplies like food, salt and petrol to my State.

Afridi soldiers in plain clothes and desperadoes with modern weapons have been allowed to infiltrate into the State, at first in the Poonch area, then in Sialkot and finally in mass in the area adjoining Hazara District on the Ramkot side. The result has been that the limited number of troops at the disposal of the State have to be dispersed and thus have to face the enemy at several points simultaneously, so that it has become difficult to stop the wanton destruction of life and property and looting. The Mahora power house which supplies the electricity to the whole of Srinagar has been burnt. The number of women who have been kidnapped and raped makes my heart bleed. The wild forces thus let loose on the State are marching on with the aim of capturing Srinagar, the summer Capital of my Government, as a first step to over-running the whole State.

The mass infiltration of tribesmen drawn from distant areas of North-West Frontier Province coming regularly in motor trucks using the Mansehra-Muzaffarabad Road and fully armed with up-to-date weapons cannot possibly be done without the knowledge of the Provincial Government of the North-West Frontier Province and the Government of Pakistan. In spite of repeated appeals by my Government no attempt has been made to check these raiders or stop them from coming to my State. In fact both the Pakistan Radio and Press have reported these occurrences. The Pakistan Radio even put out a story that a Provisional Government has been set up in Kashmir. The people of my State both the Muslims and non-Muslims generally have taken no part at all.

With the condition obtaining at present in my State and the great emergency of the situation as it exists I have no option but to ask for the help from the Indian Dominion. Naturally they cannot send the help asked for by me without my State acceding to the Dominion of India. I have accordingly decided to do so and I attach the Instruments of Accession for acceptance by your Government. The other alternative is to leave my State and my people to the looters. On this basis no civilised Government can exist or be maintained. This alternative I will never allow to happen so long as I am the Ruler of the State and I have life to defend my country.

I may also inform Your Excellency that it is my intention at once to set up an Interim Government and ask Sheikh Abdullah to carry the responsibilities in this emergency with my Prime Minister.

If my State has to be saved immediate assistance must be available at Srinagar. Mr Menon is fully aware of the gravity of the situation and he will explain to you if further explanation is needed.

In haste and with kind regards.

Yours sincerely,
Hari Singh.

Lord Mountbatten replied the following day accepting the accession of the State and adding his Government's wish that 'As soon as law and order has been restored in Kashmir and her soil cleared of invaders the questions of the State's accession should be settled by a reference to the people.' He further said, 'I will send troops of the Indian Army to Kashmir to help your own forces to defend your territory and to protect the lives, property and honour and your people.'

To gain the sympathy of the British public and justify his action Mountbatten stated that in his decision to approve the invasion he was influenced by humanitarian reasons, in that there were 200 British residents to be saved. This really was a poor excuse. If he had only asked the Quaid to get them evacuated it would have been done in no time.

General Bucher and General Russell, GOC Delhi and East Punjab had prepared the detailed plan in advance and in the evening of 26th October the troops were flown in.

Everyone was in a flap at the Army Headquarters. At Government House there was an atmosphere of war and Mountbatten was directing the operations. The Quaid was the enemy and was supposed to be sitting in Abbottabad waiting to ride in triumph to Srinagar. Mountbatten and his British staff had become totally Hindu and were determined to make three million Muslim Indian citizens forget that the division was supposed to be based on the principle of 'majority areas'. It was a crime against humanity. It will be recorded someday as a treacherous act.

The Quaid arrived in Lahore the same day and was furious when informed of the invasion.

On 27th October he ordered Gracey to move troops into Jammu and Kashmir and to seize Srinagar and the Banihal Pass. Gracey replied that he could not comply with the order and must report the matter to Auchinleck as compliance would entail the issue of 'Stand Down Order No. 2' which meant the withdrawal of the British officers from the Pakistan Army. According to Gracey's private secretary, Wilson, Mountbatten rang up Gracey and threatened that if he moved any troops to Kashmir he would ensure that he would not get his knighthood. Gracey capitulated.

The Daily Statesman was threatened with dire consequences if it did not toe the Indian line and its editor, Ian Stephens, was forbidden to bring out an edition of his paper from Karachi.

28th October: The Indian Cabinet accepted the 'Instrument of Accession'. The Auk flew to Lahore and met the Quaid. Gracey was present and emphasized the military weakness of Pakistan. The Auk pointed out the consequences of a violation of Indian territory. The Quaid was very angry and disturbed. He considered that India was using underhand methods to secure Kashmir. The Auk said that under the orders of His Majesty's Government he had no option but to withdraw the British officers if the border was violated. He was enforcing the orders in the literal sense, without appreciating the extenuating circumstances. But then the Auk was no politician.

This was a political decision and the Auk should have kept out of it. He thought that as a good soldier he was complying with orders, little realizing their implications. The Auk thought that he was preventing a major conflict between the two Dominions in which Pakistan would be crushed and dismembered. In this connection he was doing a service to Pakistan. He did not realize the resolve of the people and that they could not easily be crushed.

At the same time the army to which the Auk once belonged, which he trained and led in war, was fighting among themselves. Auk was in a very difficult position. He was being used by His Majesty's Government and Mountbatten to pressurize the Quaid. In fact the Auk should have left this task to Mountbatten himself. This was a grave error. Unwittingly he walked into the trap.

By this time it was well known that Auk had no sympathy for India. He had been dubbed as pro-Pakistan. And everyone knew there was no love lost between him and Mountbatten. If the British officers were to be withdrawn from Pakistan the Auk should have insisted that similar action should be taken in India as they had planned the invasion of Kashmir and were now conducting it.

Reluctantly the Quaid withdrew his orders. The Auk also suggested to the Quaid that Liaquat, Mountbatten, Nehru and Hari Singh should meet at a Round Table Conference and find a way out of the present impasse. As I expected, the Round Table Conference was never held. The Auk reported his interview with the Quaid to the Chief of Staff and said it was an open conflict. The Conference was postponed on the plea that Nehru was indisposed and Patel could not leave Delhi.

Mudie, the Governor of Punjab, who always supported the cause of Pakistan, was very critical of Gracey and said that he should have sent troops to Kashmir on the quiet. Mudie called him a 'wind-up merchant'. Gracey was impetuous and had no political sense. He was out of his depth and invariably turned to his private secretary for advice. It was all Gracey's fault. He had no business to inform the Auk and should have carried out the orders.

Mountbatten is jubilant but has left a legacy of bitterness. India has scored.

A proper war has started. India has sent more and more troops into Kashmir. India has also resorted to air strikes against the tribesmen who have no air cover. This action has further aggravated the bitterness. The subordinate Commanders in the field are paying little attention to their British bosses and are carrying out many atrocities. Bucher has been saying that a friendly Kashmir was vital to Pakistan defences and economic prosperity.

31st October: The Auk wrote to me thus:

SUPREME COMMANDER
NOTE

Dear Shadid,

Many thanks for your note. Glad you and Tahirah and the children are well.

The rumour in official (Indian) circles here is that you are leading the attack on Srinagar!!

However, Wilson (IMA) told me that you were in Pindi yesterday.

Yours
Auchinleck

The Blitz of Bombay has cursed me in no uncertain terms and said that I was the 'Arch conspirator'. Indirectly it was an attack on the Auk himself, implying that he was associated with the Kashmir Operations. The paper reads:

PAK'S MURDER INCORPORATED
School for Strangers Spies and Saboteurs
NEW DELHI:

Pak Army Chiefs-in-Charge of Kashmir invasion are reported to be running an Espionage Training School in Rawalpindi. There, picked fanatic Muslim young men are trained in the art of spying, sabotage, assassination and wireless communication in secret codes. Several such trained desperadoes, some of them Kashmiris, are said to have secretly slipped into Kashmir Valley, behind Indian Lines, for espionage work.

Brigadier Shahid Hamid, present Director of Military Intelligence of Pakistan Army, is in charge of this school. Before partition he was Private

Secretary to Field-Marshal Auchinleck and, later, he organized the Pakistan National Guards, now incorporated in the Pakistan Army. He has been actively associated with the Kashmir invasion right from the beginning.

Auk refused to contemplate about the past. He lives in the present and looks ahead. The past would be too much for him. He has lost interest.

November 1947

*'I am not running away or shrinking the responsibilities
assigned to me, but my task has been made impossible by
India.'*

The Auk.

6th November: There was an incident in the Second Gurkha Rifles as they
were not prepared to serve India and had volunteered for the British Army.
India retaliated by saying that they would not be allowed to serve His
Majesty's Government either.

Baldev Singh wants the Ex-Indian National Army officers to be considered for appointments in the Foreign Service as Military Attachés. He
wants them to be rehabilitated in the Army as well. He also wants them to
join the railways and certain auxiliary forces. The Auk has resisted such an
action all along. Mountbatten has supported him though in a very luke-warm
manner. Now Mountbatten is of the firm view that those who joined the
Indian National Army were inefficient and that the INA Division was
considered of less fighting value than one Japanese battalion. He said that
the appointment of Ex-Indian National Army personnel as Military Attachés
would be resented by the Regular Army officers. It may also bring India into
disrepute abroad. However, he asked the Supreme Headquarters to send the
records of the Indian National Army personnel to Baldev Singh.

8th November: Mountbatten wrote to the Auk:

My dear Claude,

. . . No one could have done more for India over an entire life's career
devoted to her Army and nobody contributed more to help find a peaceful
and acceptable solution. I hope you will not let the fact that impartiality is
no longer respected by many Indians make you feel that you have some
how failed – history will show very much the reverse.

I have felt all along that in spite of your many honours you have never
had your due – when they first wished to give me a peerage in December,
1946, I asked for it to be postponed – I also urged that you should be given
one. The King told me that your name would be considered when your

time was up as C-in-C in India. When, therefore, I wrote to the Prime Minister I knew he would immediately accept my recommendation and as I told you he immediately did.

Your name went in for the GCSI but when I am in London I can take it out again. I am glad you agree that your subordinate commanders whose names went in can remain in for you must realize that the list will be dated August 14th and will clearly have nothing to do with subsequent events.

I am also sorry but also understand your not wanting us to give you a large farewell dinner but I hope you will allow me to ask some of your real friends in to say goodbye to you at an informal lunch after the Joint Defence Committee on November 26th, or a small dinner that evening.

Finally, may I tell you again how deeply I appreciate your friendship, loyalty and help throughout this very difficult time. You are a very great man, Claude, and I am proud to have worked with you.

Yours ever,
DICKIE

Knowing how the Auk felt I am certain this letter meant nothing to him.

13th November: It was announced that the Supreme Commander's Headquarters would be wound up on 30th November.

15th November: The Auk held his last Conference with the three Service Chiefs, the Commanders-in-Chief of both the Dominions and Generals Wood and Savory. It is said that the Auk did not show any signs of emotion at this, his last conference. He said little. However, he did mention that there was no hope of reconciliation between the two Dominions and that events may lead to a war. Frank Messervy mentioned that Pakistan dreaded a war with India but that the tribesmen could not be recalled as long as the Indian troops stayed in Kashmir. Bucher was of the view that India would not do so.

Financially the Auk is a poor man. He has managed to save very little due to Jessie's extravagant ways. I know how every penny matters to him.

The Auk was due four months' leave with full pay. In his present rank he cannot get this as a Field-Marshal never retires. Neither does he get release leave but goes on half-pay. Mountbatten should have realized this and pleaded with His Majesty's Government to grant him some compensation in lieu of his due leave. Later, when someone suggested it to him, Mountbatten managed to get the paltry sum of £666 for the Auk. That, too, he broadcast all over.

The Auk received many hundreds of letters before his departure. General Bahadur Shamsher Rana of Nepal wrote 'Your departure would mean a personal loss to me but at the same time all your well-wishers and friends – if they are really so – must congratulate you on your escape from the situation that has now developed in India. I feel that it is no use remaining tied up to a thankless job. I shall always hold you in great respect.'

There was another letter from Amar Nath Jha, Chairman of the Public Services Commission, United Provinces. He said, 'I feel your departure greatly when India as a whole is in such a real need of your wisdom and experience. No one who has known the Indian Army during the last several years can fail to realize what a cementing influence you have exerted and what a great force for good it has been under your leadership. You rank with Roberts and Kitchener as one of the greatest Chiefs.'

The Begum of Bhopal wrote to the Auk and said, 'This country you cherished, loved and served with all your heart and might, little realizing the disappointment to follow. I feel very sad for you . . . You must feel so heartbroken.'

There was a letter from Field-Marshal The Earl Wavell who said:

My dear Claude,

This is just a line of sympathy for you, and of good wishes for the future. I know how deeply you must be feeling the tragic events in India, and the disruption of the Indian Army and the apparent destruction of your life's work.

It is heart-breaking indeed, but you have the consolation that no man could possibly have done more, indeed none so much as you did, that all who served with you and under you realize this and regard you with admiration and affection, and that the Indian Army under your command reached in the last war its highest point of fame, reputation and efficiency. It may never be so effective a force again or have the same spirit. But the work that you and all your officers did will live both in the past and future history of India.

With my grateful thanks again for all you did for me and with all my sympathy for the present and good wishes for the future.

Yours ever,
ARCHIE

This was a beautiful letter, sensitively written by a very great man.

Leo Amery wrote to the Auk: 'You have rendered greater service to India and the Empire than you might have done if you had marched from Alamein to . . .'

20th November: Mountbatten told Auk's sister Cherry to tell him that he has recommended him for a peerage. Auk was quite annoyed. Savory thought he would not accept it, as he was being recommended by Mountbatten, the person whom the Auk considers has made a mess of things. In any case Mountbatten now represents India.

The Sikh jathas have been sent to Kashmir to deal with the Muslim population. The Government of India cannot control the Sikhs so they are diverting their attention and their energies towards Kashmir. The Indians have conveniently forgotten that they had accused Pakistan of not controlling the entry of tribesmen into the Valley.

The Kashmir situation is going from bad to worse. The new rulers are suppressing the popular agitation in favour of Pakistan. If they suffer reverses it would mean 'loss of face to India' which they are not prepared to accept.

The holding of a plebiscite has been discussed by both sides. Nehru stands committed to it. This will mean a withdrawal of forces and their replacement by a neutral force and observers. Some people in India want a division of Kashmir.

Nehru is saying that on no account, and whatever happens, would he submit to aggression against the people of Kashmir and against the Indian Union.

India has been aggressive, and the talk of a fully fledged war between the two Dominions is not ruled out.

General Gracey, after letting Pakistan down, is now trying his level best to plead the cause of the Muslims. He maintains that a super-Nazi type of persecution is going on against the Muslims in India. At the same time they have urged the Hindus to leave East Pakistan and are putting the blame on the Government there. He further says that nothing can stop India becoming a totalitarian Government of the worst type.

25th November: Mountbatten gave a lunch as the final farewell to the Auk. It is common knowledge that Mountbatten is being shabbily treated and humiliated by Nehru and Patel, in spite of toeing their line in all matters. Some say that he is not happy. The Indians have used him and now got him where they want. He has not only sacrificed his prestige but also that of His Majesty's Government. All his actions are closely watched by Patel's henchman, V. P. Menon.

26th November: The Auk sent the following signal to the Chiefs of Staff 'Leaving today to Arthur Smith, Deputy Supreme Commander till 30th November then Commander British troops. Leaving India 1st December.'

Auk left at 8 p.m. There was no Guard of Honour. No formal departure. No formal function. The Auk considered all these as hollow mockeries. How wise he is. He went unsung. It was the end of a chapter. Who could have foreseen the manner of his departure? One day the world will realize the part he played during these momentous few months.

Savory said of him: 'Now he has gone. The flag no longer flies over his house. The sentries have gone and he has gone. One of the best friends India ever had. And one of whom, at last moment, the Indians turned. Sad. A great man who has done more for India than any living Englishman and yet who during his past few months of office was misrepresented by the Indians for their own ends.'

Mountbatten wants the C-in-C's house to be given to the British High Commission but the Russians have already laid claim to it.

On 30th November the Supreme Commander's HQ was closed. The curtain has dropped.

1st December: The Auk left for Italy to live at Villa Rustica, Paraggi, Santa Margherita, Liguria.

I shudder to visualize what his feelings must have been at the time of his departure. I am certain he was a bitter, disillusioned, frustrated, disappointed and humiliated man. His was a task unfinished.

Just before he left Delhi he wrote the following letter to my son and sent him his ribbons and badges.

SUPREME COMMANDER'S HEADQUARTERS
DELHI

My dear Hassoo,

I am sending you the ribbons and the badges of rank. I hope you will like them and wear them. I hope you and your father and mother and Shahnaz and Chotu are very well. I hope you are all happy.

I hope to come to Rawalpindi again soon and to see you then.

Yours affectionately
AUCHINLECK

This was his last act before he left India but his spirit remained behind.

PART VII

The Silent Man

The Auk was a bitter man, though he never said a word against the injustice done to him. He adopted silence, and was sustained by the conviction that 'history itself would set things right' and that 'a soldier should not defend himself.'

Mountbatten had certainly not played fair with the Auk. He was responsible for dragging his name down into the dirt and making him a scapegoat. The last year had not been an easy one for the Auk. By not allowing him to complete the job assigned to him as Supreme Commander, the Auk felt let down by the Labour Government. Because of this overpowering feeling he did not want to meet any member of the Cabinet on his return to England.

'A man who cannot adjust himself to changed surroundings has served his usefulness in life.' The Auk had often said this to me during our years together. And he himself was quick to adjust to new circumstances.

He sometimes said how he would like to 'fade away'. Though it is sad, I admire his viewpoint.

On leaving the subcontinent he did not wish to settle in the United Kingdom. He preferred to be a 'nobody' wanting to sever his connection with the saddest period of his service. However, after a rest of some months he got tired of the life in Italy and wrote to me, 'I miss your children: I expect they have forgotten me.' And again, 'But now I am feeling a bit restless and wish I had some definite work to do – in spite of my great age.' He wrote to Savory, 'No congenial intelligent society. I cannot remain contented. There is no one to laugh with and to ramble with. I feel fit and full of vigour – that is the real trouble with me. Must have some definite objective in life. I fail to feel my age. I feel that is a nuisance.' He wrote later, 'The last four months in Delhi are rapidly passing into the limbo of bad dreams. I am glad to say I am forgetting the bitterness and the source of it.'

So in fact time had cured his bitterness. He returned to a modest flat in London, before shifting to Beccles, a small town in Suffolk, where he bought a house. This house was small, though comfortable. It had a tiny garden in which he took great interest. His study was full of books and things of interest from the subcontinent.

He began a new secluded life, a life of loneliness, 'Good God, there is the Auk' was often heard in Beccles when someone spotted him on his walks. His eyes would narrow, his face would brighten and he would give a vulnerable smile which would show up his real kind and gentle self.

The Auk wrote regularly to Tahirah and I, and to our children. We met him in the United Kingdom on several occasions, even stayed with him in Beccles, where, on our arrival, he always flew the Pakistan flag. The Auk wrote to Peter Goodwin, 'Shahid, Tahirah and the two girls stayed with me here last month. It was good to see them again. I wish they could have stayed longer.'

He acted as the guardian of my children when they were being educated in the United Kingdom. He not only visited them regularly but also had them stay with him in his house. He supervised the entire education of my eldest son Hassu and grew to love him. My younger son, Ali, had joined the Army. On one of his visits to the United Kingdom the Auk had a long session with him alone.

At various times on our visit to Beccles I tried to persuade the Auk to write his memoirs and defend the actions for which he had been blamed. He invariably said, 'Who would want to read it? Nobody.'

I knew this was incorrect. It would have been the story of a man whose family had served India through three generations and who, during its worst period of turmoil, had not only displayed the highest qualities of a soldier, but had remained a normal human being with a smile and a friendly handshake for all.

'The Auk was an officer of the greatest distinction and a character of singular elevation . . . the greatest General of the War.' These were Churchill's comments about the man he had dismissed. The Auk, as a result of his dismissal, had suffered great humiliation.

Incidentally, the Auk seldom mentioned his days in the desert during a conversation. Only once he wrote to the London *Times*, correcting one of Monty's untruths, but attributed it to 'a faulty memory'.

Another time in 1961 he gave an interview to the *Daily Mail*. (See Appendix XII, p. 347.) In a lecture in London he made it known that his grievances were against India, and not Pakistan. It was Pakistan from which he had always obtained great support.

The Auk was also very popular among civilians. Many an institution and sports ground were named after him. Even a private house in Peshawar was called 'Claude House'.

Pakistan was where his Regiment was and where he longed to be. He stayed with us. His main attraction in revisiting Pakistan from time to time was that he could visit the troops. This always brought back old memories to him and past associations. It was here where he had spent the best years of his life. He could not tear himself away from the Army life. His visits had been regular. While in the country he visited his Regiment and other military establishments and his old haunts and met numerous friends.

The Auk took part in the 200th Anniversary of the 1st Punjab Regiment at Lahore. He commanded them on parade. Afterwards he wrote to Savory, 'Every time I go to Pakistan I find the good will towards us growing stronger and more permanent. In the Army this is specially so even amongst the generation now growing.'

Talking to the Auk I asked him once which classes in the Indian subcontinent did he consider made the best troops. He thought it over for a moment and then one by one he described the failings and the good points of each class. Finally he came to the Punjabi Mussalman (PMs) and said that taking all the factors into account he considered that the PMs were the most reliable as they possessed the supreme quality of being steady and consistent in battle, day in and day out. There were no ups and downs and one could rely on them always.

During one of his visits to Pakistan I asked him to address the officers of a garrison. He was reluctant as he thought that I would ask him to speak on his desert campaign or on the partition of the forces. However, when I mentioned that I would like him to speak on the Army when he joined it, he consented.

He spoke for an hour and a half and there was pin-drop silence. At the end all said that it was fascinating listening to the great Auk and all wished that the talk had been longer.

In 1963 the Auk paid a long visit to Pakistan. Apart from visiting his regiment, he visited the Frontier, the various formations, Staff Colleges, etc.

He visited the Lahore Horse Show and was fascinated by the sixteen hundred pipers and drummers playing the military tunes. He watched them play every day and said that it was a rare occasion to get sixteen hundred pipers and drummers playing together.

The Indian Government was always very suspicious about his visits to Pakistan. They thought that he was planning an 'invasion' of India. In fact, during one of the Auk's early visits Nehru officially protested to Attlee who called the Pakistan High Commissioner in London and asked him the purpose of the visit. The Auk never went to India at all, even though he was Chairman of Grindlay's Bank, lest they misunderstood his intentions.

In 1967 the Auk moved to Morocco. His name appeared in the telephone directory of Marrakesh as 'Auchinleck – Claude – soldier'.

In his dealings with Mountbatten the Auk was not blunt enough; he did not force an issue. He accepted interference. On rare occasions he said, 'I cannot do it.'

There were continued clashes with him which affected the working of GHQ. On more than one occasion the Auk told Mountbatten that he was prepared to quit, but he never forcefully threatened to resign.

The fact of the matter was that he was too British and too loyal a subject to cause any embarrassment to Britain. He just carried out the orders, fully realizing that, if in their pursuit things went wrong, Mountbatten would not support him, and that, ultimately, he would be made a scapegoat.

Auk and Mountbatten were totally different personalities. There was nothing in common between them. While the Auk carefully considered and weighed the consequences and the repercussions of any action beforehand, Mountbatten acted impulsively and could not care less as long as he could achieve his objective. Auk felt for people, Mountbatten only provided lip service.

As I mentioned earlier, Mountbatten never took the Auk into his confidence, or into his inner circle. He closely guarded many decisions he had taken and kept his papers from him. He gave no credit to the Auk.

People often said the Auk was 'unfortunate' and 'unlucky'. Neither is true. He hated self-justification. He hated the BBC investigators who jumped to conclusions. According to him they had pre-conceived ideas and seldom did their home work.

In later years he did sometimes come out into the open with his views. The Auk regarded Reggie Savory as a great friend and a tower of strength to him while in India. He used to consult him regularly. In normal course, he would have succeeded the Auk as C-in-C. The Auk told me this himself.

Auk wrote to him:

> Mountbatten made many false steps – Kashmir was a lasting disgrace and tragedy. He has a good deal to answer for – his knowledge of India and Indians was practically nil. Also he had some odd advisers. Pug Ismay I know felt all this . . . Kashmir remains and will remain an open sore and must eventually lead to another war between India and Pakistan unless India can agree to negotiate a settlement. After all it is more of an encumbrance and a danger to India than anything else. It is only because of Nehru's Kashmir ancestry that India really wanted it. . . . It is Mountbatten's fault in agreeing to such a monstrous error as the exclusion of Kashmir. Who advised him?

Then he wrote to Savory again:

> I have no idea what may happen in India. It is a continent not a country, and continents are not usually ruled eternally by one member of its many nationalities. I think India will split into several States or countries as it was before the British intervention. It is too big and too varied to submit to rule by one of its numerous principalities. Sounds nonsense but may be true. The Sikhs may try to set up a separate regime. I think they probably will and that will be only a start of a general decentralization and break-up of the idea that India is a country, whereas it is a subcontinent as varied as

Europe. The Punjabi is as different from a Madrassi as a Scot is from an Italian. The British tried to consolidate it but achieved nothing permanent. No one can make a nation out of a continent of many nations.

India will never consolidate in Kashmir though Dickie seems optimistic as usual over Kashmir. He is now in his true colours. The account of Mountbatten's behaviour at Gandhi's cremation did not leave a very good taste in my mouth.

The Auk once wrote to Peter Goodwin:

Pakistan should let East Pakistan go. They will always be a millstone about their necks and a great danger or more. Jinnah made a big mistake when he fought for their inclusion. I expect he had the jute industry in mind. I am afraid General Yakub Khan, a very old friend of mine, may have taken a fall in this affair. He was in Command in East Pakistan.

And again:

Pakistan is in a mess. Punjabis and Pathans will never mix with Bengalis; they are like oil and water. They differ so in every way except religion and I always think a Bengali is a Bengali first and a Muslim second! I think myself that they should agree to separate. West Pakistan will be stronger without the East in my opinion in spite of the loss of revenue from jute . . .

I do not myself think there is any hope of re-uniting East Bengal to Pakistan. In fact I wonder it was not a grave mistake even to have agreed to their becoming one nation which they are not and probably never will be.

In December, 1970, the Auk wrote to General Savory thus:

Pakistan's news is pretty bad and terribly difficult to handle with one thousand miles between the two parts of the country with not exactly friendly India in between. Jinnah should not have insisted on East Pakistan. It is alien to West Pakistan in every conceivable way except religion. Much more akin to Hindu Bengal. Why cannot they do a deal over Kashmir?

On 23rd April, 1971, he wrote to Savory again:

I have had no news from Pakistan. It is a complete tragedy and I can never forgive Yahya* and his stupid advisors, probably soldiers but not, I feel sure, Yaqub† and Ahsan,† who are in disgrace for showing some

---

*General Yahya Khan was the President of Pakistan.

†Yaqub was the Commander of Forces in East Pakistan and Ahsan was the Governor of the Province.

humanity. I agree with you about Mountbatten's decisions. India and
Pakistan are getting pretty near to war. I believe that East Bengal will get
Independence. If it does it will probably be eventually absorbed by India.
After all 49 per cent of the people are Hindu. It has always been a
ridiculous situation and the Pakistan troops have always looked on service
in East Pakistan as foreign service. If Pakistan can continue to exist
without East Pakistan all may settle down eventually but Kashmir remains
and will remain an open sore and must eventually lead to another war
unless India can agree to negotiate a settlement. Curzon tried to divide it
and failed. The trouble in East Pakistan is inevitable as that fool Yahya
persisted in efforts to subdue Bangladesh by force. He has only himself
to thank. . . . It is our fault – Mountbatten for being so precipitate over
partition and agreeing to such a monstrous error as the inclusion in
Pakistan of East Bengal and the exclusion of Kashmir.

Auk's 90th birthday was celebrated by the Association of British officers
of the Indian Army at the Hurlingham Club on 28th June, 1974. (His actual
birthday was on 21st June.) Nearly a thousand guests assembled.

Tahirah and I had not informed the Auk that we would be there on the
occasion. We arrived in the United Kingdom that very morning and
attended the party along with our son Hassan. While the other guests waited
elsewhere we were taken by General Henry Swinburn* to a big side room
with closed doors and ushered in quietly. It was the atmosphere of the Delhi
we had known all over again. All the faces were the same. Auk was surprised
to see us, and the delight at his face was something I can never forget. I told
him that I had to be present on this great occasion. 'Even now the ex-C-in-C
must have his ex-Private Secretary.'

Later he came out and addressed the gathering. It was a memorable
occasion, never to be forgotten. A painting of an officer of the 1st Punjab
Regiment was presented to him by General Sir Rob Lockhart and Philip
Mason presented him with his book *A Matter of Honour*.

Earlier on, the Army Board had given a luncheon to celebrate the
occasion.

In later years he used to say that he was feeling his age and that his
memory was playing tricks. He would remember his early exploits clearly,
e.g. the Tibetan campaign – but later events had become hazy. He would
sometimes say, 'I am going "gaga" and my memory is not the same as it used
to be.'

Once the Government of Pakistan issued an invitation to him to visit the
country. He had refused. When I heard about it I said that it was a wrong

---

*Major-General Henry Swinburn (1897–1981) was Director of Morale, India,
1945; Deputy Military Secretary GHQ India 1946; Military Secretary GHQ India
1946–47.

approach. Had they asked the 1st Punjab to issue the invitation to him to visit them, he would have come.

His admirers kept on writing to him without expecting a reply.

Auk died in his sleep on 23rd March, 1981, at the age of 97 in Marrakesh. I know his great wish was to be buried in Pakistan. But he was buried in the British military cemetery in Casablanca. He wanted his funeral to be private and quiet. No fuss was made and no military party was present to sound the Last Post. He was no more bitter or disappointed. He had joined the army of the heavenly soldiers.

Her Majesty the Queen said 'His brave and unstinted service to his country in war and peace will always be remembered.'

The silent warrior was sacked by Churchill and later by Mountbatten, but was vindicated by history.

A host of tributes were paid to his memory.

A Service of Thanksgiving for the life of Field-Marshal Sir Claude Auchinleck, GCB, GCIE, CSI, DSO, OBE, was held on 5th June, 1981, at 12 noon at Westminster Abbey and arangements were made by the Welsh Guards which was a pity as they possessed no knowledge of the old Indian Army and did not give due importance to the presence of the old Indian and Pakistani officers attending the service. In the list of those who attended the service *The Times* did not name one native officer. Pakistan had sent a contingent of 1st Punjab officers headed by a Lieutenant General – they were seated in an obscure corner of the Abbey. The entrance to the Abbey was lined by the Gurkhas and the Indian Grenadiers and not by the Auk's parent regiment the 1st Punjab.

The service was very impressive but the address by Major-General J. G. Elliot, late of 1st Punjab Regiment, was not moving and weighty in keeping with the achievements and service of the great Auk.

More impressive than the service was the great congregation. It was the last gathering of people connected with the British Raj. There were faces we had not seen since the partition of the Indian subcontinent. Naturally we wanted to meet them and wish them well, but there was no such opportunity. General Sir Robert Lockhart said to me that he felt as if the Auk was present and that all had come to pay their respects to him. Admiral Sir Geoffrey Miles, the last C-in-C of the Indian Navy, could not stop talking about the Auk and the difficult time they went through in 1947. Air Mashal Sir Hugh Walmsley, the last Air C-in-C, was deeply moved at the service. Aileen, Viscountess Slim and Lady Messervy were in tears. Cherry Jackson, the Auk's favourite sister, looked frail and could hardly walk.

Many of my classmates and the people I had served with were there but I never got a chance to meet them. Had some arrangement been made after the service where we could have got together, it would have been a marvellous opportunity to revive old friendships and associations. The old guard is fading out and chances of such meetings will never come by, which cement goodwill between the countries which had fought together.

The Auk in his will did not forget his regiment, the 1st Punjab, and left to them his ceremonial sword with sling and sword knot, his service sword with scabbard and Sam Browne belt and sword knot and steel scabbard and his miniature decorations and medals.

So was the end of a great statesman, a great 'Native' of the subcontinent, a man who had become a legend in his lifetime. He was the C-in-C at the most critical period in this history of the subcontiment. His lasting achievement was the reconstitution of the two Dominions Armies. He was the founding father of the two Armies, thus consolidating his true place in history.

Pakistan and India of the future will realize what it owed to him.

Epilogue

*'I preferred to remain as I am. I like my own and my
father's name best, and my own rank earned by service, is
good enough for me.'*

The Auk.

Mountbatten had said that all deaths were inevitable. 'He is a man tarnished
by hubris with blood on his hands and callousness.'

As Sir Reginald Savory put it, he 'tried to make it appear to India and the
world and to ourselves that we were committing a noble deed. . . .' We left so
quickly that all the good work has gone waste. . . . This is the result of our
magnanimous action. The British Mission in India has finished and it has
failed. This would not have happened had we possessed the determination to
govern and to hand over a running machine.'

Savory blamed Mountbatten for forcing the pace. He equally blamed the
Labour Government who 'lacked self-confidence to govern, took note of
immature world opinion and lost control, thereby creating a disastrous
situation and pretending that they were being magnanimous. The leftist
politicians should blush with post-hoc shame.

Louis Heren, who was special correspondent of *The Times* in Delhi, said
that Pug Ismay was a better source of information largely because he did not
disguise his dislike and contempt for Mountbatten. Nehru warned the
foreign correspondents not to report the intensity of the turmoil and what it
was costing in terms of human life.

Non-violence always provoked violence and finally it caused a million
lives. This was Gandhi's role! The biggest blood bath in history.

Louis Heren also said 'I was invited to dinner by the Governor-General
and Lady Mountbatten asked me what the Muslims were doing to her poor
Hindus. When I told her about the train tragedy (where 4000 Muslim
refugees were massacred) an ADC hurried me from her presence.'

Sir John Biggs-Davison, MP, was Deputy Commissioner of Dera Ghazi
Khan during and after the transfer of power to Pakistan. He recalls a visit by
Lady Mountbatten accomanied by Indian congressmen in Gandhi caps to
the refugee camps where local Hindus and Sikhs had been gathered for their
protection. Her Excellency, who was then wife of the Governor-General of

another Dominion, suggested that she use her influence with her husband to
have a Hindu regiment sent to the district. 'I restrained myself and said as
calmly as I could, "Lady Mountbatten my Muslim police have worked night
and day protecting the minorities. Many of them are worried about relatives
in India." I declined her offer.'

By presenting Kashmir to India Mountbatten had laid the foundation of
future wars between the two countries. I still wonder whether this was
intentional or naive. By treating Hyderabad in such a shabby manner he
earned the enmity of the Muslims.

After leaving the subcontinent he adopted an unreal and Utopian posture
and came out in his true colours. This manifested itself in the fact that he
started believing what he wanted to believe.

He should have tempered his judgements on the results of his mission
with a touch of modesty. In view of the terrible sufferings after independence
– caused by haste – he should not have looked upon Independence Day 'with
completely undiluted pleasure'.

A touch of humility, even shame, was perhaps called for and in subsequent years, less readiness to recall with pride and vainglory his regal, busy
days as 'the last Viceroy'. He could not have been proud of the blood bath.

Mountbatten had a guilt complex. He was at pains to justify what he
thought was his close relationship and friendship with the Quaid, and his
great service to Pakistan. He liked to think that everyone was his friend and
everybody loved him.

The people of Pakistan considered him as *persona non grata* and an enemy
of the country. Some years ago on one of his many trips to India, his pilot
felt he was running short of fuel and asked permission to land at Karachi.
When the control tower found out who was travelling in the plane they
flatly refused him permission to land. This was an unethical thing to do,
but it did show the intensity of hatred in even a common official towards
Mountbatten.

Mountbatten was most contradictory. He said that Quaid polarized him
into a force of repulsion. Though publicly he stated that Jinnah's faith in him
was absolute, he trusted him and he never doubted his (Mountbatten's)
integrity. He went even further and told an audience that the Quaid, before
his death, had said that Mountbatten had the look of a saint on his face!
Anyone knowing the Quaid would realize that he was incapable of using
such expressions. The words of Quaid keep coming back to my mind:
'I detest the man!'

Mountbatten's greatest mistake was underestimating the Quaid and the
Muslims' sentiments. He realized too late that Jinnah was the 'Muslim
League', and that he had the future of India in his hands. The partition had
been accepted by all before Mountbatten ever arrived in India. He would
have completely disarmed the Quaid if he had made a declaration to this
effect and earned his friendship.

Mountbatten was naive or ignorant enough to think that disarming of Gandhi and Nehru would make his task easier and the League was of no consequence. He never made a sincere effort to cultivate the Quaid; on the contrary he criticized him behind his back which antagonized him.

At the morning conferences Mountbatten held each day the Quaid was invariably discussed. He maintained that Jinnah had all the characteristics which made negotiations impossible. Mountbatten used to say, 'My God he is cold, it is impossible to warm him. He is arrogant, "vain", "inflexible", "unapproachable", "uncompromising", "disdainful", "frigid", and a "lunatic" as well as being an "evil genius".' According to Mountbatten Quaid said 'no' so persistently and so effectively and that his strength lay in this. He did not budge and was a fanatic and his basic failure was to grasp the realities of life and he always considered himself right and maintained that he would never be in the wrong. In fact Mountbatten was of the firm opinion that Quaid was a most difficult man.

At one time Mountbatten prided himself by telling everyone that he 'thawed the Quaid' by saying to him, 'You go to hell' and 'You are crazy'!

The fact was that Quaid was a professional advocate of the first order and used constitutional law to back his case and knew how to win it. There was no comparison between the Quaid and Mountbatten when it came to solid arguments. Invariably Mountbatten had to look over his shoulders and accept defeat. He could not tolerate his humiliation.

On the other hand the Quaid equally detested Mountbatten. He said that Mountbatten was a partisan and toed the Congress line. He could not be trusted. Later events proved that his assessment was correct.

In later years Mountbatten said that if he had known the seriousness of Jinnah's illness and that he was to die soon he would not have agreed to the partition. He also said that Jinnah was responsible for all the ills in East Pakistan and the miseries which followed.

Mountbatten boasted in later years that subconsciously he always wanted to be the Viceroy of India.

He even said V. P. Menon and Krishna Menon were his spies in the Congress camp.

Mountbatten wanted to be the hero of the British public as well as of the Indians. He wanted everyone to believe that his performance and his actions connected with the partition of the subcontinent were the only feasible ones. The image he wanted to project of himself was that he was the only person who could have done the job. Through all this he wanted to camouflage the killings that had gone on, which in fact had surpassed those of 1857 in numbers, as well as the injuries done to Pakistan when he accepted the accession of Kashmir to India. Ismay has said that a million lives were lost. Mountbatten, therefore, carried out a ceaseless publicity campaign beginning from the time he was appointed Viceroy. He encouraged people to write books on the great role he had played. To some writers he gave as many as thirty interviews, brain-washing them into believing that the course he adopted was totally justified. Magazines were full of his exploits, the texts of which he often corrected himself. He never missed an opportunity to address a gathering where he could talk about himself. Of course the Indian press, both internal and external, assisted him, as this helped them to cover their own wrong-doings. With all this publicity he gave little chance to the people to judge him, his acts or the events of the time for themselves. All writers were turned into Mountbatten's mould.

Jenkins never said a word in spite of the fact that he was blamed for the Punjab tragedy. Once when I met him and pressed him to write his memoirs, he replied that, 'It is not in the interest of the Commonwealth.' It is known that at the time of his departure from India he was warned by Mountbatten not to speak out. He was ordered to burn all his official papers, which included many connected with the Boundary affair. So there was a bonfire in the cellars of Government House, Lahore, but still a few papers including the original sketch map demarcating the boundaries between the two Dominions before it was altered by Mountbatten fell into the hands of Sir Francis Mudie, the Governor, who gave them to Liaquat. Whether Jenkins kept some papers with him is not known.

Officially the Joint Defence Council was wound up on 31st March, 1948. Pakistan's share of stores left in India amounted to one hundred and sixty thousand tons. In addition to it were the ordnance factories, plants, laboratories, docks, etc. Efforts were made to produce a new formula for the division of assets between India and Pakistan but it did not work. Stores were being moved at the rate of 8000 tons per month. They mostly consisted of items which were not required by Pakistan. A classic example was the over- and undersized army boots. In August, 1948, the stores were discontinued. It was said that some financial adjustment would be made but again it came to nothing. In this connection the *Blitz* of Bombay attacked Generals Lockhart and Bucher. The latter was described as 'a viper under Nehru's pillow'.

Appendices

APPENDIX I

Memorandum by the Commander-in-Chief in India to all Commanders on the First INA Trial

I have now been able to study a large number of reports from higher and unit commanders and other sources on the effect of the action taken in respect of the first 'INA' trial on the Indian Army as a whole.

It is most important that we should study and analyse carefully these effects, as they may influence very greatly our ability to maintain the solidarity and reliability of the Indian Army in the difficult times which undoubtedly lie ahead of us. It is for this reason that I am writing this letter to you. I have considered the desirability of making a personal public statement in explanation of my action in commuting the sentences of transportation passed by the Court on the first three accused, but I have decided that this would not be in the best interests of discipline or the maintenance of my influence and authority as Commander-in-Chief.

I feel, however, that we should do all we can to remove the feelings of doubt, resentment and even disgust which appear to exist in the minds of quite a number of British officers, who have not the knowledge or the imagination to be able to view the situation as a whole, or to understand the present state of feeling in India.

2. As I see it, the commutation of the sentences of transportation on Shahnawaz, Dhillon and Seghal has had the following effects in India:

(a) On the general public, moderate as well as extremist, Muslim as well as Hindu:
Pleasure and intense relief born of the conviction that confirmation of the sentences would have resulted in violent internal conflict.

This feeling does not, in my opinion, spring universally from the idea that the convicted officers were trying to rid India of the British and, therefore, to be applauded, whatever crimes they might commit, but from a generally genuine feeling that they were patriots and nationalists and that, therefore, even if they were misled they should be treated with clemency, as true sons of India. In this connexion, it should be remembered, I think, that every Indian worthy of the name is today a 'Nationalist', though this does not mean that he is necessarily 'anti-British'. All the same, where India and her independence are concerned, there are no 'pro-British' Indians.

Every Indian Commissioned Officer is a Nationalist and rightly so, provided he hopes to attain independence for India by constitutional means.

(b) On the Indian officers of the Indian Army:

Except for a few recovered prisoners of war who have suffered much at the hands of their fellow countrymen who joined the so-called 'INA', the vast majority almost without exception, however much they may like and respect the British, are glad and relieved because of the result of the trial. Most of them admit the gravity of the offence and do not condone it, but practically all are sure that any attempt to enforce the sentence would have led to chaos in the country at large and probably to mutiny and dissension in the Army culminating in its dissolution, probably on communal lines.

The more senior and intelligent undoubtedly realize the implications of our having established in principle the seriousness of the crime of forsaking one's allegiance and the wisdom of meeting it with a heavy punishment such as 'Cashiering' which carries with it the stigma of disgrace.

They realize that if their future is to be at all secure, discipline and loyalty must be maintained, but they too, are Nationalists, and their feelings are much the same as those of the public at large . . .

(c) On the British officers of the Indian Army:

As I have already said, the effect on many British officers has been bad, and has led to public criticism which has not been in accordance with the traditional loyalty I am entitled to expect. To these officers, perhaps not always very perceptive or imaginative, an officer is an officer, whether he be Indian or British, and they make no allowance for birth or political aspirations or upbringing, nor do they begin to realize the great political stresses and strains now affecting this country. They are unable to differentiate between the British and Indian points of view.

Moreover, they forget, if they ever knew, the great bitterness bred in the minds of many Indian officers in the early days of 'Indianization' by the discrimination, often very real, exercised against them, and the discourteous, contemptuous treatment meted out to them by many British officers who should have known better. These facts constitute the background against which the decisions should be judged, always keeping before one the object, which is to preserve by all possible means in our power the solidarity of the Indian Army, and of the RIN and the RIAF as well . . .

3. The terrible tragedy of Singapore following on the fall of Hong Kong must have seemed to the great majority of the VCOs and rank and file to be the end of all things and certainly of the British 'Raj' to whom the Army had been used for so many years of war and peace to look as its universal provider and protector, acting through their own regimental officers . . .

It is quite wrong to adopt the attitude that because these men had taken service in a British-controlled Indian Army, therefore their loyalties must be the same as those of British soldiers. As I have tried to explain, they had no real loyalty or patriotism towards Britain as Britain, not as we understand loyalty.

4. So much for the rank and file. The officers who went over present a much more difficult problem. Owing to their presumably superior education, knowledge of the world and experience generally, it is not possible to apply the same reasoning to them, except possibly to the very junior, and to those who had been promoted from the ranks, whose background was more limited and whose knowledge was less.

There is no excuse for the regular officers who went over, beyond the fact that the early stages of 'Indianization' from its inception to the beginning of the late war were badly mismanaged by the British Govt. of India, and this prepared the ground for disloyalty when the opportunity came.

There is little doubt that 'Indianization' was at its inception looked on as a political expedient which was bound to fail militarily. There is no doubt also that many senior British officers believed and even hoped that it would fail . . .

It is no use shutting one's eyes to the fact that any Indian officer worth his salt is a Nationalist, though this does not mean, as I have said before, that he is necessarily anti-British. If he is anti-British this is as often as not due to his faulty handling and treatment by his British officer comrades.

It is essential for the preservation of future unity that this fact should be fully understood by all British officers.

No Indian officer must be regarded as suspect and disloyal merely because he is what is called a 'Nationalist', or in other words – a good Indian!

5. This aspect of the business, though it cannot excuse the action of these officers in going over to the enemy, must be considered, as it does provide the background against which we must view the present and the future . . .

6. There remains the matter of the decision to commute the sentences of the first three officers from 'Transportation' to 'Cashiering'. If, as we have admitted, they were guilty of the worst crime a soldier can commit, then it may well be asked – 'Why be lenient with them?'

In taking the decision to show clemency, the whole circumstances, past, present and future, had to be considered, and were so considered most carefully and over a long period.

The overriding object is to maintain the stability, reliability and efficiency of the Indian Army so that it may remain in the future a trustworthy weapon for use in the defence of India and, we hope, of the Commonwealth as a whole . . .

Always keeping before one the difference in outlook between British and Indian, which I have tried to explain in this letter, I decided, therefore, that, in the interests of the future of both India and Britain and because of the unprecedented circumstances of the case, the only proper course to pursue was to confirm the finding and so establish the principle, but to show clemency in respect of the sentence. Some bewilderment has been caused, I believe, by the fact that Shahnawaz, who was found guilty of 'abetment of murder' as well as of 'waging war', received the same treatment as the other two accused who were found guilty of 'waging war' only. Shahnawaz's offence, which was committed by him as an officer of the 'INA' in the alleged execution of his duty, in that he ordered a sentence authorized by a higher 'INA' authority to be carried out, did, in the circumstances, flow from his basic offence of 'waging war' as a member of the 'INA'. The punishment of this – the principal offence – was 'Cashiering' in the case of all three officers. Shahnawaz did not himself commit any brutal or violent act against any person, but passed on the orders of a superior authority which he claims to have believed to have been properly constituted.

It is necessary also to remember that some 20,000 officers and men joined the so-called 'INA' and that, even if it were desirable, it would have been a physical impossibility to bring all these men to trial within anything approaching a reasonable period of time . . .

7. There is one other criticism which is often made. It is said that we ought to have dealt with the accused summarily in forward areas; that if the men were to be brought to India we should have avoided publicity, and, in particular, trial in the Red Fort; and that we ought to have put out counter-publicity from the start. The answer to the

first point is that we had to deal with 43,000 men, in one instance a whole 'INA' division surrendering without firing a shot. It was obviously impracticable for forward areas to deal with men on this scale summarily, and it was the obvious course to bring them back to Delhi where organization existed for interrogation. As to publicity, I am sure it was right to decide not to hold trials in secret because it would have been thought that the men were not getting a fair trial. Once it was decided that the trials could not be held in secret, it would have been wrong to tuck them away somewhere where defence counsel, relations, etc., could not conveniently attend, and the Red Fort was the most convenient place from nearly every point of view. We avoided counter-publicity because it was practically certain that a big publicity drive would be represented as prejudicing the accused in their trial, but in any event it is not possible for us to force papers to publish anything which they regard as propaganda and with which they do not agree. We have no control over them in this respect . . .

8. Finally let me again state the object: it is to maintain the reliability, stability and efficiency of the Indian Army for the future, whatever Govt. may be set up in India.

This can be done only if the British and Indian officers of that Army trust and respect each other and continue to work wholeheartedly together for the common cause as they have done in war.

It is your task to do your utmost to bring this about and I am sure you will: you have excellent material on which to work.

APPENDIX II

Text of the Commander-in Chief's Broadcast, 28th March, 1946

EVERY OFFICER OF THE INDIAN ARMY

YOUR GREAT DUTY

1. In the critical period through which we are now about to pass, the Indian Army requires clear and positive guidance. Here it is.

2. The duties of an Army are:

a)   to repel an aggressor;
b)   to help to keep the peace within its own boundaries.

3. The first of these duties has already been done and we hope it will not have to be done again for a long time. The magnificent divisions of the Indian Army are world-renowned. The Indian soldier will go down to posterity as among the finest fighting soldiers of the world.

LET THE INDIAN ARMY GUARD ITS GOOD NAME

4. What is the situation with regard to the second of these duties? The great event of India's history is about to take place: viz, the transfer of power from Britain to India. It must be a peaceful transfer, with the least possible dislocation.

The object of the British is to hand over a peaceful India. The object of the Indians is to take over a peaceful India. The nationalists of India, who have worked so long and hard for the independence of their country, cannot desire it in any other way; otherwise they will run the risk of failing to reap the reward of their efforts, which is a free India, strong and able to stand on its own feet.

OUR OBJECTS THEREFORE ARE IDENTICAL

5. Unfortunately there are, however, in India certain disruptive forces. There are certain to be at a time like this. There may therefore be trouble. If so, it is the duty of the police to deal with it. If, however, the police cannot deal with it, then the Army will be called on to help.

If, however, the Army, through inefficiency or unreliability in the performance of its duties in the maintenance of law and order, fails to carry out the orders of the Government in power at the time, then the internal situation may well develop into chaos. Internal chaos means suffering, misery and loss to every one and can only retard progress.

In the last resort the country depends on the Army to ensure peace and order within its frontiers.

THE ARMY IS THE ANCHOR OF THE COUNTRY

6. Remember the Viceroy's words in Calcutta in December:

India has before her great opportunities, the greatest she has ever had.

7. How can the Indian Army help?

a) By keeping itself disciplined, efficient and calm.
b) By realizing that if it does NOT do this, the NEW INDIA will be saddled with an Army unequal to its tasks of repelling an aggressor or keeping internal order.
c) By all Indian Officers realizing that anyone tampering with the discipline and efficiency of their great Army will only, to use an Indian proverb: Be cutting his own foot with his own mattock (*apne paon ap Kulhari mat maro*) or, to use an English proverb: Be cutting off his nose to spite his face.
d) By all British officers of the Indian Army serving the NEW INDIA as loyally as, in the past, their Indian comrades have served the present India.

In short the Indian Army may well be the instrument which will ensure that this great period in India's history will pass peacefully and in a spirit of goodwill on all sides.

> LET THE FOLLOWING POINTS THEREFORE STAND OUT CLEARLY:
> ALL OFFICERS, INDIAN AND BRITISH
> REMAIN DISCIPLINED, EFFICIENT, AND
> LOYAL TO WHATEVER GOVERNMENT MAY BE IN POWER.

Indian Officers

DO NOT CUT YOUR OWN FOOT WITH YOUR OWN MATTOCK.

Do not take or connive at any action which may impair the discipline, efficiency or loyalty of the Army to the Government of the day.

British Officers

SERVE THE NEW INDIA as loyally as in the past your Indian comrades have served the present India.

It is your duty to your country and to the Army to which you belong to pass on to your Indian comrades, who are to follow you, in a spirit of unselfishness and service, all the experience and knowledge that you have gained in the past so that they may, in their turn, serve the Indian Army as faithfully and truly as you have done.

THUS MAY THE INDIAN ARMY LEAD THE WAY.

AUCHINLECK

APPENDIX III

The Strategic Value of India to the British Empire

OBJECT

1. The object of this paper is to appreciate the value of INDIA to the British Empire, and to set out the strategic advantages and disadvantages should INDIA become an Independent Sovereign State outside the British Commonwealth of Nations.

FACTORS

2. *Introduction*

The strategy of the British Commonwealth is at present based on the ability to move troops and material by air and sea across the world without interference by any hostile power.

In order to be able to protect our merchant shipping we have established Naval bases on the main lines of communication in order that the necessary warships may be maintained and repaired. We are now establishing air lines of communication and air bases from which both our maritime and air L of C can be protected.

The increasing range of shore-based aircraft and the development of guided missiles has already made it difficult to protect convoys in narrow waters, and there is little doubt that we shall have to rely less on narrow waters such as the Mediterranean, and more on the broad waters of the great oceans. In effect our L of C will gradually be pushed southwards and we shall come to rely on the Cape route to the East much more than on the Mediterranean.

3. *Importance of Indian Ocean*

It is the openly expressed policy of His Majesty's Government that no potentially hostile power shall establish bases in the Indian Ocean area, and any attempt to do so would be regarded as a hostile act.

The oil from the Persian Gulf is essential to the British Commonwealth, and its safe passage must be assured.

Our normal sea communications with Australia and New Zealand pass across the Indian Ocean, but these could be deflected round the Cape or through the Pacific without undue dislocation. From a Naval point of view a hostile India would not seriously affect our position, but if India was dominated by Russia with powerful air forces it is likely that we should have to abandon our command of the Persian Gulf and the Northern Indian Ocean routes.

4. *Air Communications*
The Imperial air communications between the UK and AUSTRALIA and the Far East must of necessity pass through INDIA. A subsidiary route for Long Range Aircraft could be established using routes such as:—

a) Arabia – Ceylon – Cocos Is – Australia.
b) Ceylon – Andaman/Nicobar Is – Burma/Malaya.
c) East Africa – Seychelles – Diego Garcia – Ceylon/Cocos Is.
d) These routes could be further developed by the use of floating bases and Aircraft Carriers.
e) At present suitable airfields do not exist at all the above and services would have to be based on flying boats. In any case few existing types of aircraft have sufficient range for such long 'hops', and even with the progress that may be expected in the future, it will be many years before fighter aircraft can ever be flown over such routes. INDIA is therefore an essential link in our Imperial air communications, and without INDIA the flexibility of Imperial Strategic Air Reserves is seriously impaired.

5. CEYLON is only of value if it can be used as an effective substitute for the Naval and Air Bases now located in INDIA. It is considered that even if the island were converted into a fortress it would be of limited use in the face of a hostile INDIA, and it would be untenable if INDIA were dominated by a major power such as RUSSIA.

6. *India as a Base*
Major operations of war must be based upon a land mass which is capable of containing all the necessary base installatioins, repair shops, hospitals which are necessary for the maintenance of modern Naval, Army and Air Forces. Furthermore such a base must have an indigenous industrial capacity which can expand to meet the extra load placed upon it in war.

With the coming of Atomic Warfare there is increased necessity for space, which will allow of proper dispersion of base installations.

Should it be necessary for the Commonwealth to undertake military operations on a large scale in the FAR EAST, INDIA is the only suitable base from which such operations could be sustained.

AUSTRALIA has the space and, to some extent, the industrial capacity but has not the manpower from which to provide fighting forces and also to expand her industry.

7. *Indian Manpower*
From a military point of view one of India's most important assets is an almost inexhaustible supply of manpower. INDIA, including the Indian States and NEPAL, can produce as many soldiers as the Commonwealth can maintain.

Without this help it would have been difficult to have won the last two wars.

It must, however, be remembered that up to date all recruits have been volunteers, and by the end of the last war the limit of voluntary enlistment had been reached.

8. *British Manpower*
If the 'New Concept' is agreed, Britain, pending nationalization of the Indian Armed Forces, will provide manpower for INDIA on the following (maximum and diminishing) scale:—

	Officers	*ORs*
British Army in India	800	16,400
RAF in India	1,500	10,000
British personnel of RIN	300	
British personnel of Indian Army	4,400	7,500
TOTAL:	7,000	33,900

Britain is at present experiencing great difficulty in finding sufficient armed forces to meet her worldwide commitments. A relief of 7,000 officers and 33,900 men would be of very great assistance.

There are in addition approx. 2,000 British officials in INDIA and some 30,000 non-officials. The large proportion of these would leave INDIA, and would be available for service elsewhere.

9. *Natural Resources*

INDIA is the sole producer of jute, and one of the largest producers of tea in the world. Both these commodities are of great value to the Commonwealth.

Thorium exists in TRAVANCORE and this mineral may become of increasing importance in connection with atomic warfare.

10. *Industrial capacity*

INDIA is at the beginning of an industrial revolution. Her cotton and steel industries are beginning to rival those of any country, and there is no doubt that her heavy industries are capable of enormous expansion. In twenty years INDIA may be a highly developed industrial country, and may be capable of producing herself all the equipment required by modern armed forces. If INDIA is part of the Commonwealth this constitutes a great and increasing asset. If INDIA is hostile or dominated by a hostile power the threat to the Commonwealth would be extremely serious.

11. *Effect of British Withdrawal from INDIA*

Although potentially powerful, INDIA is at present so divided within herself that if the British should 'quit' INDIA entirely, leaving the leaders of the various parties to work out their own salvation, the country would be left wide open to RUSSIA.

It is not possible to estimate whether RUSSIA would actually establish bases in INDIA, but, with her taste for power politics, it is considered likely that RUSSIA would take advantage of an unprecedented opportunity to establish herself in a position from which she could threaten the whole fabric of the British Commonwealth. History has shown that nature abhors a vacuum and, if the British step out, we can expect the Russians to step in.

12. *Effect of a hostile INDIA*

If INDIA were hostile our naval position would not be seriously affected, but if she was dominated by a hostile power we cannot guarantee our sea communications in the Northern part of the Indian Ocean and our oil supplies from the Persian Gulf would probably be cut off.

Our strategy would have to be reoriented and our sea communications would have to be round the edge of the Indian Ocean, protected by Naval Forces based on the

East Coast of AFRICA, SINGAPORE and WESTERN AUSTRALIA. It might still be possible to move oil down the coast of AFRICA, but our Naval Forces in the Indian Ocean would have to be very considerably augmented. It is presumed that our strategy is based on the assumption that the UNITED STATES are friendly, and it is considered that we should probably have to realign our Commonwealth communications so that our normal approach to AUSTRALIA, MALAYA and CHINA was from the Pacific.

The 'Far East' would in fact become the 'Far West'.

This is probably possible from a Naval point of view, but is virtually impossible from an Air point of view unless we have the use of air bases on American islands in the Pacific. The only alternative to the use of American islands would be the construction of floating bases either across the Pacific or across the Southern Indian Ocean.

13. *ANDAMAN and NICOBAR Islands*

We have already pointed out that CEYLON would be untenable in the face of an INDIA dominated by RUSSIA. It is, however, considered that the ANDAMAN and NICOBAR Islands are just far enough away from INDIA to allow a reasonable degree of security. If we 'quit' INDIA we shall presumably continue to hold MALAYA, although it is doubtful whether we shall hold BURMA permanently. Our communications to BURMA and MALAYA will then be from the east and south-east and we shall be in a similar position to the Japanese in 1942/45.

In these circumstances it is considered that we should not give up the ANDAMAN and NICOBAR Islands, but should hold and develop them as outposts to BURMA and MALAYA.

The harbours should be developed, and airfields should be built from which to defend MALAYA against attack from INDIA.

SUMMARY

14. The disadvantages of the British Commonwealth of an independent INDIA may be summarized as follows:—

a) The supply of oil from the PERSIAN GULF is dependent upon the maintenance of our sea communications in the PERSIAN GULF and ARABIAN SEA. These could not be assured if INDIA was dominated by RUSSIA, and we consider that RUSSIA would not neglect her opportunities of influencing an Independent INDIA (Paras. 3 and 11).

b) Air communications between ARABIA and AFRICA on the one side and BURMA, MALAYA, AUSTRALIA and NEW ZEALAND on the other can only be maintained with difficulty without the use of bases in INDIA (Para. 4).

c) The value of use of Ceylon would be largely reduced if INDIA was hostile, and the island would be untenable if INDIA was dominated by RUSSIA.

d) INDIA as a base is of the very greatest importance to the successful prosecution of operations in SOUTH-EAST ASIA (Para. 6).

e) Indian manpower is an enormous asset to the Commonwealth Armed Forces (Para. 7).

f) INDIA's natural resources and industrial capacity are of increasing importance (Paras. 9 and 10).

15. The only advantage that we can see in an Independent INDIA is a relief to British Manpower Commitments (Para. 8).

16. *Conclusion*

We consider that it is impossible to guarantee that an Independent INDIA would not be unfriendly or would not be influenced by a power such as RUSSIA, CHINA or JAPAN, hostile to the British Commonwealth. Should such a situation arise, we could not maintain our power to move freely by sea and air in the Northern part of the Indian Ocean area, which is of supreme importance to the British Commonwealth.

A reorientation of Commonwealth strategy, whereby we might make use of the Pacific in place of the Indian Ocean is a palliative which may be forced upon us, but it will not adequately replace the value of the Indian Ocean to the British Commonwealth.

The object of the exercise was to keep the country or countries in the British Commonwealth. Britain is interested in preserving her commercial and strategic interest in the subcontinent at all costs.

APPENDIX IV

Policy Note on the Future of the Armed Forces

1. I have read this paper and consider that within the limit of its scope it is sound.
2. I am not, however, satisfied that our present conception of the future Army of India is sound or likely to be adequate to provide for the defence of India in five or ten years from now.

The future Indian Army that we have so far envisaged is an Army of the last war, composed, organized and equipped to meet the conditions obtaining in the closing years of that war.

This is not to be wondered at as the conception originated while the war was still in progress, and before we had had time to collect our thoughts and think seriously about what the future might have in store.

3. We have now had more time to think and more material on which to base our thoughts. It is imperative that we should think, rapidly and intensively, so that we may not commit ourselves and our successors, to whom we owe the duty of planning progressively and with foresight, to plans which will be obsolete in a few years' time.

It cannot be too strongly stressed that the re-organization and re-equipment of an Army, once launched, is very difficult to alter in scope or direction without causing great dislocation and much useless expenditure of money, time and labour.

For some months now I have been uneasy lest we were not looking far enough into the future in our planning for the future Army of India.

I am now quite sure that we are not. We must, therefore, review our plans in the light of coming developments, so far as these are now apparent to us.

4. Briefly, the developments which seem certain to affect the size, organization and maintenance of armies in the near future, possibly within the next five years, are:

   i)   Nuclear energy.
   ii) Bacteriological warfare.
   iii) Guided projectiles.
   iv) Increase in range, power and speed of aircraft. The general effect of all these developments will certainly be to make the concentration in small and relatively confined areas of men, materials and transport, most difficult if not impossible without facing the risk of losses which could not be borne.

I believe that the effect of these new developments on the machinery for the maintenance of armies will be particularly marked and drastic. I do not believe that it will be possible to operate large bases of supply-concentrated traffic on single lines of communication such as trunk railways or roads or narrow shipping lanes, except possibly for short and irregular periods.

I feel sure that armies will have to rely on many small and widely dispersed bases of supply for their maintenance. If this is so, then many lines of communication, that is roads, railways, waterways or ports will be needed, and it will be impossible to guarantee that these will exist in many potential theatres of war. In fact we know quite certainly that they will not exist.

Examples, if examples are needed, can be found in an advance that might have to be carried out on land against Kandahar, based on Quetta, or against Baghdad, based on Basra. In these and many theatres the multiplication of bases and lines of communication is simply not possible at the outset of a war, because the necessary facilities do not exist.

It follows, therefore, that either land operations will become impossible or that land forces will have to be greatly reduced in size and complication so as to simplify their maintenance to the greatest possible extent.

If it is necessary to reduce the size of armies, then it becomes essential to increase their mobility and striking power, so as to compensate for this.

5. The fact that the maintenance of armies by land is going to become increasingly difficult and may become as difficult as to make it almost impracticable, points to the necessity for substituting supply by air for supply by land.

Supply by air can be carried out with relative ease from a number of small, widely dispersed bases, and aircraft are not confined to narrow lanes of movement to the same extent as land or water transport.

If air transport is likely to increasingly take the place of land or water transport for the maintenance of armies, we must consider seriously the system under which the air transport of any Army is to be provided, controlled and maintained. It is obvious that, should air transport become a normal means of maintaining an Army in the field, the Air Force may not be the most suitable agency to provide or control it.

The transport aircraft may well become just as much an Army vehicle as the three-ton lorry or the jeep. This aspect of the problem demands urgent examination.

6. Bearing the facts set out in the preceding paragraphs in mind, I am driven to the conclusion that, before we proceed further with our plans for the Indian Army of the future, we must think again and think very hard in the light of probable future developments.

I wish, therefore, the possibility and consequences of re-organizing the Indian Army (excluding any possible British component) to be considered on these lines:

a) A number of 'Divisions': These 'Divisions', which should be of the same type and composition, would be used in conjunction with airborne forces as the offensive weapon of the Army. They should each contain a strong armoured element and a motorized infantry element to which should be added the essential minimum of artillery, engineers and administrative units. All combat troops in the 'Divisions' should be as powerfully armed, as fully protected, as mobile as it is possible to make them.

In suggesting a composition for these 'Divisions', the aim should be to continue the minimum strength in men with the maximum hitting power, protection and mobility. It is essential also that they should be completely self-contained and ready for immediate action when an emergency arises; this will demand a high degree of completeness and readiness in peace and will be correspondingly expensive.

b) One airborne division: This formation might keep the same basic organization as at present, modified as necessary to give the maximum of hitting power and mobility with the lowest possible manpower.

c) A number of self-contained 'Groups': These might be called 'Fortress Groups' or 'Defence Groups', whose task it would be to hold areas seized by the striking forces (the 'Divisions'), to control occupied enemy territory, to protect our forward bases and lines of communication, airfields, etc., and, in peace, to provide the necessary aid to the civil power when required.

These 'Groups' should consist mainly of 'Infantry', specially equipped, organized and trained for the tasks they will have to carry out. Their tasks being primarily defensive, the armament of the units comprising these 'Groups' should be designed accordingly and their power of developing fire against both ground and air attack should be as great as possible. The old idea that every infantryman must be armed with a rifle and bayonet must be abandoned and full use made of modern small arms. At the same time they must be self-contained and highly mobile, as not only will they have to move far and fast when they are called forward, but their defensive duties will demand the provision of highly mobile and powerful patrols to counter enemy reconnaissance activities and to give warning of impending attack. They will have to be provided with the best and most complete methods of warning against air attack and with the maximum of protection against bacteriological attack.

The need for the inclusion in these 'Groups' of Artillery, other than Anti-Tank, and Anti-Aircraft weapons and mortars is open to question and must be carefully considered. They must have readily available in their organization earth-shifting machines to enable them to fortify with maximum speed and efficiency any locality they may have to defend. Whether this equipment should be provided on a 'Group' or a 'Force' basis is for examination.

Each 'Group' must be self-contained and, so far as it is possible to achieve this, self-supporting.

d) 'Frontier Groups': In India, for the time being at any rate, we shall need some more or less specially organized and equipped forces on the Western Frontier and, possibly, on the Eastern Frontier also, to deal with tribal unrest and meet the first shock of any landborne incursions from beyond the frontier.

The number of troops so employed must be kept to the essential minimum, as their duties and training are likely to militate against their being able to be ready at short notice to fight an enemy equipped on modern lines.

Their organization, armament, equipment and training should, therefore, be assimilated to the greatest extent possible with those of the 'Fortress Groups' discussed above.

Although it may be necessary to give these 'Frontier Groups' some animal transport and light artillery, they should be fully trained and equipped for mechanized warfare, so that they can take their place in a major war without the need for extensive re-training or re-equipping.

e) Internal Defence Troops: In peace, duties in Aid of Civil Power should be the secondary responsibility of the 'Fortress Groups' and 'Secondary Groups'.

In war, these 'Groups' should be replaced by militia units composed of the older classes of Reservists, organized and trained for the purpose in peace.

7. If my suppositions regarding the nature and scope of future land operations are in any way correct, and I think they are, then it will be obvious that we shall have to revise our present lavish and over-luxurious ideas as to the needs of an Army in the field.

These small, heavily armed and armoured, and highly mobile striking forces which I have tried to describe in this note will not be capable of sustained or continuous fighting.

They, whether airborne or landborne, will have to be held in leash until the chance arises to strike a decisive blow at some vital point in the enemy's defence.

When they are unleashed, their action must be swift, unchecked and final.

There can be no question of long preparation for assault, of daily preparatory bombardments by masses of land artillery, or of the building up of vast dumps of material and stores behind the front before an attack is launched. Indeed, these methods of waging war will not be practicable, because of the impossibility of maintaining long lines of communication and great maintenance organizations in the face of the new weapons which are already in being.

Should an attack by these new model striking forces fail, there will be no question of sitting down and 'consolidating the ground gained'. The battle will have to be broken off and the attacking troops withdrawn out of contact, so that they can reform and be ready to try again.

When launched to the attack these forces must be self-contained and self-sufficient to the utmost extent in all their needs: food, ammunition, medical facilities, repair facilities, water (if the conditions demand it) and so on.

Their weapons must be so designed as to give the greatest effect possible with the minimum expenditure of ammunition, and this principle must also be applied to all their equipment.

While in action, they must live hard and strike hard – otherwise they will fail, and probably perish.

Should the attack succeed, it is reasonable to assume that the ground gained or the localities captured from the enemy will have the effect of forcing back his installations and bases, whence he has been using his aircraft and guided weapons against our areas of supply.

This should in itself ease our problems of maintenance and enable us to bring forward our 'Fortress Groups' to hold the ground gained and to cover the establishment of a new 'Forward Bombardment Area' of our own.

It may also allow of the forward extension of our own lines of communication by land and water.

Until this happens, however, it is obvious that we shall have to depend very largely, if not entirely, on air transport for the maintenance of our striking force during its offensive and thereafter, until it is possible to develop land or water systems of maintenance to the forward areas.

This will entail a drastic revision of our present ideas of the use of air transport. We are now apt to think of it almost entirely in terms of an emergency and supplementary means of supply, only to be used on special occasions, or in particular areas, such as the jungles and mountains of Burma.

In future we must come to look on air transport as the normal method of supply of striking forces, certainly in the initial stages of a campaign and, probably, throughout it.

This being so, it is necessary seriously to consider whether the time has not come for the Army to take over the provision and control of its own air transport, instead of relying as at present on the Air Force for this purpose.

This is only a logical outcome of modern developments and will certainly come about before long. It is highly desirable, therefore, to examine the problem now as a matter of urgency before more time and money is spent on providing and developing forms of land transport which are likely to become obsolete, or, in any event, to be in much smaller demand than heretofore.

The primary business of the Air Force is to fight, either defensively with fighters or offensively with bombers. It is no part of its business to provide the normal day-to-day maintenance transport of the Army, nor is it really fitted to carry out this task, which is radically different from the task of fighting in the air.

8. a) The General Staff should now consider and make recommendations for the re-organization of the Indian Army (exclusive of any British troops) to comprise:

i) An airborne Division (re-organized if necessary to meet modern requirements).
ii) A number of armoured and motorized Divisions organized, armed and equipped on the lines suggested in these notes.
iii) A number of 'Fortress Groups' as described in these notes.
iv) A number of 'Frontier Groups' as considered necessary to meet the special needs of Indian Frontier Defence.

b) The General Staff will also consider in consultation with Principal Administrative Officers and Air Headquarters the question of the Army becoming responsible in the future for the provision, training and control of the air transport required for the maintenance of the Indian Army in future wars, and the number of air transport units likely to be needed for this purpose.

APPENDIX V

The Commander-in-Chief's Talk to Students at the Staff College

I am going to talk to you about our plans for the future of the Armed Forces of India, assuming that India remains within the British Commonwealth of Nations as a fully autonomous Dominion. It is, I think, necessary to make this assumption a basis of our planning, and if India does not remain a member of the Commonwealth, so many unknown and uncertain factors are brought into the problems as to make any realistic planning practically impossible.

I will assume, then, that India will remain within the Commonwealth and that she will, in consequence, be ready to help in its general defence against an aggressor and also to rely on the aid of the other members of it, should she herself be attacked. It is then my task, helped by my advisers in Naval, General and Air Headquarters to try to produce and maintain in peace the Armed Forces which will enable India to defend herself against the first shock of an assault, or to help any other part of the Commonwealth, which may be threatened, to do the same. You will realize, I know, that we are rigidly limited in our planning by financial considerations and that we have to restrict ourselves to the absolute minimum forces needed to give security, and to ensure as rapid an expansion as possible on the outbreak of war.

You might well ask, in view of the uncertain political situation in the country, why we are making any plans at all.

What guarantee have I, or any one else for that matter, that the new National Government of India will not have quite different ideas as to the form and size of the Armed Forces it needs, and proceed to re-organize these on completely new lines?

I can only say that I have no such guarantee. I am sure, though, that it would be wrong to stop planning for the future and just mark time.

To do so would, I am certain, set up a rapid and dangerous decline in morale and efficiency, not only in the Headquarters of the Armed Forces, but in those Forces themselves.

I am afraid I am not one of those who believe that all wars have ceased. The planning and development of new weapons of war is going on at an alarming rate on all sides, and I have no doubt myself that in five years time many of our present-day weapons will be as out-of-date as the horse is today, so far as war is concerned.

I will now tell you briefly how far we have got in our planning.

So far as the Royal Indian Navy is concerned, we hope to have a balanced, if not very large, fleet, consisting of three cruisers as its nucleus, with sloops, frigates and other smaller vessels as considered necessary.

The Royal Indian Navy is a young force, which, through no fault of its own, grew up too quickly, perhaps, during the late war, though we all know how excellently it proved itself in many parts of the world and what high praise it earned from its big brother, the Royal Navy. All the same, it did expand to a tremendous extent in a very short space of time.

As to the Royal Indian Air Force, that too expanded very rapidly in the war years, too rapidly to allow of it being built up, as it should have been, had conditions permitted, into a balanced and self-contained Force. There was a natural and very proper desire to see Indian squadrons taking their place in battle against the enemy, with the result that, when fighting ceased, we found ourselves with ten Royal Indian Air Force Squadrons, all fighter squadrons and practically entirely officered and manned by Indians. We all know how well these squadrons fought in Burma.

Behind these squadrons, however, the Royal Indian Air Force had no maintenance organization of its own. There was, and still is, a vast repair and maintenance organization for the upkeep of the Air Forces in India but this is a mixed Royal Air Force and Royal Indian Air Force organization and depends very largely indeed on the Royal Air Force for the large number of skilled technicians and artificers required, though intense efforts were and are being made to train Indians to fill these essential posts.

To turn now to the Army.

The basis of our planning has been that in peace we must have the nucleus of a field army ready for use in emergency with the least possible delay. In other words, we hope to have our divisions and brigades complete, not only with their fighting units, but also, so far as is possible with their transport, medical and other administrative services.

We hope, too, that we shall be able to keep these divisions concentrated under their own commanders and staffs, in suitable training areas, so that they can really prepare themselves for war and keep alive the divisional spirit which has grown up so strongly in the last war. Our plans include one armoured and one airborne division as well as several infantry divisions.

The infantry divisions will keep the signs and numbers they had in the late war, though the units must change, of course, from time to time.

These divisions and brigades will consist entirely of units of the Indian Army; in fact this is already the case. As you know, up till now our divisions and brigades have been a mixture of British and Indian units and a very good mixture it has been, as anyone who has read the histories of the Indian Divisions of the last war will know. Coming constitutional changes make it necessary to put an end to this close partnership and from now on our divisions and brigades will be composed solely of Indian units.

In addition to our divisions and brigades of the Field Army, we shall need some frontier brigade groups to help the civil authorities to keep order on our western frontier and these will consist, as they have always done, of infantry, artillery, Sappers and Signals, with some armoured units to reinforce them if necessary. We have a big plan for the expansion of the Civil Armed Forces, that is the Scouts and Militia Corps, on the western frontier, so that these can more and more take over the duty of policing the tribal areas and so replace regular troops, which can then be concentrated and trained for modern war.

In addition to the Army in India, we have still a large number of divisions and brigades of Indian troops overseas in the Middle East, Iraq, Burma and Malaya, besides our occupational troops in Japan.

If the future Government of India wishes to retain British troops in this country and if the British Government agrees to their being kept, and it is an important proviso, then these troops will be organized in Independent Brigade Groups. This process has already started and there are at the present moment five or six such groups composed of British infantry battalions and British artillery regiments in various stations throughout India. This is a necessary and convenient arrangement which follows on the decision to have all-Indian divisions and brigades in the Field Army. How many, if any, British units will be kept in India will be for agreement between the future Government of India and the British Government, but, as I said before, it will be primarily a matter for India to decide.

It is the intention to have such British brigade groups as may be kept in India, concentrated under their own commanders so as to make the training and administration easy to carry out.

As for the supply of officers, you will have heard of our plans for a National War Academy, an Indian 'West Point'. An excellent site has been tentatively selected on Lake Karakvasla, near Poona, and we are now going ahead with plans to secure land.

If our plans mature, this will be a magnificent place, fully worthy of India and of the great achievements of her fighting men in the last war.

We hope it will hold some 2500 to 3000 cadets, who will go through a four-year course, organized on the best and most modern lines. As you know, it will train officers for all three services and this I hope will lay the foundations for that close comradeship and co-operation between them which is so essential to success in war.

I ask the support and help of all of you in order to make this scheme the success it deserves to become.

There is one other most important matter to which I want to draw your attention and it is this. The new weapons for war which are now being rapidly developed in many countries – atom bombs, bacteriological warfare, guided projectiles and so on – must, I am sure, have a most marked effect on the size and make-up of armies in the future.

At the moment our divisions are organized and equipped as they were in the last war but I am sure that this cannot last long. I feel that all these new weapons will have the effect of making it more and more difficult to supply large armies in the field. Enormous bases of supply and crowded roads and railways for lines of communications will not, in my opinion, be possible in the face of the long-range, accurate attack of these new weapons. I believe this will force us to reduce the size of armies in the field and that such armies as we may be able to maintain will have to be very highly protected, extremely mobile, very hard-hitting and self-contained to the greatest possible degree. I suggest that you might give thought to this problem. I have already instructed the General Staff at GHQ to give it their urgent consideration.

There is one final point I wish to make to you. It is concerned with loyalty.

An officer is bound to be loyal to his Service and to his country. He may hold whatever political opinion he likes, but so long as he is serving as a sailor, soldier or airman, he must not allow politics to affect his loyalty to his Service or to the Government which is in power, even if he thinks that it is not the right form of Government. We all know that the political situation in India today is confused and the future most uncertain. I think I can say that no one knows better than I do the difficult position in which many Indian officers find themselves. I hope that the political situation may clear up in the near future and so, I am sure, do all of you, but it may not. So long as this uncertainty continues, I hope all officers will remember their duty and their loyalty and not allow their political opinions to interfere with either of these.

If an officer feels so strongly that he cannot restrain in this matter, it is his duty to resign. I hope most sincerely that none of you will have to take such a drastic step, as the Army needs today all the officers it can get.

Setting up of the Armed Forces Nationalization Committee

The Defence Department issued the following notification:—

It is the declared policy of the Government of India to nationalize the Armed Forces in the shortest possible time compatible with the maintenance of efficiency. In replying to a Resolution in the Council of State on the 8th April, 1946, His Excellency the Commander-in-Chief, as the War Member of the Government of India, stated inter alia:—

The object is to create a completely national army, that is, an army officered and manned throughout by Indians in the shortest possible space of time without lowering the very high standard of efficiency which obtains in the Indian Army today. It is the declared policy of the Government of India that the British officer element of the Indian Army shall be replaced by Indian officers as soon as possible, compatible with the maintenance of efficiency of the army as a whole.

The latest pronouncement on the subject was made by the Honourable the Defence Member on the 9th October, 1946. In his broadcast to the Armed Forces he observed:—

We aim at building up in a truly national way a national army which will be the pride of this great land of ours. Nationalization of the Armed Forces will now be speeded up at an accelerated pace compatible with efficiency.

There is now an insistent demand for accelerating the pace of nationalization. In order to assist them in giving effect to their declared policy, the Government of India have decided to appoint a committee to go into the whole question. The committee will be known as "THE ARMED FORCES NATIONALIZATION COMMITTEE" and will consist of the following:—

Chairman
The Hon'ble Sir N. Gopalaswami Ayyangar, CSI, CIE

Members

The Hon'ble Pandit Hirday Nath Kunzru
Mr Muhammad Ismail Khan
Sardar Sampuran Singh
Major-General D. A. L. Wade, CB, OBE, MC
Brigadier Kodendera Subayya Thimayya, DSO
Wing Commander Mehr Singh, DSO, RIAF
Commander Hajee Muhammad Siddiq Choudri, MBE, RIN

Secretary

Lieut.-Col. B. M. Kaul

An officer of the rank of Major-General, Commodore, or Air Commodore will attend from the Indian Army, the Royal Indian Navy, and the Royal Indian Air Force, respectively, to advise the Committee whenever questions concerning the Army, Navy or Air Force, as the case may be, are considered.

The terms of reference of the Committee will be:—

In order to nationalize the Armed Forces of India, viz., the Indian Navy, the Indian Army and the Indian Air Force, and all Auxiliary Services, both officers and men, within the shortest possible time, with due regard to Indian national interests and reasonable efficiency, and to enquire and report on:—

a)   The ways and means, within the minimum possible period, of replacement of non-Indian personnel by Indians in each Branch or Service;

b)   the target date or dates of complete nationalization for all or each category in different Services, if possible;

c)   the ways and means of retaining, if necessary, non-Indian personnel as advisers or experts in nationalized categories;

d)   the enumeration of those departments, categories or personnel where non-Indian personnel can be replaced by Indians immediately.

The Committee will submit their report to Government within six months from the date they assemble for the first meeting.

APPENDIX VII

Division of the Armed Forces

There can be little doubt that for the overall security of India and the future growth of her military strength one Defence force, under central control, is most desirable. But, in the absence of solid political unity in the country, such a defence force would be exposed to divided loyalties, suspicion and discrimination which must, in due course, inevitably make it quite useless.

Therefore, either in keeping with the political trend, the armed forces should be divided and re-organized so that two armies, though potentially weaker but actually more dependable, are substituted for the one army now under the shadow of disintegration, or, for the sake of the future armed strength of India, politicians must be forced to agree to a reasonably united Centre. It is considered that, on military grounds alone, justification for the latter course does not exist.

This paper is, therefore, set out to show:—

Part I   — Why division is desirable and feasible.
Part II — Basis for division. And how it can be done.
Part III — An examination of details.

Part I – Why division is desirable and feasible

1. If Pakistan is established, it may have its own army or it may share one with Hindustan, but it cannot really be sovereign unless it also achieves military independence. It is appreciated that in future no small country, nor even some bigger ones, can stand entirely on their own for defence, and such absolute military independence is unlikely to exist anywhere. But this does not mean that one State should merge its forces with another's to such an extent as to lose all real control over them and thereby expose itself to unhindered hostile designs. This is precisely what can happen if a politically autonomous Pakistan shares a common defence force with Hindustan. However great the desirability of such a common organization may be, since its control must rest at the Centre it virtually becomes an army of occupation as far as Pakistan is concerned.

2. One reason why most soldiers are averse to the idea of dividing the Armed Forces is that it must result in serious weakening of the overall security of India and must necessitate a complete remoulding of the present structure of defence, which has been evolved after much thought and experience. This fear is not unreasonable, but it is not commonly realized that the existing conception of the defence of India is based on certain factors which no longer exist.

The present forces were designed to fit into a defence plan under which India was naturally treated as one unit – one huge potential base of operations in the East – one vast source of raw materials. A strong India meant a strong Britain. The Army was to provide internal security necessary for the smooth running of administration and the easy mobilization for an *Imperial purpose*. Secondly, this force was to withstand the first shock of a possible invasion, to gain time for the arrival of external Imperial assistance and for the expansion and concentration of India's own effort. Thirdly, this force was to be sufficiently strong to assist in preventing the occupation of Afghanistan, Iran and Burma by any other power (other than Great Britain).

All this added to the strength of the Empire and Britain, which in turn prevented the occupation of India by another first class power. Plainly speaking, Russia and Japan were kept out of India in pursuance of an *Imperial purpose* which incidentally gave India peace and escape from a worse master.

This purpose was well served by the present Armed Forces and the existing defence structure. *But this purpose is no longer valid.*

3. India was a target for Japan and Russia chiefly because it was the main base of British Imperial power in the East and was, therefore, a dagger permanently pointing at the flanks of these two countries. With the withdrawal of British power it ceases to be so.

Since her recent defeat, Japan is not exactly in direct contact with us. A stronger China, an independent Burma and the Anglo-American Navy intervene between us more effectively now. Long before we come into direct conflict, other countries will have been involved and we shall have become part of a larger allied defence front. This will mean careful co-ordination and adjustment *between several armies*, and as such the existence of two, instead of one, Indian Armed Force makes little difference. On the other hand if there were a threat of direct aggression, a permanently unified armed force would certainly be almost essential. Similarly if overall British supremacy were to continue in India, one force would again be advantageous because it would save much unco-ordinated labour. But a threat of direct aggression from the East is not likely to arise for a few years, and overall British supremacy in India is to end next year.

4. As far as Russia is concerned the withdrawal of British power from India will remove the most potent excuse with which she could justify an advance in our direction. However, if we do come into conflict with Russia the situation would be:—

Navy – The Indian Navy, united or disunited, would obviously make little difference, because, apart from its lack of strength, it could never run a private war of its own in the Indian Ocean – a war in which the British Navy is not already involved.

Air Force – In this age of atom bombs, jet planes, cosmic rays, rockets and expanding airborne armies, the ten Indian Squadrons, united or disunited, have no significance except as a nucleus for expansion dependent upon foreign machines for a long time to come.

Army – Against the possibility of aggression from the West the Army plan has apparently, so far, consisted of holding forward bases in the tribal territories with the object of preventing the growth of foreign influence in these areas and to gain time, in the event of attack, for the mobilization of the Field Force. Secondly, the plan provides a Field Force capable of expansion.

The basic structure of this plan must inevitably change in a free India. A free India and particularly a Muslim State or Group in the North could not possibly justify the occupation of the tribal area. On moral and political grounds all these garrisons will have to be withdrawn. On military considerations too the holding of the forward areas may become undesirable because an airborne army, landing in the wide open spaces behind them, would make the position untenable. Closer ties, political treaties, mutual trust and the opening up of new economic possibilities for the tribes will have to be substituted. This may provide the necessary security from raids for the settled districts and India as a whole. But it does mean the collapse of the present defensive structure as far as aggression from the West is concerned. And, therefore, without treaties of friendship with Russia or alternatively an offensive/defensive alliance with Great Britain (which might become pointedly anti-Russian), the position of India becomes equally weak whether she has one or two Armed Forces.

5. Thus, as far as the external defence of India is concerned (from a purely Indian point of view) division of the present Armed Forces does not materially worsen our immediate prospects. Our role must, necessarily, change to the primary object of maintaining a nucleus sufficiently large to ensure adequate training, technical progress and rapid expansion – *all with a view to fitting into some international defensive front when another war becomes imminent*. Such an object can be pursued with equal ease by two armies independently, and they should be able to achieve excellent results if they are also able to evolve a common defence policy and adopt common training methods.

It might be asserted that division will increase the danger of internal war. Should the two States be hostile, it will lead to an armament race possibly ending in a serious conflict. But this unfortunate situation can be avoided by the establishment of a common Defence Council to evolve a common defence plan for the two separate but dependable armies. On the other hand, one Army owned by two politically disgruntled states or nations will be open to complete disintegration and itself becoming a danger to law and order.

6. To sum up; division of the Armed Forces is necessary if political independence for Muslims is to become a reality. For the external defence of India division creates no immediate dangers. As the future defence structure of India must inevitably be changed and reshaped after freedom, there will be enough time to build this on the basis of two armies as easily as one. Internally, one Army suffering from divided loyalties and under the ever-present shadow of disintegration is a greater menace than two separate armies which are at least dependable in their own spheres.

The real question is whether division is feasible before June 1948 and on what basis.

Part II – Basis for division

1. The maximum share, in the Armed Forces and their equipment, to which Pakistan might be entitled should be assessed either on the present Muslim and non-Muslim ratio in the Armed Forces (30%–70%) – or in proportion to the total population of Pakistan Areas as compared with Hindustan. The latter alternative is probably fairer. The population of India, excluding States, may be approximately 300 millions of which Pakistan will have some 70 to 90 millions (depending on whether Punjab and Bengal are partitioned or not). This means an entitlement of 25% to 30%. Pakistan may not need all this or may find it difficult to support financially. This, however, is a matter to be settled after a fuller consideration of the Pakistan Defence problem and the financial position. To start with, the full share should be

made available. The division of officers, men and moveable equipment, on the above basis, will present no serious difficulty. The correct share of immoveable assets such as arsenals, schools, hospitals, accommodation, institutions and landing grounds, etc. will have to be made over to Pakistan by financial compensation where necessary. It may also be desirable to draw up a five years' agreement to permit the common use of training establishments on payment of special fees. Unless specially so desired by the two States, the new armies should not become purely Muslim and non-Muslim. Their composition should reflect community population in the States. However, in the case of officers, or at least senior officers, it may be desirable to make initial postings on Muslim and non-Muslim basis only. Later the two States will probably allow and encourage exchange on the understanding that a resident of Pakistan who serves in the Hindustan Army should cease to be a national of Pakistan and vice-versa.

2. To put the above into effect means immediate planning for division, on paper, and re-organization to lay the outlines of two balanced armies. The detailed elaboration of such a plan would take considerable time. Its execution would be an intricate and expensive operation even under peaceful conditions and with the co-operation of all concerned, because it would mean the break-up and reshuffle of practically all units, enormous clerical work in the sorting out of records, a host of committees and sub-committees all over the country to make assessments and effect division, and greatest of all the heaviest strain on our transportation services for many months. The task is a hard one, and under existing circumstances involves many additional risks. In the period of reshuffle much unpleasantness among officers and men, and opportunities for ill-discipline will arise. Some portions of the Armed Forces might become ineffective for a considerable period at a time when internal security demands may be urgent.

Yet, these difficulties are not insuperable and certainly cannot be permitted to stand in the way of vital political issues. It cannot be argued that for the sake of doubtful internal security and military convenience in the next twelve months, the future freedom of a people should be jeopardized. However short the time may be, the great advantage of this year must not be forgotten. The difficulties of today, with a neutral power in control of the Armed Forces and the Government will be magnified a hundred times after June 1948, when two interested parties are in the saddle. Therefore, the task must be undertaken at once in full recognition of the risks which should be minimised by means of a phased programme.

3. *Phased programme.* A phased programme can be designed so as to follow and fit in with the progress of political settlement. In such a case work could start immediately and further stages be introduced as and when opportune political moments occur.

If the principle is accepted, certain preliminary actions can be taken now without prejudice to further decisions. For instance, the present Northern Command covers exactly the area of NW Pakistan and a part of Rajputana. From this the separation of Rajputana would mean only a paper transaction, while the detachment of Ambala Sub-Area would remove exactly those areas which a partition of the Punjab would cut away. The territorial organization of the remainder, that is to say, Frontier Area, Punjab Area and Sind Area (covering Baluchistan) – all under control of Headquarters Northern Command – provides an ideal and fully fledged structure for the formation of the Pakistan Army. Similarly in the east, Headquarters Bengal and Assam Area (at Calcutta) and its two Sub-Areas at Calcutta and Shillong can be adopted with a little readjustment if Bengal is to be partitioned. *Thus the most important and difficult part of an Army, namely its basic framework of Headquarters, communications, installations and the necessary organization for maintenance and adminis-tration, all actually exist today on the ground.* This organization in the NW and east is not likely to be altered and there can be no possibility of it coming under dispute by rival claimants. Therefore, the first action that can be taken at once is to start posting Muslim officers to Headquarters, Bases, Services and units with predominant Muslim composition that are located in these areas. The non-Muslim staffs (other than British) can be changed over smoothly within a few months – at least to such an extent that all key positions and important appointments are held by Muslims.

The first rough and ready forecast of the allotment of major units should take very little time. From this it will be obvious, for instance, that the Frontier Force Rifles with their centre at Abbottabad and the 1st Punjab Regiment with their centre at Jhelum (Muslim proportion in both being 50% or over) must fall to the share of Pakistan. Therefore, battalions of these regiments could be given Muslim command-ing officers at once and further posting of non-Muslim officers and men stopped. Again, all expected moves of completely or predominantly non-Muslim units into Northern Command and Bengal Area can be diverted at once.

All these changes of staffs, alteration of moves and curtailment of recruiting can be commenced immediately without prejudice to final decisions, and can be completed rapidly within the framework of the impending nationalization and the normal reshuffle and demobilization that is taking place.

Meanwhile the problem of division can be examined in detail at a high level and a committee appointed to consider the re-organization of the divided army into two balanced forces. When the final General Staff plan is ready its execution will probably fall into four stages. *First*, the preliminary posting of Muslims to Headquar-ters, etc. in Pakistan Areas will already have taken place and most of the obvious units will have got Muslim COs and officers. *Second*, the officering of all remaining units, the positioning of ancillary services, and the finalization of maintenance and adminis-trative arrangements can be completed without trouble because most of these exist on the ground and only a slight reshuffle of personnel will be necessary. By now there should be no predominantly non-Muslim units in Pakistan Areas. So that if, because of political reasons, the actual composition of units has not yet started to be altered – at least the main structure of two armies will have come into existence and the appropriate staffs ready to take over control. *Third*, from now onwards the operation will have to be open and intense. This will include orders to all concerned regarding their new composition, the preparation of transfers, innumerable com-mittees and sub-committees and the execution of large-scale moves. This stage might conceivably continue up to and even after June, 1948, but the organization to carry it to completion will have been firmly established. *Fourth*, the establishment of a common Defence Council or negotiating committee to deal with problems of common defence policy, training facilities, mutual aid, treaties and the completion of division.

It must be remembered that up to June, 1948, there will be no actual split in the Army, whose allegiance will still be to the King, and everybody, wherever and how-ever posted, will still be under the Commander-in-Chief and his Headquarters. This unified command can and must ensure the maintenance of normal discipline. All that will really have happened so far will be a re-organization of the Army. When the time for handing over comes, Northern Command with Bengal and Assam Area will be detached from the rest which will really mean no sudden change as far as the component parts of the Army are concerned.

4. In conclusion, it is obvious that, in spite of all the difficulties, the task of dividing

the Armed Forces by June, 1948, is not impossible. The framework and essential maintenance and administrative organization of two armies exists now. The reshuffle necessitated by nationalization can be so directed as to create a virtually Muslim Army in the North-West. The fact that all parts of the Army continue to be under the Commander-in-Chief and owe their allegiance to the King up to June, 1948, and the fact that no structural alterations will be made in the framework of the Army, reduce the risks of the transition period to the minimum.

APPENDIX VIII

Preparation of Plan for the Partition of the Indian Armed Forces

Paper by the Honourable Member for Finance

The Indian Armed Forces, Army, Navy and Air Force, are now in the process of re-organization and nationalization. The object of re-organization is to produce the nucleus of two armies out of the wartime arms and services. The object of nationalization is to replace all British officers and men in the Indian Armed Forces by Indians as soon as possible. Nationalization affects mainly the officer cadre including the Higher Command. The question of selecting Indian officers for the appointments of Commanders-in-Chief of the Army, Navy and Air Force, Army Commanders, Principal Staff Officers and other senior posts in all the three Services is, I understand, already under consideration.

2. After HMG's statement of 20th February, 1947, a United India with a single Army, Navy and Air Force can no longer be taken for granted. In spite of this, the re-organization and nationalization of the Armed Forces are proceeding on the assumption that they are to continue as a single entity. The fundamental constitutional issue of a United or Divided India is thus being prejudged on a most vital point to the grave detriment of Muslims. The division of India implies the division of the Armed Forces for no State can exist without its own Armed Forces on whom rests the ultimate responsibility for internal security as well as external defence.

3. Another serious consequence of treating the Armed Forces as a single entity is that no regard is paid either to the organization of Muslim units or to the representation of Muslim in suitable number and ranks in all the arms and services. From such figures as I have been able to obtain from the Defence Member so far, I find that the representation of Muslims in the Armed Forces is grossly inadequate particularly in the officer cadre of all the three Services but more markedly in the Navy and the Air Force. I am trying to obtain more information on the subject and shall raise the issue at a later stage. I touch on it here to indicate that Armed Forces which do not have an adequate representation of Muslims in numbers and ranks will not have the confidence of the Muslims – a situation fraught with the utmost danger to the security of the country and of the Armed Forces themselves.

4. In order that the constitutional issue should not be prejudged it is necessary to devise a course of action which should not be to the advantage or prejudice of either political party. This neutral position would be obtained by re-organizing the Armed Forces in such a manner that they can be split up when a decision on the partition of the country is taken. An essential preliminary is the preparation of a plan by the

Commander-in-Chief and his staff for the partition of the Armed Forces. This will necessarily take some weeks and if taken in hand immediately should be ready by about the time that a decision on the main constitutional issue is reached. The time limit set by HMG demands that no time should be lost in preparing such a Plan which will in no way interfere either with the present political negotiations or the present status of the Armed Forces.

5. I suggest therefore that –

i) the Commander-in-Chief should be asked to prepare a plan for the partition of the Armed Forces, and

ii) action on the present plans for the re-organization and nationalization of the Forces on the basis of a United India should be suspended until the constitutional issue has been settled. This is of the utmost importance because if present plans are persisted in, their reversal at a subsequent stage will mean a major upheaval which may have most serious effects upon the efficiency of the Armed Forces.

Remarks by the Honourable Member for Defence

I have very carefully considered the note by HM, Finance on the 'Preparation of Plan for the Partition of the Indian Armed Forces'.

It is true that the Indian Armed Forces are now in the process of re-organization and nationalization and that this is proceeding broadly as indicated in the note. The need for re-organization arose due to the imperative urgency of return to post-war conditions within the limited funds available, with which is also intermixed the inescapable technical and scientific changes brought about by developments during and experience gained in war. The scheme of nationalization has been drawn up as a result of the overwhelming pressure of public opinion and changes inherent in the present situation which no one can ignore. Both re-organization and nationalization could only proceed on an all-India basis. No other course was either possible or practical for the simple reason that the major issue of the defence of India as a whole could not be prejudiced in any way until the larger political issue of Division – if it is indeed to take place – is finally and fully settled in all its bearings and implications. To say that the re-organization and nationalization of Armed Forces prejudges the issue of Division is to subordinate the larger interests of Defence to sectional or Group interests – a proposition which nobody will accept.

In Para. 3 of his Note, HM, Finance has made reference to 'Muslim units' and 'representation of Muslims' in all arms and services of the Armed Forces, in the light of the figures I gave him in reply to his enquiry in this respect. I do not understand the reference to 'units'. As regards the statement that '*representation of Muslims* in Armed Forces is grossly inadequate' I must take the *strongest objection to the statement as well as the insinuation* which incidentally has found place lately in the Muslim League Press as well. I note that HM, Finance will raise this question later. Meanwhile I will state that neither in the process of re-organization nor that of nationalization has any discrimination been made against Muslims or any other community *per se*. The Armed Forces, as now emerging after the war, are being organized on a set-up built on standards of the past with modification to suit the needs of the times and based on the experience of Army Commanders over a long period of time. The entire scheme of this organization is being drawn up by specialists in various technical branches and services under the direct authority of the C-in-C, and I can say with authority *that nothing has happened in this planning to the detriment of any community in any way*. If, therefore, the demand for a plan of the division of the Armed Forces, here and now, is based on the suggestion that Muslims are being discriminated against, it is wholly wide of the mark, to say the least.

I have had the implications of the proposal of HM, Finance examined by the C-in-C. His note is attached. In the short time available to him, he has analysed it in some detail with reference to the administrative, technical and financial implications involved. It is his firm view that the division of the Armed Forces into two on the *basis of Hindustan and Pakistan is not possible before June, 1948*, and indeed for quite a long period thereafter with due regard to the requirements of Defence and that is if enough funds are found. Of far greater consequence are such factors as the territorial boundaries of the two States and whether Muslims now in the Forces and residing in non-Muslim regions – defined or to be defined – are to be drafted in the scheme of 'Pakistan Forces' and if so whether with or *without any reference to* the officers and men concerned.

The Armed Forces as a whole have been built up on a non-communal basis. They have, fortunately for India, remained free from communal complications up till now. Various factors have contributed to this and among these the chief one is the general belief that, whatever the political future of the country, any attempt at the division of the Armed Forces will leave both the Muslim and non-Muslim parts not only weak in numbers but technically and strategically at considerable *disadvantage against even the weakest neighbours*. The discipline inculcated by association with British officers has been a cementing force of no small value. In the event of a Division of the country, the division of the Forces will of course have to be faced. In that event and while the process is on, the potency and striking power of the Forces will, I have no hesitation in saying, remain seriously impaired for a considerable time. That issue too will have to be faced when the time comes. What I must lay the greatest emphasis on is that if even the mere indication of splitting the Armed Forces is allowed to gain ground at this stage, it will result in creating chaotic conditions in the ranks and disintegration will set in almost immediately. In the communally charged atmosphere in which we find ourselves today – to say nothing of the international situation – such a contingency would be too disastrous to contemplate.

Nor can I ignore how the prevailing communal disturbances have affected the administration in certain areas and the repercussions thereof on internal security. Respect for law and order is rapidly waning. In certain parts large sections of population have lost confidence in the ability of the police to protect life and property. The only relieving factor in this dark picture is that the *integrity of the Armed Forces* is still unsullied. Their aid is sought after and welcomed by all everywhere, irrespective of group or communal considerations. They, on their part, have fully measured up to the expectations of the Government and the people. It would indeed be an irreparable disaster if a Force such as this was exposed to risks that would not only weaken but ultimately destroy its worth.

For these reasons –

a) I am strongly of the view that *the time is not opportune to discuss the proposal* of HM, Finance in the Defence Committee of India in terms as stated by him.

b) I cannot agree to suspend the present plans for the re-organization and nationalization of the Armed Forces which, on the other hand, must proceed in view of the urgency of many complex issues that cannot be shelved without serious loss of time and money, and risk of endangering the efficiency of the Forces.

In view of the difficulties I have stated and inherent in this problem at this stage, I would suggest instead that HE might informally discuss the issues involved personally with HM, Finance or any other Hon'ble Members as he may deem fit.

Baldev Singh
Defence Member
23rd Apr 1947

TOP SECRET

Remarks by HE the Commander-in-Chief

GENERAL

The Armed Forces of India, as they now stand, cannot be split up into two parts each of which will form a self-contained Armed Force.

Any such proposal would involve the rebuilding of two new Armed Forces of which many essential components do not at present exist in duplicate, or are not located suitably to serve two separate sovereign States.

'PAKISTAN' includes all the important land frontiers of India, and the Army and Air Forces required to defend 'PAKISTAN' from external aggression would be virtually the same as those now required to defend India as a whole.

If 'PAKISTAN' and 'HINDUSTAN' are to have separate Defence Forces, it would seem certain that the combined total of these forces must be greater than that of the Defence Forces designed to serve a United India, since the administrative overheads must be duplicated and there would be a great loss of flexibility. . . .

The formation of two separate Armed Forces is not just a matter of redistribution of certain classes of men. It is a matter of the greatest complexity and difficulty, not only in the preliminary planning stages but also, and more particularly, in the practical means of bringing any such plan into being.

Any such drastic re-organization would have to be carried out in phases over a period of several years, and during this period there would be no cohesive Armed Forces capable of dealing with any serious defensive operations on the North-West Frontier.

Meanwhile it has not been possible to suspend planning on the assumption that HMG will hand over a unified Armed Force. In the absence of any such plan, the cost of the Armed Forces could not have been calculated, demobilization could not have been carried out, and provision for the requisite officers, equipment, supplies, and accommodation could not have been made.

In short, no plan at all could have been handed over by June, 1948.

As it is likely that any rumour concerning a proposal to divide the Armed Forces would have an immediate and unsettling effect on the morale of the Muslim soldiers, ratings, and airmen, it is urged that this matter should not be discussed except on the highest level.

I wish to stress that in the present state of communal unrest in India, any publication of such discussions might well be disastrous to the continued morale and efficiency of the Armed Forces.

APPENDIX IX

The Military Implication of Pakistan

24th April, 1947

You asked me the other day to give you my opinion on the strategic implications of the setting up of an independent Pakistan. I enclose a note which sets out the situation as I see it, taking a long-term view of the problem.

I also enclose a note written by my Deputy Chief of the General Staff setting out a view which might well be taken by the advocates of Pakistan. In my opinion, this view is really a short-term one and does not take into account the potentialities of the future.

A few days ago I received from the Secretary of the DCI a paper written by Mr Liaquat Ali Khan on the subject of dividing the Armed Forces into 'Pakistan Forces' and 'Hindustan Forces', and asking for my views on it.

I enclose a note giving my own opinion on the subject, based on facts and figures as they are known today. I have sent this note to HM Defence with the original paper, as the views of HM Defence were also requested by the Secretary. I am not sure what HM Defence has done with the original paper or with my note, so I am sending this copy of my note direct to Your Excellency in my capacity as a Member of the DCI. I hope it will give you the information which you require.

Auchinleck

His Excellency Rear Admiral The Rt Hon'ble
Viscount Mountbatten of Burma, KG, GMSI, GMIE, GCVO, KCB, DSO

THE MILITARY IMPLICATIONS OF PAKISTAN

This paper is based on the following assumptions:—

a) That India is split into two sovereign independent States – Pakistan and Hindustan, with boundaries as shown on the attached map.
b) That neither Pakistan nor Hindustan remain within the British Commonwealth of Nations, though either or both may be in close treaty relationship with it.

As will be seen from the map, the two regions of Pakistan, that is the western region and the eastern region, are separated from each other by some 1500 miles.

It is true that this gap is traversed by reasonably adequate rail and road communications, but these would be completely controlled by Hindustan and available for the use of Pakistan only by the goodwill of Hindustan, who could close them at any time she so desired. The same conditions would apply to the passage of fighting aircraft wishing to pass between the two regions, as the use of facilities such as airfields, refuelling stations, and radar would depend entirely on the goodwill of Hindustan.

Any idea of a 'corridor' such as the Polish corridor can be discarded as quite impracticable.

By sea, the movement of Pakistan forces between the two regions would be an extremely dangerous operation if Hindustan were hostile.

Any strategic co-operation, except to a limited extent by aircraft between the two regions, would be most difficult, if not impossible, in the event of strained relations between Pakistan and Hindustan.

EASTERN PAKISTAN

a)   It would seem that at the most the Eastern region of Pakistan can not include a greater area than that comprised of Bengal east of the Brahmaputra and Assam, and this is the area shown on the map. This would have practically no resources of any strategical value, and its Muslim inhabitants have few warlike traditions, though they enlisted in considerable strength in the last war in transport and pioneer units. Their officer-producing potential appears to be negligible at present. Rail and road communications in the region are poor and ill-adapted for purposes of defence against aggression. There is one port, Chittagong, which, though of small capacity, reached a high standard of efficiency under British military direction during the last war. There are no mineral resources, factories, repair shops or any establishments which could contribute to the upkeep of Armed Forces. There are, however, a number of airfields constructed during the last war for the Allied Air Forces operating over Burma but the upkeep of any airfield would involve a considerable expenditure.

b)   The region would be open to attack by land from the North, though communications are not highly developed, and also from the West though a land attack on this front would entail crossing the Brahmaputra – not an easy operation. A serious land attack from the East can be ruled out owing to the lack of roads through the Lushai hills, though an enemy advance against Chittagong from the South, as attempted by the Japanese in the last war, is a possibility.

c)   By air the region could be attacked from hostile air bases to the North-East and West, and its defence would need air forces and anti-aircraft defences out of all proportion to its size or importance.

d)   Attack from the sea would always be a possibility and could be given reasonably close support from shore-based aircraft. A combined operation by an enemy against Chittagong would have to be guarded against, and this would entail the provision of seaward and anti-aircraft defences on a considerable scale.

e)   Altogether, the effort involved in providing adequate defence against aggression for this region would seem to be out of all proportion to its economic or strategic value, and certainly could not be provided from the resources available in the region itself. Help would have to be sought from the Western region of Pakistan on a large scale.

WESTERN PAKISTAN

a)   The Western region of Pakistan, as will be seen from the map, would consist of a long narrow stretch of country lying between the high tablelands and mountains of Baluchistan and Afghanistan and the plains of the Eastern Punjab. In fact it comprises the valley of the Indus and its Westernmost tributaries: the Jhelum, the Chenab and the Ravi.

The region being all length without breadth is basically difficult to defend from the strategic point of view. Whether attack should come from the West or the East, there is a lack of depth so essential in modern war to success of any defensive plan.

The average width of the region is about 300 miles only, except in the extreme South, while the distance from Karachi to Rawalpindi is about 700 miles.

If Kashmir is to be included in the region, the distance from Karachi to the Northern frontier where it meets the Pamirs would be about 1100 miles.

The region is well provided with rail communications, especially in the Northern part but the general trend of these communications, as will be seen from the map, is North and South, whereas any large scale attack by land is bound to come from the West or the East.

Moreover these communications all converge into a bottle-neck on the lower Indus about Sukkur and Hyderabad (Sind) before running into Karachi.

Karachi is the only channel through which supplies and munitions can come direct by sea from the outside world, so that if the main North and South communications are severed about Hyderabad or Sukkur, the northern part of the region will be entirely cut off from all direct overseas sources of supply. Should the neighbouring States to the West and East be hostile, or even if one were hostile and the other not, the procurement of munitions and supplies overland across the Western or Eastern frontiers would be a long and most uncertain business, dependent entirely on the goodwill of the neighbouring States – Afghanistan or Hindustan – to provide the necessary transit facilities.

b)   The region would be particularly vulnerable to attack from the air, either from the West or the East, and the lack of depth on which stress has already been laid would make a really efficient defence against such attack almost impossible under modern conditions. The advantage would all be on the side of the aggressor.

c)   The general trend of the four big rivers from North to South, though it may be held to provide successive lines of defence against attacks by land from the West or the East, is really more of a disadvantage than an advantage, owing to the handicap it would place on the free movement of troops and stores within the region, bridges over these rivers being few and far between and vulnerable to air attack or sabotage.

d)   The region contains practically none of the natural resources on which a country must depend for success in war, except wheat and cotton and a little oil near Attock. There is the possibility of more oil being found, but so far no definite proof of this.

There are no minerals and practically no industrial plants except at Karachi where there is ship repair industry. There are certain railway workshops which might in war be turned over to make munitions but their capacity is infinitesimal by modern standards.

e)   Attack by land forces across the Northern sector of the Eastern frontier, that is on the general front Jullundur-Bhatinda, would present no serious difficulty to an aggressor. In fact an advance on this front would be well served by rail and road communications leading directly to the main supply bases in the interior of Hindustan and could be well supported from the air.

Large scale attack by land on the Southern part of the Eastern frontier, that is from Bhatinda South-Westwards to Jodhpur, is not so likely, but there is nothing to prevent small hard hitting and mobile motorized enemy forces from striking across the frontier towards Multan, and the main line of railway connecting Lahore with Karachi. In fact this form of enemy activity based on the Rajputana railway system would be almost certain to eventuate.

f) From the West, the most serious threat by land is likely to be against Quetta and then down the Bolan Pass against the communications bottle-neck at Sukkur, the capture of which by an attacker would go far to paralyse the defence.

In these days of fast-moving and hard-hitting armies, which can be supplied from the air, a serious land offensive along the Makran Coast through Kalat and Las Bela against Karachi is by no means an impossibility, and adequate provision would have to be made against it. Should an aggressor attain complete superiority in the air which is quite possible in certain circumstances, a hostile land advance would also be possible through the Khyber Pass directly against Peshawar, but this is unlikely to be attempted so long as some vestige of air power is left in the defence.

g) A combined operation by the enemy for the direct capture of Karachi is always a possibility, and such an operation could be easily supported by shore-based aircraft from airfields in Kathiawar and South Western Rajputana.

Seaward and anti-aircraft defences, including Radar warning systems, would be needed on a large scale for the defence of Karachi.

h) The sea routes leading to Karachi would be open to continuous seaborne and airborne attacks from enemy bases in the Persian Gulf and on the West Coast of India, and there is little doubt that this line of supply would be most unreliable if the enemy knows his business.

i) To sum up, it may be said that the Western region of Pakistan would be strategically and economically most unfitted, at least for a long time to come, to withstand attack by any power possessing even relatively small modern armed forces and that its isolation from the outside world would be almost a certainty in a comparatively short period after the outbreak of hostilities.

The only sources of supply to which Pakistan can look for the procurement of the munitions and supplies essential in war lie in the great industrial areas of Europe, Russia, or the United States, all of which are separated from both regions of Pakistan by thousands of miles of sea or by long land routes practically devoid of any means of transit.

From the purely military and strategical aspect, which is the only angle from which the problem has been viewed in this paper, it must be concluded that the provision of adequate insurance in the shape of reasonably good defensive arrangements for Pakistan would be a most difficult and expensive business, and that no guarantee of success could be given.

NOTE BY DCGS(A) ON THE PAPER
'MILITARY IMPLICATIONS OF PAKISTAN'

(Written from the point of view of Pakistan)

The paper appreciates the defence of Pakistan from the military and strategical aspect, and very clearly and adequately states the weakness of Pakistan in the event of aggression across her several frontiers.

In my view, however, a Muslim League appreciation of the defence problem facing

Pakistan would take account of certain other factors, mainly political, not referred to in this paper.

I have therefore written in the following paragraphs what I think such an appreciation would contain. A consideration of these points may be of some help to the C-in-C should the appreciation have to be argued out with the politicians.

The possible enemies of Pakistan can be conveniently considered in three groups –

a)   Russia.
b)   Afghanistan, Persia, Burma.
c)   The Independent Frontier tribes and Hindustan.

RUSSIA

Neither a united nor a divided India can defend herself against Russia. Any such defence can only be done politically through the UNO of which Pakistan will be a member. The successful political defence by Persia against Russian aggression in Azerbaijan is an example.

The provision of Armed Forces designed to defend Pakistan against Russia is therefore not contemplated.

a) *Afghanistan*

Pakistan would expect to have a mutual non-aggression treaty with Afghanistan. Even so, she must be prepared to deal with an Afghan incursion into Pakistan territory should this pact be broken. The routes by which such incursion can take place are few, and there is no reason to suppose that a Pakistan army, with all the advantages in experience and training which their officers and men would have, could not defeat such aggression if they were kept concentrated and well handled.

It is, however, considered that hostile action by Afghanistan is more likely to be confined to stirring up tribal trouble in Independent territory.

b) *Persia*

Short of an attempt to capture the port of Karachi, an attack by Persia would serve little purpose. The Persian Army is considered quite incapable of sustaining any offensive that would bring her within reach of the River Indus. Persian armour is of little or no military value and they could not support any such offensive by air. Pakistan is, on its South-Western front, very well protected by the Baluchistan desert, and in this respect the vital port of Karachi is very favourably situated.

c) *Burma*

For many years to come there will be no Burmese Army capable of carrying out any large offensive against Eastern Pakistan. Burma will require all her military resources for competing with her own internal problems. While a minor operation against Chittagong is possible, Chittagong is much easier to defend than attack. The approaches to Chittagong are bad, and the military garrison of Eastern Pakistan should be well able to defeat the small forces that could be brought against it.

Reinforcement from Western Pakistan would indeed be long and difficult, and Eastern Pakistan would have to rely on its permanent garrison provided from Western Pakistan plus a certain number of infantry bns that could be raised from the tribes in the hill tracts south of Assam.

THE NWF AND HINDUSTAN

None of the above appear to constitute the main problem that will confront Pakistan during those difficult first years when she is finding her feet and organizing her slender resources. The real problem lies in controlling the frontier tribes in the NW and in defeating any aggression by Hindustan.

There is good reason to believe that these two would not take place together, forcing Pakistan to fight on two fronts. Any Hindustan aggression into Pakistan would call for a Jehad to which our co-religionists on the frontier may be expected to respond at least with neutrality, leaving the Pakistan forces free to deal with Hindustan.

But even when these threats are considered separately, neither will be easy for Pakistan to counter. Pakistan can ill afford to pay and employ the tribesmen as the British have done, and it would be no exaggeration to say that any serious frontier trouble would fully occupy all the armed forces that Pakistan could maintain, and leave her incapable of resisting any simultaneous attack from Hindustan. Therefore, even though an attack by Hindustan might well result in the stopping of any frontier disturbances, it might then be too late for Pakistan to turn to protect herself against Hindustan.

The main enemy of Pakistan will be Hindustan, but we think that a concerted attack on Pakistan, sponsored by a Hindustan Government, is unlikely. A Hindustan Government as a member of the UNO would be unwilling to face the UNO as an aggressor. What is far more likely is that parts of Hindustan, e.g. the Sikhs, might become inflamed over some question of the treatment of minorities and take independent action.

If this is so, then it is probably unlikely that the Pakistan forces, in countering this threat, would be called upon to fight on all her frontiers with Hindustan.

It will be agreed that Pakistan is economically a poor country, and that her resources are small. But it can be argued that she will be no poorer than Afghanistan or Persia, who have successfully retained their independence and preserved their nationality through two World Wars.

At the worst, Pakistan can have an army equal to the armies of Afghanistan, Persia, or Burma. Within the whole international set-up, why then should she be in a worse position to defend herself?

I suggest that the above is, in outline, the sort of view of the situation that the advocates of Pakistan will take. They will refuse to consider the situation in terms of any threat from a first-class power or in terms of armoured forces or air offensives. They will regard their defence problem in terms of some local third-class war which will be settled one way or another with infantry and artillery.

APPENDIX X

Minutes of the Meeting on
Liaquat Ali Khan's Paper on
the Partition of the Armed Forces

26th April, 1947

The committee had before it papers submitted by HM Finance, together with the comments thereon prepared by HM Defence and HE the Commander-in-Chief. His Excellency in introducing the paper said that he regretted that he had had to override the advice of HM Defence and HE the Commander-in-Chief in bringing this paper before the committee. They had been so impressed with the need for secrecy, because of the disastrous effect on the armed forces if it was known that this matter was even under consideration, that they had been reluctant to agree to the matter being discussed at all. He, too, fully appreciated the great importance of ensuring complete secrecy in this matter. His reasons for bringing the matter to the committee were that he required their views for inclusion in his report to HMG as to the form of Government he recommended for India. Pakistan was an issue which must be faced, and the partition of the armed forces was one of its most important implications.

HM Defence emphasized all he had written as to the effect on the armed forces of partition. Such division of forces should follow the political decision in favour of Pakistan, assuming that such a decision was taken; if it were to precede such a decision, the consequences might be serious.

HM Finance agreed that the decision must obviously follow the political decision, but there must be a plan in readiness to go ahead with separation if Pakistan was accepted. Further, nothing must now be done that would in any way complicate what was already a difficult problem.

Points in discussion were:—

a) The technical difficulties of separation were enormous, but if it became politically necessary they would have to be overcome. To delay thinking about them would make it all the more difficult to carry them out should it become necessary. A start must therefore be made now.

b) It was unfortunate that this issue should have to be considered while the political future was still uncertain. The full implications of Pakistan would require definition to provide a clear basis on which to plan separation of the armed forces. Pakistan would still leave Mohammedans in Hindustan, and vice versa, thus complicating the problems of recruitment. The problem might be further complicated by the theory of two nations whereby Mohammedans resident in Hindustan would be expected to owe loyalty to Pakistan, and vice versa. It was explained, however, that the Hindus and Muslims residing in the two areas would enjoy the full rights of citizenship in those areas, irrespective of their religion.

The political decision will guide but will not settle the armed forces' problem.

c) If Pakistan is decided upon then each of the two States will require its own forces for internal security, but it can be expected that there will be a treaty between the two to provide for defence against aggression by a common enemy. This would allow of the use of troops by both parties impartially for the common good. There is reason to hope that even if Pakistan is decided upon there will be many interests in common between Pakistan and Hindustan in matters of commerce, finance, etc.

d) It followed that training establishments and ordnance factories could be shared by mutual agreement and that it was by no means essential that the forces of each State should be entirely self-contained. In any event India, even when united, was not self-contained for war, and was dependent on outside for much of the specialized and technical equipment she needs, as also for research and design.

e) It was explained that the basis of the paper written by the Commander-in-Chief had been to point out the practical difficulties that would have to be overcome in separating the armed forces. It was in no way intended to influence the decision for or against Pakistan. There were obvious flaws in it, but these resulted from the fact that no clear terms of reference had been given as to the relations between the two States.

f) It was urged that it was important that the larger military headquarters and staffs, as well as the major units, should be re-organized while British officers were still present. It was therefore essential to delay nationalization until such re-organization was complete.

g) The implications of delaying nationalization were discussed. It was explained that a plan for nationalization prepared in armed forces headquarters was ready but that execution of it had been temporarily postponed. There was no intention of delaying preparatory measures, e.g., training of Indian officers required to take over. All that was being held up was the complicated process of cross-posting officers consequent on the withdrawal of the British element. Separation would further complicate these postings as it will be necessary to review afresh the officers suitably qualified and available in both Hindustan and Pakistan. It was explained that the re-organization taking place in the armed forces was a gradual reduction to the target figure for the new budget, and that the only changes in class-composition of units were those explained in the Commander-in-Chief's paper, which would simplify separation if it ever became necessary. It was explained that a brief delay in executing the nationalization policy would attract no outside attention, and His Excellency gave an assurance that a political decision on the subject of Pakistan would in all probability be forthcoming by the end of May. The delay, therefore, would not be long.

His Excellency summed up as follows:—

i) He suggested that the issue should not be put to the Cabinet until the political decision had been taken.

ii) He wants to stress the need for secrecy and suggested that those members of the committee who did not need their papers for subsequent reference should return them to the Cabinet Secretariat at the end of the meeting for safe custody and reissued when the subject was again put on the agenda.

iii) He thought that the armed forces could probably complete nationalization by 1st June, 1948, without reducing standards to an unacceptably low level. He felt that the Armed Forces might complete separation by 1st June, 1948, without undue risk. To attempt both nationalization and separation by that date was in his opinion running a very dangerous risk. He stressed the unique position of the armed forces and their reputation for impartiality in the existing state of communal tension. He pointed out that he bore personal responsibility for law and order which he must carry until such time as he could hand it over to one or more responsible authorities. While he bore that responsibility he had in the last resort the use of British troops to fall back on. After 1st June, 1948, there would be no British troops but the necessity for reliable and impartial armed forces might still exist; and by unduly hastening the process of separation we might defeat our own ends and produce a situation in which the armed forces would be semi-organized and not reliable. Much as he would like to see the separation completed, if it proved to be necessary, he reaffirmed his doubts as to the possibility of doing so in the time available.

iv) He suggested that it would be wiser to think in terms of pooling the forces of Hindustan and Pakistan, and, though each would have its own GHQ, there could remain a Federal GHQ in general control, until such time as separation could be completed without detriment to efficiency.

v) He agreed that there must be a plan because when Pakistan was announced it would be imperative at once to let the armed forces know where they stood, and to reassure them that preparations for their separation were in hand. He suggested that a personal broadcast by HE the Commander-in-Chief might be made indicating how he proposed to proceed.

vi) The possibility might be examined of setting up a small high level staff to consider, in secret, outline plans for going ahead with separation if it proved to be necessary; and also on the possibility of holding up measures of nationalization until the political decision was taken.

The Commander-in-Chief said that it had been brought out in discussion that there was really no basis on which he could plan the separation as so many factors were uncertain. He agreed that he could put in hand planning in broad outline only to determine the problems which would have to be tackled and the staff that he would require to undertake the work. He agreed that nationalization could be temporarily postponed.

The Committee:—

1) decided that the issue should not be put to the Cabinet until the political decision had been made.

2) directed the Commander-in-Chief to think out (a) the personnel of the small high level committee he should set up, and (b) the broad outline of the problems

it will have to tackle if the decision taken involves separation, on the assumption that the terms of reference for the committee would be drawn up in that event by HE the Viceroy on the basis of the political decision.

3) authorized the Commander-in-Chief to hold up nationalization at his discretion until the political decision was reached, the guiding principle being that no action should be taken which would prejudice or complicate separation should it finally become necessary.

APPENDIX XI

Massacres in Punjab

MUSLIMS BUTCHERED BY ARMED MOBS OF SIKHS

BREAKDOWN OF CIVIL ADMINISTRATION

By *The Times* Special Correspondent in Punjab, 25th August 1947.

As a reminder that this communal war is not one-sided, a train loaded with Sikh refugees from West Punjab was attacked by a Muslim mob west of Ferozepur yesterday and arrived with 25 dead bodies on board and more than 100 passengers with stabbing wounds of varying degrees of seriousness. Three small girls in one compartment had been hacked to death.

When the Punjab mail train was derailed and attacked on Tuesday night by Sikh mobs east of Ferozepur, a valiant and successful defence was organized by two British passengers. They were Mr Harington Hawes, Secretary to the Agent for the Punjab States, and Major Rob Major, late of the Indian Political Service who was on his way to Kashmir with his wife and daughter. The mail-train had been diverted south from Ludhiana, and east of Ferozepur it was halted by obstructions on the line. All the Sikh passengers had been tipped off at a previous station and had left the train. After being halted the train was surrounded by armed Sikhs. The Major noticed that they advanced and retired in military formation, with a Sikh in blue commanding each section of about 12 men. They were driven off by shots fired by the British passengers and a few others who had arms, and by the train's armed escort, which consisted of two Muslim Sepoys, two Hindus, and one Sikh.

As night was approaching and the train was surrounded by long grass easily set on fire, the Major and Mr Hawes decided that it would be wisest to spend the night at a deserted station up the line. About 150 passengers, all Muslims, went to the station and most of them climbed on the roof. The Sikh Sepoy killed one man in an approaching mob, and this seems to have kept the Sikhs off for the night. During the night a military patrol arrived and left one section with the stranded passengers. While looking for water Mr Hawes found four Muslim members of the station staff murdered. On returning to the train in the morning they found it had been looted clean, and several Muslims who had insisted on staying behind to look after their belongings had been killed. Although the line had been interfered with west of the station, they reached Ferozepur without any further adventure. There is no doubt that but for the presence of these two Britons the entire trainload of passengers would have been massacred, as had already occurred in several instances.

THE JATHAS AT WORK

'A thousand times more horrible than anything we saw during the war,' is the universal comment of experienced officers, British and Indian, on the present slaughter in east Punjab. The Sikhs are on the warpath. They are clearing eastern Punjab of Muslims, butchering hundreds daily, forcing thousands to flee westward, burning Muslim villages and homesteads, even, in their frenzy, burning their own too. This violence has been organized from the highest levels of Sikh leadership, and it is being done systematically, sector by sector. Some large towns, like Amritsar and Jullundur, are now quieter, because there are no Muslims left. In a two hours' air reconnaissance of the Jullundur district at the week-end I must have seen 50 villages aflame.

The Sikh Jathas, armed mobs from 50 to 100 strong, assemble usually in the Gurdwaras, their places of worship, before making a series of raids. Many Jathas cross over from the Sikh States. The armament of a typical Jatha consists of one or two firearms, army and home-made grenades, spears, axes and kirpans – the Sikh sabres, which are also religious emblems. The Muslims are usually armed only with staves. When threatened they assemble on their roofs and beat gongs and drums to summon help from neighbouring Muslim communities and prepare to throw stones at the attackers. The Sikhs attack scientifically. A first wave armed with firearms fires to bring the Muslims off their roofs. A second wave lobs grenades over the walls. In the ensuing confusion a third wave goes in with kirpans and spears, and the serious killing begins. A last wave consists of older men, often army pensioners with long white beards, who carry torches and specialize in arson. Mounted outriders with kirpans cut down those trying to flee.

British officers have seen Jathas that have included women and even children with spears. Appalling attrocities have been committed; bodies have been mutilated; none has been spared – men, women, or children. In one village, out of 50 corpses 30 were those of women. One Viceroy's Commissioned Officer found four babies roasted to death over a fire. Although the Jathas are often led by former soldiers, in whom this region abounds, they are cowardly bodies. One well-armed Jatha, which had burned a stronghold of 15 Muslim villages and murdered at least 500 people, was finally halted with the loss of six lives by a small Muslim village possessing only one rifle and one pistol but dauntlessly led by a former Captain of the Royal Indian Army Service Corps. Two British officers effectively dispersed a mob about to attack a train which had been expertly diverted into a siding. The young Indian pilot of my Auster aircraft dispersed several Jathas (only temporarily, alas!) by firing Verey lights at them.

FRIGHTENED OFFICIALS

The three battalions of the Boundary Force have lately been reinforced by a fourth; they have had to cover three large districts and have been faced with an impossible task. By the time they have received one report and acted on it, the Jatha has moved on elsewhere. Moreover, Sikh and Hindu troops have refused to fire on Sikh gangs, or else they have fired to miss. The Muslim police were disarmed before August 15th, and the Sikh police have looted and killed the mobs. The civil administration has been gravely weakened by the summary recent dismissals of several key Englishmen, and wholesale changes among the Indian officials have now caused control to break down completely. Those officials whose sympathies are not with the mobs have been threatened by the Sikhs and are frightened out of their lives. In Jullundur city the civil authorities first disarmed the Muslim police and then forbade the military authorities to post Muslim troops inside the city boundaries. The troops who had to be posted – namely Sikhs, Dogras, and Jats – made no effort to prevent last Wednesday's massacre or the subsequent looting and burning.

A refugee problem of gigantic proportions is building up which is completely beyond the capacity of the civil authorities to handle. The Army has done valiantly. Even mess orderlies and bearers have gone out on escort jobs. Refugees are pouring in. At one Jullundur camp, started by the Army, but now under the direction of the civil authorities, the majority of the 8,000 or more people accommodated have had only one meal in five days. The troops are spread out over an enormous area. They are having small success in breaking up the Jathas, and the men they do arrest are usually released almost immediately by the civil authorities, but they are succeeding in establishing a number of defended assembly points for the refugees.

The Sikhs will tell you that this is retaliation for what the Muslims did to the Sikhs in Rawalpindi in March – which was retaliation for Hindu massacres of Muslims in Bihar, which was retaliation for Noakhali, which was retaliation for Calcutta. So it goes back, violence begetting violence. But even India has never seen anything worse than this present orgy, which has already sullied the name of the Sikh, synonymous in two world wars with martial valour. Only most determined efforts on the part of the leaders can end the madness.

APPENDIX XII

Daily Mail *Interview with Sir Claude Auchinleck*

In fourteen years this nation has done more for itself than the British did in a century.

What Pakistan has achieved in the fourteen years since it became an independent country is extraordinary. In that short time this new nation has done more towards modernizing and industrializing itself than the British did in the whole of the 100 years we were there.

Under British rule those parts of the old India which are now East and West Pakistan were regarded purely as agricultural regions.

In the Punjab, now Western Pakistan, we are building a first-class irrigation system, but there were only the slightest beginnings of industrialization, a few cotton mills, one or two hydro-electric stations.

We created the city of Karachi but purely as a port for the export of grain and cotton. The Punjab, with its fertile Indus Valley plains, was looked upon as a great granary that also produced good soldiers.

Today, what a difference! The grain and cotton are still there, and so are the good soldiers, but Karachi has developed into a very big industrial area.

And North from the city industrial enterprises are also springing up.

There are cotton mills, engineering and chemical works, fertiliser factories, sugar refineries, where once only raw materials were grown for export.

Today the finished products are being manufactured, either for home consumption or to be sent abroad to bring back much-needed foreign exchange.

Whenever I go back to Pakistan – and I have managed it most years since I came home after the partition of India in 1947, on business or to my old regiment, and many old friends – I get the impression that this is a nation that *intends to go forward* and get on, making the best of all its resources.

They have discovered, and are working natural gas; preliminary building has started on a vast new capital city; dams and reservoirs are being built.

Much of what is happening now could have happened under British rule but the Pakistani people bear us no malice for the fact that it didn't.

One thing is in the minds of their leaders – the necessity to make their country into a nation. And they are doing just that; the old patriarchal country is becoming the industrial country.

In 1947 when partition came they *started with nothing*; the Army was split; the Navy was split; the Air Force was split.

The difference between the new Indian Government and the Pakistan Government was that the Pakistanis started with nothing at all. Under Mr Jinnah, their Government set up in Karachi literally without typewriters or chairs to sit on.

On the other hand the Indians, taking over in Delhi, were as well organized as the British Government in Whitehall. *They inherited Government offices and Parliament House alike ready made.*

Don't misunderstand me on this. I am not for one moment suggesting that India hasn't done the same, but they had a much better base to start from.

And, although I don't want to talk politics here, I am sure that always at the back of the Pakistani mind is the thought that India didn't want partition; rightly or wrongly the attitude is: *'They only want to see us fail and then they can walk in.'*

That thought alone is a great spur to their determination to succeed as a nation. I think they will succeed and I think they deserve to succeed, but here again, I do not want to be misunderstood in my attitude to Pakistan and to India.

I go to Pakistan because my regiment is there and because I am received as a friend but I have many friends in India too, and by far the greater part of my service was spent there.

I think I can put it this way – Pakistan has come safely through a period during which, largely because of the selfishness of some of its politicians, it might have *disintegrated.*

The President, Field-Marshal Ayub Khan, stopped the rot when he took power after the so-called revolution led by the Army in October, 1958.

Energetically, but *without bloodshed,* the political parties, with their maladministration and corruptness, were suppressed, and the Army, under the Field-Marshal, took control.

I am no militarist and no believer in military autocracies, but this Government of soldiers is probably the best Government Pakistan has had since it achieved its nationhood. The country has surged forward and its many problems are being tackled with courage and energy.

Some of my friends in Pakistan don't agree with me here, but I firmly believe that if this take-over by the Army had not happened there would have been a really *bloody revolution.*

The soldiers have done a wonderful job through insisting that the most important thing of the moment is to get on with running the country efficiently and well. But, of course, this system cannot go on for ever.

The first to realize that the country must have a proper Constitution is Field-Marshal Ayub; already it is being worked on. A Constitution Commission has been set up: it should be only a matter of months before the details are hammered out and its form adopted.

Already too, more civilians are being taken into key jobs. Already there is a system of basic democracies working with success.

Briefly, this is a system whereby the people of each locality choose a representative that they know and trust to become a member of an administrative group looking after the area.

In turn this group elects its representatives for the next tier of Government and so on.

All these trends augur well for the future of Pakistan. What part is Britain to play in that future? I am no economist, but I believe sincerely that there are two important things to remember:

There is ample and worthwhile scope for the investment of more British capital.

Pakistan is ideally situated for the easy distribution of manufactured goods to many parts of Asia.

There is an almost inexhaustible supply of labour; raw materials of many kinds are available.

The Pakistani as a *workman is very reliable.* Once trained he is excellent, and he takes as much pride in his job as he does in the soldiering.

There is, I am convinced, great need for British salesmen, supervisors and businessmen of all kinds going out to countries like Pakistan to remember that the old days are done and finished with.

We must take the trouble to learn the language, and to learn what the people are thinking. We must get out among them.

It is not enough only to mix with one's fellow Britishers at 'The Club' and ignore what is going on all around.

That sort of thing is an Imperial hangover from other days.

The Germans and Japanese don't do it. If they spend their time drinking gin and bitters with anyone it is not with each other, but with the local people they are negotiating with selling to, or working for.

The people of the country are the people that matter. In the case of Pakistan if they do as well in the next fourteen years as they have done in the past fourteen, they are going to matter a very great deal indeed.

Extracts from some of the Auk's Letters to the Author and his Family

The Auk wrote regularly to Tahirah, to my children and myself. The letters would make a book by themselves, so I am including here only a few extracts from some of them, to give a glimpse of a side of his personality which he seldom revealed.

In December, 1948, he wrote from Italy:

> It is just over a year ago since I left Karachi and it seems in some ways like a hundred years but in other ways it seems only like yesterday. I always find it difficult to make myself believe that my very pleasant life out there is all over and that all my friends are scattered. However, I am glad I have some left like you and Shahid. How often I think of your lovely parties in your garden at Delhi and wish I was back. . . .

In January, 1950, he came for the first time to Pakistan and stayed with us in Karachi. We had several parties for him and he met all his old friends. He toured the whole of Pakistan. Most of the time he spent with my children. Talking to him one day, he said in his typical style, 'I am no politician and I may be talking out of turn but, knowing your country for the past half a century, I feel that the only way you could keep East Pakistan with you is by having a "loose federation" with them.'

In December, 1953, he wrote:

> I have just finished reading Chris Birdwood's book *A Continent Decides*. I think it is worth reading as he has obviously taken a lot of trouble to get the facts about Kashmir and writes impartially on the whole – you will say – 'that is the trouble with you English you are too damn impartial – You never do anything'. I agree with you!

In November, 1955, he wrote:

> I had a very long talk with Hassu's tutor and he told me that Hassu was doing very well indeed and was much liked. He had no fears about him at all apparently, so you and Shahid can be proud of your son. I am. I really think Hassu had done very well. He is quiet and self-contained. Quite a master of himself although he did throw a stink bomb the other day and apparently got beaten for it. However, no one worries about that, he certainly does not.

In April, 1959, he and I attended the General Assembly of the World Veterans' Federation in Rome; I acted as his Private Secretary. At one of the receptions held in honour of the Delegates by the Minister of Defence we walked in together and I introduced him to a row of old gentlemen who obviously had been in the Armed Forces of Italy. After the introduction one of them approached me and asked 'Who did you say he was?' So I repeated his name. Thereupon about ten or twelve of them surrounded him and introduced themselves as various Army and Corps Commanders of the Italian forces in North Africa when the Auk was there. It was these very people the Auk had beaten in battle and they were very happy to meet him. Together they talked about the battles which they once fought. We saw the Pope at the Vatican.

The Auk wrote to Shama, my younger daughter, in 1959, 'I must say how much I admire your writing and your wonderful command of English. This is not 'Khusha-mud' (flattery) but sincere. Do not get too puffed up . . . I am sorry that your 'Koonjs' (birds) have been eaten – I liked them. . . .'

In December, 1961, he wrote:

I did not know that you were thinking of writing a book about me. I think you would be wasting your time. About papers I will lend you anything that you may think useful.

In February, 1962, he wrote:

About the book, as I told you I am honoured that you should have thought of writing it. But quite honestly, I do not think the material for such a book exists. My life was and is a very ordinary one and nothing very exciting or interesting came my way. It was an ordinary career, a soldier's life and I do not really think that there is anything to be made out of it!!! There is not any deep personal side so far that I can see. And I ought to know.

In March, 1983, he wrote to Tahirah:

It was very nice to see Shahnaz and Shama, charming as usual and very perceptive – like their mother. Tell Shahid that he must take time off now and again and relax for a bit each day. He will not listen but tell him anyway. It would not be possible for me to put into words what I feel about all of you and Shahid and all your retainers have done for me and for the really splendid generosity and hospitality you have shown me. You know, I think, how much I loved your house and being allowed to stay in it and enjoy what is going to be certainly the best laid-out garden in Pindi; indeed in Pakistan.

On 3rd June, 1963, he wrote to Tahirah:

Shahid came to lunch yesterday. When he left I felt and still feel really desolate. He brought such a breath of Pakistan and such lovely memories back to me that really I feel quite disturbed in my heart, most unusual for a prosaic matter-of-fact chap like me. He made me feel restless to be back in your country where one meets such friendship and spontaneous kindness and where one can feel relaxed and at ease, but I shall recover, I suppose.

In 1964, he wrote:

I have just heard from Shama from Peshawar. I know the Peshawar University as I have been there several times. In fact I saw it soon after building began and then again last year. I think it is a magnificent achievement and I feel it should do a tremendous lot of good. When I first saw it my immediate reaction was 'How can they build this city outside the barbed wire which still protects Peshawar cantonment? It is an invitation to the tribesmen to loot and murder.' When I was a Brigadier in Peshawar thirty years ago no one was allowed outside the wire fence after dark.

He wrote again:

I am very interested in the situation in Pakistan and I must say that it worries me a bit. It is of course part of the growing pains as they call them. Anyway Pakistan is still adolescent if I may be forgiven for saying so. Only seventeen years old. Of course history goes back a long way but this is a new life and is bound to go through a lot of teething trouble . . . One can understand of course the frustration of many able, intelligent and patriotic people but one has to look to the good of the whole. Britain and the United States of America, specially the USA, have been stupid and blind in their arms policy towards Pakistan. If they give to India they should give at least in proportion to Pakistan. But I have lost faith in politicians. I never had very much. I have said for years and I still think that we in Britain are still suffering from an Imperial hangover and are unable and are unwilling to see that our future has got to be completely different from our past two hundred years and that we can no longer go stamping about the world in Wellington boots pretending to be policemen still carrying 'The White Man's Burden'. Our policy about bases, bases for what? We have nothing to put in them. Anyway if we are really a Commonwealth and in agreement with Pakistan and India why cannot Britain say 'Let us ease your task in every way and help you'?

In the beginning of 1965 he wrote to Tahirah:

The future of Pakistan depends on the undergraduates of today. Sounds very pompous and 'nawabi' but it is true. They are the people who have to make the new Pakistan and I hope they realize it. This applies in my humble opinion, the opinion of an ignorant soldier brought up on parade discipline and wars, specially to the women. It is a girl of today, the educated emancipated girl, and you are one of these, who is going to make the Pakistan of tomorrow. However, the General and Hassu may growl. But this is true. The future is in their hands and very lovely hands too. But I mean it. Every girl who graduates is an asset from what I have seen of them; they can transform Pakistan in a generation. They can still be good Muslims and I hope they will be. Well you will now realize that I am really old and becoming *Behosh* or *Pagal*.*

He wrote to Tahirah in September 1965:

I have been so anxious and worried about you all that it was a great relief to have news of you. I hope and pray that all goes well with all of you and that no harm

*Senile.

comes to you. I have been most miserable and depressed over the whole business since it started and I am still very worried and anxious. I fear the British have lost a lot of goodwill in Pakistan and this will, I think, be difficult to recover. All the same I believe that informed opinion was heavily in favour of Pakistan and for United Nations to free Kashmir. I hope, (Inshallah) that a just settlement can be reached. I feel most depressed – not much left to live for . . . I hope and I trust that these differences between India and Pakistan may be smoothed away. They are so exhausting and really unnecessary, though I do realize very well a threat to Pakistan, real or unreal, is always there and will be there, I fear, so long as there are Brahmins who live in the past.

In 1966 he wrote to Tahirah:

I can see you and Shahid walking among the wheatfields and I shall have to come and find those tulips again. The Indian situation seems pretty serious and I hope it is not troubling your parents. I cannot myself see the future of India clearly. I always thought when Nehru died it might begin to break up again into its old kingdoms. The people are so different; religion is the only bond I suppose. If it does begin to disintegrate the whole position in the subcontinent might become extremely dangerous. I do not like much this 'Sikh Suba'* business. They are or were good soldiers but they are born intriguers and care far too much for money.

In 1969, he wrote:

I have been thinking a great deal about you since the trouble started in Pakistan and I have been anxious, perhaps stupidly, for your safety and happiness. So it was a great relief to receive your cheerful letter. You need not think that I shall ever forget you and Tahirah and the family I have known for so long and loved so well. I am very glad that all goes well with Hassan and the others. It is good to know that Shanaz is happy. God bless her and Jaffar too. He is the lucky man. I am so glad that Ali has joined his Regiment. I always thought he would become what we used to call a dedicated soldier. I am often homesick for Pakistan, but, as you know, Pakistan is really my home and not England. I never had a real home in England and when I used to go on furlough to England for six or eight months every four or five years I always wanted to get back to Hindustan before my leave was finished. This may sound strange but it is true. I still feel like that. Morocco is the nearest thing to Pakistan.

In 1979, he wrote:

My mind always goes back to Pakistan and I wish I had stayed on there but that is all past history so no use regretting it. My memory is failing fast and requires to be reminded before I can really remember what happened thirty or fifty years ago. I see you are writing a book on me. Do not hesitate to write to me if you think I can be of help and send me a proof copy if you wish to do so. I wish I could live the old days over again – Rawalpindi, the Frontier and the Punjab. I still live in hope that perhaps one day I will see them again and you and Shahid. I sometimes think I should have been wiser to return to Pakistan instead of Morocco though I am

*Sikh province.

happy here if rather lonely sometimes. I am not at home here as I might have been in Pakistan speaking the languages I knew and meeting the people I loved and admired but one cannot have everything. I am not grumbling though I often think of Pakistan, Lahore, Jhelum, my house there, Rawalpindi, Peshawar and the rest. I really belong there, I think. I do wish I could visit you in Pakistan but if I did I would want to stay. It is very kind of you and just like you to say you would send Hassan to accompany me. Wonderful but I am still quite active and able to travel by myself but I fear it is not to be. If I got to Pakistan I should want to stay there and die there. Thank you very much for all your news of the family. It has made me feel quite homesick like a boy at school. Old age creeping on but I do not feel like it.

Index